The Best American
Travel Writing 2004

GUEST EDITORS OF
The Best American Travel Writing

2000 BILL BRYSON

2001 PAUL THEROUX

2002 FRANCES MAYES

2003 IAN FRAZIER

2004 PICO IYER

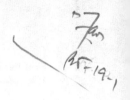

The Best American Travel Writing 2004

Edited and with an Introduction
by Pico Iyer

Jason Wilson, Series Editor

HOUGHTON MIFFLIN COMPANY

BOSTON · NEW YORK 2004

Contents

Contents

Foreword

THIS YEAR, the city council of Barcelona voted to ban bullfighting. While a number of newspapers suggested "Ernest Hemingway
is spinning in his grave," it must be said that bullfighting has never
been as popular a spectacle in Catalonia as it is in other parts of
Spain. Many see the ban as the region's desire to separate itself, cul-
turally and politically, from Madrid. Polling revealed that nearly
two-thirds of Barcelona's residents wanted the bullfights in their
city to end. Even though the municipal bullring hosted some eighteen corridas each summer, over half of the residents had never
been to watch a bullfight.

I don't intend here to enter the debate on animal cruelty, Iberian culture, or Catalan politics — though this is probably unavoidable. All I want to say is that when I read of the bullfight ban, I felt a
tiny sentimental pang. One of my fondest memories of a time spent
in Barcelona was taking a morning stroll with my wife through a
leafy park in Montjuïc, near the Fundació Joan Miró. It was a sunny
winter morning and the park walls were of course marked with
"Freedom for Catalonia" graffiti. At a clearing, we happened upon
three boys in tracksuits slowly and silently twirling long pink capes.
The youngest and smallest boy in the group, perhaps fifteen,
seemed the most serious and accomplished of the three. He held
the pink cape delicately and maneuvered it around himself in a
firm, graceful veronica.

When he finished, I asked him, a bit obtuse, "Are you matadors?"

"We are only in training," he said.

"Where are the bulls?" I asked.

"No, no," he said. "We don't get to see the bulls for a long time."

Off in a shady corner, I saw an older man, also in a tracksuit, working with a smaller, red cape and a sword. He swooped and mumbled at an imaginary bull for a while, then stopped and lit a cigar.

"He's the matador," the boy said.

My wife and I sat on a wall, thoroughly enjoying the morning as well as the notion of watching bullfighters practice in a city park — we'd never seen anything like this while walking through the park at home. One of the older boys grabbed a set of fake horns and began playing the role of the bull. He made several slow passes at the other boy's cape. A shaggy greyhound, who'd been digging in a trashcan, barked and chased after him, and together they made a dozen passes. A fat man walked by, waved his straw hat, and yelled "Bravo!"

When I read the news about the bullfight ban, I dug out two photos that we'd snapped that winter day in the park: one of the older boy pretending to be a bull, chased by the dog; another of the youngest boy, posing with his pink cape, unsmiling, trying to appear older and majestic — trying to appear more matadorlike, I'm assuming. When I showed the photos to my wife, she chuckled, and we spent the evening reminiscing about our wonderful time in Barcelona.

Yes, I know that this is all flaming nostalgia. And yes, I know that in thinking about experience this way, travel writers open themselves up to critics of the genre who call travel writing hopelessly romantic. Or worse: cultural voyeurism. I can imagine, for instance, my more enlightened friends asking, "How can you feel so warm and fuzzy about such a cruel and outdated practice?"

In their critical study of contemporary travel writing, *Tourists with Typewriters*, Patrick Holland and Graham Huggan cast a skeptical eye on travel writers. But when it comes to the nostalgic impulse, Holland and Huggan are slightly more generous: "Travel writing, like tourism, generates nostalgia for other times and places, even as it recognizes that they may have 'lost' their romantic aura. Contemporary travel writing tends to be self-conscious — self-ironic — about such losses: it is both nostalgic and, at its best, aware of the deceptiveness of nostalgia."

So maybe talking about bullfighting was too divisive a way to begin. Let me talk instead about cork.

Cork is probably not something you've thought much about. Until recently, I certainly hadn't. But over the past few years, I've been traveling around the vast green and gold plains of Portugal's Alentejo region, where most of the world's cork comes from. The back roads are lined endlessly with cork oak trees stripped bare of bark from the branches down. In the summertime, I've watched as workmen carefully and precisely unzip the bark with a sharp ax, the same way it's been done for centuries. The peeled bark is used to make traditional cork stoppers for wine bottles.

Cork forests are a remarkably sustainable resource, and they can be stripped of bark again and again without any damage to the trees whatsoever. Many cork trees in the Alentejo are more than two hundred years old, and I learned that cork takes a great deal of patience and faith to produce. A tree planted this year won't provide usable cork until about 2044.

Lately, back home in the United States, I've been opening a lot of wine bottles that have the new plastic stoppers. Friends have even given me wines — from respectable wineries — that come with a screw top. It's become clear that these synthetic stoppers are poised to take over the wine industry someday soon. Which might reasonably lead to this question: Why, with all the things that need improving in the world, would anyone feel the need to improve on the old, traditional cork? Well, wine experts contend that wines with cork stoppers are more likely to be tainted than ones that use synthetic stoppers. Cork is unreliable, they say. Too many bottles are sent back at restaurants. Too many customers complain at supermarkets and liquor stores. It's simple economics, they say. Cork presented a problem, and a well-funded company named Supreme Corq offered an affordable, artificial solution. You can't stop science.

I'm willing to grant that progress is generally a good thing and that nobody likes to open a spoiled bottle of wine. Yet I can't help but feel sad about all those cork trees I saw on my travels in Alentejo, especially the recently planted ones that are still three or four decades from making a single cork stopper. Even enlightened people worry that if the bottom falls out of the cork market, Portuguese landowners will cut down their cork forests, thus endangering some of Europe's richest wildlife habitats, home to eagles, white storks, butterflies, red deer, wild boar, and the Iberian lynx, the world's rarest cat. Most of all, I feel a little sad for the

Alentejans, the ones for whom cork has always been a way of life. My family has fond memories of these people, who have been so hospitable to us. I remember at a stand of cork trees, my year-old son laughed and waved to the smiling, weather-beaten men who made funny faces at him while they worked. I thought: Will corks still exist when my son reaches the legal drinking age? Then I thought: Am I falling prey to what critics might call the "deceptiveness of nostalgia"?

Hardly. I don't intend to tell anyone they shouldn't enjoy a wine with a plastic stopper. All I want to say is that my travels in the Alentejo gave me an appreciation, even a love, for something like cork. And now this travel memory inevitably makes me a little wistful when I open a wine bottle. Maybe it will for someone else too. Perhaps I'm simple-minded, but I believe that people enjoy thinking mostly about what they like a lot, or even love, or at the very least about what they admire. Travel writers are not much different from other people, and so it's not surprising that they write about the same sorts of things.

Pico Iyer, this year's guest editor, has famously described travel writing as akin to a love story. In his essay "Why We Travel," Iyer writes, "I remember, in fact, after my first trips to Southeast Asia, more than a decade ago, how I would come back to my apartment, in New York City, and lie in my bed, kept up by something more than jet-lag, playing back, in my memory, over and over, all that I had experienced, and paging wistfully through my photographs and reading and re-reading my diaries, as if to extract some mystery from them. Anyone witnessing this strange scene would have drawn the right conclusion: I was in love."

So it comes as no surprise that the first essay Iyer has chosen is titled "Romance," in which Roger Angell beautifully recalls the car trips of his youth. The theme of romance permeates this year's anthology, from Heather Eliot's steamy affair in the South Pacific to Michael Gorra's likening the recent rocky relations between Europe and the United States to a lovers' squabble.

Even in the more alarming or depressing dispatches in this collection, the writer searches, and finds, something admirable. In this way, we witness the optimism of building a ski resort in war-torn Kashmir, once called "the most dangerous place on earth." Or we are introduced to the owner of a diner in Vermont who is stubbornly resisting sterile corporate homogenization. Other writers find much to admire in the seemingly banal: an essay by Adam Gopnik begins simply, "Lately, I like to ride the bus."

The stories included in this anthology are selected from among hundreds of pieces in hundreds of diverse publications — from mainstream and specialty magazines to Sunday newspaper travel sections to literary journals to Internet and in-flight magazines. I've done my best to be fair and representative, and in my opinion the best one hundred travel stories from the year 2003 were forwarded to Pico Iyer, who made the final selections. He's chosen an excellent collection, full of humor, important news from the world, and, of course, humanity.

I now begin anew by reading the hundreds of stories published in 2004. I am once again asking editors and writers to submit the best of whatever it is they define as travel writing. These submissions must be nonfiction, published in the United States during the 2004 calendar year. They must not be reprints or excerpts from published books. They must include the author's name, date of publication, and publication name, and must be tearsheets, the complete publication, or a clear photocopy of the piece as it originally appeared. I must receive all submissions by January 15, 2005, in order to ensure full consideration for the next collection. Further, publications that want to make certain their contributions will be considered for the next edition should make sure to include this anthology on their subscription list. Submissions or subscriptions should be sent to Jason Wilson, The Best American Travel Writing, P.O. Box 260, Haddonfield, NJ 08033.

It was an honor to work with Pico Iyer, whose own books I consider among the very best examples of contemporary travel writing. I have known Pico for several years, and his enthusiasm and kindness have always been inspiring. I would also like to thank Stacey "Classic" Brown for her assistance on this year's anthology, as well as Melissa Grella, Heidi Pitlor, and Deanne Urmy, among others at Houghton Mifflin.

JASON WILSON

Introduction

AMERICAN TRAVEL WRITING is about looking for the light. Or so, at least, I told myself, rather loftily, as I landed in Atlanta on my first trip to the city, got into a new Aspire, and proceeded to drive around the "Phoenix of the South." I passed Perimeter Point and Perimeter Mall, drove through a web of office parks and shopping centers, passed a couple more Perimeter sites, and then arrived at my fancy hotel, in the midst of an area of jockey clubs and faux-European mansions. Afternoon tea was served in the lobby, I was told (with sterling silver strainers, no less), and a notice in my room, on "Guest Attire," reminded me that I should be formally attired for breakfast or even when passing through the lobby. Another sign in my room advised me that "for security reasons" I should call the Housekeeping Department if ever I considered leaving my shoes in the corridor for a complimentary shine.

I was taken aback to see shoes linked to security: Could tennies stage a presidential assault? Or a pair of brown oxfords represent outlaw values? Yet undeterred, I decided, my last night in the place, to take my courage in my hands, so to speak, and place my sixteen-dollar Payless Shoe Source loafers outside, in order to be polished to a Buckhead sheen. I called the Housekeeping Department to advise it of my intended maneuver, and was told, since it was close to midnight, to leave the shoes outside the door.

"But it says, for security reasons . . ."

"That's okay. It's close to midnight."

The next morning, as I got ready to check out and fly to my next stop, in California, I looked out into the perilous corridor and saw

. . . nothing. I have to check out soon, I said, calling Housekeeping, and I was wondering . . . "We'll get right on it, sir," a voice replied, with something of the firmness of Mission Control (and I was reassured just to be called "sir," as I'd almost never been before). Minutes passed, then close to an hour. I placed a call or two to the desk; it placed a call up to me. Living up to every fear of security violations, my shoes had apparently fled the hotel and might even now be hotfooting it to Mexico.

An expert was put on the case, but she was no use at all. The concierge desk summoned a woman called Ellen (or Helen or Yellin') to go out into the city to purchase for me the finest shoes that money could buy. But shopping for someone else's feet is notoriously difficult, and soon Yellin' was sending an agent to my door with shoes perfectly sized for Shaquille O'Neal. The whole process was complicated, of course, by the fact that walking shoeless through the lobby would be to violate every last item of the hotel's unbending dress code.

Finally — my flight was leaving soon, and whatever APB had been put out on my loafers had yielded no results — the hotel decided to take things firmly in its hands, so to speak: I would be permitted to walk through the lobby in my socks, indeed to check out without my shoes, so as to accompany a bellboy (the only dark face I'd seen in the place) to a Benny's shoe store in a nearby mall. Outside, as I hopped and hobbled through the lobby with my suitcase, stood a long stretch limo.

And so the day went on and on, and as the time of my check-in drew closer, I and the poor bellboy plodded glumly around a shoe shop, looking for something other than the light. At last, in order to bring the ordeal to a close, I alighted on a pair of hundred-dollar leather boots to replace the sixteen-dollar shoes that had disappeared, hardly caring that they were several sizes too large (and inelegant besides). Travel, as they say, profits not just the soul.

This is a trivial incident, of course, and one that could happen almost anywhere. And yet it bears out how travel writing can arise out of the least dramatic places and episodes, and how it is quickened, often, when things go wrong; when one falls between the cracks of one's itinerary and tumbles out of the guidebook altogether. It also can be a form of sneaking up on truth through the back entrance.

While I was traveling around Atlanta (to write about it), I visited the Martin Luther King, Jr., Center for Nonviolent Social Change, the World of Coca-Cola, the CNN Center, and Fulton County Stadium. But what seemed most characteristic, both about the city and about my experience of it, was that moment that wouldn't be found in any travel guide: the lone black worker in a place that prides itself on propriety, the collapse of simple services in a hotel that stands on highest ceremony, the elaborate atonement for what had only been a minor mistake. Besides, I'd never been in a stretch limo before.

Does such random anecdotage count as "American travel writing" (especially when it comes from someone born in Oxford, England, to Indian parents and living in Japan)? Probably not. But as someone born in Oxford, England, to Indian parents and living in Japan, I've long been interested in what constitutes the distinctly "American" component of American travel writing. Travel writing anywhere involves an extension of the passing into something more durable, and the elaboration of an incident that would be humdrum at home into something that is revealing both of setting and of self. Yet at a time when America is largely dominant in the fields of the English-language novel and serious nonfiction, we often look across the Atlantic when we're in search of classic travel writing. This is in part, no doubt, because the English, living in the national equivalent of a small town, have to go abroad to see the world; an American can sample most of the world's landscapes, both cultural and natural, without leaving his own country (nearly all the world's climatic zones can be found in Hawaii alone). But more than that, it speaks to some sense that the English, among others, have long been able to take the world as their backyard, even their private property; Americans are still more innocent abroad.

This perception is doubly curious insofar as America, in its modern form, was founded by travelers (is named after a traveler, indeed) — and travelers with a vengeance, as well as with a mission: from its earliest colonial origins, America has been a country for pilgrims longing to draw closer to their God. The centuries have passed and we may think ourselves now on a different planet from that of the early settlers, and yet this sense of searching — and a corresponding sense of a vast wilderness ready to overwhelm us in all directions ("America is a land of wonders," as de Tocqueville wrote) — has remained to this day the driving impulse of American travel writing.

In 1939, defining American literature as a whole, Philip Rahv devised a famous distinction between the "paleface" and the "redskin": the one drawn to the high refinements of the Old World he had ostensibly left behind, the other attracted to the boisterous vitality of the frontier. Though the distinction was aimed at poetry and fiction, it applies most pungently, perhaps, to American travel writing, which even now seems, with one foot, to be wandering off in the direction of Henry James (or Frances Mayes), and with the other toward Mark Twain (or P. J. O'Rourke). Open almost any travel magazine in America today and you will find elegant paeans to Paris, say, or Kyoto, check by jowl with rowdier stuff about getting drunk in Costa Rica or busted in Bangkok. Often the most interesting pieces, in which you can hear a truly distinctive American voice, are those in which someone combines the extremes to come up with what might be called an anarchic voyage of the soul: Henry Miller, for example, in his exuberant and often radiant travel classic about Greece, *The Colossus of Maroussi.*

This is all a huge simplification, of course, and yet it does help to lay down a cartography for what is the distinctively American contribution to this global form. Restlessness is part of the American way — it's part of what brought many of the rest of us to America, in fact — and it's no coincidence that Americans invented the car culture, more or less, fly more passenger miles than the rest of the world combined, and were the first to put their people on the moon. Even in the early days of the republic, Abigail Adams, wife of John, was referring to her fellow citizens, wittily, as "the mobility." And at almost the same time, one of the first official American travel writers, William Bartram, roaming around the Carolinas, Georgia, and Florida in 1791, was striking the same note his ancestors might have done: the whole world, he wrote, was "a glorious apartment of the boundless palace of the sovereign Creator," and just to transcribe its details was to give voice to a song of praise. When these two impulses coincided, America gave the world Emerson, Thoreau, and Emily Dickinson, great travelers all, who found "transports" and far-off cultures and even glimpses of eternity without straying very far from home.

Thus, whether of the New England or the Montana school, as

you could call them, or whether just a sui generis master such as
S. J. Perelman, the American travel writer has at once looked for a
kind of light and been glad to find it near to hand. For decades,
while the British were exploring Africa or Afghanistan or, for that
matter, America itself, Americans were charting the vast wilderness
around them and, in the process, asking questions of themselves
(and making discoveries) that weren't so common among Victo-
ria's men and women. From Walt Whitman, who found in the open
road a perfect model — and vessel — for the new democracy (and,
with Thoreau, among others, began to expound a whole philosophy of vagabondage), to Jack Kerouac, with his sweet reveries, to
Annie Dillard, with her hard-won epiphanies, the spiritual component of American travel writing has never been far from the surface; America's explorations have been metaphysical in a way that
travel seldom is for writers from the Old World. American travel
writing pushes and prods, you could say, where English often saun-
ters (and French dilates); American travel writing is impatient for a
resolution that older countries may have given up on. The English
traveler still carries himself often at a small distance from the place
he's exploring and is seldom naked in the way an Edward Hoag-
land or a Jon Krakauer might be. There is in American travel writing still, I think, an element of Christian in *The Pilgrim's Progress,*
and an American in India might not content himself so readily
with, say, the whimsical amusements of Ackerley's *Hindoo Holiday.*
    The Englishman, in my experience, is often traveling for a lark,
on holiday or just to escape the boredoms of home; the American,
in many cases, is on a mission, and is venturing his very being (and
those Englishmen who wish to undertake such a journey — Christopher Isherwood and D. H. Lawrence, for example — often remove themselves to America). This purposefulness can make for a
kind of naiveté and an air of self-importance — as well as a frustration — in a world that is seldom eager to give itself over to our
plans and projections, but it does confer a sincerity, an urgency, on
American travel writing that I don't tend to find in the "American
travel writing" of a Crèvecoeur, say, or a Fanny Trollope.
    In real American travel writing, I would hazard, there's some-
thing at stake, inwardly as well as practically; the American traveler
is generally looking for something, and it may be something as profound, as essential, as himself or his salvation. The result is a prose

that is less urbane often, more unguarded, even more credulous than that of the Brit, and yet there is in the air some sense of transformation. In such great American travelers as Paul Bowles (and his descendants, Robert Stone and Don DeLillo among them), this leads to a kind of reverse transformation that is annihilation; no one has written with more pitiless clarity about the traveler who is so ready to lose himself abroad that he gets taken in entirely and cannot put the pieces together at the end. Even Henry James, whom most of us would place in the other camp, exploring the mysteries of the dinner table and the courtly silence, wrote, in *The American Scene*, "The *il*legible word, accordingly, the great inscrutable answer to questions, hangs in the vast American sky, to his imagination, as something fantastic and *abracadabrant*, belonging to no known language, and it is under this convenient ensign that he travels and considers and contemplates, and, to the best of his ability, enjoys." The same James once identified Americans, as Michael Gorra reminds us here, as "passionate pilgrims."

This all has particular value today, it seems, because for many Americans, living in a country that borders few others and at a time when only one in three fellow citizens holds a passport, travel is the only way to get a living, human sense of the world around us. The major newsmagazines (for one of which I've written for more than twenty years) have cut down their coverage of international affairs by as much as 70 percent in the past fifteen years; and the TV networks, even as they tell us we're living in a global neighborhood, in which the business of one place is the business of everywhere, in practice give us less and less of the most basic information about Burma, say, or Ivory Coast. A travel writer today cannot get away with describing the wondrous surfaces of Delhi or Cairo, in part because many of his readers may have been there themselves or might be about to go there tomorrow; instead, in many cases, he's better advised to take us into some secret aspect of those places — as of a diner in Vermont or a Chinese mom-and-pop store in São Paulo — that most of his readers lack the time or opportunity to visit. Just six weeks before the planes flew into the World Trade Towers in New York, I happened to be in southern Yemen, traveling around the area near where Osama bin Laden's home village is (and where, a few months earlier, terrorists had blown up the USS

Cole). When war broke out soon thereafter, I was immeasurably grateful to be able to picture the people and the broken streets our headlines were now describing as a center of evil, and to be able to offer what firsthand reports I could to neighbors who otherwise knew nothing of Yemen except what they saw on screens.

As Thoreau wrote in his seminal essay "Walking," with a characteristic sense of intensity, "We should go forth on the shortest walk, perchance, in the spirit of undying adventure, never to return." You find that spirit today in the likes of Peter Matthiessen and Gary Snyder. And at some point in the last century, soon after the American Empire replaced the British as the leading force in the world, American travel writing seemed to begin to get its own back on its Old World master. For me some of the most engaging travel books of recent years have been the ones written by Americans in Britain (I'm thinking in particular of Paul Theroux, Bill Bryson, and Bill Buford), who have done to Britain what the British traditionally did to the rest of the world, traveling around its shores and remarking, often a little witheringly, on the strange ways and odd habitations of the natives.

Part of the fascination of much travel writing everywhere is that what used to be a simple exchange — a European writing of Peru, say — is now a much richer and more complicated dialogue: a woman half-Thai and half-Californian, perhaps, living in Paris, writing of a Peru largely filled with Japanese businessmen and German tourists. Yet even in this most contemporary of forms, the best American travel writing is still lit up, I think, by that spirit of transcendence less visible abroad. "All that is necessary to make any language visible and therefore impressive is to regard it from a new point of view," wrote John Muir, "or from the old one with our heads upside down. Then we behold a new heaven and earth and are born again, as if we had gone on a pilgrimage to some far-off Holy Land and had become new creatures with bodies inverted." Muir might have been born in Scotland, but he came to America, I suspect, in part to find that wisdom, and the wilderness that gave rise to it, and in the process offered a rallying cry for American travelers to this day.

When Jason Wilson, with his customary discernment, sifted out one hundred pieces from the year just past to give to me, leaving me with the difficult task of choosing just twenty or so for inclusion here, I was looking especially for pieces that leave travel behind, and rise out of the fact of simple movement from A to B to record something deeper and more lasting. Herman Melville, after all, was one of the most celebrated travel writers of his day (using "travel writing" in the lowest sense), and yet his countrymen stopped reading him when he began venturing out on the wilder, more uncharted seas of his memory and consciousness. Now, 150 years later, what we value him for are those inner, half-mad journeys. Many of us can get to the Marquesas and see the palmy beaches he described in his early books, but few indeed can take off on the stormy expeditions into religion and desecration that he started. Much of Paul Theroux's most memorable and enduring travel writing likewise comes, for me, in his half-invented memoirs, in which he undertakes strikingly fearless journeys into the interior.

So my criterion, in a simple way, was to find travel pieces that would be interesting to people who have no interest in travel — and to find accounts of Kabul or a Jersey truck stop that would appeal to people who hadn't known they'd want to read about those places. There are some travelers, like Tim Cahill in this book, who so excel at passing on their excitement about the road that we will travel anywhere with them (Cahill almost convinces me here that the "geographic cure" has validity and, as he puts it, that "favorite places have the capacity to heal"). And yet, when we join Roger Angell in a car, or Adam Gopnik on the local bus, we see how travel can really be a part of even the most sedentary life.

Heather Eliot (whom I've never, sad to say, read before) takes me on a transfixing journey here, and never mentions the name of the place where her transformation unfolds. Michael Byers goes to a place that seems almost impossible to make new — the National Mall — and somehow, through clarity and attention, shows it to us as if we were looking at it for the first time. Travel writing, I've come to think, is much more a matter of writing than of traveling — the hard part of the journey takes place at the desk — and I realized, making this selection, that I'd rather read Philip Roth on Newark than most of the rest of us on North Korea. As Thoreau puts it, much too memorably again, "It matters not where or how far you travel, the further commonly the worse, — but how much alive you are."

On many of these trips, the American traveler, as stereotype sug-

gests, opens out his self for inspection and lets us see what valu-
ables (or illicit substances) he's carrying around with him, declared or otherwise; the revelations in this book are often internal
ones. But at the same time, American travel writing has found itself
willy-nilly more global than before, as we've been reminded, often
shockingly, how much our destiny is bound up with that of Sudan
or Herat. Travel writing is not merely foreign correspondency in
mufti — war stories by other means — and yet it has new obliga-
tions in an age when we're persuaded that Kashmir and Congo are
not just places on the far side of the world. The most distinguished
writers of place, in my book — from Jan Morris and V. S. Naipaul to
Ryszard Kapuscinski — offer us not just a first draft of history but
an early glimpse at tomorrow.

The other difficult thing about making the selection here was
that all of us are travel writers when we go on holiday, much as we
are all travel photographers when we inflict our slides (or digicam
images) on the neighbors; unlike the Petrarchan sonnet or the
postmodern novel, travel writing is something everyone seems to
do, when e-mailing a friend or writing a fifth-grade assignment on
"what I did on my summer vacation." It is hard to do well precisely
because it is so easy to do passably. Yet reading some of the pieces in
this book, I was reminded that there are many writers around —
John McPhee, Peter Hessler, Bill McKibben, to name but three —
who can make a simple vacant lot come to life. Even if, contrary to
my original assertion, they're not looking for the light at all.

PICO IYER

The Best American
Travel Writing 2004

ROGER ANGELL

Romance

FROM *The New Yorker*

ONE SPRING SATURDAY when I was seven going on eight, my
mother brought me with her on an automobile outing with her
young lover and future husband, E. B. White. She took our family
car, a slope-nosed Franklin sedan, and we must have met Andy by
prearrangement at our garage. He did the driving. We left New
York and went up into Westchester County for lunch — this was
1928 and it was still mostly country. On the way back, my mother,
who had taken the wheel, stripped the gears while shifting, and we
ground to a halt, halfway onto a shoulder of the Bronx River Parkway. Disaster. Andy thumbed a ride to go find a tow truck, and my
mother, I now realize, was left to make this into an amusing story to
tell my father and my older sister at dinner that evening. She almost never drove — thus the screeching and scraping sounds beneath us and the agonized look on her face when she got lost in
mid-shift and we broke down. It was also unusual, an adventure, for
me to be alone with her and her office friend Mr. White, as she'd
described him. I think I wasn't meant to be there; maybe a Saturday
date with a schoolmate had fallen through, and she'd had no re-
course but to bring me along. But she never would have taken me
off on an outing that would require me to lie about it to my father
afterward, so the trip must have been presented beforehand as a
chance for her to practice her driving, with the reliable Andy White
as instructor. I had no idea, of course, that she and I were stranded
in a predicament, but I recall sitting beside her on the running
board of the ticking, cooling Franklin while we waited, with the
pale new shrubs and pastoral grasses of the parkway around us, and

the occasional roadster or touring car (with its occupants swiveling their gaze toward us as they came by) swooshing past. Then a tow truck appeared around the curve behind us, with Andy White standing on the right-hand running board and waving excitedly. Yay, I'm back, we're rescued! My father would never have done that — found a tow so quickly or waved like a kid when he spotted us.

The story stops here. I don't remember that night or anything else about our little trip, but in less than two years my parents were divorced and my mother and Andy married and living on East Eighth Street. They soon had their own car, or cars: they kept changing. The Depression had arrived, but they were a successful *New Yorker* couple — she a fiction editor; he a writer of casuals and poetry and the first-page Comment section — and they loved driving around in an eight-year-old Pierce-Arrow touring car, with a high-bustle trunk, side mirrors, and flapping white roof. After their son was born — my brother Joel — they moved up to a staid seven-passenger Buick sedan. In the mid-thirties, Andy also acquired a secondhand beige and black 1928 Plymouth roadster — country wheels, used mostly around their place in Maine. The Buick still mattered to him. Back when it was new, thieves stole it out of a garage on University Place one night and used it in a daring bank stickup in Yonkers. Andy was upset, but when he read an account of the crime in the newspapers the next day, with a passage that went "and the robbers' powerful getaway car swiftly outdistanced police pursuers," he changed sides. "C'mon, Buick!" he said. "Go!"

Every family has its own car stories, but in another sense we know them all in advance now, regardless of our age. The collective American unconscious is stuffed with old Pontiacs, and fresh reminders are never lacking. Weekend rallies flood the Mendocino or Montpelier back roads with high-roofed Model A's and Chevys, revarnished 1936 woodies, and thrumming, leaf-tone T-Birds; that same night, back home again or with our feet up at the Hyatt, we click onto TCM and find *The Grapes of Wrath* or *Bonnie and Clyde* or *Five Easy Pieces* or *Thelma & Louise,* waiting to put us out on the narrow, anachronism-free macadam once again. (A friend of mine used to drive around the Village in his 1938 De Soto hearse, except when it was out on lease to still another *Godfather* movie.) Grandchildren, slipping 50 Cent or Eminem into their Discmans in the back seat, sigh and roll their eyes whenever the old highwayman starts up again. Yes, car travel was bumpier and curvier back then, with more traffic lights and billboards, more cows and hillside graveyards, no air conditioning and almost no interstates, and with tin cans and Nehi signs and red Burma-Shave jingles crowding the narrow roadside. Give us a break.

Still, we drove, and what startles me from this great distance is how often and how far. I was a New York City kid who knew the subways and museums and movie theaters and zoos and ballparks by heart, but in the 1930s I also got out of town a lot, mostly by car. I drove (well, was driven) to Bear Mountain and Atlantic City and Gettysburg and Niagara Falls; went repeatedly to Boston and New Hampshire and Maine; drove to a Missouri cattle farm owned by an uncle; drove there during another summer and thence onward to Santa Fe and Tesuque and out to the Arizona Painted Desert. Then back again, to New York. Before this, in March 1933 — it was the week of Franklin Delano Roosevelt's first inaugural — I'd boarded a Greyhound bus to Detroit, along with a Columbia student named Tex Goldschmidt, and we picked up a test-model Terraplane sedan at the factory (courtesy of an advertising friend of my father's who handled the Hudson-Essex account) and drove it back home. A couple of months later, in company with a math teacher named Mr. Burchell or Burkhill and four Lincoln School seventh-grade classmates, I crammed into a buckety old Buick sedan and drove to the Century of Progress Exposition in Chicago; we came back by way of Niagara Falls, and, because I had been there before and knew the ropes, took time also to visit the Shredded Wheat factory, some tacky mummies, and a terrific fifty-cent roadside exhibition of dented and rusty, candy-wrapper-littered barrels and iron balls in which various over-the-brink daredevils had mostly met their end. With one exception, all of us in our party were still speaking.

If I now hop aboard some of these bygone trips for a mile or two, it is not for the sake of easy nostalgia — the fizz of warm Moxie up your nose; the Nabokovian names of roadside tourist cottages; the glint of shattered glass and sheen of blood around a tree-crumpled gray Reo; or the memory of collies and children, unaccustomed to auto-motion, throwing up beside their hastily parked family vehicles — but in search of some thread or path that links these outings and sometimes puts Canandaigua or Kirksville or

Keams Canyon back in my head when I wake up in the middle of
the night. Effort can now and then produce a sudden fragment of
locality: the car stopped and me waking up with my sweating cheek
against the gray plush of the back seat as I stare at a mystifying message, "VEEDOL," painted on a square of white tin so bright in the
sun that it makes me wince. Veedol? Beyond it, against the stucco
gas station wall, is a handmade

sign, wavery in the gasoline fumes rising outside my window. Where
are we? I want to sit up and ask my father, standing out there in his
sneakers, khaki pants, and an old shirt with rolled-up sleeves, who
is fishing his thick brown wallet — we're on a long haul to somewhere — out of a hip pocket, but I'm too dazed to speak.

The first day of that 1933 school trip to the Chicago World's Fair
went on forever, and it was after dark when we topped a hillside in
Ligonier, Pennsylvania, slowed at the vision of Pittsburgh alight in
the distance, and felt a little lurch and jolt as the right rear wheel
fell off the Buick. I can't remember dinner, but it was past midnight when, rewheeled, we pulled up at the McKeesport YMCA and
settled for two double rooms, plus cots. Jerry Tallmer, a surviving
member of the party, tells me that a fellow traveler, less suave than
the rest of us, confessed to him later that until this moment he'd
held a childhood notion that if you weren't in bed by midnight
you died. Out in Chicago, we took in the House of Tomorrow and
Buckminster Fuller's Dymaxion Car; ogled Sally Rand's "Streets
of Paris" but didn't attend; went to the Museum of Natural History;
laughed at Chicago's dinky elevated cars; and in our little notebooks wrote down that Depression soup-kitchen lines in Chicago
looked exactly like the ones in depressed New York. We were smart
and serious, and would be expected to report on this trip in Social Studies, come fall. The Century of Progress, we concluded,
was mostly about *advertising*. One afternoon, the temperature went
down twenty-nine degrees in an hour and a half as a black storm
blew in from over Lake Michigan; the next morning we read that

the sightseeing plane whose ticket window we'd seen at the fair had crashed, killing all aboard. Three days later, wheeling south from Niagara Falls, my companions (including the heroic Burkhill or Burchell, who did all the driving) offered to pay me two dollars apiece if I'd just *shut up* for a change and not speak another word for the rest of the trip. Unaffronted and short of cash, I agreed, and collected my princely ten bucks while we were passing under the new George Washington Bridge, just about home.

Breakdowns happened all the time. A year earlier, headed for Missouri with my pal Tex Goldschmidt, our car, another family Franklin, quit cold on a hillside in Liberty, New York. Towed to a garage, we learned that the replacement part we needed would arrive by mail in two days. We put up in an adjacent boarding house, where the large brown cookies permanently in place in the center of the dining room table were just possibly varnished. Sitting on porch rockers that evening with our feet up on the railing, we were terrified by a Catskill lightning bolt that flew along a grounding wire from the rooftop rod and down a viny column a yard or two from our toes. We sat on, listening to the thrash of night trees and the gurgle of water through the gutter downspouts, when — *bam!* — it happened again: an explosion and a blaze of white down the same path, and the smell of immeasurable voltage in the air around us. "Well, so much for *that* adage," Tex said, rising. "I'm going to bed."

Arthur Goldschmidt, whom I've written about before, came from San Antonio, and was knowledgeable about cars and roadside stuff. He'd been hired by my father, with whom I lived on weekdays, to come down from Columbia a couple of afternoons a week and spend some time with me when I got home from school, but he was so smart and engaging that he became a fixture. Here, a few months later, he'd been given the family car and the family wiseguy to take out west; my father would come along by train a little later, while Tex continued south to see his folks. Driving, Tex smoked Chesterfields and talked about the Scottsboro boys, asked if I thought Babe Ruth wore a girdle, and wondered how much I knew about the corrupt but colorful governor of Texas, Ma Ferguson. We had no radio but stayed alert anyway. Tex was the one to spot the first buzzard aloft and the rare passing North Dakota license plate, and to pick up on roadside or billboard names. ("Sweet Orr Pants," he said musingly. "Coward Shoes?") He challenged me to recite all the Burma-Shave jingles we'd encountered ("The bearded lady / tried a jar / she's now / a famous movie star / Burma-Shave"; "Rip a fender / off your car / mail it in for / a half-pound jar / Burma-Shave") and make up some of our own. He made me rate the girls in my class for looks and then for character, and said, "If our left front tire is six feet around, how many revolutions will it make by the time we reach Cleveland?" Late in our trip, wheeling down an unpopulated gravel highway west of Edina, Missouri, Tex slowed as we came up to three black sedans, oddly parked crossways on the road at a little distance from each other. As we passed the first one, to our left, the second moved forward from the right to block our path, but Tex spun us hard right, spewing gravel, passed behind him, and floored it up the road and away. Prohibition revenue inspectors, he thought, or maybe a highway stickup. Bonnie Parker and Clyde Barrow were around here somewhere, making do in hard times.

I keep forgetting how hot it was, driving. Two summers along, in late August of 1934, my father replanned the second part of our trip by leaving my uncle's place in Green Castle, Missouri (the same haven Tex and I had been heading for), around noon and driving nonstop to Santa Fe. We'd do Kansas by night and stay cool. Our party — Father, my eighteen-year-old sister Nancy, her Concord Academy classmate Barbara Kidder (the two had just graduated), and I — were experienced car people by now. We hated motels, carried water in our two big thermoses (later, in New Mexico, we bought a waterskin and slung it on a front fender), and favored gas stations with the old-style pumps that were cranked by hand like an ice cream freezer while you watched your Sunoco or Gulf slosh into a glass ten-gallon container up on top, then empty into your tank. We knew how to open a Coke by sticking a silver dollar under the cap and banging the bottle with your fist, and we'd learned to stop wincing or weaving when another languid or headlight-entranced rabbit in the road — *ba-bump* — went to the great cabbage patch in the sky. The floor in the back of the car filled up with crumpled sections of the *Kansas City Star* or the *St. Joseph News-Press* that we'd picked up at the last diner.

Nancy was driving by now, and could spell my father for two-hour stretches. She was a better driver than he was. Her hair was tied up with a string of red yarn, keeping it off her ears; at the wheel, she'd fire up a cigarette with the dashboard lighter, then hold it in the air in her long fingers, a ring of scarlet lipstick around the nearer end. Too classy for Bryn Mawr, I thought. I liked Barbara Kidder, who wore a blue neck bandanna and shorts, and had a nice store of rattlesnake and Gila monster stories; her parents were archaeologists — she was joining them later at a dig in Nevada. My father overcorrected while driving and favored long silences, but he was a soldier, a *comandante,* at the wheel, good for a five-hour bore through the blazing Indiana afternoon while we dozed and told dumb jokes. He didn't go for jokes, but laughed out loud when we imitated him trying to order his breakfast café au lait from a waitress at our creaky small-hotel dining room. This always started our day. "I want a glass of milk," he began, speaking loudly and fashioning the shape of a glass in the air. "*Cold* milk, in a glass. Then, and in addition, I'd like a cup of coffee" — his hands moved to one side, forming an invisible cup with a saucer underneath — "and with it a pitcher of *hot* milk, to put into the coffee. Now, again: cold milk, please, in a glass" — he poured it and pushed it carefully to the side — "coffee, hot coffee" — he made a happy sniffing sound, at the Maxwell Houseness of it — "and over here our hot milk" — little finger waves to show heat rising — "to put into the hot coffee. Is that clear?" But of course it wasn't. The waitress, bewildered by this mixture of mime and command and terrified by the lawyerly glare in his dark eyes, had long since paused with her pencil. What Father got was generally coffee with cold milk in the pitcher, or coffee and boiling water, or, at least once, iced coffee. It never came out right. We shook our heads helplessly, knowing that he wasn't cruel or unfeeling: he just liked things nice.

That night, in Kansas, Father held to course, upright at the wheel through the eight- or ten-mile straightaways, with the bright headlights forming — for me, in back — an outlined silhouette of his ears and bald head and strong forearms. I would fall asleep, and when I woke again it would be Nancy driving and smoking, with Father asleep on the right-hand seat and Barbara asleep beside me in back. The night air rushed in about us through the tilted wind por-

tals at the front of the front windows and the smaller ones in back
(we were in the zippy Terraplane that Tex and I had brought from
Detroit), and with it the hot, flat scent of tall corn; a sudden tang
of skunk come and gone; the smell of tar when the dirt roads
stopped, fainter now with the hot sun gone; and, over a rare pond
or creek as the tire noise went deeper, something rich and dank,
with cowflop and dead fish mixing with the sweet-water weeds.
I had a Texaco road map with me in back, and when we came
through a little town or stopped at a ringing railroad crossing I got
out my flashlight and tried to follow the thin blue line of our passage: Chapman and WaKeeney, Winona, and now — we must have
turned south a bit — Sharon Springs. I fell asleep again. Sometime
in the night, my hand found Barbara's hand and held on. When I
awoke with the first sun behind us, we'd climbed out of heat, and
the field dirt around us had a redder hue. "Colorado," Father said
softly. I lay back in my nest and Barbara's hand came out from under her thin Mexican blanket and took mine once again. That
morning, we went through La Junta and Trinidad and over the
Raton Pass into New Mexico. (We'd stopped earlier at a lookout
where four different states were visible, surely, in the haze to the
east and south.) The Sangre de Cristos came into view and the first
soft-cornered adobe houses, and that night we ate at La Fonda with
my Aunt Elsie, who worked for the Indian Bureau, and had Hopi
snake dances and San Ildefonso pottery makers and Mabel Dodge
Luhan in store for us in the coming weeks. Almost the best part was
still ahead.

I learned how to drive early, and in June of 1936 sent five dollars
to the Bureau of Motor Vehicles in Augusta, Maine, along with a
note saying, "I am fifteen. Please send my license in enclosed enve-
lope." That was all it took. I appropriated the Whites' yellowy old
Plymouth roadster, with its splayed fenders, wooden-spoke wheels,
cracked leather front seat, and leaky ragtop roof. (I carried a thick
roll of Johnson & Johnson adhesive tape under the seat for rainy
day patch-ups.) There was a little hole in the floorboards, near
the brake pedal, and if you glanced down there on a daytime er-
rand you could see the grainy macadam streaming by under your
foot. Soon I was taking girls to the movies on Tuesday or Saturday
nights, upstairs at the Town Hall in Blue Hill, or to the Grand, in

Ellsworth. I kept my headlights on low beam on foggy nights, suavely navigating through sudden thick blankets of damp, and found quiet places to park in East Blue Hill or out on Naskeag Point. I had become Andy Hardy. Making out in parked cars puts me into the movies or into a thousand cartoons, but what memory presents about these chilly long-gone summer evenings is the first five minutes under way, with my hands at ease on the nubbly wheel, and with the white highway ahead and the gleam from the looped roadside power wires giving back tanned knees, a sweet nose and strong chin, just there to my right. Intimacy.

Late on a Sunday afternoon in February 1938, somebody called up the stairs of my boarding school dormitory, "Angell, there are three women from Smith down here to see you." We were in the hilly northeast corner of Connecticut, far into the dreary winter term stretches of my senior year, with spring vacation still six weeks away. A gag of some sort. Muttering, I came down and found Cynthia Coggin's blue Ford phaeton waiting by the door, and her tickled smile behind the snap-on winter side window — a friend from Maine, with crinkly blond hair and her own low, late-model white-wall speedster, the snazziest wheels I knew. She was about my age, but a year and a light-year ahead. Now, with two classmates for company, she'd driven seventy or eighty miles from Northampton on impulse, to press a surprise Sunday call. I rushed upstairs for a coat and permission, and in another minute was turning around from the cozy front seat to meet the new ladies in back as we sped away, delightfully in motion. I only had an hour — time enough for tea and cake at an inn in the next village, it turned out — and they got me back barely before compulsory evening vespers. Walking into the chapel, I knew that every eye was on me and that my school clout had just taken a gigantic upward leap. I didn't have to tell anybody that Cynthia was a friend, not a girlfriend, or that the difference didn't matter to me. All I could think about was the ride and the compliment.

Driving nowadays is nothing like it was. Mostly, it's a time of day: where we are before the mall, or around nine and six and — thank you, God — not later. On longer reaches, noise and wind rustle have been abolished, traffic-free stretches appear only late at night or in the moments after a red light has swept the road clean, and horsepower provides an airliner sort of lift that does away with iner-

tia and topography. We move in ceaseless company, each of us
wrapped in an expensive and imperturbable anonymity. Only
now and then, easing at 76 mph past the Audi going 72, do we
throw a glance at our neighbors three feet to the right and are startled — it nearly makes you jump — by pure genre: two or three
young men gesturing and laughing at something in there, or an
older woman holding up her book and reading out loud to her
driver husband. Driving, for all its drags and trouble, puts us together — I'm amazed that its immense advertising never quite gets
this right — and on some trips delivers a complicated fresh sense
of ourselves. I think that pause with my mother on the Bronx River
Parkway first stuck in my memory as an adventure but later on because she and I almost never had something happen just to the two
of us. And if she thought back to that outing it could have been to
see Andy White — perhaps they were not quite lovers yet — finding a boyish and confident joy in the unexpected. My Lincoln
School classmates didn't hate me for my nonstop blather in our
crowded Buick; they craved a little quiet, and bet that perhaps I'd
enjoy it too, given a chance. It was a long shot, but maybe I'd find,
along about Poughkeepsie, that I didn't have to be on all the time
to stay alive. Tex Goldschmidt never looked at his watch in the day
and a half we hung out together in Liberty, New York, waiting for
that distributor part, while my father would have seen the mishap
as a test of some kind, and gone all stern and strong in response.
But Father trusted Tex because he'd seen that he really believed in
jokes; there was something easy and silly there that he longed for. I
don't know what Barbara Kidder made of our holding hands like
that. She was almost a woman that night and I still almost a boy, and
I can't say why I'm so sure she never mentioned it to anyone.

   There's a famous story by John Updike called "The Happiest I've
Been," which ends in a long car trip. In it, the narrator, John, a college sophomore, is driving back to Chicago after a Christmas visit
home in the middle of Pennsylvania. The trip back is a seventeen-
hour haul and he shares a car with a friend named Neil (it's his
father's car). Before heading west, they stop at a drunken party,
and late that night John holds a girl in his arms on a sofa, mostly
because they're both so cold. He kisses her a little and she falls
asleep. Dawn is coming when the trip begins at last (the girls are
gone), and Neil unexpectedly lets John drive the car. Then Neil

falls asleep too. As I read this story for the first time, in 1959, when it came out in *The New Yorker,* my mind went back, as if on radar, to Barbara Kidder.

"When we came into tunnel country" — the last passage goes — "the flicker and hollow amplification stirred Neil awake. He sat up, the mackinaw dropping to his lap, and lit a cigarette. A second after the scratch of his match the moment occurred of which each following moment was a slight diminution, as we made the long irregular descent toward Pittsburgh. There were many reasons for my feeling so happy. We were on our way. I had seen a dawn. This far, Neil could appreciate, I had brought us safely. Ahead, a girl waited who, if I asked, would marry me, but first there was a long trip; many hours and towns interceded between me and that encounter.... And there was knowing that twice since midnight a person had trusted me enough to fall asleep beside me."

FRANK BURES

Test Day

FROM *WorldHum.com*

FROM THE DOORWAY, I can see the last of my students walking up the dirt road into the school grounds. They're late as usual, but Mr. Ndyogi isn't here to beat them, so no one is running. Their crisp blue and white uniforms move slowly beneath the outline of Mount Meru. I can see they're even less eager for class to begin than normal, less enthused about English grammar than ever.

They know, as they drag their feet through the dust, that today is test day.

The last students straggle into class as I write the final questions on the blackboard. When the talking and the scraping of wooden chairs dies down, I tell them to put their notebooks away and begin.

Testing is a futile exercise in so many ways. For most of these students, all forty-seven of them on a good day, English is their third language, after Swahili and Masai. My own Swahili is very bad, and even though we've been working on prepositions for some time, I still have no idea what the Swahili word for "preposition" is, or if there is one.

Instead, I'm reduced to crude hand gestures and bad drawings on the board. Walking around the room, glancing at the papers, I can see this hasn't worked as well as I thought it would. Instead, judging from their writing, preposition roulette is the favorite strategy once again.

"Go apologize to your brother *by* punching him in the nose."
"Where should I get *inward* the bus?"
"What sort of things are you interested *nothing*?"

Our school is a small one, not far from Arusha, the semi-cosmopolitan urban center of northern Tanzania. We have eight classrooms, which are staggered at intervals down a hill. The students begin at the top, and after a four-year downhill slide they end up with their "certificate." My students are about mid-slide, in Form III. I'm here for the year on a mostly self-funded teaching program, the idea being that, as an English speaker, I should have enough grasp of it to pass it along. This, in other words, is test day for me, too.

The walls of our classroom are whitewashed and the room is packed tight with desks and stools. The blackboard at the front is badly chipped, and overhead are corrugated iron sheets, with one plastic panel to allow the sunshine through. Our school is called Ekenywa, which in Masai means "Sunrise," because (as our head master told us) with education, the area around the school is waking up.

If some of my students would wake up, they might do better on this test.

My only real ambition here has been to leave them with a few practical English skills — how to write a letter, for example, or what the plot of *No Longer at Ease* is. Something to help them get a job in town, or at least pass their national exam.

On test day, walking between the desks, I see how far we are from such lofty goals. Take their "letter to a friend." I don't know how many times I've told them — how many times I've made them write in their notebooks — to end a letter, any letter, with "Yours sincerely."

Around the room, there are many interpretations of this: "Your thinthially," "you thinkfully," "Yours sincefully," "Your sincilier," "your sceneially," "Senceally," "Your friendly," "Yours be love friend." A few students do get the basics. John signs his, "Yours in the Building of the Nation," which I'm quite happy with. But mostly test day is the day I wonder why I'm here.

My students wonder this too. Imani even writes in his letter: "The aim of sending this letter to you is to tell you about my exam I do. The test I taking was very hard. I try to think, but I am not understand anything in this test. The teacher who make this test was not like the Form III to go in the Form IV."

A good effort, and not a bad letter, as they go. Rukia takes a more flattering tack. "I study in Ekenywa Secondary School, and the teacher is the very good and the teacher of English is come from America so they teach very well." Or, "Frank was teach me English very well. I like it because I trie to speak English and I want to go some o my town to teach a young girl and boy, like Frenck teach me." Or, "I will get 18 points on this test are very big points."

Her points, I'm afraid, will be the same size as everyone else's. But they try so hard, in spite of everything working against them. At primary school everything is taught in Swahili. Then they hit secondary school and suddenly all their classes are taught in English. In this kind of immersion, most students drown. The school provides no life rafts either, such as dictionaries or grammar books or workbooks. Never mind school supplies. Some days there aren't even any teachers.

Nonetheless, the Ministry of Education sets a huge task before them. Form III students, it says, should "develop the habit of reading for pleasure and for information," as well as to increase reading speed. It says they should complete thirteen books during the third year.

But our school has only five of the books on the syllabus, and enough copies of only three to actually use.

Of the two we finally read — *Things Fall Apart* and *No Longer at Ease,* both by Chinua Achebe — we had fourteen and twenty-three copies, respectively, and only a handful were in good condition. These were shared by groups of three or four students. But their actually reading them would be like my reading *Don Quixote* in Spanish. Impossible.

Of course, this shows on test day. We spent several weeks going over the books, and I wrote explicit outlines of everything that happened on the board, which I watched them copy down.

But on test day, students who once seemed to have mastered the plot, or at least memorized the characters, answer questions about Obi and his grandfather, Okonkwo, like this:

"Okonkwo Obi is falling apart."

"Obi is republic."

"Clara was very dislike because Obi's parents they don't want Clara to be wife of Obi. So Clara want to kill himself for that. THIS IS NOT GOD TO WANT TO KILL YOURSELF. EVEN YOU MR. FRANK."

Hmm. The thought hadn't crossed my mind. But with many more days like this, it just might.

On the other hand, sometimes on test day a previously illiterate student mysteriously becomes a brilliant literary critic.

"Okonkwo," writes Godson, "through his fears, becomes exiled from his tribe and returns only to be forced in the ignonimy of suicide to escape the results of his rash courage against the white man."

Godson is the class Rastafarian and knows the words to every Bob Marley song. I know he doesn't know anything about Okonkwo.

"Obi Okonkwo," writes Tumaini in suspiciously good English, "returns from his studies in England to try to live up to the expectations of his family and his tribe and at the same time to breathe the heady atmosphere of Lagos."

Such is the heady atmosphere of test day. Martin writes in his letter, "Just a quick note to let you know that I've had a rather serious accident in my holiday, and my leg is now in plaster. The doctor said that I've fractured it, and that I'll be laid up for about six weeks. After that I should be right as rain. I will tell you more in another letter. For now, let me end here. Yours ever, Martin Paul."

There are about three students in the class who might be able to write something like this. Martin is not one of them. He is one of the other forty-four who come to school, sit, talk, use cheat sheets I can never find, and don't pay attention, except on days when I give up on grammar and answer questions about America.

"Is it true," they would ask, "that the government gives every American a gun at age eighteen?" "Is it true that even the poorest Americans have twelve cars?" "What's up, man?" they would ask. "Hey," I'd say. "Not much."

Those days were the best of all, the days when I felt that I really had something to offer, something they wanted to know. These were the days we connected. These were the days when they sat rapt as I unlocked the secrets of America, and they, in turn, unlocked their own country, giving me all the street lingo I could use.

But there was no slang on the national syllabus, and it didn't help them on test day.

"So," I ask again as we go over the test (we've been over the material before). "Obi and Christopher went out with some Irish girls. Does anyone know what 'Irish' means?"

"Irish potatoes!" someone shouts.

"Yes," I say, "like Irish potatoes. But what does 'Irish' mean?"

"Beautiful!" someone else shouts.

Next question: "So, the girl tried to bribe Obi with sex. What . . ."

Suddenly they are all fluent. "Explain! Explain!" they yell.

"No!" says Seuri. "Don't explain in words. Give demonstration so we can see."

The students hand in the tests, and the scores are abysmal again. I'm not even sure how to grade them. If I make it on a curve, it will be a very small bump. The hardest part is that I know they could do it if they had the chance, if they had some hope. But there are too many obstacles and too few incentives. Most of my students will be married off or end up putting their certificate to work in the fields.

Yet as with so many things in Tanzania, we move on. Life is hard here, but giving up is even harder, and it's not really an option. So we go forward, to the next test, the next lesson. Along the way, we look for hope and laughter and comfort where there is little, and make our own where there is none.

As class finishes, wooden chairs scrape across the floor again as the students stand up to leave with their tests. I too move to the door, but accidentally step on Matthew's foot.

"Oh, sorry," I say.

"It's cool," he says.

"Where did you learn that?" I ask.

He looks at me and smiles.

"You."

MICHAEL BYERS

Monuments to Our Better Nature

FROM *Preservation*

GROWING UP IN THE SEVENTIES in Bethesda, Maryland, a suburb of Washington, D.C., I had the good fortune to be taken regularly to the National Mall by my mother. She was a scientist, and in
the aftermath of the Vietnam War she found much to be disheartened by. The immense Smithsonian museums on the Mall acted,
for her, as repositories of truth and exactitude in an age of cupidity,
paranoia, and evasion; they were her solace.

In the National Museum of Natural History, the gargantuan blue
whale hanging above us with its great grooved throat was a *fact*
about the world that could not be denied. The stuffed African elephant on its circular dais in the rotunda was composed of billions
of skin cells and tiny cilia, and its ivory tusks wore an unfalsifiable
brown patina of age. The chambered skull of the brontosaurus, the
irrefutable chain of his vertebrae, his ponderous thighbones, and
his sculpted metatarsals — each the size and heft of an anchor —
had been painstakingly recovered from a stony Canadian grave,
cleaned, and finally pieced together again, eons after the original
owner had ceased to have any use for them.

Certain truths, the museums assured us, were undeniable. The
meteorites upstairs had roamed the vacuum of space for billions of
years until at last, following the Keplerian laws of orbit and velocity,
they had collided with Earth, their nickel cores becoming polished
by the final scalding plunge through the atmosphere. What a wonder it all was, and how true. And how could anyone not grasp that
these truths were, in so many cases, utterly beautiful? This was the
sort of thing my young mother wanted to be reassured of in those
days, and it was an idea she wanted me to appreciate, too.

But my secret love was not the museums themselves but their grand exteriors and their placement among the other monuments and memorials. Looking ghostly in the distance, these stone structures spoke of a grandeur whose reach and glory had no measure. While for my mother these temples were tainted by chauvinism — in them she saw the young, rough-edged country trying to polish its image — for me they were transcendent. Even as a very young boy I knew they had the power to draw me across the grass, and they still do.

Washington, particularly the vast, open Mall, is the place where I first felt like a *citizen*. Standing in front of this monument or that memorial, I understood what it meant to belong to a country so populous as this one. This is the first purpose of these places, it seems to me: to inform citizens of the nation's collective character. They are massive, and beside them we are tiny. So it is politically. Alone, each of us is almost without value, but in the aggregate we are the point of the whole improbable enterprise. One is lost in the multitude, but the multitude itself is essential. It is no mistake that the White House — often the scene of great reputations made and lost — is on the back of the twenty-dollar bill, while Lincoln and his memorial find themselves on the penny. You are only a penny, the monuments tell us, but you are dearly counted.

And in life, while the White House may resemble an overbuilt embassy, the Lincoln Memorial is sublime. What American can approach Henry Bacon's temple to the humble son of Illinois and not feel his own soul beginning to rise eerily through the top of his head? What a glory to mount the broad stairs; what a thrilling incantation to count the thirty-six Doric columns, one for every state of the Union in 1864. And what a pleasure it is to call out the rank of states whose names, inscribed here above the entrance — VIRGINIA TENNESSEE GEORGIA — bring to mind not demagogic governors or backward pockets of creation science but ideal, benign subrepublics run by citizens much like ourselves. All around us, as we climb the stairs, fellow Americans are dressed in logo-covered T-shirts and careless blue jeans, and many are young, and loud. But there they are beside us anyhow, and at the top of the stairs we all stop and turn — we cannot help ourselves — to see where we have come from. And how far indeed it is that we, as a people, have traveled. Below us lie the steps where in Easter of

1939 the contralto Marian Anderson, black daughter of a coal dealer, sang "America" and "Nobody Knows the Trouble I've Seen," as seventy-five thousand looked on in the April cold. On these steps, Martin Luther King, Jr., shrugged himself away from his prepared text and in that extemporaneous moment produced a supreme example of American oratory — his long Whitmanesque lines echoing with the names of the states carved high on the temple's walls behind him: "Let freedom ring from the snowcapped Rockies of Colorado! Let freedom ring from the curvaceous peaks of California! But not only that; let freedom ring from Stone Mountain of Georgia! Let freedom ring from Lookout Mountain of Tennessee! Let freedom ring from every hill and every molehill of Mississippi!"

What a glory it is to stand where Anderson sang and King spoke — and what a glory to have been permitted to climb these steps unwatched, unquestioned, without a ticket of admission, and at last to arrive at the portico, where the simple Indiana limestone pillars are much larger than they appeared from below, and where the Tennessee pink marble floor is scuffed with millions of our footsteps, and where, as we pass inside, the Alabama marble ceiling — soaked in paraffin to make it translucent — casts a pale light. Hushed, we stop. There he is, Lincoln, on his throne, looking down at us all, while at the other end of the Mall the messy business of the Capitol goes on under his tireless, admonitory gaze.

Americans are not known for good behavior in public, but here we become subdued, reflective. It is a long way to the ceiling, and our voices fade. Who is not moved by the sentences carved into the walls? "With malice toward none; with charity for all; with firmness in the right . . . Let us strive on to finish the work we are in; to bind up the nation's wounds . . . to do all which may achieve and cherish a just and lasting peace, among ourselves, and with all nations." At this, who does not feel grateful, and feel a lump in the throat? And even those few of us who are ignorant, or disdainful, who choose to snap gum or answer cell phones — well, we are Americans, and this is our monument, and whatever we do here is by definition permissible because it is ours.

Everyone goes to the Lincoln Memorial. Not everyone goes to the Jefferson. You can drive there and park, but from the Lincoln Memorial you must walk along the Tidal Basin and cross a busy bridge. The monument faces the water, so you must approach it obliquely, or from the back. Jefferson stands, bronze, his coattails flared, his proud calves on display, his handsome head erect. Under the dome, pigeons flutter from place to place like thoughts moving in a great curved brain. The building, designed by John Russell Pope, is modeled after the Pantheon in Rome, but where is the dramatic soaring reach of the ceiling? Jefferson seems too large for his temple.

Disappointment may come from our feelings about Jefferson himself: we appreciate the need for him, but still we do not much like him. Surely we take him too much for granted. He is remote, a rationalist. And what are we to make of the arcane inscriptions? "I am not an advocate for frequent changes in laws and constitution, but laws and institutions go hand in hand with the progress of the human mind. . . . We might as well require a man to wear the same coat that fitted him when he was a boy." All right, but where is the poetry? We have left it over there across the water, in the big rough hands of Lincoln.

We approach the third great presidential monument, Robert Mills's stark tribute to George Washington, without much excitement. It is the Mall's least lovely structure, and its most primitive. Thirty-seven years in the making, and what do we have? An obelisk, which seems to the eye not quite vertical as it rises above the city. But maybe it is fitting that this most distant figure of the American pantheon should have this least expressive tower built in his name: the first president as Zoroaster, a demigod whose name we have heard but whom we do not know personally. This monument seems Egyptian, and as such out of place here on the green among the more welcoming Greek and Roman temples. But this is fitting too. Washington, we know, was himself somewhat uncomfortable in civilian life, by turns noble, humble, and clumsy. Like some of the other lifelong military men who would later find themselves in the presidency, he was never quite sure where he stood. At the top of his monument, people shove their way to the windows. If we swoon at the drop and step back from the glass, our place is quickly taken.

There is no shoving at the Vietnam Veterans Memorial. Behavior here is impeccable, and we have its intuitive, minimalist design by Maya Lin to thank. This monument is public architecture at its finest: open, instructive, and moving. The ambivalent descent, deeper and deeper, along a sinister black wall, exactly mimics the national experience of the war: the early trickle of bad news, the growing sense of obligation, the gradual realization that we are in over our heads, and at its nadir, the dark hopelessness from which there seems no escaping. We catch our breath as we descend. We are silent, knowing that some of the visitors here will have lost a brother, son, father, friend.

Adults climb out of this hole sadder and wiser. But do the twelve-year-olds also behave well here only because of the crying man in the army fatigues? Or do they, like their parents, feel that something terrible has happened, and been preserved somehow in black marble? And will their children feel the same way, or will they need to learn the lessons of Vietnam again?

At the top of the ramp we are released again onto the green. We walk to the Korean War Veterans Memorial but leave with a bad taste. It tries too hard to move us, and it fails. And so we look suspiciously at the construction under way at the foot of the Reflecting Pool where the World War II Memorial is at last taking shape. We are willing to suspend judgment, but we are concerned about the loss of open space.

Because ultimately the defined space of the Mall is its greatest asset. It is one of America's most venerable and trafficked pedestrian public spaces, where you can fly a kite alone or stand among a hundred thousand and hear a speech being given half a mile away by a barely discernible figure. It is the *distance* between monuments that I find myself appreciating every time I visit. The buildings appear on the horizon and resolve, slowly, as you approach them on foot across the grass. In this way the Mall itself functions like an enormous museum, and these imperfect places are what we have so far in our national display case, laid out on the green velvet of the enormous lawn.

As adults, we eventually learn that the brontosaurus is now called apatosaurus, and half of its bones are informed reconstructions. We discover there were ten million African elephants in 1930, and that now there are only thirty-five thousand. We see that government is bought and paid for, no matter what party is in power. But still: Who can stand on the top step of the Lincoln Memorial and not think *I am a participant in a world civilization, I have history entrusted to me, we are all in this together* — and feel it, for a minute or two, as the simple, honest truth?

TIM CAHILL

The Accidental Explorer's Guide to Patagonia

FROM *National Geographic Adventure*

I WAS ON MY WAY to my favorite place on earth. I hadn't ever been there before and wasn't exactly sure where it was, but I knew, in the way a man knows these things, that we were drawing closer and that the place I found would be my new favorite place on earth. Never mind the slight tug of airsickness.

The floatplane was following the deep valley of a mud-choked river. It wheeled this way and that against glacier-clad spires glittering in the sun. The colors were intense in this corridor of ice: the river below ran over gold sandbanks that rose sharply to become grassy hillsides, bright green against the dazzle of the ice above. It was incredibly beautiful.

"Isn't this incredibly beautiful?" Eric Hertz shouted over the howl of the engine. He was so pumped up and so sincere that I just couldn't help myself.

"If you like this sort of thing," I said.

In fact, I *love* this sort of thing. I had an aviation map of the area open on my lap. Our plane had risen out of the lake called General Carrera here in Chile. We were in the lower portion of South America, at about 46° south latitude. The floatplane was flying at about 2,500 feet, under jagged icy peaks that rose to more than 6,000 feet. The guy sitting beside me, Dave, a pilot himself and an aviation buff, pointed out the advisories stamped all over the map: "Relief Detail Unreliable." In other words, this area of Chilean Patagonia was so little known that no one could say precisely how high the mountains were.

Mark, our floatplane's pilot, followed the Río Leones as it ascended into what is known as the Northern Ice Field. Combined with Patagonian glaciers just a bit to the south, in the Southern Ice Field, this area is sometimes called the "third pole." It carries a lot of frozen water, all of it cascading lickety-split down the mountains. There's a lot of geology happening here, and it's happening right in your face.

We topped a ridge, and an immense lake, Lago Leones, surrounded by mountains and ice, lay before us like a dream. The water was pea-soup green where it was shadowed by shards of wind-whipped mist and emerald green where slanting shafts of light fell on its surface this bright summer day early in December.

Mark put the plane down, helped offload our camping gear and inflatable kayaks, then went back to pick up the rest of our crew. This was an "exploratory" trip mounted by Earth River Expeditions, the adventure travel company owned by Eric Hertz and his Chilean partner, Robert Currie. Some commercial clients — I count myself among them — prefer exploratories. Eric had come to find a new place to bring clients, and I was looking for my new favorite place on earth. These weren't necessarily antagonistic ambitions.

Except that Eric thought we might find a place "where no other human being has ever been." Since it is generally impossible to prove a negative — no one has ever been here — this sort of claim is usually an exercise in what I call GCB, or gratuitous chest beating. Eric Hertz, however, is not a chest beater; he's simply enthusiastic and so obviously sincere that his fervor is contagious whether you agree with him or not. Over the years he's led clients, journalists, and celebrities to speak out about saving this bit of wilderness or that. The guy's heart is in the right place, and several months ago, when we began talking about a trip to Patagonia, I was swept up in the current of Eric's passion. He said he was looking for a discovery. Me? I'd settle for a new fave.

Read the literature: Patagonia is either an Eden of soaring mountains and alpine lakes or it is a monotonous revelation of the merely horizontal — more than 300,000 square miles straddling portions of Chile and Argentina in the southern cone of South America. The *Encyclopaedia Britannica* calls the Argentine portion a "vast area of steppe and desert" stretching from 37° to 51° south latitude. Of course, the topography offers a bit more drama if you include the lower spine of the Andes along the international border. But many travelers have nonetheless come away with the image of unrelenting flatness as the primary impression of the area. Charles Darwin, who visited the region on the voyage of the HMS *Beagle,* said that "these plains are pronounced by all wretched and useless. They can be described only by negative characters; without habitations, without water, without trees, without mountains, they support merely a few dwarf plants."

These wretched and useless plains, I must confess, have used up a goodly portion of my life. They came to my attention a quarter century ago, when I met the climber Yvon Chouinard. In 1968, Yvon and several friends had driven a van down to Patagonia. A summit flag taped to the back window identified the occupants as "Phun Hogs," and indeed, they scaled peaks, climbed glaciers, rode horses, walked mountain trails, and caught several dinners' worth of large, dumb trout. They never made it all the way to Tierra del Fuego, the archipelago at the end of the Americas that is politically split between Argentina and Chile and that some geographers say is part of Patagonia proper. The actual borders are a bit hazy: Patagonia is as much a state of mind as it is a region. Chouinard, impressed with this state of mind, visited the region again in 1972, which is when he decided to call his garment company Patagonia. Maybe you've seen some of his clothes?

And Charles Darwin, having cogitated on Patagonia for a time, wrote, "Why . . . have these arid wastes taken so firm a hold on my memory?" Darwin said he could "scarcely analyze these feelings: but it must be partly owing to the free scope given to the imagination. The plains of Patagonia are boundless." Who, Darwin wondered, "would not look at these last boundaries to man's knowledge with deep but ill-defined sensations."

Not me. There have been a lot of deep but ill-defined sensations in the half-dozen times I've visited Patagonia since I first talked about it with Chouinard twenty-five years ago. Clearly, the region was not all arid plain and desert. On the Península Valdés, three-ton elephant seals lie like slugs on the beach, or they battle one another in bloody contests of sexual domination. Orcas motor up onto the beach and eat baby sea lions like canapés, while southern right whales breach in the deeper waters.

Not too far inland, there is a kind of cowboy heaven just east of the Andes, near the towns of El Bolsón and Esquel. If you were to drive a gravel road out of El Bolsón, you'd notice fat cattle and fast horses in the fields and old log cabins on the riverbanks. Butch Cassidy, the Sundance Kid, and Etta Place lived in a few of those cabins, on land they ranched for four years.

The old cabins are tumbling down now, and bees hum in the fields. The river flows into a large lake, and glaciers glitter in the mountains above. All in all, this place is a Southern Hemisphere mirror image of my home in south-central Montana, except that when the snow piles up above the windows in January where I live, people in Patagonia are enjoying sixteen-hour summer days. Riding horses. Having barbecues.

Aside from this seasonal inversion, Patagonia can be conveniently compared to the American West: there are endless scrublands and deserts and canyonlands and mountains and glaciers and any number of extraordinary places to send the soul soaring. It is a place of special oddities. In 1905, for instance, Butch and Sundance were said to have robbed a bank in Río Gallegos, about seven hundred miles south of their ranch.

I've seen the robbed bank at Río Gallegos — it still stands — and later on the same day I visited the nearby penguin colony. It was the American West all right, but a bizarro version, with hints of another dimension leaking into the scene. I was forced to imagine a daring daylight bank robbery, accomplished on horseback, with penguins strutting about underfoot.

And people ask me why Patagonia is my favorite place on earth.

There were thirteen of us standing on the shores of Lago Leones, all men. "We had one woman who wanted to come," Eric said, "but she runs marathons for fun and didn't think this trip would be strenuous enough for her." People find Eric's trips on his Web site, Earthriver.com, or are attracted by word of mouth, but most everyone on this go-around had traveled with Earth River before. Aside from gender, there was no common denominator: Ed was a doctor; Fermin was an accountant from Mexico; José Luis, from Chile, and John, from Canada, were businessmen. Some guys were wealthy; some were just scraping by. All knew that things seldom run absolutely smoothly on an exploratory trip like this. They liked that.

So we were an all-male expedition, ready to endure any hardship, and we might have felt pretty macho out here in the Northern Ice Field, except that the only woman who took the time to investigate the expedition thought it was a sissy trip.

I believe the marathoner might have changed her mind that very afternoon when we went looking for a waterfall we'd seen from the plane. It was several ridges over from our campsite, and we sidehilled it through thick, intensely annoying, ankle-grabbing vegetation. When you fell, and everyone did now and again, the vegetation caught and enfolded your body so that it was difficult to get up, in the manner that it is difficult to get up when you've fallen into deep snow on a steep hill. Every once in a while we'd pass red flowering plants with woody stems that sported flowers like hands with way too many fingers. José Luis, who as a Chilean knew such things, said the plants were called *ciruelillos*. They grew from two to twelve feet high and were our friends. We could grab the whiplike trunks and take a few easy steps over the matted vegetation. Our feet never touched ground; we moved on uneven, springy beds of branch and vine. We looked, altogether, like a bunch of drunks stumbling over the hillside.

An occasional tree, looking vaguely tropical, rose out of the low vegetation. Thunder rumbled in the distance, but this late afternoon was perfectly blue and cloudless. We were hearing the sound of the glacier pouring into the lake as it calved off great icebergs. I contemplated the glacier, juxtaposed with the seemingly tropical vegetation. Here was a good slice of Patagonia bizarro: a world of ice framed by red flowers and lush plants.

A mist rose from the drainage one ridge away: it was the waterfall, less than a mile off and, we calculated, about, jeez, another hour and a half away. Hell with it: we abandoned the waterfall. Probably wouldn't have been a favorite place anyway.

For the hike back we moved to the high ridges, which were less choked with vegetation, and it took us only twenty-seven days to get to camp, or so it seemed. My infallible adventure watch, with time and date and altitude and compass functions, said that we had been fighting through the foliage for only about five hours total. We were beat, and it would have been easy to think of ourselves as highly robust hikers except for one fact I've neglected to mention: Eric's ten-year-old son, Cade, was along on the trip and had done everything we'd done, only faster.

Cade was writing a diary for a school project, and it is instructive to see a ten-year-old cover the same day with a good deal more dispatch than I can muster: "My dad the guides the clients and me went on a float plane to Lago Leones which mean Lake of the lions because there are so many mountain lions there." We did, in fact, find the scat and tracks of a lion near our campsite. Cade describes our walk in this matter-of-fact manner: "Then everybody went on a hike to a creek. We did some bushwhacking but did not see much except for bushes."

The next day we inflated the kayaks and paddled down the lake toward the glacier. The sun was bright, and there were more thunderlike rumblings that grew ever louder as we approached the ice, a wall perhaps 80 or 100 feet high. Some in our party, Eric in particular, thought it was closer to 250. Let's call it 150 feet.

Occasionally a chunk of ice the size of a three- or four-story building calved off the ice cliff, and this calving occurred in what appeared to be slow motion. The ice, exhibiting a great deal of leisure, tumbled lazily into the water below, eventually sending a fountain of spray 30 or 40 feet into the air. These calvings generated waves several feet high, and the waves became a concern as we approached the glacier. It was, according to my watch, 65°F out, but there was a cool breeze from the glacier, as if someone had left the refrigerator door open.

Lago Leones, according to the infallible adventure watch, which is usually right plus or minus a few hundred feet, was only 1,070 feet above sea level. A lowland lake. It is true that there are glaciers at sea level in high latitudes — in Alaska, for instance — but this was 46° south. Portland, Oregon, is close to 46° north and also near sea level, but you seldom hear of glaciers stopping traffic on the interstate there.

Beyond this glacier, to the west, there were some pretty substantial mountains, including Monte San Valentín, which, at 13,240 feet, is the highest point in Patagonia. So it was staggering to think that if all these glaciers were grinding away down here at a thousand feet, there was surely ice beyond comprehension at 13,000 feet.

Our kayaks were doubles, and I was paddling with a guy who prefers to be nameless in this instance. We decided to defy the thunder and paddle close to the glacier. A line of calved-off icebergs floated near the place where ice met water. We calculated the risks and moved in among the bergs. Every now and again we could hear this odd clicking. It was the sound you hear when a really cold ice cube is dropped in a glass of water. We moved in closer yet and sat in the kayaks, staring up at all the ice in the world. My paddling partner said, "Makes me think of my girlfriend."

I looked up at the frigid world above and almost said "I'm sorry." Silence seemed the best course. He said, "It's the blue color."

In places, parts of the glacier had fallen away in huge, hundred-foot-high pillars, and the underlying ice was a deep and clean cornflower blue that seemed to glow, as from within. "She has blond hair and blue eyes," my partner said.

"Yes?"

"So I'm thinking lingerie."

A few judicious questions established that the woman did not presently own any blue lingerie. That situation would be rectified immediately upon my partner's return.

Thus occupied with our thoughts, we threaded through the icebergs floating at the base of the glacier. None of them was much bigger than a house. The smaller ones were not blue but white in the sun, all pocked and melting, with small rivers flowing off their backs. The sun was sculpting these bergs into various fantastic shapes. One looked like a fox's head with water dripping off the nose.

I was contemplating the oft made assertion that there is no geographic cure. If you're an alcoholic in Maine, you'll be one in Missouri, or so they say. The observation, I think, is both smug and erroneous. My favorite spots have all been something a good deal more than a photo op. Once, I climbed to the foot of a glacier in Torres del Paine National Park in Chile. No big thing, except that I was recovering from a back operation I'd needed after a climbing fall. For two months before the operation, I had been unable to walk. Torres del Paine is a favorite place. I learned to walk there.

I visited the Península Valdés during a career crisis that involved a lot of angry, high-volume negotiations. On the peninsula, I took some pleasure in watching three-ton monsters battle on the beach. And outside El Bolsón the wind whispered that a sudden and unexpected vacancy in my love life was all for the best. For both of us.

So it is my contention that favorite places have the capacity to heal. I wasn't presently in any particular mental or physical turmoil. But, as every Boy Scout knows, it is wise to be prepared. I was looking for a new favorite place, just in case.

It was the warmest part of the day, and the glacier was calving frequently. Massive quantities of ice fell, and the rumbling thunder was constant for twenty or thirty seconds at a time. A few moments later, a wave formed at the base of the glacier and radiated outward, lifting the icebergs all about. It was no good running from the wave: the awful thing could simply crest up over you and drop several dozen tons of ice on your head. No, we wanted to face the wave and paddle over the crest, dodging ice as we rose five or six feet on the swell and then fell down the other side, drawing ever closer to the glacier. In the interval between calvings, we retreated rapidly.

"Lingerie?" I asked my partner.

Ice clicked suggestively on all sides.

"Lingerie," he said.

Our party lunched on a rocky point overlooking the glacier, which creaked and groaned beside us. Below, it cracked and boomed into the lake. Eric thought it was possible no one had ever been here before. "I doubt it," I said. There was the matter of the trail up to the lake that we'd seen from the floatplane, for one thing. For another, I had read a report about a Chilean climbing team that had entered the Northern Ice Field by way of Lago Leones and spent twenty-two days on the ice, climbing Valentín, among other peaks.

"Okay," Eric said. He could accept that. You could see the wheels turning in his head. "But," he said, "we may be the first to kayak this lake."

"It is not well known," said José Luis, who lives in Santiago but has a cabin a couple of hours north of where we were sitting. "I've been coming to this area for over twenty years, and I never heard of Lago Leones before."

I thought that "not well known" was a better formulation than "the first human beings to stand on this spot."

Presently Eric said, "Let's go find that high lake we saw from the plane." It had looked pretty good from the air — a potential favorite place for sure — a small alpine lake set up against a headwall maybe 2,000 feet high.

It took us two hours to climb 600 feet. The high lake was still
about 1,400 feet above us, which meant we were only a third of the
way there. I didn't think I could get up to the lake and down to the
kayaks before dark and decided to turn back. Eric thought otherwise. Ed the doctor and John the Canadian elected to come with
me. Eric's partner Robert also joined us, and we chatted on the way
down the rolling boulder slope.

Robert was Chilean, but as a child he had lived in the United
States and Mexico. Back in Chile he had owned and operated a garage for a while, then got into the import-export business, bringing
T-shirts from Brazil into Argentina, for instance, while taking advantage of various currency devaluations. That business kept him
away from his wife and kids too much, so he bought a farm and
worked it hard. Then, in 1989, he met Eric Hertz on a train and
found himself riding a high tide of sincerity and enthusiasm.

Robert felt as if he'd been a guide in training and hadn't even
known it. "Because of my background I can fix mechanical things,
and I'm pretty good at dealing with officials and customs officers,
and the farming made me strong." Robert was still plenty strong.
He looked like he could pull a stump up out of the ground with his
bare hands.

We arrived back at the lake, and it didn't look good at all. A late-
afternoon wind was howling off the glacier, and Leones was a sea of
whitecaps. The icebergs that had been floating at the base of the
glacier were off in the far distance, congregated near our campsite
several miles away, sailing on the katabatic wind that poured off the
ice. John the Canadian and I launched first, and that was the last
we saw of Robert and Ed. The lake required our full attention.

We knew we had to cross quickly or the wind would drive us past
our camp, which was on the other side of the lake. If we missed it,
there'd be no paddling back. This required that we take the shortest possible route across, which put us broadside to the wind and
waves. It was scary out there, and John, who's run his share of Class
IV and V rivers, shouted over the wind.

"What?" I hollered back.

"Never . . . thought . . . sea kayaking . . . was . . . an adrenaline
sport," he yelled.

But it was. If the kayak flipped, we wouldn't survive long in the
frigid water. There were four- and five- and six-foot waves coming in

sets, and they slopped over into the kayak, which, thankfully, was a self-bailing model, or we'd have been sunk. John thrust his paddle into the belly of the waves as they reared up on us, and I steered in a manner that put us three-quarters broadside on the crest of the waves, which brought the rudder out of the water and rendered it useless for several moments. All that was required in that situation was a quick corrective backpaddle. In this way, zigzagging through the wind and waves, we crossed the lake and neared the icebergs, which were spread out in a defensive line blocking the promontory we had to round in order to get to camp. They glittered in the sun, melting to death in various evocative shapes as the waves exploded against them, sending spray ten feet into the air.

John and I decided not to chance the icebergs and made a pretty fair surf landing on a small stone beach one ridge away from our camp. We hadn't stopped paddling once in almost two hours. John dropped to his knees. "I'm doing a pope," he said, and kissed the ground.

Presently we began to wonder what had happened to Robert and Ed. They weren't out on the water, or we'd have seen their bright yellow kayak cresting the waves every once in a while. We climbed up the ridge for a better view and stood facing the wind-whipped lake. We scanned the water for ten minutes or more.

There was a rustling behind us. "You guys just get in?" Ed asked. He and Robert were carrying their gear to their tents. They had followed us across the lake, zigzagging in the same manner, but had made it through the line of icebergs and around the promontory.

"We were worried about you guys," I said.

"You didn't look back," Robert asked, "check on us once in a while?"

"You're a guide," I said.

"Guides are people, too."

The winds died down, and the surface of the lake glassed off and mirrored the sunset. Eric and the rest of the group came paddling back through the various reds and pinks around ten o'clock. They hadn't quite made the upper lake, just as we hadn't quite made the waterfall a day ago. Eric said he wasn't going to push things too much with Cade along. If his son got hurt, he'd have to answer to his wife, and then he'd be in the cat box.

"The cat box?"

"It's a step down from the doghouse," Eric explained.

"Anything lower than the cat box?"

"Hell."

I slept like a rock and woke late the next morning. It was 10:70. Apparently, everyone had left except for Robert, who offered me a cup of coffee without a trace of sarcasm.

"Where is everyone?" I asked.

"Asleep," Robert said.

And it occurred to me that there was no such time as 10:70 and that I was looking at the altitude calibration on my infallible adventure watch. I punched a button and discovered that it was actually 6:15.

The next day we broke camp and made our way to another, higher lake called Lago Cachorro, Chilean Spanish for Puppy Lake. We found a rough trail hacked out of the bush, but other than those few machete cuts, there were no signs of human visitation: no plastic bags or bottles or candy wrappers. We didn't even find a single fire ring.

"And," Eric said, "probably no one has been to the narrow arm way down on the other side of the lake."

I didn't say anything.

"You know Mark, our pilot? He's been here ten years. He doesn't know anyone who's been there."

"Okay," I said.

That afternoon, as we set up camp at Lago Cachorro and reinflated the kayaks, horseflies assailed us in a continuous swarming attack. I found myself wishing it would rain and drive the insects away. So, of course, the next morning dawned cold and gray and a steady rain drummed down on the tents. The sun bullied its way through the clouds by about eleven, and we paddled off down the lake through various shafts of light that angled down out of dramatic, even operatic, cloud forms. We made directly for the end of the lake, where a snowcapped mountain stood behind the others like the fin of a shark.

The lake ended at a perfectly vertical rock wall that rose three thousand feet (at a guess) out of the water. We turned left, into the narrow arm of the lake, and paddled down a fjordlike channel with rock walls rising close on either side of us. I was beset by a sudden vertigo. The rock loomed over us. A dizzying assortment of ledges ran every which way: they rose on a diagonal and then dropped like a bad day at the stock market. Waterfalls fell silver against the slick black walls that now towered between 4,000 and 6,000 feet above us. There were more than a dozen falls, and they dropped down obvious drainage patterns or followed the rock ledges for a time. They braided back and forth or pooled up on shelves, then poured over flat, vertical slabs in wide sheets, an effect architects attempt in the fountains of buildings that aspire to grandeur. One of the more substantial falls plunged down rock carved and weathered in such a way that it resembled a ski jump. The water was propelled out into space and fell 150 feet or so to the rocks below.

All of which was dizzying enough, but when I followed the water-falls to their source at the top of the cliffs — it was necessary to crane my neck and lean back — I saw any number of glaciers peek-ing over the ridges of rock several thousand feet above us. Streams of meltwater flowed out from lingerie-blue caves under the gla-ciers. The ice was poised, hanging there and ready to fall at any mo-ment, so that the slender arm of Puppy Lake was filled to the brim with the certainty of imminent avalanche.

We felt reasonably safe in the center of the channel, though a few immense rocks poked five and ten feet out of the water, and it was pretty clear where they'd come from. Every fifteen minutes or so we heard a sharp *crack* and then a rumbling that echoed through the high rock canyon. It was difficult to pinpoint the location of the avalanche, and we looked up at the assortment of hanging glaciers overhead. The sound grew in volume, overwhelmed the echo, and drew all eyes. The ice that had broken off the glacier above was bat-tered violently against the cliff so that it was cracked and finally crushed high above us, and then it fell like water, silver against the black rock, a mobile margarita kicking loose a few Volkswagen-size rocks that bounded joyously above and beside the waterfall of crushed ice.

The banks of the lake were narrow, and it was no more than a hundred yards to the cliff face, I suppose, but the ice hit this gently sloping apron and piled up on itself, forming large ice fields where you didn't want to be standing when the daiquiri of death came thundering down the cliff. Streams from the waterfalls flowed un-der the piles of ice and emptied out into the lake.

This was my new favorite place on earth.

We beached our kayaks on a gray, pebbly shore at the end of the channel, where the largest of the streams poured into the lake, and then just stood there for several minutes, silent and stupefied. After some moments, we attempted speech. Eric was keen to come up with a name for the place. He didn't think people would want to travel thousands of miles to see Puppy Lake. We tried the Ice Palace, the Glacier Gymnasium, the Coliseum of Ice. Eric conferred with Robert, who, in his farming days, had worked with Chile's Mapuche Indians. They had a word meaning "where heaven meets the earth."

"Too pretentious," I said.

"The Shackleton Arm," Eric said without a moment's pause.

"Historically inaccurate."

Eventually, Robert and Eric came up with an evocative Spanish name: Cañon Cascada de Nieve. I liked it: the Canyon of Cascading Snow. As we contemplated the name, another avalanche dropped a daiquiri of death on an ice field just a couple of hundred yards away. The name seemed appropriate.

I stood there, looking up, and felt something inside me rise with the rock. It was strange. Here was all this violent geology going on all around, and it seemed to inspire a certain tremulous serenity. I suspected that the sensation was something you might feel after sitting in an empty room meditating for a couple of decades.

Dave, the aviation buff, and I talked about it for a bit. We'd both paddled kayaks in Alaska, where the lakes were bigger and the mountains higher. "But," Dave said, "everything is always somewhere off in the distance." Here, the mountains and glaciers rose directly out of the lake, right in front of you, and there was something in that proximity that generated grandeur. Dave, with his aviation background, called all this sudden rearing up of rock and ice "immediate vertical relief."

I liked the phrase and wrote it down in my notebook. If life ever got the best of me again and I started going bughouse, I think I'd take a pass on the pills and come down to Cañon Cascada de Nieve for a couple days of immediate vertical relief. It was a place that kicked and pummeled you into a state of reflective tranquillity. And I'd already scouted it out.

The others had turned their attention to the rushing stream at our feet that was pouring out of the only nontechnical climbing drainage in the whole canyon. It rose about two thousand feet in a series of ridges that terminated at another cliff wall crested with glaciers. Eric expressed his opinion that there was a lake up top, probably located between the last ridge and the headwall. Eric always thinks there's a lake up top, and even if there isn't, inconclusive walks are the very essence of exploration.

We climbed for a couple of hours, rising up over gray granite, moving ever closer to a small glacier at the base of the headwall.

I was walking alone, at a meandering pace, when Eric and Cade passed me on the way down.

"No lake," Eric admitted.

"Look at it this way," I said. "Cade is almost certainly the only ten-year-old from Accord, New York, to have ever stood on this spot."

By the time I got down to the kayaks, most everyone had left for camp. Fermín from Mexico and Ed the doctor were standing on the shore. José Luis from Chile was still up there, as was Robert the guide, who is a person, too. Those of us on the shore thought it was best to wait for Robert and José Luis, just in case.

Presently it began to rain. After twenty minutes Ed and Fermín and I got really good at standing in the rain together. A stiff wind sprang up and drove the rain horizontally into our faces. We retreated up-canyon to a house-size granite boulder, where we perfected standing in the rain behind a rock in about ten minutes flat. Ed and I walked down to the shore, emptied out a kayak, and carried it back to the rock. Then we practiced huddling under a kayak in the rain for an hour and a half. Where the hell were Robert and José Luis?

I stepped out into the rain and tried walking over a boulder. Rain had made the rock as slick as ice. The guys were going to be a while getting down. This was unfortunate, because Fermín was wet and very lightly dressed. He was beginning to shiver, and it was odd to see and a little scary because his face was absolutely white, rather like a mime's. He had been badly sunburned on the first day. Now he was using the only lotion he had, a cream that, whatever it was, never really dissolved on his face, not even a little bit. Huddling miserably in the rain, he looked like a zombie in the first throes of convulsion. I thought it a graphic evocation of Patagonian weather: here was a place where you could easily freeze to death while slathered with suntan lotion.

God, I loved Patagonia.

It was eight in the evening before Robert and José Luis got down all that treacherous rock. We piled into the kayaks and paddled hard, racing the approaching darkness. Back at camp we drank mugs of steaming tea while Eric talked about tomorrow, our last day. The floatplane would come late in the afternoon. In the morning, if it was clear, we could climb the ridge just across the lake, where there would be a fantastic view of the mountains and ice fields. "There might even be a lake up there," he said.

Dave the aviation buff doubted it. So did I. The two of us went back to the Canyon of Cascading Snow: my new favorite place. The folks doing the real exploring did not have a great deal of fun.

From Cade's diary: "The rest of us went on a hike to a good view of the mountains and a glacier. We did not make it. We went through prickers over my head and down a giant slide full of rocks." The next line is my favorite in the whole diary: "I went on that hike with pants and came back with shorts." The very last line of the diary rings with conclusive finality: "The floatplane came and picked us up."

And that's exactly the way it happened. There is no mention of Eric's contention that it is possible that no other human being had ever seen the Canyon of Cascading Snow, which, I think, is really just my friend Eric's way of saying that it is one of his favorite places: a setting where a human being might come in a time of emotional or spiritual crisis and experience immediate vertical relief.

The Screenwriter's Vacation

FROM *McSweeneys.net*

Saturday, July 19

THE KIDS FOUGHT in the car the whole trip up. Good for establishing character but seven hours is way too much exposition. Next time we have to start further along in the story. Plus, their arguments are just too generic. That old "Your arm is on my side!" is so clichéd. With lines like that they could be anybody's kids. What they need is some kind of cute quirkiness that lets us know their backstory right away. Couldn't Katie have some kind of nervous tic? It would be great if she would stare out the window wistfully or bite her nails or react with dread to the word "sandwich."

The ride just did not provide the hook we need to grab our attention and make us want to know more. Who are these people? Where are they going? What do they hope to get out of a week by the ocean? Frankly, after an opening sequence like that one, I just don't care.

As usual, Susie was the only one who provided the kind of detail we need to ground the whole scene with some gritty realism. Just as we pulled up to the house I told her I'd brought along some work and there was a great close-up when she glared at me. Good foreshadowing — signals the beginning of an interesting subplot.

Sunday, Noon

Big problem — we're halfway through the second day and still no inciting incident. I was sure we had one when Timmy fell off the deck and it looked like he was out cold. A trip to the hospital would have sparked all sorts of conflicts, and maybe even revealed some long-hidden family secrets. Of course, a kid in a coma might be over the top for a light family comedy, but not for an *As Good As It Gets*–style dramedy. But he was only faking it. Great tension for a few minutes, but another dead end for the through line.

Sunday, 11 P.M.

Can't figure out whose story we are telling. Is it mine or Susie's? I thought it was mine, but then after supper she delivered a near-perfect tag line: "Is this a vacation or a story meeting?" I can already see it on the poster. She also delivered the first plot point right on schedule when she refused to have sex with me. No sex didn't seem to create a crisis for her, but it sure did for me, so I guess this is my story.

Monday

The second act began taking shape today. Susie's character arc is really clear and she hammered it home at the beach when she dumped the contents of the cooler in my lap. She really knows how to raise the stakes! Plus, it was a great image. That definitely goes in the trailer!

There's still the problem of the kids' subplots. Katie threw up after swallowing too much sea water — another great visual but it didn't really advance the action. Tim found a dead crab, which I thought might turn out to be a wonderful recurring image, kind of a poignant echo of the main theme. But then he kept chasing Katie with it and Susie got angry at me for "just sitting around and not taking any responsibility for what goes on." That led to the cooler-dumping episode, so I guess the dead crab was a useful device. Note: make Susie's dialogue more convincing.

Tuesday

Rained all day. Trapped in the house and the kids were climbing the walls with boredom. Tried to make some notes, with Tim and Katie screaming at each other and Susie bugging me to find something for them to do. Finally, some real conflict! My ignoring her drove Susie into a rage, which brought us exactly to where we were supposed to be — the point of no return, the halfway point in Act II, where the protagonist has to fully commit himself to the journey.

What I really needed was a little more adversity, like having the storm turn into a hurricane. Then, in the process of saving the family from drowning, I could have rediscovered the true meaning of love, parenting, and the restorative powers of vacationing. No such luck. All I could come up with was an old Monopoly set I found in the hall closet. The board was moldy so Susie wouldn't touch it, Tim said Monopoly was lame, and Katie started whining after about forty-five minutes. This could be a dysfunctional-family art film.

Wednesday

A montage day. Hit the beach early, ate at a clam shack, played miniature golf, bought some tacky souvenirs. Things were going great. Then it happened — the second act reversal. I should have seen it coming. After all, we were almost on page 90.

We were getting into the car when Katie looked down at her legs and asked, in that eerily calm *Sixth Sense* way, "Mom, what are these spots?" Flashback to taking that shortcut to the parking lot. Close-up of legs brushing innocent-looking green plants. Jump-cut to rash-covered hands holding first-aid book, open to page titled "Poison Ivy."

Thursday

The crisis. Up all night, itching like mad, taking turns giving the kids Aveeno baths. Everybody is exhausted, miserable, and ready to call it quits. Is the vacation ruined? Should we just admit defeat and go home a day early? Susie and I look at each other across the kitchen table, battered yet unbowed.

Who am I kidding? Poison ivy? A crisis? That sucks. A crisis is a shootout or a car chase. I tried driving extra fast when I went out for more calamine lotion, just in case they were about to close. Wouldn't you know it? It was a twenty-four-hour convenience store.

Would an armed holdup and some hostage-taking be too much to ask for?

Friday

The climax occurred this morning around page 104. Susie threw her suitcase toward the minivan and shouted that this was the last vacation she was ever going to take with us. Tears and everything. Shot the right way, and with the right music, it had the potential to be devastating. The kind of star turn actors go nuts for. Maybe even Oscar-worthy.

After that, the resolution practically wrote itself. At the rest stop about three hours later Katie looks up and says, in that cute little girl from *Monsters, Inc.* kind of way, "Hey my itchies are all gone!" Then, right on cue, Tim looks up from his Gameboy and says, "I had fun. Are we going back next year?"

Susie turns in her seat, her eyes still red, sighs, and says with mock resignation, "I suppose." Then — and this is the clincher — she looks at me with that perfect wifely mixture of love, annoyance, and contempt, and adds, with just the right touch of sarcasm, "If your father can spare the time." The perfect button to go out on! Pull back, car travels down interstate, disappears in traffic. Music swells! Fade to black! Roll credits! And what a terrific setup for the sequel!

DOUGLAS ANTHONY COOPER

Canadian Gothic

FROM *Travel & Leisure*

I HAVE MADE A CAREER out of not enjoying Canada. It is one of
the few things I do well. My radical malaise, Canada-wise, is associated mainly with Toronto the Good, and my hellish adolescence in
that winter-benighted place. (I was Not Very Good.) Both my novels — and most of Canadian literature, come to think of it — take
as a given that my country is a bitterly repressed thumbscrew of a
place, in which the human spirit thrives only in willfully exotic opposition to dour, Scottish-tinged emotional bondage.

Now, if you look closely, you'll see that "Nova Scotia" is transparent code for "New Scotland." Am I going to be happy here? I don't
think so.

The capital of this maritime province is Halifax, and that's where
I first intend to be miserable. I check in at the Waverley Inn, a notorious bed-and-breakfast downtown. How many B&Bs can properly
be called notorious? The Waverley is where Oscar Wilde stayed during his 1882 sojourn in Nova Scotia, and if most cozy inns might be
compared to polite Scottish matrons, this place is a drag queen. I
sleep in the Antique Chinese Wedding Bedroom, where the bed is
a real Chinese wedding bed, raised and canopied, and not so much
kitsch as just odd. Oscar Wilde is misquoted as having said on his
deathbed: "Either that wallpaper goes, or I do." At the Waverley it is
clear that Oscar left, but the wallpaper stayed.

So I am immediately disappointed: to my surprise, Halifax turns
out to be quite weird — an attribute I can't help but enjoy. Weird,
in fact, becomes the theme of my journey through Nova Scotia.
Robertson Davies once pointed out that Canada is in fact a mystical

northern race, though it prefers "to present itself to the world
as a Scottish banker." Americans in general refuse to acknowledge
the weirdness of Canada, dismissing our more flamboyant demonstrations of the grotesque — the filmmakers David Cronenberg
and Guy Madden, for example — as exceptions. Time to visit the
Maritimes.

The Bleak

I don't spend much time in Halifax. I rent a Sebring convertible —
nominally a sports car, in reality a quasi-hearse — and drive to the
western shore of the island. Here Digby produces the world's most
exalted scallops, and Acadians remain a strong presence despite
a nearly successful effort to ethnically cleanse them in the eighteenth century.

The British expulsion of the French Nova Scotians gave rise to
Longfellow's tearjerker, *Evangeline,* and it's hard to take a step on
the North Shore without encountering this theme. The highway
here follows the Evangeline Trail. You can shop at the Evangeline
Mall. You can buy little bound copies of Longfellow's poem in
the most unlikely places — grocery stores, for instance. I sympa-
thize with this, as a Jew: *You made us wander, and we're not going to let
you forget it.*

The exiled French made their way down to Louisiana, where
"Acadian" became "Cajun." Those who stayed in Nova Scotia, or
returned, share with Cajun culture an indomitable pride in the
face of poverty and minority status, and a cheerful addiction to improbable cuisine. Here the defining dish is rappie pie, a heavy
potato concoction forged in Vulcan heat and served in roadside
shacks. Not bad stuff, actually. Poutine, another characteristic
preparation, is generally dire: French fries embalmed in congeal-
ing, greasy cheese and gravy.

This delicacy aside, I have a great fondness for all things French
Canadian: those oppressed by Anglo Canada often find personal
redemption (or at least wild, Continental abandon) through encounters with the French. It's not unlike white America's complicated relationship to black culture. Montreal, for instance, was the
city in Canada where I first glimpsed the remote possibility of not
being eternally miserable.

Acadian cheerfulness on the North Shore arises in opposition to a physical environment that is, for long stretches, unremittingly bleak: low, scrubbed land eroded by a tide that is in places the highest in the world. It is a bleak to be celebrated, however; the American poet Mark Strand particularly recommends the weather-bitten churches. I am torn between the weather-bitten baroque (Catholic) and the weather-bitten austere (Protestant): both represent high points in eastern clapboarding.

The Quaint

Nova Scotia offers nothing if not variety. As you round the shore to the south, prepare yourself, aesthetically, for the exquisitely quaint. This is the aspect of Nova Scotia best known to outsiders: the little painted fishing village, casually arranged by the unseen hand of genius around the perfect Atlantic inlet.

The Heart of Quaintness is Peggy's Cove. It's a one-view town — an entire community devoted, touristically, to a single ideal postcard of a view. I buy the postcard and skip the village. You see, I was in Peggy's Cove some years ago. Nice landscape. Nice lighthouse. *Shame about the seventeen buses full of eager landscape aficionados lined up to experience the one view.* Besides, I'm here at the anniversary of the 1998 Swissair disaster — the plane came down just off Peggy's Cove, and the locals famously consoled the families of those lost — and I don't really feel like mixing my shallow view-gathering with genuine, authentic, human activity.

Instead, I check into the Rose Room at 100 Acres & an Ox, an extravagant B&B near Mahone Bay. Ardythe Wildsmith, the benevolent matriarch who presides over 100 Acres (which really does occupy a property of that size, complete with lake, but no ox), has put together one of the world's great B&B experiences. The South Shore is about Getting Away From It All, and Ardythe's estate — quite brilliantly — is devoted to Getting Away From All Those People Who Are Getting Away From It All. It's about twenty minutes from the coast, and everyone else is scrambling with Darwinian zeal to occupy the coast itself.

The day begins with an obscene breakfast — blueberry pancakes made with blueberries picked (by Ardythe) just down the road; maple syrup that is, yes, better than anything south of the border; real whipped cream and scones and cereals and eggs and butter. It's a communal affair: the entire B&B gathers about a dining table, and is forced to be social as the coffee kicks in. Luckily, those breaking fast prove convivial and diverse. I meet another Canadian writer; a leather-clad biker, who advises me to trade in my Sebring for a Ford Mustang; and a man with a scarred lip.

The wounded American is a pleasant guy whose story emerges when I ask him whether he plays the French horn or the trumpet: I associate the round scar on his upper lip with professional brass players. No, he explains, this is where his lip was reattached, after a brief encounter with a Scottish ghost.

Thank God — I knew I was in for a ghost story sooner or later. Some things just go together: love and marriage, plaid and ecto-plasm.

It turns out that he and his wife were traveling in Scotland when — against advice — he took a picture in a haunted castle. That night, at a nearby inn, he woke violently in a pool of blood, to discover that a huge wooden valance had fallen off the wall above his head, disturbing his sleep and severing his lip. The lip was sewn back on by a crack plastic surgeon who happened to be in town for a convention. And — here's where things get shivery and pale — my scarred storyteller later discovered that the room next to his — the room into which the bolts holding the valance emerged after piercing the wall, the room where those bolts myste-riously loosened in the middle of the night — *had the same name as the haunted castle.*

Phew. Pass the blueberries.

One Hundred Acres makes a good base camp from which to tour this section of Nova Scotia, rightly compared to Maine: an area in which brine-inclined Americans build summer homes where they get to rub shoulders with lobstermen and Yalies. Near-by is Lunenburg, one of those absurdly scenic fishing villages. It has a long history as a shipbuilding town — some of the world's most elegant schooners were hammered together here, and houses often bear a plaque honoring the shipbuilder who tossed that par-ticular dwelling together in his spare time. If you paint your house bright mauve in Lunenburg, your neighbors don't even notice.

The Cliffs

I am not really a partisan of the quaint. Give me the urban or its opposite: I don't condone twee half-measures. Five hours to the east, at the entrance to the Cabot Trail on the vast island of Cape Breton, the landscape winds and rises to wild grandeur: cliffs and crags and spray, in lieu of population.

I stay at the Keltic Lodge, the most famous resort in Nova Scotia. It is owned by the provincial government, and has a great deal in common with the mountain hotels associated with the Canadian Pacific Railroad — Banff Springs, Jasper Park Lodge, Chateau Lake Louise — a kind of packaged Canadian grandness.

I have mixed feelings about the grand old Canadian hotels, and, to be fair, they have mixed feelings about me. My career as a travel writer began with a piece about the Banff Springs Hotel; I wrote what I considered a humorous riff, as a result of which Canada's most respected magazine was pulled from newsstands across the Rockies, and my name dragged across nails on national radio. All because I interviewed the chambermaids instead of swooning over the scenery. Their colleagues called them "chamber sluts," I noted, and nobody would dance with them except pot washers, dubbed "dish pigs." I'm still fond of my original title for that piece — "Dead Brides and Dish Pigs: An Appreciation of the Canadian Rockies" — which was bowdlerized, alas, to "Rocky Mountain Highs and Lows."

These legendary hotels are all about vastness, about public spaces and vistas. The room you actually sleep in tends to be on the tiny side and generally disappointing. Few hotels, however, can boast a location as spectacular as Keltic's. The property sits on an isthmus at the far reaches of the Cabot Trail, thought by many the most impressive road and hiking path in North America: a stormy, Scotlandish coastline, with dense green forests standing at the edge of precipitous cliffs.

The lodge hogs one of the nicest bits of the trail, but there are hundreds of miles more: if you're not a hiker, driving the trail is a transcendent experience (insofar as a highway can be life-transforming). I drive it a bit too fast — it's the Mustang — and probably should set aside more time to wander off the highway to the myriad coves and inlets, where the scenery is even more staggering.

There, you're generally at the foot of the cliffs, looking up, as opposed to careering around the top, trying desperately not to look down.

The Celts

Cape Breton is the home of another exotic microculture forged by poverty, pride, and isolation, although in this case it's not so much Louisiana as Appalachia. It is here that my Fear of Scottish Stuff gives way to unbridled, intoxicated admiration. (It helps that I'm staying at a distillery.) Cape Breton has preserved and intensified a kind of Scottishness long lost in Scotland itself, just as the French spoken in Quebec bears an accent forgotten centuries ago in France. The locals feel no sense of inferiority beside the motherland; in fact, Scotland has turned to Cape Breton in order to revive its own traditions.

My "hotel," the Glenora Inn & Distillery, brews the only single malt native to Canada, and it's fine stuff: not so much a peat-heavy bog of an experience, but a golden, almost brandylike liquor. The distillery will also rent you a chalet — primitive except for the Jacuzzi — with a view of the green, green valley, where tiny white farmhouses flash with sun.

"Weird" is, I'll remind you, a term wed immortally to all things Scottish by the bearded sisters in *Macbeth*. I don't meet anyone transparent, green, or headless, but I do feel, during my stay in Cape Breton, that I have encountered a people and way of life as mysterious and affecting as anything this side of the Atlantic and the Middle Ages.

Cape Breton culture (perhaps all culture?) has music at its root, and its specific flavor of Celtic music might well have died out were it not for the influence of a documentary. Canada has a peculiar relationship with the documentary film, which is an important national genre. Elsewhere, things happen and then get documented; here, things get documented and then they happen. *The Vanishing Cape Breton Fiddler*, televised in 1972 by the Canadian Broadcasting Corporation, so jolted the endangered species that fiddling enjoyed a massive revival. (A resident, remarking on the island's epidemic of unemployment, cracks to me that someone would do a great public service if they made *The Vanishing Cape Breton Worker*.)

I never imagined that I would be much taken with fiddling. Who knew? I'm behind the times here; a local fiddler, Ashley MacIsaac, brought the music of Cape Breton to the outside world a decade ago. MacIsaac ("Ashley" to everyone on the island) doubled the tempo and began to play the grunge clubs of Toronto, came out of the closet, and — after flashing his genitals on *Late Night with Conan O'Brien* — saw his career peak in a blaze of flamboyant drug abuse and sordid behavior. Cape Breton music is in fact very similar to what Ashley took to New York and Europe: virtuosic fiddling, sans vibrato, with heart-stopping changes in tempo and uncanny, almost telepathic interaction between band members.

The thing to catch is a *ceilidh,* pronounced "*kay*-lee," which is a traditional kitchen party. I don't manage to witness one in an actual kitchen. The town of Mabou is the epicenter of Cape Breton music, and overcivilized *ceilidhs* are held regularly at the community halls. You can hear some superb players, but it's very much a sit-down concert experience, as opposed to the Scotch-drenched, reeling debauch that I imagine I missed.

And then there's the foot music. Ashley MacIsaac gained early fame, before the age of thirteen, not as a fiddler but as a step dancer. Step dancing in Cape Breton is known as "close to the floor" and involves very little of the body north of the knees. Amazing thing to watch, really: a guy standing loose and motionless, looking almost bored, as his feet and ankles put Fred and Ginger to shame.

To experience Mabou, you can't do much better than to stay at the Normaway Inn & Cabins, about thirty-five miles away in Margaree Valley. Normaway has for years been an instigator of all things Celtic; it holds regular barn dances and invites local acts to play after dinner.

Dave MacDonald, the proprietor, is a fierce advocate of Cape Breton culture. He records the music, promotes it, defends it. God help any act that snubs Mabou. Ashley MacIsaac, who danced at Normaway when he was a wee tyke, is only now beginning to undo the damage he caused by behaving too much like a standard-issue celebrity. Even the famed Rankin Family is expected to play fundraisers in order to avoid alienating its fan base.

In other words, this is a culture composed of actual people interacting face-to-face with actual people — as opposed to viewers interacting nose-to-screen with product. The CD or video of your music, in Mabou, is incidental: what matters is the thing that happens in the kitchen.

In the lounge at Normaway I am privileged to see musicians and step dancers Rebecca and Guillaume Tremblay, ages eighteen and sixteen. Relatively unknown, they generally perform in a three-some, the Tremblay Family, except that their older sister has gone off to study cosmetology. I know I'm gushing like those naïve college kids who first "discovered" the blues in the sixties, but who cares? The culture of Cape Breton is enjoying something like the folk revival in America forty years ago, and it's about time. I'd be amazed if anywhere else in North America was routinely producing teen performers like Rebecca and Guillaume Tremblay: shy, and gormless, and preternaturally good.

For Celtic music, Cape Breton is the Mississippi Delta. Or it's the Delta, Houston, and Chicago all rolled up into one.

A great portion of the young locals, of course, have been infected by pop culture and haven't the faintest idea what they have at home. One waitress, itching to leave, informs me that "it's the most boring place on earth." Where does she come from? Bras d'Or, in the center of the island. "I wouldn't call it a town. It's more of a road, with people."

And what precisely does this girl miss? "Well, I was down in Florida at the House of Blues, and 'N Sync walks in! I mean, that doesn't happen in Cape Breton. You go away, and suddenly you see stars."

Well, before I moved back to Montreal, I used to see stars every weekend at my neighborhood café in Manhattan. All I can say about the experience is that stars are generally a lot shorter than you expect. I know I'll never convince my shining waitress of this, but I hope that, after seeing a few of these stunted celebs, she'll go running back to Bras d'Or.

With a bit of sleuthing, in fact, she could find more than a few celebrities of a different sort living quietly right under her nose. Robert Frank, the photographer. The composer Philip Glass. The essayist Calvin Trillin. All have found this province inspiring and congenial, and a welcome respite from 'N Sync.

It's a road, you see. With people.

JOAN DIDION

History Lesson

FROM *Travel + Leisure*

THERE IS in the collection of the E. G. Bührle Foundation in Zurich an 1880 Renoir portrait of a gravely beautiful French child, eight or nine years old, her long hair tied back, her small hands folded in her lap. The name of the child was Irène Cahen d'Anvers, and at age eighteen she married Moïse de Camondo, the thirty-one-year-old heir to much of the wealth of a Sephardic banking family that had migrated from Spain in the fifteenth century to Constantinople to Trieste and finally, in the nineteenth century, to Paris. Before running away with the Italian who trained her husband's horses, this gravely beautiful French child bore Moïse de Camondo one son and one daughter, Nissim and Béatrice. Nissim de Camondo volunteered to fly for the French in World War I and was killed in combat, leaving his father and sister alone in the house on the Rue de Monceau that the father had built after the mother defected. The sister married in 1918. The father died in 1935. In accordance with his wish, the house on the Rue de Monceau, and the perfect examples of eighteenth-century French furniture with which he had filled it, were given to France, to be maintained as a museum named for the lost son, Nissim. Only a small plaque at the entrance to the courtyard of the Musée Nissim de Camondo now gives us the fate of the sister: "Mme. Léon Reinach, born Béatrice de Camondo, her children, Fanny and Bertrand, the last descendants of the founder, and M. Léon Reinach, deported by the Germans in 1943–44, died at Auschwitz."

I paid a visit to this house on the Rue de Monceau late last November, during a week in Paris when the dark was already stretch-

ing late into the day and falling back over the city not long after
lunch. I felt the weight of the copper pots in the pristine kitchen. I
counted the places set at the long table in the servants' dining
room, and already forget how many there were. Twelve, fourteen?
More? I counted the place settings in the wall of Sèvres off the main
dining room, and lost track. I stood at the windows and watched
the rain blow the branches in the Parc Monceau, its lawns and fol-
lies largely deserted, none of the small children for which the park
is famous, only an occasional jogger sufficiently determined to ignore the rain. Just one thing had changed since I first visited this
house, several years before: at that time there had been, hanging
from the racks in an upstairs bathroom, monogrammed towels, the
monograms threadbare and the toweling itself worn thin by repeated laundering, a sharp reminder of the life once lived there.

It had been the towels, on that first visit to the house on the Rue
de Monceau, that brought tears to my eyes. This November it was
something else. There is upstairs a dressing room in which glass
cases have been placed, for the display of letters and documents
in one way or another meaningful to those who had lived there.
There are many documents from the Louvre, of which Moïse de
Camondo was a director and to which his cousin Isaac bequeathed
his Fragonards and Watteaus and Monets and Cézannes and some
thirty works by Degas. There is a letter of condolence from Marcel
Proust, delivered to Moïse de Camondo after the death of his son.
There are medals, honors, accountings of expenses. There is also,
and this is what stopped me in November, an engraved invitation to
a weekend shooting party at the country estate of the Camondo
family — just a card, one such invitation of what must have been
many, yet it spoke to me that day in a way I did not immediately understand.

I did nothing much else, that November week in Paris. I watched
CNN and the BBC. War in Iraq, and whatever might follow, was by
then a foregone conclusion to all but the most wishful. A worldwide disruption seemed for the first time since my childhood a distinct possibility. My husband and I had dinner with friends whose
sense of foreboding matched our own, an American reporter and
his wife who were leaving the next day for Amman. The imminence
of war was very much with the four of us that night: the reporter's
son was an Army officer already serving in the Middle East, and my

husband's nephew was a Marine officer due to leave for Kuwait in January.

Days passed. We started out to see a Modigliani exhibition and ended up walking instead in the Jardin de Luxembourg, the wet leaves underfoot, the only greenery remote behind the glass of the locked greenhouses. We started out to see the Monets at the Musée Marmottan and ended up sitting instead in the Ranelagh gardens, watching the children play soccer. We lit candles at Saint-Sulpice. We walked through a flea market behind the École Militaire, one stall after another filled with monogrammed coffee spoons, amateur watercolors, faded table linens folded in pale tissue, the detritus of comfortable bourgeois lives. The dark, wet days allowed a sadness, a gravity that offered relief from what had come to seem through the fall in New York and Washington an increasingly histrionic enthusiasm for confrontation and its collateral damage, "security." It did not escape my attention that there was at the entrance to the Élysée Palace an absence of the kind of visibly brandished security we in the United States had come to take for granted. To enter the Élysée Palace one rings the bell, and someone answers the door, yet I do not imagine the official residence of the president of France to be unprotected.

I had gone to Paris to think about what I should be writing, to think where the world was going, but when I tried that week to contemplate fundamentalism and tribalism, confrontation and "security," it was the Camondo family that kept coming back to me. There was the glory of the Sèvres, there was the sweet thrift of the worn towels on the bathroom racks, there was the engraved card with the invitation to the shooting party. The Sèvres and the towels and the engraved card all told the same story: This was a family with reason to believe that it had managed over the centuries to obtain the right visas, negotiate an escape from the woes of tribalism, arrive in a place where its members would be honored. This was a family that had thought itself exempt from history. This was a family that had been wrong.

BILL DONAHUE

Under the Sheltering Sky

FROM *The Washington Post Magazine*

THE COOLEST PEOPLE in the world do not wear their baseball caps backwards or pierce their navels with diamond studs. They are old and their cool is subtle, carrying hints of wisdom and poise. Johnny Cash, Marlon Brando, Georgia O'Keeffe: we behold their weathered sang-froid and we are ineluctably intrigued.

As I was, years ago, watching the 1990 film *The Sheltering Sky*. Based on a 1949 novel of the same name, by the American expat Paul Bowles (1910–1999), the movie follows three aimless Americans who land in Bowles's adopted home, Tangier, Morocco, and wander south, only to be destroyed by primal Third World realities: thieves, mystical religion, and illness. Bowles makes a cameo appearance as narrator, and, in the end, we see him watch one of the stars drift into an ancient Tangier café. He just stands there, motionless, an old man with white hair and rheumy gray eyes. All he says to the woman before him is "Are you lost?" And yet somehow he embodies existential grace, and a link to a bygone era.

Bowles first lived in Tangier in 1931. During the fifties and sixties — when the city was controlled by nine Western nations — and for a brief time after Moroccan independence in 1956, he was the reigning spirit over a glamorous and largely gay artists' colony. Tangier loomed then as Paris had in the thirties. William Burroughs wrote *Naked Lunch*, the definitive novel of heroin addiction, in Tangier, tossing the manuscript pages onto the floor of his fleabag hotel as he typed (Jack Kerouac and Allen Ginsberg helped him assemble the trampled clutter of papers). The Rolling Stones' Brian Jones showed up to hear the mesmerizing Master Musicians of Jajouka. Timothy Leary came to Tangier, too, to lead experiments using mind-expanding mushrooms, and Bowles's novelist wife, Jane, hosted grand parties.

Jane Bowles was a lesbian whose marital bond was primarily literary, and around the time of her death, in 1973, Tangier's colonial flavor faded. The scene fizzled, and only Bowles remained. He wandered constantly, living for a time in Sri Lanka and Mexico, but always he came back to Tangier. In old photographs he wears white canvas trousers and a benevolent grin, smoking cigarettes on a long silver stem as exotic Morocco (The camels! The adobe forts with darkened slit windows!) shimmers behind him. He knew everybody in town, and yet he always retained that analytic detachment you hear in his cold-blooded gothic prose — in words such as these, from *The Sheltering Sky*. "The wind at the window celebrated her dark sensation of having attained a new depth of solitude."

Gore Vidal once wrote that Bowles "has few equals in the second half of the twentieth century . . . [He] has glimpsed what lies back of our sheltering sky." The Library of America last year published a 940-page compilation of Bowles's major works. But none of the three Bowles novels that followed *The Sheltering Sky* — *Let It Come Down* (1952), *The Spider's House* (1955), and *Up Above the World* (1966) — sold especially well, and late in life Bowles was known more as an icon than a writer. When he visited New York City in 1995, for the first time in more than four decades, there were two sold-out celebratory concerts at Lincoln Center, replete with standing ovations. His primary gift to Americans was a dream: here was a man who flew free of the doldrums of Middle America to live with aplomb in a faraway place. I envied him. So when I was in Morocco last year with a spare week, I went to Tangier and searched for the ghost of Paul Bowles.

Tangier is on the temperate northwest coast of Africa, just ten miles from Spain, across the Strait of Gibraltar, and washed in the breezes coming off both the Atlantic and the Mediterranean. But to the average Tanjawi, Europe is a distant dream. Tangier, population 600,000, is extremely poor, almost entirely Muslim, and, like many African cities, growing rapidly. Tangier is a place where you see an amputee child hunched on the sidewalk with a begging cup beside the dusty stub of his truncated leg. Much of Morocco's homegrown hashish travels through the port here, and the quieter beaches outside town are a prime launch point for destitute Africans who risk their lives, and pathetically seek First World fortune, by sneaking makeshift boats across the strait, toward Spain. Old movies don't tell the whole story.

But still, I made sure that there would be a certain bohemian splendor to my Tangier visit. I stayed in the Kasbah, the mud-walled old fortress city overlooking the burgeoning metropolis, in a decrepit home rented (but not occupied) by three young American expats/artists who'd given Tangier a whirl after college, then fled. I'd met these fellows one night at a bar in New York's Greenwich Village, and in Tangier their painter friend, Abdel-Aziz Boufrakech, picked me up at the airport.

Aziz is forty-one. When he pulled up in his battered Citroën station wagon, I was unshaven and ragged from seven days in the Sahara, but Aziz just laughed when he saw me. "You will like the house," he said. "There's hot water for showers."

Aziz had lived in Paris, L.A., and Switzerland. Now he was married and raising three children according to Muslim law, pretty much, and painting tranquil and earthy Moroccan scenes that sold well in galleries. "You are inside four walls in Tangier," he said, "blocked. There are almost no other artists to talk to."

We turned onto a narrow side street, and at once there was an explosion of Mediterranean color: green doorways, turquoise shutters, splashes of soft red and lavender. We parked and walked into the Kasbah, where a few hundred people live, and there the streets were ten-foot-wide footpaths that wound through the ancient mud buildings and into dimly lit tunnels that led to massive wood doors.

I stowed my bags in the Americans' house, and then I strolled down to the Cervantes Theater, a splendid art deco building that drew international stars in Bowles's day. The building was shuttered. I visited the Grand Hotel Villa de France, where French romantic painter Eugène Delacroix stayed in 1831 as he sketched Tangier street life. All I could see through the locked gate was the weeds in the driveway.

Finally, I went to Guitta's Italian restaurant, a one-time beacon for expats. There were actually a few people there, most of them ancient white men dining alone. I talked to an eightyish British gentleman, who was wearing an ascot inside his bright mustard blazer, and he assured me, "There's still a few expatriates left. You can go down the boulevard and meet them, you know."

A broad-boned and ample old woman sat beside us, so we could see her in profile. She gazed into space, her arms crossed, her lower lip quavering slightly and her eyes burning with what I took to be an ire at the world in general.

"The matron," the Brit said tentatively. "She knows quite a bit of the history."

"Does she, um, speak English?"

She answered herself, without ever shifting her gaze. "I don't give interviews anymore," she said crisply. "And I don't like you talking to customers, either."

"Do you want me to leave?"

"You're finished here."

I left.

Gradually, Tangier blossomed for me. Bowles wrote that the city had "the classical dream equipment of tunnels, ramparts, ruins, dungeons, and cliffs," and the place seemed surreal to me, too. The streets twist over a series of seaside hills, scantly marked by signs, and often I'd find myself cracking out my map to get directions from strangers. They puzzled over the document as though it were in hieroglyphics. One man stared long and hard at the blank back of the map before shaking his head in confusion.

There are camels on the beach in downtown Tangier, and one afternoon, as I watched them pick at the grass amid some old ruins, I met a man named Omar Charif. Omar identified himself as a travel agent and said that he knew Aziz. He said he was his uncle. And beyond that, he'd been acquainted with Paul Bowles himself. "A very nice man," Omar said. "He spoke Arabic like a Moroccan."

Omar was forty-seven and wearing a green mesh baseball cap and plaid polyester trousers. Eventually he offered to show me the apartment in which Bowles lived the last two decades of his life. There are no official Bowles walking tours in Tangier. There is not even a Bowles museum, and I was curious to see where this excursion was going. So we meandered off the beach, then up a hilly, traffic-choked street and through a market, progressing at a dawdling pace.

It is no secret that Bowles, who was gay, had a fondness for the bronze-skinned young men of Morocco. Omar told me that he was once one of Bowles's favorites, and that he and Bowles had numerous trysts. "But that's life," he said with a gruff shrug. "That's life."

We kept walking. At one point, we crossed paths with a long-haired young German who waved curtly at Omar before rushing away. "That man," Omar confided, "is a very famous writer."

"What's his name?" I asked.

"I can't remember," said Omar.

"How much longer now?" I said.

"Soon, you know — five minutes."

Roughly half an hour later, in the blazing sun just outside Bowles's apartment building, Omar paused at a cross light. "I am not a boy hustling you on the street," he said, his voice raspy and insistent, more proud than desperate. "I am a guide — that is my job. And I am doing something very special for you, and afterwards, my friend" — Omar cackled nervously, then clapped me on the back — "you can do something for me. Right, my friend?"

"Right."

We went inside and knocked on the door of apartment 20, and, not getting an answer, we went downstairs, where the manager's daughter addressed us impatiently. "Mr. Paul Bowles," she said, "he is dead, and every week twenty people still come here. Why? His books are gone; the people who knew him are gone. Why? What do you want?"

Omar looked at me and shrugged, and then held out his hand.

The house I was staying in slowly filled up. By odd coincidence, several other itinerant friends of the renters wandered into town simultaneously, and at one point I was domiciled with a French painter, a Canadian documentary filmmaker, a British banker, and a Moroccan photographer. We interviewed one another. The French painter said things like, "The culture in France is finished — *done.*" We drank a lot of beer.

Aziz kept a bemused distance from the whole scene. He did not drink because, he said, he wanted to set a good example for his children. But still he came by, evenings, in the spirit of hospitality, and we'd talk. He spoke of painting in a precise and workmanlike manner, sounding almost technical when he noted, "Matisse came here because of the light and the warm Mediterranean colors. And the colors came from the hand-embroidered clothes of the country people — the Arabs who live outside of Tangier, in the Rif Mountains. You go up there and you'd think you were in Andalusia, in Spain."

Some days Aziz got some painting done. Other days one of his kids was sick, or he got tied up renovating one of the ten houses he owns and rents out. He was unfazed either way, and I appreciated his long vision, his understanding that making a life as an artist is ultimately about making compromises — about taking care of the kids and the mortgage (or whatever) as you try to remember, somehow, your original burning ambitions. It was nice to come to a place so far from home, and so steeped in crazy-artiste legend, and find an artist so steady.

I kept hearing stories about Bowles. Abdessalam Akaaboune, a café owner, told me, truthfully, that Bowles persuaded the Rolling Stones to record the tune "Continental Drift" in Akaaboune's basement. He also spoke of Bowles, age eighty-eight and dying, being carried through the streets of the Kasbah in a plastic chair, so he could see the leader of the Jajouka masters play flute. "It was the last time he went out of his house," Akaaboune told me.

Every story I heard about Bowles depicted him not as a friend, really, but as a treasure — an aloof and inscrutable icon. I should have expected this. Bowles's autobiography, *Without Stopping*, was so unrevealing that Burroughs nicknamed it "Without Telling," and I'd read that, while living, Bowles had stymied hundreds of admirers — hippies, grad students, journalists — who'd come to Tangier in hopes of communing with the master. They were all welcome in his home, but he endured them silently, smoking hashish with a weary look on his face. "I don't know why he comes," he sighed to a reporter after one frequent guest left in 1991.

I can understand his disdain. I have my own doubts about the whole literary pilgrimage thing. We experience the nuance of books alone, in the mind, and what sings for us isn't really the place that inspired the writer. Rather, it's the place the writer invented — a place you can't reach on a tour bus. For this reason, I have always been skeptical of guided tours to, say, the pubs of James Joyce's Dublin.

Still, I was hopeful that in Tangier I could somehow see through

Bowles's patrician exterior and find some glimpse of the person beneath. This wasn't happening, in part because Bowles left behind very little tangible evidence. He fathered no children, and like most nomads he was a minimalist; he didn't collect stuff. You'd think there'd at least be a gravestone in Tangier, but there is not. Paul Bowles's ashes were interred near his parents' graves in Lakemont, New York, in November 2000. A man named Joe McPhillips bore the urn west from Tangier.

McPhillips, sixty-seven, is the executor of Bowles's estate and also the headmaster of the American School of Tangier. I visited him at the school one morning. His secretary, an American, was typing on an electric typewriter, and McPhillips himself was enjoying a cigarette as he puttered about in a rumpled tweed jacket and wide-wale cords. The scion of an old Alabama family, he likened the school to his prep school alma mater, calling it "the Andover of the Mediterranean. We provide an old-fashioned education," he explained. "Students rise when adults come in the room. They read *Lord Jim* and *Julius Caesar.* There's not a lot of ancillary nonsense in the curriculum."

McPhillips arrived in Tangier in 1962, following a Princeton classmate, and caught the last chapter of the city's halcyon era. He spoke wistfully of the "old days" when, he said, there were 100,000 Europeans in Tangier and "no traffic lights. You could walk into the Parade Bar and you knew everybody, and things were incredibly cheap," he said. "Tangier was small and charming then, and yet it was incredibly sophisticated. You'd go over to Paul and Janie's, and there would be Leonard Bernstein; there'd be Gore Vidal. That time will never be replaced."

Bowles had trusted McPhillips, I knew, because McPhillips was the last guardian of an old order — and a man who bore this mantle seriously. After a few minutes, McPhillips opened the top drawer and with great care took out a plastic bag containing a passport — the last passport Bowles ever owned. It was an American passport. McPhillips handed the document to me, and then gave me a minute with the hunched and withered old man in the photo. "You know," McPhillips said, "I asked Paul once, 'You've lived outside of America so long and you've traveled so extensively. Do you still feel American?' He simply said, 'I am American. I always will be.'"

"But he lived in Morocco for most of sixty years," I said. "Why isn't he buried here?"

McPhillips began shouting, literally screaming. "I can't tell you," he said, "how many people asked me, 'You're going to lug Paul Bowles all the way back to America?' Look, I am the executor of Paul Bowles's estate, and it was Paul Bowles's will to be buried in America. I can't just go and bury Paul Bowles wherever the hell I feel like it." McPhillips flung himself down on a couch, and then, depleted, red-faced, with a trail of smoke rising from his fist, he added, "Yes, I buried Paul Bowles in America."

The whole performance was a bit much, but McPhillips, who directs his school's theater program, enjoyed soliloquizing, and I enjoyed listening, so that evening I went up to his home, on Tangier's affluent Old Mountain Road, for drinks. He kept his necktie on for the cocktail hour. "I never saw Burroughs without a tie," he said, "and Paul, too, abhorred sloppiness. He lived within the frame, and the frame held everything together for him. If you don't have a frame, you fly off in all sorts of directions. But inside the frame you are secure; you can observe what happens. Paul came here to observe," McPhillips said, "and to write what he saw. He was fascinated with the exotic, and that fascination was rooted in his own New England Puritanism."

McPhillips's butler, Ali, came around now, with vodka tonics and a silver tray bearing Ritz crackers. Ali was a striking young man in a white waist jacket. He wore white satin gloves to deliver the food and the drinks and went barehanded at all other times. I took my drink, and then McPhillips and I went out onto the terrace, where it was dark and we could see the lights of the Moroccan coastline glittering below in the distance.

"Tangier has changed so much since Paul first arrived," McPhillips continued, "but it is indestructible; it will always have mythical qualities. Tangier is possessed of this very intense creative force — it comes up out of the earth."

I knew what he meant, but way up high on the mountain, that earth force of Morocco seemed, like Paul Bowles himself, so far away.

The next day was the first day of Ramadan. Aziz was fasting and abstaining from all drink, even water. He offered me tea when I stopped at his house, but I felt weird about taking it, so we just sat there in his airy, tile-walled living room, awkwardly stoic, trying to make conversation as his giggly four-year-old son, Jabir, took running dives into his lap.

My plan was to leave Tangier that morning and take the train a few miles south to a popular beach. But Aziz had friends in a more distant coastal village reachable only by bus, and he said, "It is beautiful in Moulay Bousselham. Why don't you go to Moulay Bousselham?"

That is what I ended up doing. I rode in the back of the bus, surrounded by young men who stared straight ahead, not eating, not talking, keeping the Ramadan fast. The bus wound to the edge of the city, where there were goats on the road, and then on into rolling potato fields. Almost no one spoke. They simply rode. Night fell; the fast ended. Strangers passed a sweet pastry called chebakia from seat to seat in the cramped, unlit bus. "*Kul,*" said the man seated beside me. "Eat." The chebakia tasted of almonds and honey, and I looked in my guidebook and came up with "*hada bnin*" (this is delicious), and the man smiled and gave me another chebakia. Then the bus stopped.

A young man got on with a boombox blasting a haunting and undulating Ramadan tune and, as the bus started again, held the box to his chin and sang in high, soulful tones, his gaze cast into the distance. I could not tell which words came from the box and which from his mouth, and I was aware suddenly of how little I understood the spiritual tides surging around me. I was not in control; I was outside the frame.

In time, of course, I would come back within the frame, back to my familiar habits of observing and writing. But right then, on the bus, I was learning how rich it is to venture into that strange territory of the mind where you are bewildered and vulnerable — lost, even. I just listened to the music.

HEATHER ELIOT

Sandbags in the Archipelago

FROM *WorldHum.com*

TWO WEEKS AGO, I was next to him on the lumpy double bed of my rented South Pacific island bungalow. Outside, an afternoon rain fell, dogs fought, scooters buzzed down the road. Under the shadowy light of the mosquito netting, I was on my belly reading Jeanette Winterson, in a cami and bikini, as he snored softly beside me. I had given him Tums — he was ill from too much beer and fatty food — and in his boxers he slept off his heartburn. I wiped his forehead with a damp cloth. A man I'd known for twenty-four hours. If the air were cool and dry instead of warm and moist, if the smoke of the mosquito coil, irritating my sinuses, were not drifting around us, we could be in my California apartment, napping after a Sunday morning of brunch and languid afternoon sex. Now, I am alone in my California apartment, typing at my laptop, drinking tea, a Massive Attack CD on repeat, writing of him.

On what was meant to be my last morning before heading back to the main island of the archipelago, I had just opened Winterson's *Written on the Body* when a shadow fell across me. I looked up. It was a man.

"Hi," he said, "I'm Derek."

I introduced myself. I had seen him earlier that day walking across the yard, and thought then that he was the most beautiful man I'd ever seen — shoulder-length dreadlocks, arched eyebrows, wide smile, wearing a Fubu shirt and board shorts. He said, "We're doing renovations on the bathrooms. Is it okay if I check yours out?"

"Sure," I said, and he gave the bathroom a perfunctory inspection. I'd heard worse opening lines from men.

This is a fantasy of travel. Not an actual fantasy, because it happened to me, but a fantasy of a relationship that might have been, realized through the movement of my body to an alternate space. I crossed the Equator, I crossed the International Date Line, and found myself in bed with a man. I had found myself in bed with a number of men in the past eighteen months, since the relationship I'd wanted to last forever painfully and caustically ended. I had coped with the anguish by taking a six-month break from sex, and then by having as much as I could get. Other men's bodies became sandbags, forming a protective barrier between myself and my past. On the first page of my travel journal, I had written, Stay away from boys.

After inspecting my bathroom, Derek returned to the foyer. As he lounged in my doorway and began to chat, I found myself liking his self-confident ease, his awareness of his body, his casual knowledge of the pleasure of looking at him. The polite, distanced formality I'd experienced with other locals was less apparent. Where was I from? He had been to California; his sister lived in Los Angeles, and his parents, who owned the bungalows, were there now for medical care. He and his brothers helped their father build the bungalows and were looking after things in their parents' absence. He finished high school in New Zealand, played semiprofessional rugby, was injured, did a chef's course, lived in South Africa for a year, worked as yacht crew between San Francisco and Honolulu. He traveled through Europe, staying with people who had visited the bungalows throughout his childhood. We were the same age.

He asked me what I was doing there.

"Just hanging out," I responded. "I'm a teacher and a writer. I'm interested in local art."

I didn't say, I'm on the run from sleeping around after having my heart broken by a man who valued his habit more than he valued me.

What did I think of his island?

"It's great," I said. "But I'm meant to head back to the main island on this afternoon's flight."

"You're going back today? That's too bad. I'm taking a boat out to a friend's *motu* tomorrow. I'd be glad to take you along."

I knew about *motus*, the small deserted islands that flanked larger inhabited ones, but I had never thought about them belonging to anyone.

"Your friend's *motu?*"

"He leased it from the government. He's building a house, and he wants me to supervise the crew. He hired some men from the village to clear the bush." He paused a moment. "I'm going to watch the rugby match up the road. I'll be back before you leave for the airport."

As Derek walked across the yard, I considered the implications of a beautiful man and a deserted island. *Stay away from boys.* I didn't doubt that his offer of transport to the island included sex on the island. I had always experienced travel through my body, as a physical and erotic process, my attachments to places mediated through sexual relationships. Through travel the trajectory of meeting, dating, sex, and breaking up became compressed into a few hours, days, perhaps a week, until our journeys took us in separate directions. I experienced a social shift — suddenly no one would ask me if I was traveling alone, when I would get married, or if I had a man back home. As part of a couple I became safe, I became figured out, I lost some of my mystery. Sharing my narrow guesthouse bed, I also put down some emotional roots, if only temporarily. Places on a map became places where I'd slept with someone. I returned home and developed my photographs and there were always one or two of them, rarely one of us together. On past travels I had woken up next to local men, Peace Corps volunteers, an English medical intern. Sex in hotel swimming pools, on my sarong spread out on the beach, in a stolen moment in a shared hostel room. One summer spent traveling across Europe with the addict, our itinerary defined by where he could get a bag, us either fighting or sleeping together. Wanting him, and wanting just as desperately to leave him.

I went into the bathroom to pee, using the bumpy pink toilet paper found in formerly colonized countries. Afterward, washing my hands, I considered myself in the small mirror above the sink, and considered the possibility of Derek. When traveling, I am radiant. A few days on the main island's beaches, swimming in warm salt water, digging my toes into sand, and my hair and skin were glowing. My leather jacket, stretchy pants, and chunky city shoes traded for a sarong and tank, barefoot, a toe ring. Tanned, coconut-oiled skin.

Hair curled around my shoulders, from humidity and letting it go without washing, coppery sun highlights coming out. I stroked the smooth inside of my arm, let the strap of my cami fall from my shoulder, the curve of my breast visible.

I continued to consider Derek, and the airport, as I packed the small rucksack I'd brought along. *Stay away from boys.* Needing to break a cycle, I had wanted, planned, this time, to have a trip that wasn't defined by who I'd slept with along the way. I rolled my clothes — a few rayon skirts, a few tanks, a bikini. My silk sleep sheet in its pouch. A flashlight, insect repellent, camera, film. Basic toiletries in a Ziploc bag, sunscreen, lip gloss, shimmery body powder, tampons. A plastic bag with some nonperishable food. My ticket for the local airline, to head back to the main island at 3 P.M. Check-in time, 2:30 P.M. Derek's powerful shoulders, his engaging smile, his easy manner. A deserted island. A downshifting sensation in my lower belly, my period coming soon. Would he mind?

When Derek returned from the rugby match, I was curled up again on the large chair in the foyer, my bag packed, reading. He was holding an open beer, from the small restaurant and bar opposite the bungalows.

"Still leaving this afternoon?"

"I'm thinking about it. How was the rugby? Did you play?"

"I can't play anymore since I got injured. But the match was good. Do you want to get a beer while you think about leaving?"

We walked across the verdant yard around which the several bungalows were arranged, passing the friendly black dog who seemed to belong to no one in particular but received a diet of kitchen scraps and coconut in exchange for watching over things. The grass was damp and fresh-smelling from the rains. I entered the small open-air structure with Derek, the only woman other than Emma behind the bar, whom I'd befriended the day before. Emma was also my age, not married, which was unusual for the islands. We'd spent some time discussing her *moa*, who worked at the airport. He had a jealous nature; they had been arguing and hadn't talked for two weeks. She asked if I had a *moa* back home and said she liked the color of lip gloss I was wearing. She called it "lip shine." Today she was serving up beers to the various men, younger ones in rugby jerseys and shorts, grimy from the match, older men who had watched the match. They ranged from the drunk to the extremely drunk.

Derek and I got a table. He sat across from me, and Emma brought over two opened beers. "Are you going to the *motu* with Derek?" she asked.

"I'm supposed to leave today. Isn't it bad if I miss my flight? In the States, if you don't show up, there's hell to pay."

Emma and Derek laughed. "No one here cares if you miss a flight," Derek said. "You go into the airline office on Monday and pay five dollars. They'll reschedule you."

Derek and I toasted beers. His knee was against mine under the table. I hardly ever drank beer at home, usually cosmopolitans, or bottles of red wine at dinner with dates. They paid with their Visa check cards. I was not sure who was paying for the beers in front of me, which were multiplying. Was I leaving or not?

Two men arrived on scooters, wearing the uniforms of the local airline, for beers before they had to be at the airport to check in the passengers and baggage for the afternoon flight. I saw Emma bristle, and I realized: her *moa*. She'd said I'd be sure to recognize him when I got to the airport: he was tall and had a long ponytail. I saw them talking, and she relaxed a bit.

Derek called the airport guys over and asked them to explain the process of missing a local flight. They laughed. Emma's *moa* said, "Five dollars. We'll take care of it for you. We're going to the airport now. No worries."

I took a breath. For the briefest of moments I questioned allowing myself the pleasure of sleeping with this man, who was so entirely unlike the various engineers, computer programmers, and MBAs I'd been dating for the past eighteen months. I knew that Derek and I would not recount our childhoods over Thai food. We would not rent DVDs of romantic comedies, and he would not take me to a sex shop and offer to buy me nipple clamps.

"Okay. I'll stay."

A cheer went up around the bar, and Derek smiled and stroked my leg under the table. I would not, after all, stay away from boys. An extra day, spent on a deserted island with a beautiful man, then back to the main island, to the family at the guesthouse who may or may not be expecting me; everything was so fluid here that they wouldn't be concerned if I didn't turn up when I'd said I'd be back.

Flashes of moments under the mosquito net, the light from my travel candle glowing warm across our bodies. The smooth broad expanse of his skin, padded with layers of muscle. His mouth tasting of seawater, of the Australian cigarettes he smoked. The wet slipperiness of our bodies moving together, the sweat from his temples dripping onto me, running down my breasts, pooling on my belly. His dreads in my face, scratchy, as I felt the enormous strength of his body behind his thrusts. I began to bleed, so he showered afterward. Returning from the bathroom, toweling off, he said, "It's been five months for me."

The next morning, Sunday, Derek got up early to help a friend slaughter and roast a suckling pig. He said he would be back by 10:30 A.M., as we had to head out to the island before the tide changed. After he left, I surveyed the bungalow. The sheets resembled a murder scene, so I washed them in the sink, scrubbing the stains with my facecloth, and draped them around the bungalow to dry. Our clothes were scattered on the floor. I picked up the one good bra I'd brought with me, and then Derek's T-shirt, pressing it to my face, inhaling, his scent moving through me. Folding the T-shirt and his rugby shorts, I left them on the dresser. His return time came and went. The sheets, now nearly dry, I spread out on the bed, leaving them untucked against going sour. On my belly, on their cool dampness, I picked up my book again, soon to fall asleep to the sound of late morning rain.

I awoke when Derek returned. Smiling apologetically, he explained that it was too late to go to the island today, that the tide had already changed. He parted the mosquito netting and climbed in. "Stay another day, go to the island with me," he said, curling up around me. I felt the instant ease of travel relationships with him, my body adjusting comfortably to the presence and shape of his.

"I knew there was no way you'd be back in two hours." I nuzzled into his chest, stroking the smoothness of his arm. The smoke from the pig roast was in his hair, on his skin. His lips brushed my throat as his hand moved under my skirt, his fingers sliding into my panties. I pulled his hand away, sucked his fingers until they were slick, then replaced his hand. I felt him pressing into me, under his shorts.

A car horn honked outside the bungalow. "Let's go eat," Derek said, pulling away, adjusting himself, and I followed him out the bungalow, wishing I'd had forewarning, time to comb my hair. A new Isuzu SUV had pulled up. It was his friend Simon, a good-looking man with short curly hair, in his late thirties, wearing Oakley sunglasses. Derek hopped in the front seat and I got in the back. Simon asked me, "Do you like Kid Rock?" and slid a CD into the player. Driving down the bumpy road, music blaring, I looked back into the cargo area and saw some tinfoil-wrapped bundles and the remains of the suckling pig, roasted, headless, on a platter.

Simon lived in a large, Western-style house with a tennis court and a patio overlooking the harbor. The building site that Derek was supervising on the island would be his weekend home, though I was not sure what activities distinguished Simon's weekends from his weekdays. On the patio, Derek unwrapped the foil bundles: taro roots, taro leaves cooked in coconut milk, and, strangely, turkey and stuffing, like American Thanksgiving. While we ate, the men talked about tides, wind directions, currents, a conversation in which I couldn't possibly participate.

Afterward, in the kitchen, I began to do the dishes, but Derek said, "Leave it. The housegirls will do them." As I stood at the sink, he was behind me, pressing himself into my back, his arms around my waist. I leaned back into him, a drawn-out sensation within me. I was letting him under my skin, in the way I hadn't let a guy under my skin for two years, since I'd said goodbye to the addict. We'd been living on separate coasts by that time, and the goodbye scene had occurred in an airport parking lot. I hadn't wanted him to go inside with me. A searing pain throughout my body as I let go of him, aching from days of doubling-up crying. Dreading the fear of loss spreading through me, a pain so all consuming it was numbing, from loving deeply the absolutely wrong person. A rupture like an infected wound. Moving back from the space of memory, I felt Derek's lips on my neck.

Derek and I returned to the bungalow. His stomach was upset, and thinking of the accumulating beer bottles, the fatty pork, I dispensed Tums and Tylenol. I made him drink lots of water, filling my Nalgene bottle from the spigot at the rainwater cistern. We spent the afternoon and evening drifting in and out of sleep and sex. Later, I took peanut butter, crackers, oranges, and my Swiss army knife from my rucksack and spread out my sarong on the bed like a tablecloth. We picnicked under the mosquito net, to the sound of buzzing insects, chirping geckos, the occasional grunting pig outside. We compared tattoos. He liked the Celtic design on my leg; like the local tattoo work, it was flat, black, symmetrical. Derek had a turtle on his left breast, and his name was tattooed on his bicep in cursive. I placed my mouth over it, tracing it with my tongue, repeating his multisyllabic surname in my mind: its many vowels, its soft consonants.

"If I lived in the States, would you date me?"

The question startled me into imagining Derek in my world, in my California beach town, playing volleyball by the pier, shopping with me at the farmers' market, at a cookout with my friends, eating guacamole. There was an unexpected fit with him that I didn't normally experience with travel relationships. Usually I didn't even attempt to imagine the possibility of a future beyond the immediate present. Perhaps because he was a traveler too, because he navigated with ease in and through multiple worlds. Perhaps because, with his smarts, his beauty, his sureness of himself, and his sense of cool, he could have had anyone, and as I had made the choice to not stay away from boys, I felt that he had also chosen me. "Definitely," I told him. In the dark, warm room, under the mosquito net, his fingers curled around mine, calloused and strong.

The next morning, I packed quickly for the trip to the *motu*. I bought bread, two pineapples, and some bananas from a woman at the market beside the wharf, and Derek purchased a basket of taro. We climbed into Simon's motorboat, tied to the dock, and Derek took his position at the wheel. He was self-assured as he piloted the boat, even through a shallow bit, avoiding sandbars and hunks of coral reef. He told me the names of the coastal villages we passed, and pointed out a sea cave opening onto the water that was the home of a rare bird.

The *motu* looked like Gilligan's Island: small, flat, with coconut trees, palmettos, and tangles of vines. The workmen waved at us from the beach as we anchored the boat and waded to shore. Derek and I put our rucksacks, the basket of taro, and bottles of rainwater under an open-sided shelter. I tied the plastic bags containing the loaves of bread and the fruit to the roof with string, to keep the ants out. Several dome tents had been pitched along the beach. Derek and I chose one and moved it away from the others, for us to sleep in. He began cutting up the taro to make a stew for the workmen.

Leaving him to his work, I took my camera and wandered along the beach. The waves crashed beyond the reef, about fifty feet out, but within the reef the pools of water were warm and shallow. Wading barefoot, holding up my sarong, I found sapphire-blue starfish, a dead purple jellyfish, avoided urchins. Triggerfish dove at my toes. I dipped my fingers into the water and sucked the saltiness from them.

Later, in the darkness of the new moon, Derek and I wandered nude from our tent into the cool shallow water just outside, lying on our bellies, supporting ourselves on our elbows. The constellations were different, disorienting me. Derek pointed out the Southern Cross, and I gained my bearings, also remembering the direction the sun had set. The lights from the main town on the island glowed to the north. The nighttime water was illuminated by phosphorescent creatures, like glitter, which sparkled when we splashed.

We returned to the tent. In a moment he was on top of me, teasing me with his mouth in the darkness, moving quickly from nipple to thigh. I giggled, enjoying the joke, the tiny unexpected nips from his lovely teeth. Was this a rugby strategy, darting across a field? Feeling the heavy dampness of the sand beneath my sarong and the tarp bottom, his hands confidently massaging my breasts, never doubting his abilities, or mine. Afterward, I rinsed in the sea, washing the fluids from my thighs. We slept curled up together, in a world silent but for the sounds of the water lapping the shore just a few feet from the tent.

When I woke up, the sun was streaming into the tent and Derek had already gone out to check on the fishing nets. I'd heard the workmen jeering at him when he'd crawled naked from the tent, teasing him as he'd scrambled into his board shorts. There was sand in my underwear, in my scalp, sticking to all my possessions. Derek returned with a report: the nets were empty. I emerged from the tent, wrapping myself in my sarong, which Derek had used as a sheet, and washed myself in the sea. I made peanut butter and banana sandwiches for myself, Derek, and the workmen, arranging them on a large fresh leaf. Derek peeled and sliced the pineapple with his bush knife. The workmen first protested that they couldn't possibly take advantage of my generosity, as I would starve if they were to eat my food, but when I insisted that they eat, that I wouldn't be needing the food, I was leaving that day, it would only be wasted otherwise, they marveled at the ingeniousness of the peanut butter and banana sandwiches, and seemed to enjoy them.

After breakfast, Derek rushed me into the boat, to get me back to town before the tide changed again. He anchored the boat to a dock opposite the bungalows and accompanied me up the steep pathway. I had imagined a Casablanca ending, an extraordinary conclusion to an extraordinary few days, but I didn't get one. After a few awkward moments, Simon arrived in the SUV, and Derek "had to go." He pulled me into the main house and kissed me, asked if I could send him some AA batteries, and then was gone. I waited in the bar with Emma for the driver to take me to the airport.

"Where's Derek?" she asked, bringing me a beer.

I shrugged, "Gone."

I caught the plane back to the main island, caught my plane to California. I returned to work, where people remarked on my tan. I broke things off with the current guy back home, deciding to stay away from boys after all, for the meantime at least. I sent Derek a care package with batteries, condoms, and a bottle of Aqua Lube, marked "religious materials" so it wouldn't get opened in customs. I included the photos I took on the island: him kneeling in the tidepools, gathering shellfish, smiling at the camera and me. Sometimes I let myself travel into the fantasy of something more than a sandbag, something more than a quick fix, something more than dinner and a DVD. Sometimes I let myself imagine that Derek will call me from his sister's place in Los Angeles, that I'll drive south on the freeway to pick him up, or that he'll appear at my apartment with his cute smile, his speargun, and his rucksack. He slipped in and out of my life like a triggerfish, gloriously beautiful and bold.

KEVIN FEDARKO

Kashmiri Extremism

FROM *Skiing*

IT'S 4 A.M., and outside the fog shrouded windows of the Kashmir Alpine Ski Shop, the Indian village of Gulmarg sleeps in the shadow of a 13,576-foot ridge that looks directly into Pakistan. The door opens and Hamid blows in with a blast of cold night air, grabbing a seat near a tiny charcoal brazier that is the shop's only source of heat. At the table is Hamid's friend and business partner, Yaseen, surrounded by a pile of gear that looks like a cross between a vintage ski swap and a United Nations garage sale: some battered Völkl Tour Extremes given to them in 1983 by a New Zealand trekker; worn Dynastar boots donated by a German climber in 1989; goggles, gloves, and gaiters left by guests from Europe, Asia, and the Middle East; and some safety straps I'll apparently be using, which Yaseen is now jury-rigging from a roll of frayed Bengali baling twine. While I wolf down toast and tea, Yaseen and Hamid exchange a remark in Kashmiri, which is followed by a rueful chuckle. I ask what they're talking about.

"We are just remembering," Yaseen explains. "In the days before the fighting came to Kashmir, we used to start out all the time like this, at three or four in the morning. We are reminding each other how many foreigners used to come here from all over the world. Australia, America, Denmark, Switzerland, Brazil, Hong Kong, Sweden, Japan, France, Norway . . ."

"Dutch," adds Hamid, helpfully.

"Yes, Holland too."

Yaseen glances at the disused skis stacked against the table, the snowboards languishing in the shelves on the back wall. "But look around. Now there's nobody." He sighs and reaches for the nozzle of his hookah — a Turkish-style tobacco pipe sometimes used for smoking hashish. I don't know what's in the hookah this morning, but Yaseen draws a deep, satisfying inhalation that burbles flatulently through the water in the bong, then emits a string of wet, hacking coughs. "This war has made me old," he declares, casting a hard look at his watch.

Time to go. We clomp into the milky starlight, throw our skis over our shoulders, and begin a predawn, 4,592-foot climb through the snow-draped forests to the alpine heights above Gulmarg, gateway to the finest war-zone skiing on earth.

Cupped in a meadow high above the Kashmir Valley, Gulmarg is dotted with small tin-roofed homes, tiny tea stalls, and elaborately carved wooden hotels, several of which have been abandoned by their owners and are now being remodeled by the winter wind. The village is a "hill station," a mountain sanctuary where India's colonial rulers used to flee in order to escape the choking heat of the plains below. In the nineteenth century, British army officers and civil servants spent their summer vacations up here cavorting on the highest golf course in the world, while in winter they hired ponies to haul their wooden skis to the top of the beginners' runs (which are now served by a handful of modest lifts). More recently, Gulmarg has emerged as a honeymooners' haven, a place where besotted Indian newlyweds come to gaze at the mountains, fling snow at each other, and pay to get dragged through the slushy streets on blocky, wooden sleds pulled by underworked porters.

All this is charming, to be sure — but it's the three-mile ridgeline above Gulmarg that induced me to fly ten thousand miles to get here; that, and the fact that Himalayan snow typically falls in the form of dust-light powder. Beneath the northeast-facing ridge, the terrain consists of 35° rollovers that merge onto open slopes comparable to the Back Bowls at Vail. The bottom section flows through forests of widely spaced, hundred-foot fir trees whose branches resound with the chatter of monkeys. The forest floor is laced with the tracks of leopard, deer, and black bear. Surrounding the village is nearly ten square miles of skiable terrain that would rival some of the largest resorts in North America and Europe — that is, if Gulmarg actually had a lift to the top. The ten-square-mile figure, however, applies just to the ridge above Gulmarg. To the southeast lies an adjacent 15,500-foot massif called Sunrise Peak, and between Gulmarg and the valley floor, an additional 2,000 feet of vertical drops steeply through yet another forest of conifers. This more than doubles the skiable area and makes Gulmarg perhaps the greatest untapped big-mountain resort in the world. The operative word here, of course, is "untapped," because Gulmarg also happens to sit in the middle of the most intractable military standoff in Asia. Just getting here from Kashmir's capital city of Srinagar requires a two-hour drive into the mountains that runs a gauntlet of soldiers and machine-gun emplacements.

The origins of the conflict date back to 1947, when, in a process referred to as Partition, Britain divided its South Asian empire into two new nations: the Hindu-majority republic of India and the Islamic state of Pakistan. Partition's upheavals produced one of the largest migrations of refugees in history — some ten million people — and the slaughter of nearly one million Hindus, Sikhs, and Muslims. Another casualty was the princely state of Jammu & Kashmir in the mountainous north, which had a Muslim-majority population ruled by a Hindu maharaja. Two months after Partition, Pakistan invaded Kashmir. India — at Kashmir's request — then airlifted in Sikh troops to meet them. When the fighting ended fourteen months later, India controlled two-thirds of the state and Pakistan ruled the rest. The de facto border was the military ceasefire line, which started near the Indian city of Jammu and cut a diagonal, northeastward swath toward China. Along the way, it skirted the edge of the ridgeline just above Gulmarg.

This border was dubbed the Line of Control, a term that revealed wishful thinking on both sides: in 1965 and again in 1971, India and Pakistan fought two more wars in Kashmir (both of which Pakistan lost). It wasn't until the mid-1980s that Delhi and Islamabad finally began taking tentative steps to iron out their problems. The prospect of peace encouraged tourists, and by 1988, 600,000 Indians and 60,000 foreigners were pouring into Kashmir annually. This, in turn, inspired Kashmir's state government to begin building a gondola at Gulmarg in the hopes of transforming the place into a world-class ski resort. It was a heady time when people voiced serious speculation about Gulmarg making a bid to host the Asian Winter Games and, eventually, the Winter Olympics.

One person who took particular interest in all this was a man named Mohmad Yaseen Khan.

Yaseen, forty-eight, grew up in a small village just below Gulmarg that is surrounded by apple and cherry orchards. His skin is leathery, his hands are impervious to cold, and he looks a bit like Paul Newman, if you can imagine Paul Newman addicted to smoking a hookah and missing two-thirds of his teeth. Having spent the winters of his boyhood working at the resort, Yaseen had dreamed for years of owning his own ski-industry enterprise but was hampered by the fact that he had never learned to read or write. Then, in the spring of 1989, he decided to partner up with Abdul Hamid Dar, thirty-five, a friend who possessed enough education to help manage the business, and whose family owns land in Gulmarg. Hamid has a soft voice that is offset by an impressive black mustache that seems to bristle when he negotiates ski and snowboard rental fees.

Together, the two Muslim men bought a tiny studio near the center of Gulmarg and opened the resort's first privately owned rental shop and guide service. The Kashmir Alpine Ski Shop doubled as their living quarters; there was no toilet and they had to bathe at a friend's house. Their rental stock consisted of two sets of skis and two pairs of boots purchased from some cash-strapped Austrian tourists, which they leased for five dollars a day. Two months after their grand opening, Kashmir's latest war broke out — a civil conflict that pitted more than sixty Islamic guerrilla groups against half a million Indian troops. In the ensuing mayhem, which consumed newspaper headlines all over the world, and which continues to this day, more than thirty-six thousand Kashmiris have been kidnapped or killed. During the mid-1990s, the guerrillas also began targeting foreign visitors. In July 1995, six trekkers were taken hostage. One American escaped, but a twenty-seven-year-old Norwegian named Hans Christian Ostro was decapitated. The rest were never found.

High in the mountains, Gulmarg remained relatively untouched, but down in Srinagar, hotels were surrounded by barbed wire and virtually every street corner was guarded by Indian soldiers in sandbagged gun emplacements. Tourist numbers plummeted by 98 percent, Gulmarg's dozen-odd hotels were all but abandoned, and construction of the gondola, which could now transport visitors 1,320 vertical feet to a terminal halfway up the mountain, came to a halt. Then, on the night of March 17, 1999, an electrical fire started in the shop adjacent to Yaseen and Hamid's store, and in twenty minutes their entire business burned to the ground. They lost their skis, their equipment, and all their personal belongings. Not even Yaseen's socks were spared. "That was my biggest bad day," he recalls. "We had no money, and we had no resources."

A month later, about a hundred miles east of Gulmarg, more than eight hundred Pakistan-supported militants launched a surprise attack across the Line of Control and started shelling Indian army posts. By midsummer, each country was threatening to use nuclear weapons to wipe its rival off the face of the planet, provoking Bill Clinton to declare Kashmir "the most dangerous place on earth." At the time, the comment seemed to mark the final phase of Kashmir's excruciating slide from paradise-on-earth to living hell. In fact, though, Clinton's words evoked a violent paradox that has plagued Kashmir for centuries, and that is illustrated most chillingly by an incident that took place more than 1,400 years ago in the same mountains that encircle Gulmarg.

The story is about an elephant belonging to a Hun warlord whose army was invading Kashmir via a pass high in the Pir Panjal Range. Somewhere in the middle of the pass, the elephant lost its footing, stumbled off the path, and trumpeted in plaintive horror as it plunged to its death. Finding himself stimulated by the otherworldly shriek, the warlord immediately ordered that a second, then a third, and eventually one hundred elephants be pushed over the precipice, so that he might savor the exquisite sound of their terror. The point of this story is that in Kashmir, beauty is gratuitous — but so, too, are cruelty and pain.

In the spring of 1999, the weight of this truth bore down crushingly on the owners of the Kashmir Alpine Ski Shop as they confronted bankruptcy and ruin. It was at this point, however, with a few dozen foreign skiers showing up over the course of a season and the lifts running only intermittently, that fate decided to cut these two beleaguered Muslim ski guides a break and dispatched an unusual emissary to lend them a hand.

He arrived in the winter of 2000, a hash-smoking ex-commando from Israel, whose apparent mission was to become the Jewish snowboarding messiah of Kashmir.

Ido Neiger was raised just south of the Sea of Galilee and learned to snowboard at Mount Hermon, the highest peak in Israel, where a tiny ski resort looks into Syria and the slopes are occasionally shelled by Hezbollah. In 1994, Ido was drafted into the Israeli army, earning a spot in an elite commando squad which ran demolition operations that included blowing up the homes and buildings of suspected Islamic terrorists in southern Lebanon.

For the past six years, Ido, twenty-eight, has traveled almost constantly, earning money working for land-mine-defusing projects run by the United Nations, and snowboarding in New Zealand, Slovenia, the Dolomites, and Breckenridge. When he's not riding his Air Burton or unscrewing the detonators on tank-busting land mines with his Leatherman, he can often be found attending full-moon backpacker raves in places like Australia or Thailand, where he dances to trance music and consumes prodigious amounts of psychotropic drugs.

In February 2000, Ido's quest for untracked powder took him to Gulmarg, where he met Yaseen and Hamid and decided to stay for the winter, bunking down in the attic above their rebuilt ski shop. He was maddened by Gulmarg's many problems, which included a lack of well-maintained slopes (Gulmarg does not even publish a trail map) and the fact that the gondola — which, thanks to rampant Indian nepotism, has 150 people working for it — can't manage to open up at the same time every morning. Ido also understood, though, that such glitches were, in a backhanded way, part of the charm of a place where a one-day lift ticket costs five dollars. "Because there are virtually no skiers here, you feel like you have your own private resort," he said. "It doesn't even matter what time you wake up in the morning — you will always have the first run, and you will always have the fresh snow. Plus it costs only fifteen dollars a day to ski, survive, and smoke the best hash on earth. Tell me where else you can get away with that."

When he left in March 2001, promising to return, Yaseen and Hamid weren't sure they'd ever see Ido again — a suspicion that grew stronger when they didn't hear from the guy for nearly two years. Unbeknownst to them, however, Ido was working on a bold plan.

First he got a lucrative mine-defusing job in Croatia, which enabled him to save more than five thousand dollars. With the extra cash, he started buying up used snowboarding gear, eventually amassing fourteen boards, seventeen pairs of boots, and sixteen pairs of bindings, as well as a formidable stash of wax, goggles, gloves, and P-tex, plus an old laundry iron. He assembled everything in Tel Aviv, bundled it into a five-hundred-pound package, then sweet-talked Royal Jordanian Airlines into flying the whole thing to India for free. After landing in Delhi early last January, he rammed the shipment through customs with the aid of a few bribes, rented a jeep, and hauled the gear six hundred miles up to Gulmarg. He appeared at the door of the ski shop with no warning, dumped his gift at the feet of a flabbergasted Yaseen and Hamid, and told them that it was time to get down to some serious business.

Meanwhile, the government of Kashmir, apparently infected with the same viral strain of rabid optimism that is driving the Kashmir Alpine Ski Shop, decided to restart construction of the final phase of the lift. When the cableway is complete — supposedly in November — Gulmarg will boast the third-highest gondola (12,990 feet) in the world.

The fact that this is all taking place in an active combat zone, and would thus seem to qualify as the most asinine business venture in the history of industrialized snow sports, doesn't appear to have had the slightest effect on anyone.

I spent four days in Gulmarg, and never quite managed to escape the feeling that I'd blundered into a place that has been cruelly — and perhaps irrevocably — screwed up. The war is now in its fourteenth year, which means that the resort long ago slipped off the radar of the international adventure-travel set. Yet nearly everyone connected with Gulmarg clings ferociously to an irrational mixture of hope and denial. "The government is not giving proper information to foreign tourists," groused Hamid one afternoon as we walked down the road. "Here there are no guns. Here there is no danger." He seemed oblivious to the fact that he was making these remarks within direct sight of a heavily armed Indian military convoy. "See our mountains — so much potential!" Yaseen exclaimed during a backcountry climb the next day. "You can ski anywhere you like." Fifteen minutes later, we were kicked off our traverse by a platoon from India's High Altitude Warfare School, which was training for winter combat along the Line of Control.

On my final day, as I was preparing to write Yaseen, Hamid, and Ido off as victims of their own propaganda, we made our pre-dawn climb to the ridge to preview what skiers and boarders will see next season when they disembark from the completed gondola. It was a surreal moment. There was Yaseen pointing out Pakistan and warning me not to drift too far right, lest I be spotted by an Indian army patrol and arrested. And there, too, smack in front of us, was one of the most stunning views of any ski resort in the world.

Crowning the vista was the sweep of the eastern Karakoram, dominated by 26,658-foot-high Nanga Parbat and dozens of 20,000-plus-foot peaks. Directly at my feet stretched a deliciously steep, alabaster mantle of powder broken only by our own boot tracks and the paw prints of a contouring fox. It was a half mile to the first tree, a quarter mile from there to the gondola, three miles to Gulmarg itself. And from there, if we wished, we could continue over the lip and plunge another two miles to the village of Tangmarg: an unbroken descent of nearly 7,000 feet. As I pushed off, it occurred to me for the first time that maybe these guys weren't suffering from delusional blindness but from something quite a bit more treacherous, and infinitely more forgivable. They had simply fallen in love with Gulmarg. And in that moment, I think I understood why.

Launching into my first turn, I failed to experience any grand epiphanies regarding the cosmic connection between skiing and the Oneness of the Universe. Instead, I found myself just concentrating on how to link turns through snow that had the consistency of spackling compound. More to the point, though, for the first time in four days I *wasn't* thinking about kidnappings, hand grenades, or Hans Christian Ostro's missing head. For a moment I was completely liberated — a state of mind encompassing just about everything that poor, shackled, benighted Kashmir dreams of touching, and that remains tragically beyond its grasp. Something about this was both dreadfully sad and, at the same time, incorrigibly human. Who could fail to be seduced by such magic?

The questionable ethics of inducing others to come to a place like this, however, remained. The next morning, I was walking through the village with Ido to catch my taxi back to Srinagar just as one of the Cheetah helicopters that the Indian army uses for high-altitude warfare clattered overhead. Shouting to make myself heard, I demanded to know how he, Yaseen, and Hamid could, in good faith, propose to bring tourists into a war zone.

"Maybe I'm a bit extreme when it comes to danger," Ido replied. "My line of work deals with death all the time. Also, I'm an Israeli, and right now Israel is the most dangerous place in the world. But because of these things, I know that death and terrorism can catch me anywhere, at any time. I know that no place is truly safe, because these days the entire world is a dangerous place. And I also realize that this knowledge can actually make you free. If you realize that death can reach you anywhere, you can go wherever you want. You can do whatever you want. That's why I've had such a wonderful time here. And that's why I want other people to come to Gulmarg."

In recent months there have been some encouraging developments in Kashmir. In May, India and Pakistan announced plans to restore diplomatic relations and hold their first talks in two years. If all goes well, the ski dreamers at Gulmarg might eventually see their hopes vindicated. It's worth noting, though, that India and Pakistan have cycled through similar phases in the past, and each time, hope was shattered when somebody decided to push an elephant off a cliff just for the sake of hearing it scream.

I was afforded a glimpse into how this works when, on the return flight from Srinagar, I found myself sitting next to Arun Joshi, an Indian public relations executive returning home to Delhi from a holiday. As the plane skirted the snowy crest of the Pir Panjal and soared out over the hot, green plains to the south, Mr. Joshi affably explained that he and his wife had been staying with a close family friend in Srinagar who also happens to be the lieutenant general in charge of the entire Kashmir Valley, one of the most important posts in the Indian army. "So how does the commander feel about the situation?" I asked.

"Oh, he is extremely pleased," Mr. Joshi replied. "Things were very bad, it's true. But now they are much better. Stability has returned to Kashmir."

The next morning in Delhi, I picked up the newspaper and learned that around midnight on the day I had left Srinagar, eight

Islamic militants dressed in olive-green fatigues and pretending to be Indian soldiers entered a small village called Nadimarg, about seventy miles from Gulmarg. The militants had ordered every Hindu in the village to line up for identification and then proceeded to gun them down with automatic weapons. Of the twenty-four unarmed civilians who were murdered that night in Nadimarg, eleven were women, and two were infants, shot to death in their mothers' arms.

Segways in Paris

FROM *Slate.com*

From: Tad Friend
Subject: Three Cheers for American Engineering!
Monday, May 19, 2003, at 2:48 P.M. PT

My wife and I arrived in Paris in the middle of a general strike — something about pension funds, though the French never seem to require an excuse to strike. Buses and metros were basically out, and it took us two hours in heavy traffic to get from Charles de Gaulle airport to our hotel on the Left Bank. We were here to ride Segway Human Transporters, the new two-wheeled scooters, around Paris's crooked sidewalks and to have a cultural exchange on the fly with our favorite cheese-eating surrender monkeys. The strike seemed almost too apt for our purposes; it made our first foray out with the Segway HTs as overdetermined as the opening scene of a Hollywood movie:

We open on a swirling, helicopter shot of the EIFFEL TOWER, then take a fast AERIAL TOUR of the CHAMPS ÉLYSÉES before the camera comes to earth midway down the traffic-snarled Boulevard Saint-Germain, which is filled with EXCITABLE FRENCHMEN, who stand beside their Renaults and Citroëns waving BAGUETTES over their heads, dashing their BERETS to the ground, and gesticulating at the state of their beloved CITY OF LIGHTS, which has not seen so much CHAOS since the GERMANS arrived in 1940. We hear angry voices (*"Mon Dieu!* What a

folly of mankind it was to build cities zat no one can navigate" . . .
"Who can save us from zees catastrophe of our own devising?"
Etc., etc.)

Suddenly, all heads turn as a devastatingly charismatic team of
three Americans (the bespectacled and bookishly sexy TAD;
AMANDA, his incredibly chic and provocative wife; and CHRIS-
TIAN, the team's bearded, gnomic, all-knowing technology guru)
blaze down the sidewalk on SEGWAYS, the miracle scooters that
will solve all of PARIS's transportation problems!

They move with such EASE, going where they will simply by leaning FORWARD and BACK, that they seem to herald a JOY of
FLYING that mankind had hitherto found only in dreams. Before
anyone can stop them they ZIP around the corner in search of new
adventures, and we . . .

CUT back to the faces of the FRENCHMEN, who have lowered their BAGUETTES and now seem SCANDALIZED but PI-
OUS. Once again, the AMERICANS have arrived to bail them out,
as we did in WORLD WARS I and II and by generously going along
with that whole BEAUJOLAIS NOUVEAU SCHEME, and these
OVERCIVILIZED DENIZENS OF OLD EUROPE cannot help —
despite their grievances with us about IRAQ and McDONALD'S,
and our ADAM SANDLER–STYLE CULTURAL IMPERIALISM —
feeling . . . what is it? The Frenchmen seem to rack their memories
for the feeling, it is so foreign to them — *Mais qu'est-ce que c'est le mot
juste? Ah, oui!* GRATEFUL.

Oddly enough, when we began training on our Segways outside
our hotel, that is more or less what happened. It took us about
twenty minutes to learn the basics from three Segway representatives: lean forward on the machine and you go forward, lean back
to stop, keep leaning back to go backward, and twist the left han-
dlebar to turn right or left. The machine has a zero turning radius
— you can spin on a dime, and it's really fun. There were a few
small accidents — Christian unhorsed himself, and I took a strip of
green paint off a building trying to thread a narrow sidewalk —
but within half an hour we were all able to navigate even the heavy
medieval cobblestones in front of the church of Saint-Germain-des-
Prés with ease. We were flying along at two or three times pedestrian speed. And we were grinning like schoolkids. Going where
you want to go just by following your own inclination is like having
a magic carpet.

Everyone — everyone — was transfixed by us. A burly man ran out of a brasserie and whistled down the street; when I turned he gave me a huge thumbs-up. Two stylish women in blue raincoats grabbed each other and laughed from sheer pleasure: *"C'est superbe!"* A homeless man threw his arms over his head when Amanda went by: Hallelujah! "It's like being Jennifer Aniston!" Amanda said. "And I'm so tall!" (The platform gives you an extra eight inches in height, putting my head right at awning level.)

Whenever we stopped at a corner, we were surrounded: "What is it?" (A Segway Human Transporter, invented by Dean Kamen and produced in Manchester, New Hampshire.) "How does it work?" (Each wheel is driven by high-speed electric motors that you recharge simply by plugging the Segway into an outlet overnight. The machine has five gyroscopes and two tilt-balancing sensors that determine, one hundred times per second, what the terrain is like and how your body is arrayed.) "How fast does it go?" (Up to 12.5 miles per hour in top gear; we had them in sidewalk mode, where the top speed is 8 miles per hour.) "Is it available in France?" (In a few weeks, the Keolis Group, Segway's partner in Europe, will start a pilot program along the Champs Élysées for 150 "responsible citizens.") "How much does it cost?" ($4,950 in the United States — they're available exclusively on Amazon. You can't buy them in France, but Keolis is planning to rent them out for about eight dollars an hour within a few months and eventually expects to set up "Oxygen Stations" at metro stops around the city where you can pick up a Segway, zip around for a while, and then drop it off at another Oxygen Station.)

The prevailing mood was curiosity and wonder: thumbs-up, applause, admiring head-shakes. But on two separate occasions very serious men with brush cuts parked their BMW motorcycles and came over to write down all the Segway's specifications, assessing the undercarriage with frowns, as if they planned to reverse-engineer the machine that very evening on their lathes.

And one fortyish woman, her Joan Jett hair dyed that dark shade of henna that only French women consider stylish, stared at us on Rue de Seine, her left foot on the floorboard of a low chrome scooter, her face a mask of deep injury. When I looked back ten seconds later, she still hadn't moved. She was yesterday's future and we were tomorrow's, blowing on by and leaving her in our noiseless, emissionless, dust-free dust.

From: Tad Friend
Subject: The Force Is with Us
Tuesday, May 20, 2003, at 1:02 P.M. PT

As I write this, Amanda is sitting cross-legged in a chair by our hotel room window, eating petits fours out of a pink box from Ladurée and reading French *Vogue*. "Who are you, Kate Moss?" she murmured just now, staring at the supermodel's druggie-chic cover photo. I laughed, and then saw that the cover line was actually, *"Qui êtes-vous, Kate Moss?"*

Only the French, still in thrall to the *nouvelle vague*'s belief that style is character, would expect that a two-page magazine article should plumb Kate Moss's soul, and that its failure to do so might even be — *Qui êtes-vous, Kate? Qui? Qui?* — cause for despair. In America, we expect only to audit Moss's newest incarnation. She is not a soul to be understood but an amalgam of views and accomplishments to be downloaded. Ever practical, our cover line would read, "Newly Fit and Focused, Kate Moss Talks — About Sex, Men, and How She Stays So Thin."

The French have Voltaire and Sartre; we have Eli Whitney and Thomas Edison. Of course, we have philosophers, too (Will Rogers, Fred Rogers), and they innovators (the French invented pasteurization, coquilles St. Jacques, and the Maginot Line, along with two or three other things). But it is universally understood that an educated Frenchman's cultural role is to be the *philosophe* who produces nothing but can explain everything, while an educated American's — *mais, quel paradoxe* — is to be the idiot savant who can fashion wondrous things (DDT, thalidomide, bunker-buster bombs) but always uses them incorrectly.

Some of these thoughts occurred to me as Amanda, Christian, and I were Segwaying this afternoon from the Hôtel Bel Ami on the Left Bank to the Radisson on the Right. We had gotten comfortable enough on the machines to use the advanced "red key" to start them up, meaning we could now travel at their top speed, 12.5 miles per hour. We crossed the bone-colored crushed gravel paths of the Tuileries, rising and falling over the small ridges as if we were riding through the desert, three abreast in our raincoats, and Christian said, "*Star Wars* police." It was the perfect image. At the next crosswalk, Amanda said, "It's funny you said that. I was just thinking that all the other people there on foot looking at us were like the weird creatures in *Star Wars,* and we were the normal ones: Luke, and Leia, and Han Solo."

Christian stands erect in his Segway with an absent-minded air, like a man out walking his dog: he is Han Solo. Amanda grips her handlebars, lowers her head, and braces her legs as if she's manning the helm during a fierce sou'wester: she, clearly, is Leia. And I like to push the speed limit and slalom between bollards or oblivious pedestrians, but sometimes I lose the Force and bang a curbstone: I am Luke.

The assumption that we are the normal ones is not shared by Parisians: they see us as the circus come to town. Along the Champs Élysées, I parked my Segway against a tree and went to look at a mile-long exhibition of French trains, from a stunningly restored old wagons-lits parlor car to the newest TGV locomotive. When I returned, there were thirteen people gathered around Christian and Amanda; all of them had come to walk the railway timeline, all of them were now much more interested in the Segway. I found myself giving a Segway lesson to a friendly man named Jean, explaining with great authority the techniques I'd learned the day before. An orotund, P. T. Barnum–ish note came into my voice, and I found myself accepting Jean's praise as my own just due. Simply by being American, and in temporary possession of a Segway, I felt at least partially responsible for its reverse-torque braking mechanism.

Near Place Clemenceau, a policeman sitting with a few colleagues in a white van gestured to us to halt, then put on his cap and squared it before stepping out to address us. You're not supposed to ride Segways in the street, as we had briefly been doing. As we discovered this morning, when we went shopping in the Sixth Arrondissement for shoes (Amanda) and birthday presents (that is, shoes), it's much easier and more fun to blast down an alley on your Segway rather than beetle it along the tiny, crammed sidewalks.

As it turned out, this policeman simply wanted to understand what the hell this thing was. While Amanda explained the Segway's specifications, he nodded as if it all had been foreseen. Young and assured, he had roses in his cheeks and an air of good humor. He touched the machine. *"Anglais?"* he asked.

"*Américain,*" I said.

"*Beh!*" He gestured and walked away — then turned back with a grin. A crowd had gathered by now, and he was enjoying the audience, embracing his cultural role as the true interpreter.

"Who uses them?" he asked.

I explained that police at the Atlanta airport and the Los Angeles Metropolitan Transit Authority were using them for security patrols. In a confusion of bad French, I used the word "*flics*" for cops — slang roughly equivalent to calling an American policeman a "pig." He smiled, enjoying the gaucherie, then turned his mouth down at the corners (not for us, such vehicles). An older woman in a lime-green raincoat walked by and assessed the situation: the *Star Wars* police being interrogated by the real police. "Is it an American thing?" she asked.

"Yes," the policeman said, pausing with the relish of a man who knows he's about to get off a zinger. "But for an American — not bad."

From: Tad Friend
Subject: Segways and Social Stratification
Wednesday, May 21, 2003, at 12:40 P.M. PT

A cold, rainy day in Paris; this morning Amanda cocked one eye at the window and declined to arise for our Segway trip to the Eiffel Tower. She had, in any case, to exchange a pair of black sandals on Mouffetard; both shoes had proved to be for her right foot. When she phoned the store, the salesman denied the mistake and then refused to countenance her suggestions for how they could fix the problem without making her bring the shoes all the way back. "*Je suis désolé,*" he said, and hung up. You hear that a lot here: No, there is no iron in the hotel that works; no, the hotel staff does not know of a manicurist in Paris; yes, we told your caller from the United States that you were not staying at the hotel: *Je suis désolé.* In theory it means "I'm sorry," but it is invariably said with a curt shrug that translates as, "I'm sorry that I have allowed you to intrude upon my consciousness for one instant with your ridiculous needs."

Christian and I had gotten advance permission to take our Segways up the Eiffel Tower's elevator to the second platform, 380 feet above the city, but when we arrived we were told that security had been tightened after the terrorist bombings in Casablanca, and so the Segways must remain earthbound. *"Je suis désolé,"* etc., etc. As it turns out, the platform was a gauntlet of girders, staircases, and rain-drenched tourists, so it was just as well that we didn't have them with us. As we looked out on the city, feeling sleepy and aimless and somewhat trapped high in the air, a Nepalese man with a windblown map asked me to point out Notre-Dame, and we fell into conversation.

Indara, a middle-aged clerk with a kind smile and bad teeth, was one of the fifteen thousand Nepalese who work in Kuwait. He sends money home to his family every month. After fourteen years, he had finally saved enough to make his first trip to Europe, but not enough for any of his family to join him. He talked eagerly and confidingly about how the Kuwaitis treat all Asian guest workers like animals; how the massacre of the Nepalese royal family was never properly investigated by the government, which is sickeningly corrupt; and how, if you support the government, the Maoist rebels will kill you, but if you support the rebels, the government soldiers will kill you. After ten minutes, we shook hands, wished each other a safe journey, and parted.

As Christian and I were trudging down the stairs, it occurred to me that Indara would never have approached us if we had been standing on our Segways. All the people who have come up to talk to us about the machines — the hundreds of people, by now — have had the look of being able to afford one, or at least to rent one for a few hours. The poor don't approach. The other day on the Rue Mouffetard, a few yards from Dr. Evil's shoe store, we bought two boxes of extremely tasty raspberries from a fruit vendor in his traditional French blue coat. (After eating the first one, Amanda said, "It's like you put a small, furry animal in your mouth that dissolves into a cloud of sweetness.") The vendor eyed our Segways but said nothing, even when other shoppers began to ask questions. After I explained about the gyroscopes and the tilt sensors, he said *"Technologie"* in a low voice, as if it were an idea, such as "celebrity" or "immortality," that would be forever beyond his grasp, and handed me my change and turned away.

Like cell phones and computers, the Segway will commence its life as a device for the rich. And like those earlier technologies, it will gradually develop an accompanying etiquette. The two hotels we have stayed at here have seemed delighted to have us ride our Segways into the lobby, to park and recharge them for us in their luggage rooms, even to have us ride them in the elevators up to our rooms. Their sensible belief is that the hotel itself shines in the glow of our cosmopolitan style. After Segways become commonplace, they will be viewed by hotel managers not as a branding opportunity but as a burden on physical space and employee time.

When that happens, it is by no means certain that the Segway will continue to be ridden indoors; propriety, for now in bewildered abeyance, may come down against these frolicsome man-chariots. The verdict will occur when we decide — probably at about the same time as we finally come up with a name for the current decade — whether the Segway is at heart a form of aided walking, like a wheelchair, or of regulatable transportation, like a bicycle.

That determination will affect a host of other questions: Where will one park them? How fast should one go on a crowded sidewalk? Should one pass on the left or the right? As the machine has no horn, how will one warn pedestrians of a wish to overtake? Walkers don't respond quickly to an "Excuse me" — they don't expect trouble from the rear — but "Segwaying on your left" is cumbersome and inscrutable, and "Make way, lowly biped!" is probably not quite the thing. One wants to convey apology together with lordly resolve, a tricky combination. Perhaps the French have a phrase that would suit.

From: Tad Friend
Subject: Segways: Toys or Useful Tools?
Thursday, May 22, 2003, at 11:02 A.M. PT

Great buckets of café au lait could not get me started this morning. It was cold and rainy for the third straight day, and I was hung over. I had no wish to venture out and buttonhole Frenchmen about their views. My body shrank from responsibility. I was like a spacecraft that fails to achieve the proper angle of reentry and bounces off Earth's atmosphere into deep space.

Amanda and I went to dinner last night at one of the ten three-star restaurants in Paris. She wore a beautiful black frock and I a jacket and tie, and we Segwayed stylishly up to the doorstep of Pierre Gagnaire and hovered, waiting. The maitre d' appeared and thrust his hands out in horror, giving us the full Heisman. After some alarmed back and forth — yes, we had a reservation; no, we need not bring the vehicles to our table — he found room for the Segways by the fire exit, and we sat down for a five-course, five-hour meal with our voluble friend Jeffrey Steingarten, the food writer for *Vogue*.

Meals with Jeffrey are always fascinating — we learned all about the role of the Jews under the Ottoman Empire, as well as the history and manifold virtues of spelt and neffles, two foods I had never heard of until they surfaced on Pierre Gagnaire's menu — but can also remind one, by the shank of the evening, of being stuck with Jack Nicholson in *The Shining*'s Overlook Lodge. Acres of food, a crazy man with an ax, and no way out.

When we finally left at one-thirty in the morning, we discovered that Segwaying is even more fun when you're a little drunk. (The author is strongly opposed to people operating machinery in the dark while drunk. I mean it. All Microsoft's many lawyers mean it. Now, back to the story.) Like dancing and sex and most excitements, Segwaying comes more easily if you don't think about it too much. I have no idea where in one's brain the "Segway handling" protocol gets lodged, but it must be near the driving and skiing regions, as it borrows from each. Sometimes you borrow from the wrong one, and instead of squatting into a snowplow-style skiing stop, you press on the Segway's foot brake. There is no foot brake.

The Segway is not always perfectly intuitive: you can't step off the machine and walk away or it will take off and then topple; the kickstand breaks easily; it's a pain to line up the holes in the wheel well so you can thread a bike lock through them; the battery recharging light is impossible to see unless you kneel and crane your head sideways; and, as there are no shock absorbers, your calf muscles quiver after an hour's ride. On the whole, however, it is a wonderful machine.

But the jugular question is whether it is a toy or a useful tool. After riding a Segway for a few weeks in his sidewalk-free subdivision, the *Wall Street Journal*'s Walter S. Mossberg concluded, "It's not easy to use in the suburbs." Nor is it always easy to use in Paris. Cobblestones and narrow sidewalks make for a jerky ride, and if you come to a curb higher than four inches, you have to step off, put the machine into "power assist" mode, wheel it over the curb, and get back on. I had never before realized how many five-inch curbs there are in Paris.

Ideally, from Segway's point of view, cities would be reconceived to suit the new technology, as cities were remapped to make way for freeways and underground parking garages. Sylvain Pernin, the gallant, optimistic Segway project director at the Keolis Group, acknowledges that there are difficulties at the moment. "But when we have ten thousand Segways here, it may be different," Pernin says hopefully. "This machine is so beautiful, I think that the government will have to widen the sidewalks."

In the city's Marais or Latin Quarter, there is no room to widen the sidewalks without paving over the roads. Segways may be better suited to Paris or London than to, say, Los Angeles, but even Paris is currently configured — often badly — for cars. Which gives me an idea. What about building a Segway car, one that would run on batteries and accelerate as you leaned forward in the driver's seat? I have a feeling the Segway car would be anathema to Dean Kamen, the Segway's inventor — gravel-voiced, brilliant, with an eraser nub of black hair, in interviews he often seems dismayed by the world as it is — but, you know, Dean, the thing about roads is, we already have them.

The other big thing a Segway car could do is protect its driver from the elements. The current Segway is no fun when it rains. So, this morning, when we finally stirred ourselves and went to the Pompidou Center to see some modern art — which mixes so beautifully with hangovers — we took a taxi.

The Pompidou turned out to be closed because of the ongoing general strike. We walked, in the drizzle, to the Musée Picasso. It, too, was closed. We angled sleepily down Rue Vieille du Temple to the Seine, looking in at the shops, most of which were also closed. We walked across a bridge to the Île Saint-Louis and then to the Île de la Cité and came upon the rear of Notre-Dame. Every tourist in Paris, driven by the twin horsemen of storm and strike, had gathered beneath its dirty gray buttresses hoping to get in.

We turned away and sought a taxi. On a corner a few blocks up, we found three cab drivers, all wearing black sweaters and smoking. Two were in side-by-side white Renaults, and the third had his foot up on the first car's bumper. The driver of the car in the middle of the road reluctantly agreed to take the fare. He had been lying fully reclined in the driver's seat, and when he raised himself, he had bushy gray hair and circumflex eyebrows and the toothy grin of a mad professor. He would be the ideal driver of my Segway car, I was thinking as he eased in the clutch, still talking to the others through the open passenger-side window. "*Oui, oui!*" he said, laughing. "*Absolument oui!*" Picking up speed, he shot them a kiss.

From: Tad Friend
Subject: *Liberté, Égalité, Fraternité* — and Segway
Friday, May 23, 2003, at 9:12 A.M. PT

Paris is a walker's city, built for sauntering, window-shopping, the sideways topple into the café chair. On our last day here, we finally realized that the best way to get around on Segways is to use the bike lane rather than the sidewalk. The ride is fast and uncluttered, and you aren't constantly giving pedestrians heart attacks. Technically, Segwaying in the street is illegal, but the policemen who stared us down at intersections and in front of President Chirac's house all seemed to be following the same penal-code decision tree ("Not a bicycle, yet has two wheels and moves in a leisurely manner: ALLOW TO PROCEED").

Our belated epiphany came courtesy of David Mebane, the owner of Mike's Bike Tours, which conducts bicycle tours of the city. (Yes, he knows it should be called David's Bike Tours; long story.) David, an easygoing twenty-seven-year-old Texan, led us around Paris for four hours on his Schwinn as we followed on our Segways, *Make Way for Ducklings*-style. Every once in a while he would stop, lean over the handlebars, and explain something: "Marie Antoinette's head was lopped off in the *place* there, totally decapitated by the guillotine"; "If you go over to the third window to the right of that arch of the Louvre, you can look in and see the Venus de Milo for free"; "Down there in the Hôtel des Invalides, my favorite building in Paris, so beautiful when it's all lit up at night, the French Resistance built a false ceiling in the dome — just below that second level of windows. They hid U.S. airmen who'd been shot down, bomber crews and so on, between the two ceilings."

He had the patient manner of someone who must explain to American visitors, several times a day, why the ATMs here don't dispense dollars. While an implacable enemy of French bureaucracy, he loves the French and their history. At Place Clemenceau, he wheeled up beside a dark green statue of Charles de Gaulle and said, "Little World War Two story. Obviously, de Gaulle was leading the Gaullist resistance, but there was also a Communist resistance, and when the Allies took Paris back, there was a void of power — who's going to take over? August 1944, de Gaulle flies in from London to take command but gets extremely low on fuel, it's a near thing, is he going to make it?" I guessed that he would. "He lands with nothing in the tank," David continued, "then walks down the Champs Élysées in a big parade with all the soldiers and citizens, from the Arc de Triomphe to Notre-Dame, with German snipers on rooftops taking potshots at him, whatever, craziness, but nobody hits him and he takes the keys to the city. There's just this tremendous celebration of liberation."

Amanda looked up at de Gaulle in his uniform and kepi. "He looks like he belongs in *Singin' in the Rain*," she said. The figure did look rather as if it were beginning to pirouette and break into song.

"Or like the Morton Salt girl," David said.

It was a sunny day at last, and all Paris seemed to be out and in a cheerful mood. It might well have just been coincidence, but cultural understanding of the Segway seemed to have seeped into the collective consciousness. On our first day here no one knew what the machine was, but today four different people seemed to know all about the Segway and its gyroscopes and began explaining it to other bystanders as we talked nearby.

As we slalomed around I. M. Pei's glass pyramid in the Louvre's courtyard, a photographer who shoots Polaroid photos of tourists there at six euros a snap began asking rapid-fire questions. A short, intense man in a red windbreaker, he was curious about the Segway's range. When I said that it was seventeen to twenty-five kilometers, he frowned and seemed to take against the whole idea. "But that's nothing," he said. "Paris is very large — what can you do with twenty kilometers? You can't get to the office and back!"

David took up the cudgels. After riding the Segway in the courtyard, he had decided that he wanted one for leading his tours. "You can always recharge. It takes no time." (Well, five or six hours.)

"Four hours of use before you need to recharge, it's nothing," the photographer said. "My cell phone has a five-hour charge! And whose boss will let them charge the machine at the office?"

"The Segway engineers are working on extending the battery life," David said, which is true, but he was winging it. "The newest technology, magnesium —" He looked at me.

"Cadmium," I said, not entirely sure if that was what you use for batteries or enemas.

"Cadmium," David repeated confidently. "All the problems will be solved. Now, if this machine were a little cheaper and had a larger range, would you be interested?"

The photographer lowered his sunglasses and looked at it again, up and down, then broke into a charming smile. "It is very interesting," he said. "Very."

After we wound through the crooked streets of the Marais and had some superb sandwiches at Lina's, just off the Rue de Rivoli, I noticed that my battery indicator was getting low. Halfway up the Champs Élysées, it indicated that I had no reserve at all, and as we were entering the home stretch on Rue de Bassano, the user interface screen began flashing red: nothing in the tank! My Segway was slowing, creeping, humming just a little. Would I make it?

I guessed that I would. And indeed I coasted up to the front door of the hotel with nothing in the tank. There was no tremendous celebration of liberation, just a chance to get off and recharge and think happy thoughts about the imminent possibility of dinner. The French helped liberate us in 1776, we returned the favor later, and now both countries are free to be provoked and intrigued by each other and to disparage each other's wine.

Amanda had been following right behind me, to give me a push if necessary. "*Liberté, Égalité, Fraternité* — and Segway," she said.

ADAM GOPNIK

The People on the Bus

FROM *The New Yorker*

LATELY, I like to ride the bus. I don't mean the double-decker tourist buses that, half empty, warily circle the city, like dazed displaced troop carriers, or the long-distance buses that come sighing into the Port Authority Terminal, where it is eternally three A.M. and everyone looks exhausted before the journey starts, or even the yellow-and-blacks that still delicately deliver children from downtown to uptown at eight in the morning. I mean the ordinary city buses, those vaguely purposeless-looking, bulbous-faced, blue-and-bone M2s and 3s and 4s and 5s that chug up and down the avenues and along the cross streets, wheezing and whining, all day and night.

For twenty-odd years in New York, I never rode the bus at all — not, at least, after a single, traumatic bus experience. On the very first day I visited Manhattan, in the anxious (though, looking back, mostly unfrightened) summer of 1978 — the summer when Jimmy Carter turned down the air conditioning all over town — I got on a bus outside the Metropolitan Museum, saw that the fare was fifty cents, and, with the unquenchable cheerfulness of the visiting Canadian, proudly pulled out a dollar bill — an American dollar bill — folded it up neatly, stuffed the dollar in the fare box, two fares, and looked up, expecting the driver to beam at my efficiency. I will never forget his look of disbelief and disgust, mingled, I think, with a certain renewed awe at the enormities that out-of-towners were capable of.

From that day on, I don't think I ever rode another bus. I suppose I must have; transportational logic says that I must have —

there must be a crosstown M86 or an uptown limited in there somewhere — but, if I did, I don't know when. Even if I had been on a bus, I don't think I would recall it. Bus-blindness is a standard New York illness; of all the regularities of life here, the bus is the least celebrated, the least inclined to tug at the heart, or be made into a symbol of our condition. The taxi has its checkered lore, the subway its legend, the limo a certain Michael Douglas–in–*Wall Street* icon quality — but if there is a memorable bus scene in literature, or an unforgettable moment in a movie that takes place on a New York City bus, I have not found it. (If you Google New York buses in movie scenes, you end up with a bus enthusiasts' site and a shot of a New York City bus from a Sylvester Stallone movie called *Driven*, and this bus turns out to be dressed up like a Chicago city bus, and filmed on location in Toronto.) There is nothing about buses that makes them intrinsically symbol-repellent: the London bus has a poetry as rich as the Tube's — there is Mary Poppins, there is Mrs. Dalloway. In Paris, Pascal rides the bus, Zazie rides the metro, and that is, evenly, that. But as a symbolic repository the New York City bus does not exist. The only significant symbolic figure that the New York bus has had is Ralph Kramden, and what he symbolizes about the bus is that being stuck in one is in itself one more form of comic frustration and disappointment; the New York City bus might best be described by saying that it is exactly the kind of institution that would have Ralph Kramden as its significant symbolic figure.

If you had asked me why I avoided the bus, I suppose I would have said that the bus was for old people — or that taking the bus was one step short of not actually living in New York at all, and that if you stayed on the bus long enough it would take you right out of town. Riding the bus was one of those activities, like going to Radio City, that was in New York but not really of it. My mother-in-law rode the bus when she came to New York to visit, and that, I thought, said whom the bus was made for: elegant older women who didn't mind traveling forty-five minutes every morning to visit their grandchildren.

And then I didn't ride the bus because I loved the subway so. Compared with the vivid and evil and lurid subway, the bus seemed a drab bourgeois necessity — Shirley Booth to the subway's Tallulah Bankhead. When I began to ride the subway, particularly in the late seventies and early eighties, it was both grander and stranger than a newcomer can imagine now. The graffiti, for one thing, were both more sordid inside — all those "tags" — and more beautiful outside. When the wild-style cars came roaring into a station, they were as exciting and shimmering as Frank Stella birds. The air conditioning was a lot spottier, too, and sometimes the windows were open, driving the stale and fetid air around in an illusion of cooling. When the air conditioning worked, it was worse. You walked from steam bath to refrigerator, a change like a change of continents, and your perspiration seemed to freeze within your shirt, a phenomenon previously known only to Antarctic explorers.

Feral thugs and killer nerds rode the subway together, looking warily at one another. And yet there was something sublime about the subway. Although it was incidentally frightening, it was also systematically reassuring: it shouldn't have worked; it had stopped working; and yet it worked — vandalized, brutalized, a canvas and a pissoir, it reliably took you wherever you wanted to go. It was a rumbling, sleepless, snorting animal presence underfoot, more a god to be appeased and admired than a thing that had been mastered by its owners. If the stations seemed, as people said, Dantesque, that was not simply because the subway was below-ground, and a punishment, but also because it offered an architectural order that seemed to be free from any interfering human hand, running by itself in its own grim circles. It was religious in the narrow sense as well: terror and transportation were joined together, fear propelled you to a higher plane. (The taxis, an alternative if you had the money, were alarming then, too — a silent or determined driver in a T-shirt resting on a mat of beads and demanding, fifty blocks before your destination, which side of the street you wanted — without being at all sublime.)

Coming home in 2000 after five years abroad, I took it for granted that I would return to the subway and the taxi, only to be stunned by the transformation in them both. The subway, now graffiti free, with dully gleaming metal cars (though obviously made to be as resistant to vandalism as a prison), had recorded announcements, and for a while a picture of the station manager at every stop. It seemed obviously improved but somehow degraded, grimly utilitarian, intended to suggest the receding future vision of *RoboCop:* automatic voices encased in armor. The chaos was gone from inside the cabs, and held on only around them. After five years in Paris, where one phones for a cab or lines up in an orderly manner at a station, logically and fairly, I nearly wept tears of frustration at the anarchy of the street system — you waited for fifteen minutes and someone waltzed out into the middle of the block and stepped in front of you as a cab approached. (There is, of course, an implicit system of fair dealing in this — one block away is legitimate; the same corner is not — but I could no longer remember the rules, much less find the patience to practice them.)

And so the bus. Almost every day for the past year and a half, I've found myself taking a limited bus down an East Side avenue, and then, a few hours and frustrations later, taking it back uptown on the adjoining avenue. I stand or, in good hours, sit among the usual bus riders. The bus I find humane, in several ways. There is, first of all, the nonconfrontational and yet collaborative nature of the seating. You look over people's shoulders, closely, and yet only rarely look directly at them, face to face, as you must on the subway. There is a hierarchy of seating on the bus, far more articulate than that of the subway. There are seats you must give up to handicapped people, seats you ought to give up to handicapped people if you have any decency at all, and seats — the bumpy, exhaust-scented row in the very back — that you never have to give up to anyone, if you're willing to sit there. (The reason for all those designated spaces is that law and propriety dictate that when someone in a wheelchair rolls up to a bus stop, the bus has to stop and let him on.) There is also on almost every New York bus a little single seat tucked in near the back door, which has the air of a dunce chair in a classroom. You can sit there, but you wouldn't want to. Late at night, there is even a policy of optional stops. You ask the driver to stop the bus where you're going and, if he can, he will.

The bus also has order, order as we know it from the fading patriarchal family, visible order kept by an irritable chief. The driver has not only control over his world but the delight of the exercise of arbitrary authority, like that of a French bureaucrat. Bus riders learn that, if your MetroCard turns out to be short fifty cents, the driver will look at you with distaste, tell you to find change from fellow passengers (surprisingly, to a subway rider, people dig into their purses cheerfully), and, if this doesn't work, will wearily wave you on back. You are included, fool though you are, and this often at the moment when the driver is ignoring the pounded fists and half-audible pleas for admission of the last few people who, running for the bus, arrived a second too late. The driver's control of the back door is just as imperious. A red zone of acceptability exists around the bus stop, known only to the driver, who opens and closes the door as he senses the zone appearing and receding.

It is uniquely possible to overhear conversations on the bus. The other morning, for instance — a beautiful morning of our time, the sky blue, the alert orange, and the *Times* sports pages ominously upside down — a man behind me was trying to remember the names of popular Drake's snacks from his childhood.

"What are those things? There were Ring-Dings and Drake's cakes."

"You mean Twinkies," the man he was with said, with assurance. I couldn't see either face, but their voices had the peaceable quarrelsomeness of those who have just passed from middle-aged to elderly.

"No, I don't mean Twinkies," he said angrily. "I mean them other things."

Long pause. We couldn't resist. "Devil Dogs," someone said. "Devil Dogs."

"Yes, thanks, Devil Dogs. How come you don't ever see Devil Dogs these days?"

This is a typical bit of bus talk. (In a taxi you would stew on the issue all by yourself. The millionaire in his limo could ask the driver, I suppose, but he would be too embarrassed to answer. On the subway, no one would hear, in the first place; and if the words "Devil Dog" were said with enough emphasis to be heard, it would cause a panicked mass exodus.) On another morning, a man and a woman were riding together down Fifth Avenue and saw the new, comically twinned, comically misnamed AOL Time Warner Center — the Delusional States Building, as it will doubtless someday be known — come into view. (And those two towers rising, however plainly, have become a source of pride: *something's* rising.) "That Trump," the man said, chuckling. "He always does things in twos. Have you ever noticed how he always does things in twos?"

"I've noticed that. That's his thing, his signature, doing two of everything."

"Well, there he does it again. Two towers again."

Sage nods. The fact that, as it occurred to me later, the towers are not by Trump, and that, in any case, Trump, in his long career, has never done two of anything, should not diminish the glory of this exchange. If you were on the subway, there would be nothing to look at; if you were in a limo, you would actually be Trump, building things, gloriously, in nonexistent pairs.

When I first started riding the bus, I mentioned it to people sheepishly, almost apologetically, as one might mention having had a new dental plate put in, or the advantages of low-fat yogurt — as one might mention something that, though not downright shameful, might still seem mildly embarrassing. But, to my surprise, almost everyone I talked to (and women, I think, in particular) turned out to feel the same way I do about the bus. "The bus lets you feel that you're in control, or that someone's in control," one woman said to me, and another friend said flatly, "You can see what's coming." The bus feels safe. Of course, there is no reason for the bus to feel safe. (A friend from Jerusalem got on the bus with understandable watchfulness.) Yet we have decided to create in the city a kind of imaginary geography of fear and safety that will somehow make us safer from It — from the next attack, of course, from the Other Shoe, the Dreadful Thing that we all await.

I have thought about it a lot while I am riding the bus, and I have come to the conclusion that, while anxiety seeks out the company of excitement, fear seeks out the illusion of certainty. People tend to write these days about anxiety and fear as though they were equal, or anyway continuous, emotions, one blending into the other, but anyone who has felt them — and anyone who hasn't felt them, at least a little, hasn't been living in New York in the past year — knows that they are as distinct as a bus from a subway, as a Devil Dog from a Ring-Ding. Anxiety is the ordinary New York emotion. It is a form of energy, and clings, like ivy to a garden wall, to whatever is around to cling to, whether the object is nationalism or the Knicks or Lizzie Grubman, as readers of the *New York Post* recognize. At the height of the bubble, anxiety was all around us: the anxiety of keeping up, of not falling behind, of holding one's place.

Fear, well earned or not, is a different thing. People who live with the higher kinds of fear — the ill, soldiers — live with it mostly by

making structures of delusional domesticity. They try to create an
illusion of safety, and of home. At Waterloo, soldiers welcomed the
little signs of farm-keeping evident around them; in the dugouts of
the Somme, every rat-ridden alley had a designation and every rat
itself a pet name. The last time New Yorkers were genuinely afraid,
as opposed to merely anxious, during the great crime wave of the
sixties and mid-seventies, they responded in the same way: by con-
structing an elaborate, learn-it-by-heart geography of safe and un-
safe enclaves, a map of safe rooms. The knowledge that the map
could not truly protect you from what you feared then, any more
than riding the bus can save you from it now, did not alter the need
to have a map. People say that twentysomethings have sex out of
fear — it is called terror sex — but twentysomethings have sex out
of sex, and the adjective of the decade is always attached to it. In
the eighties, they had safe sex, and in the nineties boom sex, and
they will have sex-among-the-ruins, if it comes to that.

What we have out of fear is not sex, or any other anxiety-ener-
gized activity, but stillness. It's said that people in the city are nicer
now, or more cooperative, and I suppose this is true. But it is true
for reasons that are not themselves entirely nice. The motivation of
this niceness is less rectitude and reform than just plain old-fashioned fright. There are no atheists in foxholes, but there are no religious arguments in foxholes, either. The fear we feel isn't as immediate or as real as the fear soldiers feel. But our response is the
same. These structures of delusional domesticity are the mainstay
of the lives of many of us in New York now. The bus, a permanently
running dinner party among friends, a fiction of family for a dollar-
fifty, a Starbucks on wheels, is the rolling image of the thing we
dream of now as much as we wanted the Broadband Pipe to wash
away our sins three years ago, and that is the Safe Room. For the
first time, the bus has something to symbolize.

On the bus the other morning, the worst regularly scheduled thing
that can happen on the bus happened. A guy in a wheelchair held
things up for three minutes — no time at all, really, but an eternity
on television, or in the subway, or, usually, in the city. As bus riders
know, buses are equipped to stop and, by lowering a clever elevator
device, let a wheelchair-bound rider board the bus. This, though a
civic mitzvah, involves a sequence where the driver locks the front

door, works the elevator at the rear door, hoists up the wheelchair on the lift, and then folds up the designated seats to give the wheelchair man room (it is nearly always a man). There is something artisanal, handmade about it — the lock, the voyage, working the elevator — in which a municipal employee is reduced, or raised, to a valet.

"It's the lame and the halt on the bus," one woman said.

"What's the difference between the lame and the halt?"

"The lame are, like, lame, and the halt, halt."

"You mean the halt don't walk."

"I mean they halt. But they halt because they're lame."

It is the kind of conversation — discursive, word-sensitive — that is possible on the bus right now, and nowhere else. I keep meaning to look up the difference

MICHAEL GORRA

Innocents Abroad?

FROM *Travel + Leisure*

ONE DAY IN THE SUMMER of 2001 I found myself in the old ec-
clesiastical city of Würzburg, not far from Germany's geographical
center, walking up the great staircase of the Residenz, which was
begun in 1720 by Balthasar Neumann for the town's ruler, Prince-
Bishop Johann Philipp von Schönborn. Built of warm golden sandstone, with an interior of marble and gilt, it was an extravagant
place even by the standards of eighteenth-century absolutism. The
philosopher David Hume, on a visit in 1748, described it as "more
complete and finished" than Versailles — and that was before the
paint job. In 1752, Gianbattista Tiepolo was hired to work a fresco
over the entirety of the ceiling toward which I was now climbing,
and in the process transformed the already majestic flight of stairs
into one of the grandest spaces in Europe: the Continent's largest
fresco, all the guidebooks say, so large that it's impossible to see
the whole thing at once. There's always something behind you or
hidden by the turn of the stairs, and each step, each twist of the
head, reveals something new, as though the picture were moving
around you.
    Certainly the vault's subject enforces that sense of cinematic
motion, for Tiepolo's project was to paint an allegory of the four
continents. As I ascended the first steps, America began to rise before me, a vision dominated by an enormous alligator and a bare-
breasted, feather-headdressed maiden. There were palm trees and
bows and arrows, Indians and the banners of the conquistadores,
high mountains and a cannibal feast, all of it on a dim north wall
where the colors seemed misty and low. Then I reached the land-

ing and turned, and on the opposite wall saw bright Europe. Far fewer people here were naked. Instead, there were musicians and painters, crosses and crosiers, Europa with her flower-horned bull, a greyhound, some fragments of architecture, and, away in the corner, Tiepolo himself, looking rather tired.

In making the turn toward Europe, in walking up those stairs, I began, in that summer that now seems so distant, to spin a theory about the whole business of being an American. It was a theory forged during a time of peace and goodwill, when for a few brief moments we Americans seemed as welcome in Europe as at any time since World War II. And it comes back to me today when the newspapers and broadcasts on both sides of the Atlantic are so full of mutual accusations and suspicion. Now that many of us are experiencing a new and alienating wave of European distrust, when we may fear being reviled for our nationality on a continent whose culture we share, it seems necessary to think hard about just what our relation to Europe has been. What has it meant, as a destination rather than a place of origin? What has it said to us, as Americans?

In that June of brilliant, peaceful sunshine, surrounded by Tiepolo's splendid world, I could not help but see myself as having stepped for a moment into one of Henry James's stories about the American encounter with old Europe. "A Passionate Pilgrim," the title story of his first book, tells the tale of an American who believes he has an ancestral claim to an English manor. The piece is sentimental and far from James's best, but it does supply a necessary phrase, as does a letter he wrote not long after to Charles Eliot Norton: "It's a complex fate, being an American, and one of the responsibilities it entails is fighting against a superstitious valuation of Europe." In fact, the main character in "A Passionate Pilgrim" dies of that superstition, broken by his discovery that England cannot provide a home for him. I had some of that superstition, too, and like James I had a sense that as an American I was both a latecomer to and the inheritor of the world that lay painted on the wall above me. (Though for me that world had been in no way fatal, and the passion part had taken the substantive form of my own marriage to a Swiss art historian.)

Americans used to go to Europe — "old Europe" — in search of a larger life. We went because living abroad expanded our sense of what an American could be; offered, paradoxically, a different and richer and grander way of being an American than we could find at home. In James's day we came to grasp at an antique culture, to talk with a history that stretched back beyond our grandparents; in the 1920s, Ernest Hemingway and F. Scott and Zelda Fitzgerald joined Gertrude Stein in Paris, escaping the insular prohibitions of Main Street. Later, black writers and musicians (James Baldwin, Louis Armstrong, Miles Davis) traveled to Europe, because there they could be American in a way that they couldn't in America itself. But in a sense this was true for all Americans, James included: Europe allowed us to see ourselves in purely national terms, to shuck the more local affiliations of race or region or even family. And the fiction of expatriation, from *Portrait of a Lady* to the early work of Hemingway and on to James Baldwin's *Giovanni's Room* and even Patricia Highsmith's *Talented Mr. Ripley,* has used Europe as a kind of litmus paper against which to test an abstract American identity.

Or at least that's what such fiction used to do. A decade after "A Passionate Pilgrim," and back in Boston for the first time since he had made his own choice of London, James observed that the American writer "*must* deal, more or less, even if only by implication, with Europe; whereas no European is obliged to deal in the least with America." *Not true,* I couldn't help thinking, as I looked up at the camel caravans of Tiepolo's rather Arab-dominated Africa, *not now, not anymore.* We Americans were still nearly all of us superstitious about Europe, we bought its food and cars and cosmetics, its furniture and clothing; it still set the fashions, or some of them. But often it no longer seemed necessary, no longer something with which we were "obliged to deal," and our own country stood in its place, as even James had suspected it someday might. The complexities of our fate might still be worked out in relation to Europe, but not to it alone.

Standing beneath Tiepolo's Asia, with its ruins and elephants and cavalry, it struck me that the books that today use a foreign land to probe our peculiar fate tend to choose a different setting and to belong to a different genre. When he'd settled in Europe, James wrote home: "I take possession of the old world — I inhale it — I appropriate it." Even then, such words no longer seemed a figure of speech. Not America's aspirations but its power, not its innocence but its culpability: those are the terms that today would shape James's "international theme." And now that theme belongs not to the novel of manners but to the thriller, to fiction that in chronicling the American imperium finds its most congenial settings in such places as the Southeast Asia or Central America of Robert Stone's *Dog Soldiers* and *A Flag for Sunrise,* or in the unnamed Middle Eastern kingdom of Henry Bromell's recent *Little America.*

Perhaps Patricia Highsmith's Ripley books marked the moment of change. For Highsmith's Tom Ripley the New World is not fresh and promising; instead he finds in France and Italy a chance for the self-invention denied him at home — an ironic inversion of what America itself had offered to so many of the Continent's tired and hungry and poor. Yet Europe is also for him a place free of consequences, a playground where he can literally get away with murder, and in the post-Highsmith novel of expatriation Europe becomes an entirely conventional setting. The Americans in Paris whom one finds in such expertly made novels as Diane Johnson's *Le Divorce* and *Le Mariage* are awkward and ingenuous and perhaps even criminally naïve. The Europeans aren't and lean toward duplicity instead. The terms are all known and settled in advance, the rules firmly and predictably established. In a way, they're the fictional equivalent of the act my wife and I have developed over the years, a practiced routine in which *la différence* can be endlessly discussed and each other's cultural limitations deplored. But neither those books nor that routine itself offers much in the way of surprise. Europe might still provide a sense of individual liberation, I thought, but the cultural stakes in such an awakening were low, a matter of lifestyle.

Yet I felt uneasy with the thrust of that argument even as I carried it down the stairs and across the square in front of the Residenz. It seemed odd to think of Europe as irrelevant in Germany of all places, especially while walking across a square on which the brownshirts had mustered and books had been burned. Here, more than anywhere, was where our hunchbacked era had been determined and deformed. Europe wasn't irrelevant. But it was no longer the inescapable term of comparison.

Or was it? The months since I stood beneath Tiepolo's ceiling seemed at first to confirm Europe's diminished role in shaping our condition, and yet later to give it a renewed importance, the sense that it remains our necessary cultural counterweight. It hasn't always been comfortable to see the debate I had with myself in Würzburg become the material of op-eds and headlines, to find the terms of what had seemed a long-settled relation tossed and turned and argued over. The familiar faults that Diane Johnson describes no longer seem just a question of manners, are no longer the stuff of comedy. They have consequences once more, and have left each side with grave doubts about the other, with the fear that our interests — or maybe just our governments' interests — now diverge, in a way that they haven't for a half century and more. Yet those debates — those doubts — have also revealed the degree to which we remain each other's interlocutors, and in the end our disagreements recall nothing so much as the doubts of marriage itself; a bad patch in something that will nevertheless be patched up. My own marriage has made Europe into a place with which I am indeed obliged to deal and from which I continue to learn, even as our alliance ensures that my wife, too, will have to keep on coming to terms with America. And so it is for our two continents: linked as in any marriage by time, by what's been shared and squabbled over, by what amounts in the end to history. However disagreeably America and Europe may now strike each other, a divorce remains unthinkable.

TOM HAINES

Facing Famine

FROM *The Boston Globe*

Burtukan Abe braces against the hard mud wall as Osman, her two-year-old son, wails and wobbles on stick legs.

Are there others? I ask.

Yes, one, she says. A boy, one month old. He is inside.

There is no turning back. Through the low, narrow doorway, in the darkness that guards cool by day, heat by night, lies little Nurhusein.

May I see him?

This journey began weeks earlier, when yet another report described widespread drought and the threat of famine across much of Africa.

What can that life be like?

Travel often approaches boundaries of wealth and health. But what does it feel like to cross those boundaries and enter a place that is, everywhere, collapsing? What comes from knowing people who, with an empty grain basket or a thinning goat, edge closer to death?

The route led first to Addis Ababa, a highland capital, then east and south, down into rolling stretches of the Great Rift Valley. In the tattered town of Ogolcho, Berhanu Muse, a local irrigation specialist, agreed to serve as translator and guide.

A narrow road of rock headed south, through one village, then another, for one hour, then two.

In late afternoon, before evening wind lifted dirt from north to south, east to west, we stopped and parked near a hilltop. A man and woman collected grain from a tall stick bin on the corner of their rectangular plot of land.

Gebi Egato offered his hand from his perch inside the bin. Halima, his wife, smiled warmly, then carried a half-filled sack toward the family's low, round hut. Abdo, a three-year-old with determined eyes, barreled out the door.

I asked if we could stay.

"Welcome," Gebi said.

For four nights, a photographer and I would sleep here, beneath open sky, then wake to wander this village of one thousand people. We would step into a schoolhouse, a clinic, and other thatch-roofed huts, including the one that held Nurhusein.

But that first afternoon, the village came to us. They were mostly old, all men, a group of perhaps two dozen. Many held walking sticks, one a long spear. One man said he would like to show us something: a hole, not too far, that used to hold water. The hole was shallow and wide, perhaps the size of a Boston backyard. It was empty, nothing but hard earth.

The men calmly debated how many months it had been since water filled the hole. Flies buzzed and jumped from eyelids to lips.

A young schoolteacher, a specialist in math and science, sat at my side, his legs crossed, hands in his lap.

"Thirst is thirst, hunger is hunger," he said.

Hours later, I awoke to a setting moon and could imagine this land as it long had been: Beneath my cot, wheat, barley, and teff shot from the ground. Birds swarmed tree branches, trading throaty, bubbling calls. Water pooled in ditches and holes. Thick green hedges framed the farmyard.

Gebi would describe to me what this can feel like. The land offers so much bounty, so much comfort, he said, that even when the sun is high and hot, you want to lie down on the earth, close your eyes, and sleep.

In the hut's outer room there is a low wooden bench, but little else. The food, furniture, even a grandmother and three uncles have gone.

Now five people remain: Burtukan, the mother, age nineteen; Abdurkedir Beriso, her husband, twenty-seven; Abduraman Beriso, his brother, sixteen. And the children, Osman and Nurhusein.

They have no animals, no money. Neighbors share hard bread and flour.

"I have nowhere to go," Abdurkedir told me. "I will die here."

From behind a curtain, in the hut's back room, I hear the rustle of blankets, a whimper, a soothing voice: sounds of a mother gathering a baby in her arms.

On our first morning, as nighttime hilltop sounds — a howling hyena, a barking dog, a farting donkey — gave way to those of dawn, we were outsiders, in the cool air, listening.

Beneath Gebi and Halima's thatch roof, Abdo squealed and pouted. Bontu, barely a year old, cried for breakfast.

Soon, with the fire made, the children fed, Halima strapped plastic canisters on the back of the family donkey and began to walk. Gebi followed with the ox.

Halima sauntered gracefully, as though out for a stroll. She crossed a parched soccer field to a footpath lined with huts. She greeted a woman walking toward her. They held hands and talked.

Farther along, in an empty cradle of land set back from the trail, a stack of branches and twigs covered a hole roughly twelve inches in diameter. Three times, the government had tried to dig a well in this village, which sits far from any river. The last time, a powerful machine made the narrow hole and bore in search of water. Villagers gathered and watched as earth spit upward. Then the drill bit broke, 820 feet underground. It was there still.

Halima walked on for more than an hour, then stopped in a spot of shade. She untied the canisters and knelt by a wide pond of muddy water. The pond teemed with salmonella, the root of typhoid fever, and parasites that thrive in intestines, infecting 70 percent of Adere Lepho's children.

Another young woman leaned at the pond's edge and filled every last ounce of space in her canister. She stuffed the spout with a plug of withered grass.

Hundreds of people came each day to this pond, the only water source for Adere Lepho and two neighboring villages, and carted home water to quench the thirst of thousands.

A month earlier, this pond, too, had been nearly empty. Then two days of heavy February rain filled it. How long would it last? Even village elders, men and women forty, forty-five, and fifty years old, had never seen this kind of drought.

Two years earlier, and two years before that, meager rains had fallen. Families had to sell animals, eat thinner harvests, and spend precious savings just to survive. But this was worse: the February downpour was the first time it had rained in nearly a year.

Late the next afternoon, rain fell. As the drops landed thick and heavy, men, women, and children took shelter in the low, open building that houses the village's grain mill. After three, maybe four minutes, the rain stopped.

Women heaved sacks of grain, some of them holding well-rationed harvests from years past, others gifts from farmland half a world away, onto a scale. Across the room, the mill owner sat alongside a conveyor belt spun by a howling generator, the only power in the village. The owner opened sacks into the mouth of a grinder that turned kernel to flour. Dust filled the air, sticking to hair and eyelashes.

Outside, dozens of men gathered beneath the branches of a wide tree.

Gebi Tola, elected leader of a local farmers' group, explained that the government had offered land for ten volunteers to move to another region. The government owns all land in Ethiopia. This resettlement program provided a rare chance.

The men, sitting on the ground in orderly rows, faced Tola. He explained that some plots of land were north, in a neighboring district. Most would be farther, three hundred miles to the west.

Voices rose. How can we know this land is good? one man asked. How can we trust that life will be better there?

Kedir Husein, a young father who had stood to ask many questions, stepped away from the group. He told me he had decided not to volunteer to leave.

"I am afraid," he said.

Nurhusein emerges, his head resting in the crook of his mother's left elbow.

A soft cotton blanket opens to shocks of slick, curly hair. Tiny fingers spread in the air. I touch Nurhusein's forehead, cool and smooth.

"He is beautiful," I say.

Nurhusein bleats softly. His lips often latch on to a dry breast. He has a small stomachache, Burtukan tells me.

The bleating rises then falls, just beyond the blanket's edge.

Nurhusein is already too wise. It is as if he knows.

*

Morning inside Gebi Egato's hut. Glowing coals. Boisterous children. Hearty porridge. A calf, head low, softly chewed its cud.

Shilla, the oldest at five, licked her fingers and pondered her favorite foods as Abdo crammed both hands full of porridge.

"Milk," she said. She raised her head and smiled. "And sugar."

Finished, Shilla and Abdo scrambled to waiting friends. Gebi and Halima took turns digging a wooden scoop deep into a jug decorated with shells.

Each bite brought more peril.

Gebi's tired cow and thirsty goats were giving little milk. The porridge was made from wheat that had been meant as seed for planting if the spring rains came. Neighbors with less were already selling cows and goats, driving prices down.

As the coals darkened, I asked how long the family could last.

Gebi told me that in two weeks the family's wheat would be gone. He would then sell his goats, then the cow. Then the ox and, finally, the donkey. He paused.

"Five months," he said.

Gebi, like most villagers a Muslim, said he was confident rain would come. Then he could partner his ox with that of a neighbor and together they could churn the dark, moist earth.

"We have seen so much hardship already, God will not add more," Gebi said. "I hope."

After breakfast, Gebi took the donkey and walked beneath the high sun for three hours. He crested three low ridges and crossed three shallow valleys. The first was carpeted in six inches of dust. The second traced the steep gorge of a dry creek. The third, staggered with acacia trees, opened widely toward the village of Cheffe Jilla.

A group of men, women, children, and donkeys swayed in the village's main square. White sacks of grain sat in lopsided piles. Gebi joined the hopeful and registered his name in a government office.

I saw Gebi Tola, the leader of Adere Lepho's farmers' association, standing beneath a tree. He told me families from his village would take home five hundred sacks of grain. But they could use a thousand. How do you judge the needy when a whole village is staggering?

He spoke quickly. A crowd of dozens, young, old, pressed in around us.

I asked Gebi how he felt.

"I feel sorry," he said.

I had grown used to stoicism. But sorry? I stepped aside with Berhanu, our translator. "Sorry" does not feel like the right word, I said.

In English, I explained, "sorry" often has a light sense. Sorry I stepped on your toe. Sorry I'm late for dinner. It is not something felt by someone watching his friends and neighbors beginning to starve.

Berhanu is a compassionate, intimate man. He raised his hand to his chin.

He told me that, in that case, "sorry" was not the word he meant.

The crowd moved in again and curious eyes followed our exchange.

I asked Berhanu to choose another English word that more closely matched the Oromigna word Tola had used.

He could not find an exact translation. I asked him to describe the feeling.

"Well," Berhanu said, "it is the feeling you have when something bad happens. Say, for example, when you lose your lovely brother. Is there a word in English for that?"

Misery?

Yes, Berhanu said calmly, that is part of it.

Emptiness? Yes, he said, that too.

Anguish, despair?

His eyes sparked at the connection.

Anger? Yes.

Frustration? Yes.

Fear? No.

Fear, Berhanu said, like sorry, was too light a word.

Terror?

Yes, Berhanu said, "terror" is a good word.

I stand before Nurhusein and start to cry.

Is it empathy? I have a ten-month-old son, a spirited boy with muscles across his back and a quick laugh.

Or am I crying from fear?

In the hot sun, looking from hut to hut, from face to face, the problem was always too vast.

I stare at Nurhusein. I cannot look again into his mother's eyes.

PETER HESSLER

Chasing the Wall

FROM *National Geographic*

THERE IS ALWAYS at least one happy person at a Chinese funeral.
I learned this while driving across the north of China, where lessons were plentiful. I also learned to avoid driving at night, or in
the rain, or on the tiny red roads that squiggled like aimless capil-
laries across my map. I learned that most Chinese gas station attendants are young women, and they often give you a free pair of white
cotton driving gloves with a fill-up. I learned to be wary of black
Volkswagen Santanas, because in rural China they are frequently
occupied by low-level Communist Party officials, who are among
the most aggressive motorists anywhere in the country. There are
lots of black Volkswagen Santanas in the north of China.

I was heading west. I had a rented Jeep, a tent, and a sleeping
bag. I had my worries — I didn't know how the Chinese authorities
would react to a foreigner taking a solo road trip, and as a precau-
tion I planned to divide my journey into two parts, fall and spring.
From my home in Beijing, I drove to Hebei Province, where I began my journey at the edge of the Bo Hai sea. I intended to follow
rural roads along the path of what has come to be known as the
Great Wall.

The Great Wall has become a symbol for China, and yet it has
been consistently misunderstood over the past century. In the popular consciousness, the Great Wall is a unified concept, but in fact
northern China is crisscrossed by many different walls built by
many different dynasties. It wasn't until modern times, through a
combination of foreign misconception and Chinese patriotism,
that the ancient walls were symbolically linked by the use of a singular term. Many of the Great Wall's supposed characteristics — that

it is continuous, that the entire structure is over two thousand years old, that it can be seen from the moon — are false.

I was chasing a myth, and on the road I hoped to meet people who could help me untangle the truth. Scholars or specialists didn't particularly interest me — instead I hoped to meet average Chinese who, living near the ancient fortifications, would have their own view of the past and the present.

I began in autumn, when the Hebei harvest had been deliberately left out in the road, waiting to be threshed by passing cars. Millet, sorghum, wheat — the chaff cracked beneath my tires. The ancient walls hovered like stone mirages atop the hills. I could gauge my distance by a glance at the glove compartment. Steadily it filled with white cotton gloves as the Jeep cruised west.

I stopped for funerals all the way across Shanxi Province. The first was in the small town of Xinrong, where the main street had been blocked off by a crowd of five hundred. They had gathered to watch a traveling folk opera troupe perform in memory of a departed businessman named He Yu. He had owned the biggest shop in Xinrong — the Prosperous Fountainhead Store — and the opera troupe had been hired to perform directly across from the shop entrance. Even in death, He was doing good business — it was a seven-day funeral, and mourners wandered into the store and browsed whenever the actors took a break. The troupe's stage was a converted Beijing 130 truck, its railings removed and replaced by loudspeakers. Wei Fu, the head of the troupe, grinned beneath his greasepaint and told me that 80 percent of his business comes from funerals. "Of course I'm sorry for the family," he said, "but this is my living."

Zhang Baolong wore that same grin the following day. I was driving south and west from Xinrong, and the landscape had become barren — low, dry hills punctuated by the occasional signal tower that had been part of the Ming dynasty (1368–1644) defense system. I pulled off the road to look at one of the ancient towers, and then I heard the wails of the funeral nearby. When I approached, a pudgy man handed me his business card. It announced in Chinese: "Zhang Baolong / Feng Shui Master / Red and White Events: Services for the Entire Length of the Dragon, From the Beginning to the End."

Twenty-seven separate services were listed on the back of the card. Some were easily defined as red, or joyful ("selecting marriage partner"), and others were clearly white ("choosing grave sites"), but occasionally the colors blurred. Zhang also handled "unusual diseases," "house construction," "evaluating locations for mining," and "towing trucks." "I'm very busy," said Zhang. He had been hired to choose today's burial site.

The family members took turns prostrating themselves before the tomb. Nobody seemed to mind that I was watching. First the men kowtowed, burning paper money and moaning softly. In a whisper I asked Zhang if the ancient signal tower had any influence on the tomb's feng shui, or geomancy — the relationship with the surrounding landscape, a traditional Chinese concept that determines fortune. In the past the Communists had banned feng shui as old-fashioned superstition. But over the past twenty years, as the economy has opened up, the old belief has been revitalized — and repackaged to fit business cards.

"The position of that tower is very important," Zhang said. "You see, this place is good because it's high, and there's water in that stream to the east. And you have the signal tower above, which serves to protect the tomb." Then he slipped into official feng shui jargon, jotting the words into my notebook: "A person buried in this location will have many wealthy descendants, who will rise to high civil, military, and scholarly positions."

Now the women kowtowed, their wails echoing across the valley.

"My father and grandfather were both feng shui masters," Zhang said. "We've always done this in my family. And everybody in my family lives for a long time. My father lived to be ninety-five, and my mother was eighty-eight when she died. My grandfather lived to be ninety-nine!"

The keening rose another pitch. I wondered if this conversation might be more appropriate at another time, but Zhang kept talking. As far as he was concerned, he had already guided this particular dragon to its end.

"I have three sons and three daughters," he said. "My sons are feng shui masters! And one of my daughters" — he beamed at the thought of security, in this world and the next — "is a nurse!"

The funerals gave way to ancient forts as I continued toward the autonomous region of Inner Mongolia. Today Inner Mongolia lies within China's territory, but in ancient times this was a border region whose rule was often uncertain. As a result the northern

Shanxi landscape is studded with ruined defensive works that are made of tamped earth — hard-packed yellow soil that has faded in the sun. I passed signal towers and walls that stretched for dozens of miles and villages that were entirely contained by high-walled forts. Many of the town names included the characters for "fort," "barracks," and "checkpoint." Once these had been garrisons for Chinese soldiers; now they were sleepy villages. The peasants here grew potatoes. They worked steadily under a sunny sky, and the forts seemed out of place, like an ancient fear turned to dirt and left to crumble.

The majority of these defenses dated to the Ming dynasty — the builder of the greatest walls in Chinese history. Most of what we now think of as the Great Wall was built during the Ming, which was the only dynasty to construct long sections in brick and stone. Here in Shanxi, where they had defended against the Mongols, some of the Ming fortifications had been fourfold — quadruple lines of parallel walls.

But long before the Ming and the Mongols there had been other fortifications, other threats. Traditionally, the Chinese classics had taught that eventually all peoples will succumb to the appeal of culture and become civilized. But theory and practice parted company along the northern frontier, where early states often defended against the Hu. The Hu's origin is mysterious; they are thought to have included horse-riding nomadic peoples from Central Asia who were linked by a key characteristic: they showed no interest in assimilating Chinese culture. The name first appeared during the Warring States period (403–221 B.C.), when the nomads initially came south and wall building accelerated, as it did again during the Qin dynasty (221–207 B.C.), the first to unite the empire. The Hu were viciously effective warriors, and their appearance in this part of the world was as sudden and anomalous as these ancient forts seem to a modern motorist who happens to be driving north.

I stopped in Ninglu, the last village in Shanxi before the Inner Mongolian border. The population was 120, and the settlement was surrounded by an ancient garrison wall nearly a mile in circumference. Old people sat in the village square, soaking up the sun.

In Chinese villages I often asked if there was anybody who understood local history, and sometimes the people pointed me to a local sage or an amateur historian. Sources of Chinese history can be humble; official archaeologists and historians are so overworked and underfunded that they often don't have much time for a place like Ninglu. Whenever I spoke to scholars, they emphasized the same thing: don't underestimate the value of local memory.

The old people in the square answered my question immediately. "Talk to Old Chen," they said.

His name was Chen Zhen, and he was fifty-three years old. He was a potato farmer — he worked less than two acres of dusty farmland — and he owned five sheep. His annual income was around two hundred dollars. He wore heavy black-rimmed glasses, and his silver hair was cropped close to his head. He took me to his home, where he opened a drawer and pulled out a sheaf of rice paper that had been stapled together. On the front cover he had written: "The Annals of Ninglu / Research Established January 22, 1992."

I opened the book and read Chen's careful script: "The town wall was built in the twenty-second year of the Jiajing emperor (in 1543), and encased in kiln-fired brick in the first year of the Wanli emperor (in 1573)."

There were dozens of pages, hundreds of dates. There were sketches and maps. I leafed through the book, wishing there was a photocopy machine within three hours' drive. "I researched the county archives," Old Chen explained, "and then I talked to old people in town who remembered things. Some of them have died since I started. I just finished last year."

He showed me some pottery fragments that he had found near a Han dynasty wall. Three different dynasties had left fortifications in this region, and Old Chen offered to take me out to the ruins. We drove north into the mountains, where he led me into a high valley of scrub grass and dusty gullies. Old Chen had the slow, deliberate walk of the Chinese peasant: hands clasped behind his back, head bowed thoughtfully.

He pointed out the Northern Wei dynasty (A.D. 386–534) wall, a faint two-foot-high ridge running northeast. The Han dynasty (206 B.C.–A.D. 220) wall was so small that I wouldn't have noticed it without his help. Running parallel to it was the Ming wall, six feet high and marching eastward across the hills. It was intersected by the road, where a stone tablet, stuck into the heart of the wall, proclaimed Inner Mongolia. The Ming wall still serves a political purpose, marking the border between Shanxi and Inner Mongolia. It also represents an economic divide — because parts of Shanxi have lower land-use fees, peasants in this area told me they prefer to farm the southern side of the wall.

Back at his home, Old Chen pulled out a map and said that the village was originally called Ningxi Hulu. The name translates as: Pacify the Hu.

"Basically it means kill the foreigners," he said with a smile. "Look at this —" He pointed to another village on the map, ten miles to the east: Weilu. Overawe the Hu. Fifteen miles to the west: Pohubu. Destroy the Hu. Another twenty miles beyond that: Shahukou. Slaughter the Hu. Today these villages use the character for "hu" that means "tiger" — a change made during the Qing dynasty, whose Manchu rulers came from northern tribes and were sensitive to the portrayal of people from beyond the border walls.

Old Chen shook my hand when I left. "Next time you come," he said, "try to bring an archaeologist."

I drove into Inner Mongolia. These were high, empty steppes, and at twilight I pulled off the road to camp. The night was cold and clear, with massive stars overhead, and the Big Dipper hung heavy in the western sky. I fell asleep thinking about the border towns whose names bristled along these mountains: Pacify the Hu, Destroy the Hu, Slaughter the Hu. At midnight the tent was suddenly bathed in light and I sat bolt upright, thinking that it was the headlights of a truck. Then I realized that the moon had just broken the horizon. I sat still for a moment, listening to the wind and the pounding of my heart.

My trip had not been officially approved, and occasionally I passed through areas that were not open to foreigners. I tried to move quickly when I was in sensitive regions, and I often camped or stayed at truck stops, to avoid registering at a hotel. For this fall trip, I hoped to make it to Shanxi Province, and then in the spring I would continue to the far western end of the border walls.

People in these areas rarely saw foreigners, and sometimes they asked if I was Mongolian, Tibetan, or Uygur — a Hu, more or less. I often picked up hitchhikers; usually they were going back and forth between rural hometowns and new urban settlements. China's migrant population is estimated to be 150 million, mostly peasants who are searching for work in the cities. Many of my riders were small-town sophisticates — former peasant women who had made the leap to the city and now worked as waitresses or beauty parlor attendants. Their hair was dyed unsubtle shades of red and they entered the car in a cloud of cheap perfume. They sat stiffly, their backs hardly touching the seat, as if riding in a car was a formal experience. Typically they waited ten minutes before asking, politely, "You're not Chinese, are you?"

One morning in rural Inner Mongolia I picked up a young woman and her grandfather. They were both migrants — they shared an apartment in Jingbian, a small city eighty miles away. She was named Wang Yan; the given name means "swallow." She had elegant, small-boned features and almond-shaped eyes the color of coal. A tiny beauty mark had been tattooed on her forehead. She wore a red silk dress. Her appearance in this barren landscape surprised me as much as if a bird had come and settled in my Jeep.

Her grandfather was slightly deaf. He carried two enormous bags of salt, harvested from the family farm in Inner Mongolia. It occurred to me that the family had probably sent him to live with the young woman so she wouldn't get in trouble in the city.

The moment he entered the car, the old man asked, "Do you know Han Heliu?"

I shook my head, confused by the question.

"He's from our village!" the old man shouted. "He's gone to Beijing to work! I was wondering if you've met him yet!"

I told him I'd keep an eye out. Swallow smiled and shook her head.

The old man shouted questions at me while I drove. He asked what Beijing was like, and whether I was Chinese. He asked how much I planned to charge them for the ride. Swallow stared straight ahead and hardly spoke. But one of the few things she said was, "All of the young people leave our village. I'm not going back."

My fall journey ended in the Loess Plateau of central northwest China. The plateau covers 300,000 square miles, and in appearance it is one of the least hospitable landscapes in China — dry yellow mountains, craggy gullies. Centuries ago these hills were forested, but generations of farmers and years of drought have left the land as bare as a beach. Because the region represents the last northern stretch of arable soil in a crowded country, it's still heavily farmed; since 1949 the population of the Loess Plateau has more than doubled. Farmers rely on extensive terracing to coax crops from the earth, which is rock-hard when dry but falls apart when wet. Rainfall is rare — around ten inches annually — but even this small amount of water is enough to tear through the fragile land, taking the topsoil with it. Over time, tiny creeks create immense canyons. People live in caves that pockmark the crumbling hill-sides.

I always noticed the propaganda more in these empty landscapes. Whenever natural features like trees and ground cover disappear in China, words take their place, often carved straight into the earth. Sometimes their prescriptions were obviously impossible; I drove past brown barren hillsides that had been tattooed with fifty-foot-high words: "Make the Green Mountain Even Greener." But there was something mesmerizing about driving past a mountain that said "Marry Late and Have Children Late."

In Shanxi Province's Youyu County, I passed a section of the bor-der wall where four massive towers had been converted into propa-ganda. Each structure had been whitewashed with a single forty-foot-high character. Together they read: "Protect Water Solidify Earth."

I realized that the words and the walls were a perfect match. Chi-nese walls also have a tendency to fill empty landscapes, and, like the slogans, the defense structures' inspiration had usually been more philosophical than practical. Over the course of Chinese his-tory there was often an inverse relationship between pragmatism and wall building. The Tang dynasty (A.D. 618–907), one of the most powerful in Chinese history, never built long walls. The Tang ruling family had some Turkic blood, and they were skilled at inter-acting with Central Asian tribes through a combination of war and diplomacy. But centuries later the Ming refused to adopt either of the two time-trusted methods of dealing with nomads: the Ming were too weak to drive out their neighbors, and too proud to offer trade or subsidies to people they considered barbarians. Instead of choosing one approach, the court bickered for decades, finally building walls out of a failure to commit to either war or peace. The Jiajing emperor, frustrated by Mongol raids during his rule from

1522 to 1567, decreed that the character for barbarian, *yi*, should be written as small as possible on official documents. The Ming fortifications were born of the same impulse: more a message than a tactic. They scrolled across the northern emptiness, telling a long tale of human stubbornness and indecision.

The four towers — Protect Water Solidify Earth — led up to an ancient garrison fort. The tamped-earth structure stood at the summit of a massive mountain, overlooking a half-dozen valleys where the loess soil had been carved into a riot of stunningly intricate patterns. Terraced fields descended hillsides like curling staircases. In some places there were galaxies of tiny squares, each of them two feet across and a few inches deep, designed to contain and protect thousands of saplings that had yet to be planted. The fort's wall had been whitewashed with another message: "Use the World Bank's Opportunity Wisely / Help the Mountainous Area Escape from Poverty."

I drove to the Youyu County water bureau, where an official accompanied me on a tour of the area. Along with other parts of the Loess Plateau, this region was home to one of the World Bank's most widely praised Chinese projects. The official told me how the development organization's loans were being used to encourage the planting of trees, solidify terraces, and prevent erosion. He introduced me to Han Jixiang, the Communist Party secretary of Xiaojiang, a village of four hundred. "In the past, whenever it rained, everything washed away," Han told me. "The roads just disappeared. It's so much better now." His comments echoed what I had heard in the past from other visitors to the Loess Plateau — in this difficult landscape, the World Bank has had success battling poverty and deforestation.

I drove away, dazzled by the reformed loess landscape. Signs of work were everywhere along the road, and I stopped again to look at the fort's propaganda. That dazzled me as well — this structure, once built to keep foreigners out, was now touting the benefits of international aid.

Near the tower that said "Water," I passed a work crew of ten peasants. They were using shovels to carve squares into the hillside — tiny dirt forts for future saplings. I asked the peasants what they thought about the project.

"They've been doing this kind of thing since I was young," a twenty-eight-year-old man said. "In the past it wasn't the World Bank, but there have been other campaigns. You see all of these holes? They're empty. For two or three generations people have been digging holes and you still don't see any trees here. Why not? Because our labor is free, but they'd have to pay for the trees. The local officials embezzle the money instead."

The other peasants told me that in recent years the population of their home village, Dingjiayao, had dropped from two hundred to eighty. They said that much of their topsoil had been removed and carted to roadside plantings, which were important for inspections. These saplingless squares served the same purpose — despite the World Bank's success elsewhere in the north, this particular village was creating a Potemkin hillside.

"We see the World Bank officials in their cars when they have inspections, but we can't talk to them," the young peasant said. "The county leaders don't let us. Actually, I don't even know what 'World Bank' means. All I know is that it has something to do with investment. They just tell us slogans: Protect the Land, Turn the Land into Forest."

He asked me not to use his name, but he wanted the name of his village published — like many people in rural China, he still had faith that higher levels of the government would rectify local wrongs. While we were talking, a tiny tractor puttered up the hill. The driver handed each of the workers five packages of instant noodles — their pay for the day's digging. The peasants ate the noodles dry, because the only water on this hillside was the word painted on the ancient tower. I noticed that the packages said "Islamic Beef Noodles."

"Are you Islamic?" I asked.

"No." The peasant grinned. "But these are the cheapest brand — no pork. A nickel each!"

In spring I set out to finish the journey. This time I hoped to reach Gansu Province, home to the westernmost ruins of Han and Ming dynasty forts. Again I started in Beijing, but this time I followed a northern route, intending to pass quickly through Inner Mongolia. On the map it looked simple — but I never imagined that it was possible for a traffic jam to materialize on the barren steppes of Inner Mongolia.

A sudden storm had blown south from Siberia, and the temperature plummeted. Fuel lines froze solid — enormous blue Liberation trucks stopped dead in their tracks on Highway 110. Most of the other vehicles on the two-lane road were black Volkswagen Santanas. They had been better designed for the cold, but black Volkswagen Santanas have a psychological weakness: impatience. They wouldn't wait for the truckers to maneuver their vehicles off the road; each Santana kept nudging ahead as far as possible, pinning the car in front, getting pinned in turn from behind, until at last the highway was gridlocked for a mile. Meanwhile the truckers clambered down beneath their rigs, where they ignited flares and held them hopefully against the frozen fuel lines. Nearby, a highway safety sign proclaimed, "This Road Has Had 65 Crashes and 31 Fatalities."

I arrived just as the tableau was complete: the snow-swept steppe, the frozen vehicles, the flares glowing in the distance like joss sticks. Or fuses.

The scene wavered between the dangerous and the surreal — a common condition for Chinese motorists. Once, near a Ming wall outside Beijing, I met an eighty-two-year-old woman with bound feet who had never made the two-hour trip to the capital. "I get car sick," she said when I asked why she had never traveled, and over time I came to appreciate her simple wisdom. During my journeys, the vehicle got stuck repeatedly in snow, sand, and mud. Car sick. Locals yanked me out and gave directions. Roads were mixed — occasionally there was a perfect stretch of new asphalt, but often it lasted for only a few miles before fading into potholes. Everything seemed to be half built. Maps were unreliable. A couple of times I drove on roads that deteriorated into dried creekbeds. Another time I passed an automobile, smashed almost beyond recognition, that was suspended on stilts fifteen feet above the road. It promoted highway safety; on the door somebody had painted: "Four People Died Inside." Car sick. Outside Baotou, a city in Inner Mongolia, I paused to marvel at the wreckage of an enormous truck that had somehow wedged itself sideways into a tollbooth, like a Chinese puzzle: a carved pagoda within a jade egg.

The crumbling walls were never far away, a companion piece to the halfway stage of China's rush to progress. In Ningxia Autonomous Region I passed through Xingwuying, a desert village whose residents received good cell phone coverage only if they climbed the local Ming dynasty fort. They stood atop the faded ramparts, dialing furiously, gazing into the distance as if searching for invaders. In these regions the motorcyclists fixed compact discs to their mud flaps as makeshift reflectors. High-tech intersected with the ancient, as if modernity had arrived with the suddenness of an invasion — what does it mean when smoke signals are replaced by cell phones, but you still have to climb the wall to use them? In Xingwuying, the ancient wall was now an accessory: attached to cell phones, it fortified reception.

The country swept past. There was movement everywhere, but the symphony of migration also had antiphonal strains of settling down. The descendants of the Hu were coming to rest. In Uxin Qi, a small Inner Mongolian town just outside the Ming border wall, the ethnic Mongols had shifted to a settled life of farming and herding. Government programs had planted willow trees across the Mu Us Desert; the leaves could be harvested in autumn and fed to the sheep. Locals called it "the pasture in the sky." I visited Mongols who had grown up in felt tents; now they had brick homes, televisions, and video compact disc players. They told me life was better than ever before. On their mantels the peasants erected small shrines to both Mao Zedong and Genghis Khan.

But when I stopped at the Genghis Khan Mausoleum, seventy miles away near Ejin Horo Qi, a young tourist pulled me aside and said that there are still more Mongols in China than in independent Mongolia. "We're a fallen race," she said. "We don't have a united country, and yet at one time we were the greatest race in the world. Have you noticed that Mongols drink a lot?"

Certainly I had noticed that her breath sang of grain alcohol. And I had noticed that virtually everybody else at the Genghis Khan Mausoleum seemed to be drinking as well. Guides, tourists, ticket takers — all of them staggered under a bright blue sky. Some of the more sober mausoleum employees told me bluntly that Genghis Khan's remains weren't really here. Most historians say he was buried. The Chinese claim that his tomb is in Xinjiang; Mongolians claim that it's north of Ulan Bator. The controversy has raged for years, and yet the only tangible monument is the mausoleum outside Ejin Horo Qi — nothing more than a symbol and a tourist destination. The young woman asked me where I was from, and then she smiled wistfully. "The Great America," she said. "It's like Genghis Khan used to be."

After Inner Mongolia I crossed the Tengger Desert — an emptiness of graceful dunes and golden sand. I followed the Yellow River westward into Gansu Province and then turned north. In ancient times, Gansu had been the western hinterland, and the old fortifications were heavy here. Miles of earth wall ran alongside Highway 312.

At Jiayuguan I met Yang Yongfu, who was rebuilding part of a Ming dynasty wall. It wasn't the first time I'd seen old-style walls under construction — along the North Korean border in Liaoning Province, I once visited a site where the local government was erecting a massive 1.3 mile long stretch of brick and stone.

There is something appropriate about the fact that even today the Chinese are still building — and finding — the Great Wall. Its significance has never stopped developing — in a sense, it has come a long way since the Ming dynasty collapsed in 1644. The next dynasty, the Qing, viewed the walls as a reflection of the Ming's failure to defend borders through diplomacy and military power, and the fortifications were left to deteriorate.

But starting in the 1600s, Europeans who visited China began to return home with exaggerated reports about the walls. Many falsely believed that all sections dated to a single period, giving rise to a popular misconception that the entire structure was built during the Qin dynasty. Travelers saw the impressive Ming fortifications near Beijing and assumed that they continued in brick and stone all the way across China, when in fact most of the structures had been built of tamped earth. In the first decade of the twentieth century, Western writers declared, with absolutely no evidence, that the Great Wall could be seen from the moon. The length was often exaggerated. While experts say that the Ming fortifications are roughly 1,700 miles long, there is no accurate figure for the length of China's border walls, because so many parts haven't been surveyed.

Even the term "Great Wall" — used to describe a structure with almost mythic characteristics — was originally a foreign phrase. The old Chinese wording *changcheng* was understood simply to mean a "long wall," and the great Ming walls were called *bianqiang* — border walls. But by the early twentieth century some Chinese started using the phrase *Wanli Changcheng* (literally, "ten thousand *li* long wall") to render the Western concept of a Great Wall of China.

Leading Chinese scholars criticized this trend as historically inaccurate. "Chinese geographers lamented the loss of the original concept," said Arthur Waldron, a historian at the University of Pennsylvania. "They used it as an example of how terminology can become profoundly misleading and misunderstood."

But Chinese nationalists realized the symbolic value of a unified Great Wall. Both Sun Yat-sen and Mao Zedong used the Wall to represent the nation, and in 1984 Deng Xiaoping commanded that patriotic Chinese should restore the structure. His proclamation became a well-known slogan: "Let us love our China, let us restore our Great Wall." Over the past century, even as the walls have grown in symbolic significance, they have steadily deteriorated, victims of new roads and buildings. Last year a foreign organization applied its own phrase to the structure: the World Monuments Fund, based in New York, added the Great Wall to its list of "most endangered sites." William Lindesay, a British preservationist who lives in Beijing, has campaigned to save what he calls the "wild wall" — untouched fortifications in rugged natural settings.

Tourist development represents another risk. At Jiayuguan, Yang Yongfu told me that he had put his own spin on Deng's phrase. "I like to say, 'Love my China, *I'll* rebuild the Great Wall,' " Yang said. "In the past the government restored and protected it. But now I'm the one investing here."

Yang claims to be the first Chinese businessman to gain permission to rebuild a section of the border walls for his own profit. He is forty years old, a former peasant who in the late 1980s oversaw the government-funded reconstruction of another local wall section. Yang applied that experience, and an investment of more than $120,000, to his current stretch of wall, which runs through the desert near the Black Mountains. The surrounding hillsides are riddled with cement-lined bunkers built in the 1960s to defend against possible attack by the Soviet Union. Today the bunkers are abandoned and open to tourists.

When I visited, Yang's workers had already built more than a quarter mile of tamped-earth walls, burying the original low structure. Tourist admission to the wall would cost seventy-five cents.

Down the road, the government-run section was charging a dollar. Yang said that it wouldn't be hard to turn a profit. After everything I'd seen the ancient walls used for — feng shui, propaganda, cell phone coverage — Yang's defense of pragmatism made perfect sense. Nearly four hundred years after the fall of the Ming, the Great Wall had finally become useful.

"It's not enough to simply protect something," Yang told me. "You have to actually use it. If it's not valued, then sooner or later it will get destroyed."

The final line of Han dynasty forts is in the desert west of Jiayuguan. I was on my way there, passing through the small town of Subei, when I finally got caught. I had pulled over to use a public toilet. A policeman approached and flashed his badge, telling me that Subei was closed to foreigners, which I hadn't realized. It looked the same as every other place I had passed through that week — snow-topped mountains, open grasslands. I had driven exactly 4,956 miles.

Subei was in an ethnic Mongolian county, and two Mongol officers escorted me to the police station. I assumed the Jeep would be seized; there would be a massive fine; expulsion was inevitable. The region must have been closed because of military installations, ethnic tensions, or poverty — things the Chinese don't want outsiders to see.

Waiting for the interrogation, I wondered if the police might respect the fact that a foreigner had driven alone along the border walls. But I doubted that they would understand my journey. The fortifications had been built to keep people like me out, but now it was clear that the walls' most powerful characteristic wasn't exclusion but rather a sense of narrative. The Great Wall told a natural story, crossing both the landscape and the history of China, and that intersection of time and place touched at the roots of a civilization. And I had come within a few miles of finishing the story.

The interrogation began. Where was my passport and driver's license? What was my Beijing address? How long had I lived in China? What was my work unit?

They jotted my responses onto official forms. They worked quickly, leafing through dozens of pages, and suddenly I realized that there wasn't any real investigation. There were no phone calls to Beijing, no contact with the foreign ministry. They didn't really care who I was, or why I was in Subei, or where I planned to go next. My threat was purely abstract — the troubling part about foreigners was the idea, not the reality. It was something to be handled with paperwork.

They prepared a confession that said I had violated the national laws regarding closed districts. I signed it three times, accompanying each signature with a fingerprint in red ink. Then they announced the fine: twelve dollars.

I wasn't allowed to pay directly — nobody wanted to be accused of corruption — so they escorted me down the street to the local post office, where I mailed a money order. The officers smiled, shook my hand, and left me standing next to my Jeep. As far as they were concerned, the foreigner was already gone.

I kept driving on Highway 215, heading toward the mountains of Qinghai Province. The final Han dynasty fort slipped past; the Great Wall was behind me now. A sign proclaimed: "Due to Speeding, 53 People Have Died on This Turn." The highway rose to over twelve thousand feet, and I crossed into the vastness of Qinghai. There were no towns, no gas stations, no cars. The land was so empty that nobody had bothered to carve propaganda into the mountains. It looked like the end of the world.

After twenty-five miles I saw a pair of dirt roads branching off the main highway, marked by a sign. From the words on it, I guessed that the two destinations were government-run — military installations, perhaps. A left turn led to a place called "Build." A right turn went to "Unite." I took a deep breath and drove straight through.

MARK JENKINS

The Ghost Road

FROM *Outside*

DUCK OFF THE ROAD, RUN.
Down dark passageways, right at one corner, left at the next, no
idea where I'm going. On a main street in the town of Namsai, I
spot three armed Arunachal Pradesh border policemen up ahead.
It is the spring of 1996, and I'm traveling in this northeastern Indian state illegally. I slide into the flow of tasseled trishaws, pedestrians, clicking bicycles.

A vintage white Ambassador — that lumpish fifties-era sedan still
found throughout India's hinterland — creeps along within the
bright human throng. Behind it a young tribal girl carries two
buckets of water on a bamboo pole. I step up alongside her. She
smiles, then covers her face. I snap off my baseball cap and place it
on her head. She laughs and unwinds an orange cotton wrap from
around her shoulders and hands it to me. I knew she would do this;
it's not possible to give a gift in this part of the world without receiving one in return. I dive both hands into one of her buckets, slick
back my shaggy hair, and whip the fabric into a turban around my
head. Then I step to the rear passenger door of the Ambassador
and jump in the back seat.

I find myself sitting beside a large Buddhist lama in maroon
robes. I adjust my disguise and scan the crowd outside.

"You are being chased," says the lama.

"I am."

The lama speaks to the chauffeur. The chauffeur taps his horn,
maneuvers around a brahma bull seated in the road, speeds up.
In the outskirts of Ledo, we roll onto a long grassy driveway, pass a

freshly gilded stupa, and stop in front of a group of wooden buildings. The lama lifts his frock above polished black shoes and steps out.

"My name is Aggadhamma," he says in British-accented English. "This is the Namsai Buddhist Vihara, a monastery for boys. You are safe here."

That evening I have dinner with the lama and a dozen shaved-headed acolytes. We are seated on the floor around circular tables. The walls are Easter-egg blue. A tin plate heaped with rice, dal, vegetables, and burning-hot, fuscous curry is set before me. I eat with my right hand.

After the meal, the boys slug back a last tin of water and scatter into the warm, lampless dark.

"Now," says Aggadhamma, "please tell me, what brought you to this distant corner of our earth?"

I don't have any reason not to be truthful. "I want to travel the old Stilwell Road and cross into Burma."

I outline my obsession. Six decades ago, during World War II, American soldiers under the command of General Joseph "Vinegar Joe" Stilwell carved a 1,100-mile road, starting in Ledo, in the Indian state of Assam, through a wilderness of dripping mountains and leech-infested jungles in northern Burma, and across the border into southwestern China.

No one even knows if this old military road still exists. Perhaps it has vanished entirely, consumed by the jungle like a snake eaten by a tiger. It's a mystery I've been hoping to solve.

"This is your plan, despite the fact that Arunachal Pradesh is in the midst of civil unrest — car bombings, assassinations, and the like — and therefore closed to foreigners," responds Aggadhamma. "I take it you are here without government permission."

I admit that I do not have a Restricted Area Permit.

"It's not as serious as it sounds," I add. "Mostly just a game of cat and mouse with the border police."

Aggadhamma eyes me. "You can get away with this in India," he says. "India is the greatest democracy in the world. The government here is like an old elephant: vast, but slow and avoidable. Clever people can keep from being stepped on."

I don't tell him that I have already been arrested, and escaped, a half-dozen times, but he already seems to know.

"You are clever, then," he continues, "and yet you wish to sneak into Burma and play this same game?"

I just nod.

For the next three days I hide out in the Namsai Vihara. I help spade black soil in the vegetable garden and teach the eager pupils American slang in their English classes.

My last night in the monastery, Aggadhamma tells me he has someone for me to meet. After supper, he introduces me to a nine-year-old boy named Myin. The boy is as beautiful as a girl, with brilliant eyes and a perpetual grin. He is also an amputee, his left leg vanished at the hip.

"Myin is from Burma," says Aggadhamma, and tells the boy's story as Myin stares at me with a guileless smile.

Myin is a Jinghpaw, or Kachin. The Kachins are an ethnic group whose homeland includes most of northern Burma; they are one of seven major ethnic minorities — along with the Karen, Karenni, Mon, Chin, Shan, and Arakanese — that make up about 30 percent of the country's population (68 percent of the 50 million citizens are Burmese), each with its own state. All told, there are some 140 ethnic groups and 100 dialects in Burma.

Two years earlier, soldiers under the military regime burned Myin's village to the ground and took all the boys. They were tracking pro-democracy Kachin guerrillas through the jungle. The soldiers knew the trails were booby-trapped, and they used Myin as a human minesweeper, forcing him to walk alone in front of the soldiers. He was seven years old and couldn't have weighed forty pounds when his leg was blown off.

"We have several boys from Burma here," says Aggadhamma. "Each has been maimed in one way or other. This is what Burma does to humans."

After dark I leave Namsai Buddhist Vihara. Aggadhamma shakes my hand with both of his hands, holding on tightly even after I release my grip.

During the late eighties and early nineties, I went to the Himalayas on a mountaineering expedition every two years. When I was stormbound at high altitude, the best escape was always a good book, so I blame historian Barbara W. Tuchman for my original fascination with the Stilwell Road. Deep inside my sleeping bag at twenty-three thousand feet, with waves of graupel slamming the tent, I read her 1971 Pulitzer Prize–winning book, *Stilwell and the American Experience in China, 1911–45*, and was transported to another world and another time.

By the time the United States entered the Second World War, imperial Japan had been penetrating ever deeper into China for more than a decade, gaining control of nearly one-third of that weakened giant. In the first five months of 1942, Japanese forces rapidly subjugated much of Southeast Asia: the Philippines, Hong Kong, Singapore, Malaysia, Indonesia, and a large swath of Burma. If China fell, all of Asia was threatened, from the rice fields of India to the oil fields of Baghdad.

America had been attempting to bolster the Chinese Nationalist forces of Chiang Kai-shek by supplying his forces via the back door, through India. Pilots were flying ordnance and ammunition from India to China over "the Hump" — the dragon's tail of the Himalayas that hooks south into northern Burma. But China was still losing. General Stilwell, commanding general of the China-Burma-India theater, believed these supply flights weren't enough. A tough, wiry West Point graduate who had spent years on clandestine missions in China, Stilwell was a military traditionalist. He was convinced that in order to adequately supply the Chinese, an all-weather military road had to be created from India through the unknown mountains and swamps of northern Burma. This 478-mile road, dubbed the Ledo Road, would connect with the old Burma Road, a convoluted 717-mile track built by the Chinese that ran northeast from Lashio, Burma, to Kunming, China — creating a 1,100-mile supply route called the Stilwell Road. (Today it's popularly, if erroneously, known as the Burma Road.)

British prime minister Winston Churchill characterized Stilwell's endeavor as "an immense, laborious task, unlikely to be finished until the need for it has passed." Stilwell was undeterred.

Completing the road cost $150 million and required the labor of 28,000 American soldiers, almost all of them black, and 35,000 ethnic workers. It was a dangerous job; casualty rates were so high that it was dubbed "the Man-a-Mile Road." Japanese snipers, monsoon floods, malaria, and cholera took the lives of 1,100 American soldiers and untold numbers of Asian workers before the Stilwell Road was completed, in January 1945. Over the next seven months, 5,000 vehicles and 35,000 tons of supplies traveled it. Then the atomic bombs were dropped on Hiroshima and Nagasaki, and the Japanese surrendered.

In October 1945, the United States abandoned the road. Churchill had been right.

Over the following decades, the old Burma Road across southwestern China remained in use, but the stretch of Stilwell's highway that crossed the remote fastness of northern Burma reverted to a blank on the map, an enigma that became my obsession.

Detouring on the way home from various mountaineering trips, I managed to travel the entire Chinese section of the road by the early 1990s. I would sit on the roofs of listing, overloaded trucks grinding up and down hundreds of switchbacks across the gorge-scarred Yunnan Province. It was my own private adventure. I didn't talk about it, didn't write about it.

But minor triumphs gradually set the foundation for great expectations. Over the years, my desire to get into Burma and traverse whatever was left of the Stilwell Road began to displace my passion for mountain climbing. Mountains were simple, predictable beasts, compared with nations. I knew the unknowns — the brutal cold, the avalanches. I knew how to suffer, how to summit, and how to fail. What I didn't know was Burma, a different kind of impossible challenge.

In late 1993, during an expedition into eastern Tibet, I tried to enter Burma from the north with a partner. We were caught by the Chinese border patrol, interrogated, and jailed for a couple of nights. We signed a confession and were released.

In the spring of 1996, I traveled to the Indian state of Assam to write a magazine article about wildlife poaching, then veered off to Ledo to try my luck again. Two weeks after leaving the Namsai monastery and traveling most of the twenty-mile stretch of the Stilwell Road through Arunachal Pradesh to the India-Burma border, I was nabbed. I was detained for three days in Tezu and politely interrogated (tea and scones were served) by Indian army officers, all of whom assumed I was a CIA agent. On the fourth day I was placed in a jeep with two armed guards, driven to the banks of the enormous, mud-brown Brahmaputra, put on a leaky tug dragging a mile-long raft of timber, and deported downstream to Assam.

Still, I felt that I'd successfully completed my apprenticeship in duplicity. I knew how to operate alone, how to lie, how to stay calm while looking down the barrel of a gun. I had completed the Chinese and Indian sections of the Stilwell Road. All that remained was the 458-mile ghost road in Burma.

Back home, I wrote to the Myanmar embassy in Washington. (Since 1989, Myanmar has been the military government's name for the country.) In 1996, with great fanfare, Myanmar launched a campaign to promote tourism, and visitors could obtain a visa to travel in the southern part of the country, but northern Burma, including the region the Stilwell Road passed through, was off-limits to foreigners.

After pestering the embassy and its representatives for several months, I managed to get an appointment with U Tin Winn, Myanmar's ambassador to the United States. I did my political homework before our meeting.

General Aung San, leader of Burma's Anti-Fascist People's Freedom League, demanded independence from Britain in 1947. While writing the constitution, Aung San, along with six of his ministers, was assassinated, igniting a series of bloody coups and bringing Prime Minister U Nu into power when independence was granted, in 1948. In 1962, General Ne Win overthrew the civilian government and abolished the constitution. A gallows hood was dropped over the face of the nation. Through coercion, repression, state-sponsored murder, and Stalin-style domestic terror, Ne Win maintained control for nearly thirty years.

By 1988, conditions were so unbearable that pro-democracy demonstrations erupted throughout the country, led by returning exile Aung San Suu Kyi, daughter of Aung San and head of the National League for Democracy (NLD). These demonstrations were brutally crushed by the dictatorship — between three and ten thousand peaceful protesters were killed — and the State Law and Order Restoration Council (SLORC), a cabal of Burmese generals, was created to run the country.

In 1989, SLORC declared martial law and placed Aung San Suu Kyi under house arrest. Diplomatic pressure and agitation by the NLD forced SLORC to hold general elections the next year. When the NLD won a landslide victory, the generals declared the results invalid and subsequently imprisoned hundreds of NLD members.

In 1991 Suu Kyi was awarded the Nobel Peace Prize — perhaps the main reason she is still alive. In short, Myanmar has the dark distinction of being one of the last totalitarian regimes on earth.

At my meeting with Ambassador Tin Winn, I outlined my plan for traveling the Stilwell Road across Burma, tracing the route on a World War II–era U.S. Army map. Ambassador Tin Winn was enthusiastic about my "daring historical journey" and introduced me to an embassy official named Thaung Tun, who was to arrange a special visa and assist me in navigating the Myanmar bureaucracy.

On the phone and in a series of letters, Thaung Tun was invariably gracious and upbeat. "Everything looks good — we're on course. Proper papers are assembling," he told me. "Things take time only." At first I believed him, but as the months passed, I came to recognize this behavior as classic puppeteering. After more than a year of strategic confoundment, Thaung Tun suggested I break the impasse by seeking permission in person. He knew whom I should talk to. I flew to the capital, Rangoon (renamed Yangon), in the fall of 1997.

For three days I sat in a hot, dank hallway waiting to meet Thaung Tun's government colleague. Making you wait is how bureaucrats exercise dominance. I took to bringing bread crumbs for the rats that scurried along the walls. When I finally met the man, a pinched homunculus with nervous eyes and no eyebrows, he pushed me right out of his office.

"Stilwell Road gone!" he screamed. "Disappeared! No possible!"

This only served to incite me. Stilwell and his men had faced countless obstacles, too — torrential rains that raised rivers twenty feet, titanic mudslides, jungle diseases — and Stilwell had been repeatedly told that it was impossible to build a road across Burma. I began to envision defying the Myanmar junta as not merely just, but obligatory. I was still young enough to believe — bewilderedly, arrogantly, passionately — that through sheer force of will I could bend the world to my ambition.

In February 1998, I return to Assam and the town of Ledo, the beginning of the Stilwell Road. After several weeks of bureaucratic wrangling, I manage to sidestep obtaining a Restricted Area Permit and inveigle permission to travel the road up to the border of Burma. A platoon from the 28th Assam Rifles garrison, led by

Commander Y. S. Rama, is enjoined to escort me on foot from Nampong, the last Indian outpost, up to Pangsau Pass, on the border, and then directly back. It is illegal to cross the border in either direction.

The night before our hike, I pull out several bottles of whiskey and start pouring drinks. The soldiers regale me with tales of the horrors unfolding nearby in Burma. There is a command post somewhere past Pangsau Pass, and the soldiers there are almost starving. Many have malaria. Rice is in short supply, and they never have salt. Salt is worth anything to the Burmese soldiers. They sneak over the border with something they have taken from the Naga or Kachin tribes — a bearskin shield, a wooden mask — and trade it for salt. Pangsau Pass, they say, is a punishment posting for Burmese soldiers who have run afoul of the military leadership.

Commander Rama, in his blue uniform and white ascot, sits ramrod stiff after polishing off most of a bottle of whiskey by himself. "Across the border is the end of the world," he declares. "You can go backward in history, Mr. Mark. Americans want to believe that everything goes forward. But if you went forward on this road, you would go backward."

When I leave at five the next morning, the platoon is fast asleep, as if the warm night air were an anesthetic. I know I have a head start of only a few hours at most. The road hooks uphill, disappearing into the black Patkai Range, taking me with it.

My intention is to cross over into Burma, alone and illegally. I don't think I'm delusional; I have a plan. I also know that my plan might fail. The difficulty itself is no small part of the appeal. If success is a certainty, where is the challenge? I am still entranced by the road, but now the seeds of something darker have taken root inside me.

The Stilwell Road was built to stop the spread of totalitarianism. For two thousand years, from Caesar to Stilwell, building roads was how one nation conquered another. That ended with the rise of air power: planes in the sky, not trucks on a road, would thenceforth largely determine the course of warfare. Some generals could envision this not-so-brave new world, but Stilwell was not one of them. It was an airplane that dropped the atomic bomb and pushed us across a new Rubicon of technological morality.

The Stilwell Road is a paradigm for failure, another one of humankind's grandiose exercises in futility. As I know in my heart, this means that my own attempt at traveling the Stilwell Road is stained with the same futility. But of course this doesn't stop me. On the contrary, I charge forward, carrying through with my complicated, contradictory convictions. Is this not what all humans sometimes do? We deftly lay out snares and then proceed to walk right into them.

I leap the giant tropical trees that have fallen across the track and move between the moss-sheathed embankments. The road narrows to a tunnel. I step through spider webs larger than me, strands clinging to my face.

In two hours I reach Pangsau Pass, a road cut through mud walls. There is a rotting concrete sign atop the pass. I snap a photo and walk into Burma.

Just over the border the road begins to disappear. Light and sky are closed off by vines thick as hawsers, leaves large as umbrellas, bamboo stalks rooted as densely as prison bars. I begin to wonder if the trail might be booby-trapped.

A queer uneasiness comes over me: I'm being watched. It makes me want to stop, but I don't. I keep walking. When I finally look over my shoulder, two soldiers, as if on cue, part the jungle with the barrels of their rifles and step onto the road. Two more soldiers appear in front of me.

They are small men in dark green fatigues and Chinese-issue camouflage sneakers. They have canteens on their belts and AK-47s and bandoliers of rounds across their shoulders. One wears a large knife on his hip, another a black handgun in a polished black holster.

I wave to the two soldiers ahead of me and move toward them eagerly, as if I am a lost backpacker. Their jaws tighten. I hold out my hand, talking and smiling. The soldiers train their weapons on me, their faces flat and strained.

The soldiers behind me begin to shout. One soldier starts prodding my stomach with the barrel of his rifle, as if he's trying to herd me back where I came from, but I won't move. A soldier behind me grabs my pack and starts to pull me backward. I spin around and he lets go.

This is the moment — they know it and I know it. The soldier in charge, the one with the black handgun, steps forward and holds my eyes in a cold, searching stare. I stare back. I know what he's looking for: fear. Fear is what he most wants to see, what he is accustomed to seeing.

But I have a secret weapon: I'm white. My whiteness protects me. My whiteness is a force field around my body. I know it is unjust, immoral even, but my whiteness means he can't act unilaterally. White people can cause trouble. He knows this.

The soldier shouts in my face but drops his eyes. His men begin to march me down the road, deeper into Burma, barrels at my back. Eventually we arrive at a burned-out building in a clearing. Laborers in rags are squatting in the mud in front of the building. Using machetes, they're hacking long bamboo poles into three-foot spears and hardening the points over a campfire.

From the color of their sarongs and the way they wear their machetes in a shoulder scabbard, I know they are Naga tribesmen. The Nagas were headhunters until the early twentieth century (British colonial authorities outlawed the practice in the 1890s); although the Nagas have their own language, architecture, religion, and customs, the junta lumps them in with the Kachins.

As I come close, the squatting men do not look up. There are soldiers all around. The soldier with the handgun continues up steep stairs cut into the mud embankment, while the other three remain to guard me. I drop my pack and lean against the roofless building and watch the laborers. Their machetes make muted hacking sounds, the sounds you hear in a butcher shop. The men themselves are silent, as if their tongues have been cut out.

I realize that this is exactly what I was not supposed to see. This is why northern Burma is closed, why so many remote regions of Burma are closed. According to the Free Burma Coalition, an international alliance of activists dedicated to the democratization of Burma, most ethnic minorities across the nation have been viciously persecuted; more than 600,000 have been removed from their villages and forcibly relocated. By interviewing refugees, Amnesty International has documented forced-labor camps hidden throughout the country.

I wait for seven hours, tearing engorged brown leeches off my legs and watching the blood run down into my boots. Late in the afternoon, the soldier with the black sidearm comes down the embankment, grabs me by the hair, and jerks me to my feet. I knock his hand away. He wants to hit me so badly the muscles in his cheeks quiver.

I am pushed up the mud steps. Seated against the building, I could see only the laborers and the rolling jungle. When I reach the top of the mud steps, I truly confront the world I have entered. It is medieval, something from the Dark Ages.

Before me is a four-hundred-foot-high hill, stripped naked. Cut into the base of the slope, circling the mountain, is a trench, twenty feet wide and ten feet deep. Two-foot bamboo spears, sharpened pungee sticks, stab upward from the bottom of the trench. Just beyond the pungee pit is an eight-foot-high bamboo wall. The top and outer face of the wall are bristling with bamboo spikes.

Past this is a strip of barren dirt too smooth and manicured to be anything but a mine field. Beyond that is another lethal bamboo wall. There are five walls and four strips of mined no man's land ascending the hill in concentric circles. The only break in the stockade is a narrow passageway that zigzags up the middle.

I am dragged over the first pungee pit on a bamboo drawbridge and through the first wall via a small, heavy door with bamboo spikes. We enter a tunnel, the walls and stairs dug out of the wet mud, the ceiling roofed with logs. Passing through the tunnel, I try to imagine some purpose for this surreal jungle fortress. It lies on a forgotten, forbidden border and would be a ridiculous target for any combatant. It can only be protecting the Burmese soldiers from the local people they have enslaved.

After I pass through four doors, the mud steps rise back up to daylight. We are on top of the hill. I am taken to a table set in the red dirt beneath a canopy of leaves, behind which is seated a fat man with a pockmarked face. Underneath his sweat-stained fatigues, which have no insignia, I can see red pajamas. He is wearing green flip-flops.

There are four armed soldiers standing behind the man. He says something to them and my pack is torn from my back and a bamboo chair forced against the back of my knees. I sit down. One of the soldiers dumps the contents of my pack onto the dirt and starts rummaging through my stuff. I stare at the fat man, wondering who will interpret, when he speaks for himself.

"Passport. Give."

I take my passport out of my money belt and hand it to him.

His eyes don't leave my face. Without ever looking down, he flips through the pages, then throws the passport back, hitting me in the face.

"Visa. Show visa."

I open the passport to the correct page and hand it back. He studies the stamp. I make every effort to appear bored. I have an official visa for Myanmar. It is a large stamp that fills one page of the passport. At the bottom of the page, in blue ink that matches the stamp, I've blotted out the words ALL LAND ENTRY PROHIBITED.

He shakes his head and shuts the passport.

"Not possible. No one come here. Border closed."

I expected this. I am already unfolding two other documents from my money belt. I hand them to him. One is a personal letter from Ambassador U Tin Winn, written and signed on embassy stationery, inviting me to Myanmar and urging all officials to help me travel along the Stilwell Road. The other is an official Myanmar Immigration Department Report of Arrival. My photo is affixed to this document, and it, too, has an official stamp from the Myanmar government. Along with my name, passport number, and visa number, there is a list spelling out my itinerary and the towns in Burma I have permission to travel through: Pangsau Pass, Shingbwiyang, Mogaung, Myitkyina, Bhamo.

These are all forgeries, but I have confidence in them. He has no way of checking their authenticity.

The documents make him angry. "Where you get?" he demands.

"From the embassy of Myanmar. I had lunch with Ambassador U Tin Winn. He invited me to your country." I surprise myself with the calmness of my voice. I tell him I have brought gifts. I gesture for one of the soldiers to bring over a sack from the pile of my belongings. Inside he finds a five-kilogram bag of salt, a package of twenty ballpoint pens, and three lined notebooks. Each notebook has a hundred-dollar bill paper-clipped to the cover.

He looks back down at the documents. All of his fingernails are short and dirty, except for the nail on his right pinkie, which is clean and long. I can only assume that he is the warlord of this lost jungle fiefdom — beyond civilization and beyond the fragile wing of morality — and that there is no law here, no God. He is God.

But I have these troublesome documents. I can see his mind working. Someone must know I am here. Why wasn't he informed? If these documents are real, he would've been notified of my arrival. I would've had a military escort.

He raises his small black eyes, stares at me, and says something in Burmese. Two soldiers leave. A few minutes later, a boy is dragged up to the commander. He is clearly a prisoner. Skeletal, wearing nothing but torn trousers, he has an angular head, protruding ribs, legs so thin his knees are larger than his thighs.

The commander barks at him and the boy cringes, then speaks to me.

"Why are you here?" His English is catechism-perfect.

"I told him already," I reply, feigning weariness. "I have been invited by the Myanmar government to travel the Stilwell Road."

The boy translates this.

The commander stands up and slowly walks toward me. He stops with his face in front of mine. Then he walks over and stands like a bear next to the emaciated boy and says something.

"He doesn't believe you," the boy tells me. "Why have you come here?"

When I give the same answer, the commander turns sideways and slams his heavy fist into the boy's rib cage. The boy screams and crumples to the ground.

The fat commander looks at me and laughs. The message seems to be: I may be someone it would not be prudent to harm. But this boy, this boy is perfectly expendable. This boy could easily disappear without a trace.

I am sickened by my naïveté. I've been willing to imperil my own life to travel this road, but not the life of someone else — that's why I chose to go alone. I should have known better. I've read shelves' worth of books about Burma.

When I refuse to answer any more questions, my audience with the warlord is abruptly terminated. I'm hustled back down through the mud tunnels and out of the compound. At dusk, my pack and my passport are returned to me, but my forged documents have disappeared. The film has been ripped from my camera, and all pages with writing have been torn from my journal.

I am marched back up to Pangsau Pass. Commander Rama and his platoon are waiting for me at the border. Rama stares at me with his old, oily eyes but doesn't say a word.

This should have been the end of it. But what began as a private passion I now twist into a professional goal. I secure a contract with a publisher to write a book about the Stilwell Road. This, I think, will legitimize my bewitchment. Although my editor believes I already have enough material for the book, I insist I have to complete the route.

I return to India in the fall of 1999, hell-bent on finding a way around the Pangsau Pass military compound. The Naga tribesmen I manage to speak to refuse to guide me. No amount of bribery will change their minds, and I can't do it without them. I briefly consider bushwhacking my way into the jungle in a parallel traverse of the Stilwell Road, or whatever is left of it.

Instead, I decide to attack the problem from a southern approach. I'll take a train from Rangoon to Mandalay, then another train up toward Myitkyina, a city of seventy-five thousand on the Stilwell Road. Recently opened to foreigners, Myitkyina is accessible only by plane or train, the region between it and Mandalay remaining closed. I intend to secretly hop off at the closed city of Mogaung, twenty-five miles southwest of Myitkyina, and light out from there, to the west and north, along the Stilwell Road.

I buy a black backpack and a dark green bivy tent and dark Gore-Tex raingear. I conceal a knife and cash in the sole of one of my boots and obtain declassified Russian and American maps.

This all somehow seems appropriate to me. I have only one crisis of confidence.

While studying the maps on the flight to Bangkok, trying to guess where the military checkpoints along the road will be, I suddenly experience a visceral foreshadowing of my own death. It isn't a vision, just a profound blackness, a terrifying emptiness. My body goes cold, and my mind feels as if all the synapses are short-circuiting and exploding. Then I begin sweating profusely, soaking my seat. It is such a powerful presentiment of my own death that I begin to cry.

For several hours I convince myself that I will get on the next plane home. Instead, I write farewell letters to my wife, Sue, my eight-year-old daughter, Addi, my six-year-old daughter, Teal, and my parents. I mail the letters from Bangkok, but they never arrive.

Heading north from Mandalay, I climb onto the roof of a passenger car to avoid the conductor. The train lumbers along, stopping at every rice-pig-child village, then chugging slowly back into the country. Water buffalo chest-deep in black mud. Women bent in half in green rice paddies. Deep teak forests. Bicyclists on dirt paths. Asian pastoral — just like the brochures.

Twenty-four hours later, as the train slows outside Mogaung, I hop off, run down a dirt road, and leap into the first trishaw I see. The driver pedals me through Mogaung, but there is a roadblock on the far side of town. He wants me to get out right there, in front of the soldiers. Wagging cash, I get him to pedal down a side street before I step out. Not five minutes later, the police pick me up off the street. They don't say a word. They are very young — adolescents with weapons, driving a souped-up Toyota Corolla. The driver flips on flashing lights, plugs in a bootleg tape of an Asian girl singing Cyndi Lauper songs, and flies north out of Mogaung.

We're on the Stilwell Road, heading toward Myitkyina. After half an hour, we pull into a compound across the street from the railroad tracks, on the edge of town. I peer out and shake my head in surprise and relief. They've taken me to the Myitkyina YMCA.

I register and am given a spare, clean room with a high ceiling. I shave, drop the key off with the clerk, and go back onto the street to explore. I like muddy cobblestone streets between squat, nondescript buildings. I try to speak with people here and there, but no one will say a word to me. They ignore me, their eyes darting left and right. I end up in an outdoor market where wide-faced women sit under umbrellas amid a cornucopia of brilliant, alien fruits and vegetables.

Back at the Y, the desk clerk asks me how I enjoyed the market.

The next morning I hire a trishaw driver to take me out to the Irrawaddy River. When I come back, the clerk asks me how I enjoyed the river.

In the afternoon, it rains and I go for a walk alone, zigzagging randomly and speedily to the outskirts of town. At a wet intersection, I find one of the trishaw drivers who usually hang out in front of the YMCA waiting for me. I yank a handful of grass from the side of the road before accepting his offer to give me a lift back to the Y.

Early the next morning, I repack my bag, folding tiny blades of grass into my clothes and equipment. I leave and walk the streets of the town, returning to my room at noon. I find my pack right where I left it, everything folded precisely the way it was, but there are blades of grass scattered on the floor.

That night, I slip through the window of my room and steal away, carefully climbing over a block wall with pieces of broken glass embedded along the top. I find an unlocked bicycle and take it, pedaling through the darkness to a corner where several old women, perhaps lost in opium dreams, sleep on the street. I lift a conical hat off the head of one of the women and slip a wad of bills into her shirt pocket. Now I'm disguised.

For the next five nights I leave my room and ride right past the roadblocks, with their sleepy sentries, and pedal out to the villages around Myitkyina. At dawn I return the bicycle and sneak back into my room at the Y.

In these neighboring villages, under cover of darkness, I finally find people who will talk to me. They are Kachins who are dying to speak to someone. A deluge of stories, always told behind closed doors, beside candles or oil lanterns that are frequently doused — and always in whispers. They are everywhere.

A shopkeeper who says that everyone is an informer here: "Trishaw drivers, businesspeople, teachers," he says. "Even good people are informers. This is the only way to protect their families: to give up someone else. It is poison."

This shopkeeper takes me to see a former government official who was tasked with beating tribals used for road gangs in the Karen state, in far eastern Burma.

"I was expected to hit them with a club," he says. "Not systematically, because then they could plan and train their minds to resist, but randomly. This works very well. It maintains the fear of the unknown. This is how to create terror in a human heart."

Sometimes I ask questions about the Stilwell Road, but they have stories of their own. What happened to me at Pangsau Pass is happening again: traveling the Stilwell Road is becoming irrelevant, almost insignificant — a profoundly selfish misadventure compared with chronicling these stories of suffering and struggle. On the third night, an interpreter is provided and people are brought to me at a secret location, an outbuilding on the edge of an old teacher's enormous vegetable garden.

A truck driver who uses the Stilwell Road delivering construction materials: "My wife washes clothes in the river for the bribe money," he says. "I must pay the soldiers every time I pass through a road-block; otherwise they will take a part from my truck."

Two ancient soldiers who tell me about fighting for the Americans during the construction of the Stilwell Road, traveling ahead of the bulldozers and clearing the forest of snipers: "We knew the jungle," one says. "We could kill the Japanese. The Americans were brave but did not know the jungle, so we helped them. Then they left us. Now we are in another war against our own government, but America has forgotten what we did for them."

The son of a father who was imprisoned for friendship: "The bravest of all, Aung San Suu Kyi, came here in 1988," he says. "My father knew her; they were schoolmates. Just friends. When she left, my father was taken away. He managed to get letters out to us. How they tortured him with electricity. How they used an iron bar rolled on his shins. How they used snakes with the women. Put snakes inside the women's bodies. He was released after five years, and then he died."

A middle-aged woman who tries to speak but can only cry and wring her hands.

I write pages of notes, hiding them in a jar in the grass behind the YMCA.

On the fourth night, the woman who wept brings her daughter. The mother sits quietly in the shadows while her daughter speaks. She tells me she is nineteen years old. She learned to speak English from Christian missionaries. She has dense black hair braided into a long ponytail.

"My mother came to tell you my story, but she could not do it," she says. "We have heard you are interested in the Stilwell Road." She tells me that, except in the far west, between Shingbwiyang and Pangsau Pass, the road still exists. She knows — she has been on it. Junta warlords have been logging in northern Burma and, in places, are rebuilding the road in order to transport the trees to China. Kachin households must provide one family member for the labor.

She was fourteen when she was taken away in a truck and put in a work camp with thirteen other girls. At night they were locked in a large bamboo cage in the compound. Nearly every night, she says, a different girl was dragged out and gang-raped by the soldiers. One of the girls in her crew bled to death. Another girl went mad. After a year, she was set free to find her way back home, walking barefoot back down the road.

She does not pause or weep as she tells me this, but her lower lip trembles.

"We have heard you want to travel the Stilwell Road. It could be done, but it would be very dangerous. I mean, not for you. For the people who would want to help you. But we would do it."

She tells me that since Myitkyina is now open to foreigners, tourists are coming. She believes someday there will be tourists on the Stilwell Road, and she wants them to know the truth. That it is not a road built by Americans. That was history. History is over. It's a road built by the Kachins.

"Do not believe it is a noble road. It is a road of blood. A road of death."

With both hands, she wipes away the tears now in her eyes, stands up, bows, and leaves with her mother.

My hands are trembling too much to write. I cannot listen to anyone else. I ride the bicycle around in the dark for the rest of the night, looking up at the cloudy Burma sky, asking myself, What am I doing here?

The next morning, the desk clerk asks me how my night was.

I look him in the eyes. He looks at me. He's on to me. I realize I've been endangering the people who shared their stories with me.

That night, to reduce suspicion, I decide to go drinking with the trishaw drivers. We end up in a bar, a dark, low-ceilinged place where women walk out on a little stage and sing pop songs under a ghoulish red light. When I'm ready to go back to the YMCA, my companions insist I have one more drink. A toast. It doesn't taste good. I drink some and spill the rest down my neck.

Something starts to happen with my eyes. Things begin to slide. My glass glides off the table and I reach out to catch it and knock it onto the floor. It shatters into little pieces that turn into cockroaches that scrabble away. I can't move my feet properly; they spill and flop like fish. Someone is slapping me, and I stand up swinging, screaming, spinning around.

I open my eyes. Nothing. Darkness everywhere. There's a bird over me in the dark, flapping.

I wake. My head is sideways. I try to focus. Lift my head. I'm naked, bloody, and filthy, covered with feces and dried urine. It's broad daylight. Two wide-eyed little boys are looking down at me. I sit up. I'm in the alley behind the YMCA.

I make it back to my room and fall asleep on the floor. The next time I wake up, I crawl into the shower, wash off the blood, and look at my bruises and cuts. Just beat up. Then I notice the words written in black ink on the palm of my right hand: LEAVE OR DIE.

Adventure is a path. Real adventure — self-determined, self-motivated, often risky — forces you to have firsthand encounters with the world. The world the way it is, not the way you imagine it. Your body will collide with the earth and you will bear witness. In this way you will be compelled to grapple with the limitless kindness and bottomless cruelty of humankind — and perhaps realize that you yourself are capable of both. This will change you. Nothing will ever again be black-and-white.

I spent a year of my life trying to complete the Stilwell Road, but I gave back the advance and didn't write the book. I wasn't ready. To this day, my arrogance, ignorance, and selfishness appall me. Adventure becomes hubris when ambition blinds you to the suffering of the human beings next to you. Only at the end of my odyssey did I fully accept that traveling the road didn't make a damn bit of difference. That wasn't the point. It wasn't about me. It was about Burma and the struggle of its people. And I plan to return the day the junta falls.

Since 1989, Aung San Suu Kyi has spent more than eight years under house arrest; according to Amnesty International, 1,850 peaceful demonstrators have been taken into custody, interrogated, and, in many cases, tortured as political prisoners.

In May 2002, after twenty months of house arrest, Suu Kyi was released by the junta. She immediately picked up where she'd left off, guiding the nonviolent democracy movement in Burma as much through her defiant, selfless bravery as through her words and speeches. "In physical stature she is petite and elegant, but in moral stature she is a giant," Archbishop Desmond Tutu said in 2001, on the tenth anniversary of Suu Kyi's Nobel Peace Prize. "Big men are scared of her. Armed to the teeth and they still run scared."

On May 30, 2003, while Suu Kyi was on a lecture tour with members of the National League for Democracy near Mandalay, her small convoy was ambushed by members of a pro-government militia. Four of her bodyguards and some seventy supporters were reportedly killed, and hundreds injured, including Suu Kyi herself, who suffered face and shoulder wounds. Suu Kyi was arrested and held incommunicado at an undisclosed location. In late July, Red Cross officials met with her but were not permitted to give any details of her detention.

"Courage means that if you have to suffer for something worth suffering for," Suu Kyi told reporters prior to her recapture, "then you must suffer."

RIAN MALAN

The Wrong Side of the Cape

FROM *Travel + Leisure*

IN THE FINAL ANALYSIS It was all the contessa's fault, she being my wife, a chic and glamorous Latina who grew up in Coral Gables, studied at Brandeis, left the United States in disgust during the Reagan era, and lived for many years in Paris only to wind up in Johannesburg, a vulgar city of new money, low culture, and rising crime. She learned Zulu and tolerated the city for a year or two but never quite saw the point of all the guns, guard dogs, and paranoia, the ugliness of the city in winter, the harshness of the light, the veldt burned gray by frost and cold, and the houses on our street grimly disfigured by steel burglar bars and electric fences. When our neighbor was carjacked in his own driveway, she put her foot down. "I hate it here," she said. "It's this country or me."

She wanted to get out of Africa, but for me, leaving was unthinkable; my interests and obsessions are entirely African, and my roots in this country are more than three centuries deep. I love Africa, even love Johannesburg, in spite of its problems. On the other hand, I love my wife, too, so we drove down to Cape Town in search of a compromise.

And here I must confess that I was ashamed to tell friends I was even contemplating such a move. Cape Town may be the most beautiful city on the planet, but we Jo'burg dudes see it as something of a fool's paradise, a last refuge for white colonials driven out of black Africa by the winds of change. The first such settlers were rich Belgians displaced from their coffee estates in the Congo by the troubles of 1961. In their wake, as empires toppled, came white hunters from Tanganyika, tobacco barons from Southern

Rhodesia, tea moguls from Nyasaland, and a band of aristocratic white Kenyans led by the Honorable Mrs. Patricia Cavendish O'Neill, daughter of the Countess of Kenmare, who set her beloved lions free on the Serengeti and retreated to an estate near Cape Town in the early seventies.

The trickle became a flood in 1980, when Robert Mugabe rose to power in neighboring Zimbabwe. The flood doubled after 1984, when Johannesburg and its surrounds were convulsed by a bloody anti-apartheid struggle, and doubled again in the early 1990s, when South Africa seemed to be sliding into a race war. We were spared that fate by Nelson Mandela and F. W. de Klerk, but their triumph precipitated a new influx of paradise hunters, lured this time by the perplexing (to outsiders) victory in our epochal 1994 elections of the conservative and mostly white-led National Party, which regained leadership in Cape Town and the Western Cape Province.

For apprehensive whites, this was an amazing development: history seemed to be allowing whites to eat their cake and still have it, offering them the chance to practice democracy in Africa while continuing to live in a society where power was in the reassuring hands of "people like us." Thousands pulled up stakes in the hinterland and flocked to the Mother City. Immigrants arrived. Investments poured in. The economy boomed. Cape Town mutated almost overnight into one of the most stylish tourist destinations on the planet, thronged by aristocrats, film stars, and Eurotrash. Michael Jackson came shopping for real estate. Margaret Thatcher's son Mark settled here, as did Earl Spencer, brother of Princess Diana. By 2001 Cape Town had become, for me, a place where fools sat on sea-view terraces, sipping white wine and congratulating one another for finding a corner of Africa that was somehow immune to the chaos engulfing the rest of the continent. The contessa wanted to join them. I had reservations.

It's difficult to explain, but moving to Cape Town struck me as an admission of defeat. "This isn't really Africa, you know," Capetonians are always saying, and they're right, in a way. There are streets in downtown Cape Town that resemble New York or London, and in summer the city is overrun by camera crews shooting international TV commercials. The Atlantic seaboard is sometimes mistaken for the French Riviera. Out in the nearby Winelands, the oak groves and pastures are somehow European in their gentleness, and the arid west coast easily doubles for Spain. As for the better suburbs, frame your shot to exclude dramatic mountain backdrops and smoke from the shacks where poor blacks live, and you're in an upper-middle-class anywhere: Connecticut, Marin County, Surrey, or Neuilly.

Look at this, I told the contessa. It's totally unreal, a citadel of delusions, a generically Western whites-only moon base in Africa. No way, I said; my friends in Johannesburg will laugh at me. I wanted a log cabin in the wilderness near Cape Point, where we could live a simple life of spartan purity among trees tormented into strange shapes by howling gales, uncompromised by such bourgeois comforts as electricity and running water. You're nuts, she said, so we looked at Franschoek, in my childhood a lovely valley of whitewashed cottages with plots out back where one could keep dogs and grow vegetables. Three decades on, it was still lovely, but it had somehow become more Provençal than even Provence. African farms had mutated into wine estates with names like L'Ormarins and Haute Cabrière, and the main road was lined with restaurants serving pretentious French cuisine. The contessa was enchanted. This is even worse than the moon base, I sneered. Our marriage was apparently in deep trouble, but we were saved by St. James.

St. James is a suburb on the Indian Ocean side of the Cape Peninsula — the wrong side, in the estimation of real estate agents who kept trying to steer us to the Atlantic seaboard, where you pay millions for a water view. So what? Sea is sea, and on Cape Town's Atlantic side it's always freezing and thus of little use other than as a backdrop for parties on terraces. The sea at St. James was something else entirely, a giant horseshoe of sparkling blue, ringed by mountains, warm enough for swimming in summer and full of interesting sights besides. On the day we first came, the bay was full of whales. There were surfers on the reef at Danger Beach, swimmers in the breakers. There was a real fishing harbor nearby, with real fishermen, real fish stink, and real winos on the dilapidated boardwalk. There was even a slum, a once grand holiday resort now running to seed and populated mostly by French-speaking Africans who had fled Zaire when the dictator Mobutu was toppled by rebels in 1997.

Intrigued, we returned the next day for a closer look, parking on the far side of Muizenberg, a mile north, and walking south along "millionaires' row." Here, capitalists with vast gold and diamond holdings once maintained stately summer houses on a beach so huge and empty you can still ride a horse for four hours in the direction of the sunrise and not come to the end of it. The great British imperialist Cecil John Rhodes established the vogue, buying a cottage here in 1899. He was followed by Williams and Rudd, his right-hand men. Then came Sir Ernest Oppenheimer, South Africa's richest man, soon to be joined by Sir Herbert Baker, a society architect whose houses of sandstone and Burma teak were all the rage among Johannesburg's smart set. Sir J. B. Robinson stayed with his daughter, Ida, the Countess Labia, who built a rococo palace next door to another mining magnate, Sir Abe Bailey. On a midsummer's day in the 1920s, the concentration of wealth in this mile of rock, sand, and mountainside would have rivaled anything outside the United States.

By the time we arrived, it had all vanished. The great capitalist dynasties had died out or moved their bases of operation to London. The grand houses along Beach Road had become sad Baptist seminaries and the like, and the waterfront hotels were slum tenements. Also lost to time and emigration was the Jewish community that once thrived in the warren of crooked alleys and old stone houses away from the seashore. Bernard Bendix's electrical shop had become a speakeasy. Alf Rohm's kosher dairy stood empty, and the store next door was a Congolese barbershop, gaily painted in the French national colors and surmounted by the inscrutable slogan "The Molokai Is One." Beyond Rhodes's cottage we came to St. James, a place from the time before cars, where Edwardian houses stood on terraces cut into the mountainside, reachable only by steep lanes overhung by rioting bougainvillea. In its day, St. James was to WASPs what Muizenberg was to Jews: a very English, very colonial outpost populated by merchants and bankers who would trip down the lanes of a morning in pinstriped suits and take the steam train into Cape Town, a journey of about forty minutes. Their wives cultivated English gardens and croquet lawns, and were at pains to stress that they did not live in Kalk Bay, the enclave adjoining, because Kalk Bay had Creole or "Cape colored" people in it, once considered very déclassé. Today Kalk Bay is fashionable (at least among white bohemians) for much the same reason: it is one of the pitifully few racially mixed communities to have survived apartheid largely unscathed.

This was at least inadvertently the doing of a policeman named Tommy Carse, who came to Kalk Bay in 1940 to keep watch over the mostly Cape colored fishermen who lived there, working the bay in small wooden boats. Carse was white, but his heart was open. He started writing down old men's stories about disasters, miraculous rescues, whale hunts in open rowing boats, and the community's battle against storms and corporate trawlers. He eventually published a book that in turn became a state-sponsored documentary about a magical little village with cobblestoned alleys, where Cape colored fishermen lived simply but happily under the guardianship of their benevolent white superiors. It won awards at Cannes and Edinburgh and was seen by eighty million people worldwide.

Twenty years after Carse moved in, the mad scientists of apartheid arrived in Kalk Bay and were disturbed to find people of various races living in attached houses, and even, God forbid, intermarrying. Arguing that this was counter to the laws of nature, they decreed that all those with dark skin or curly hair were to be banished. The citizens of Kalk Bay took to the streets with protest placards, cut down the "Whites Only" signs on their beach, and threatened to let the whole world know that the community immortalized by Constable Carse was about to be destroyed by heartless racists. The government backed off, and the Cape colored fisherfolk of Kalk Bay lived on to be far more sorely threatened by gentrification, or more exactly, by people like me, yuppies who cringe at the thought of being mistaken for foolish colonials on the run from African reality.

I was not alone. The local real estate agent, Dalene, told us she had twenty-seven buyers lined up with cash in hand, but there were no Kalk Bay properties for sale at any price. She did, however, have something in St. James, an ugly modern house high on the mountainside, with awe-inspiring views of mountains and sea. Standing on the veranda, we could see all the way from Cape Point northeast to the brooding peaks of Groot Drakenstein, almost ninety miles in the distance. The contessa thought a neighborhood so quaint could not fail to rebound again. I thought its charm lay in the fact that much of it was in decline, and thus mercifully free of delusion and vanity. We bought the place and saved our marriage.

Before we came to live here, I had always sensed something odd about Cape Town. For a visitor, the city is maddeningly difficult to come to grips with, a place of enclaves, each introverted and provincial in a different way, inhabited by people who seemed quietly abstracted and self-absorbed, as if their minds were on higher things. "Pretty place, stupid people," says my friend Adrian, who avoids Cape Town when possible — an astute summation, but not exactly right. After living a month or two in St. James, it dawned on me that the people among whom we had settled were less stupid than stupefied, so overwhelmed by beauty and so profoundly humbled by nature that displays of wit had come to seem superfluous.

Curious changes take place in your brain when you move to Cape Town. You get up in the morning, scurry out to make your fortune, and come face to face with an awesome sight — the sea, a storm, clouds streaming over mountain crags — that reminds you of your utter insignificance in the grand scheme of things. Your ambition starts flagging. You buy fewer and fewer newspapers, and grow less and less interested in what's happening across town, let alone in the larger world. In due course, visitors from more exciting cities start yawning at your dinner table, appalled by the banality of your conversation. The other night we spent hours analyzing the strange behavior of a great white shark that patrols our stretch of coast, nudging canoeists but never eating them. Then we moved on to another pressing issue: What are whales actually doing when they stand on their heads and wave their giant flukes in the air?

Our visitors rolled their eyes. You could see they felt sorry for us, but the feeling was mutual because they had no conception of the unbearable bliss of fine summer days when the water is warm and the figs are ripe and you are woken at dawn by a murderous sun rising over the peaks across the bay. The day begins with breakfast on the terrace and a plunge into the cool green depths of a rock pool at the foot of our mountain, followed perhaps by a cappuccino in one of Kalk Bay's sidewalk cafés. By now it's nine and time to work, often difficult on account of the ceaseless drama outside my windows: tides rising, whales blowing, birds diving, shoals of fish passing through, and in the early afternoon, the boats coming back to Kalk Bay.

We whistle up the dogs and walk down to meet the boats, joining a great convergence of gulls, seals, fishmongers, and housewives coming to witness the daily landing. Crewmen sling their catch onto the wharf; hawkers cry the prices; dealers step forward to bid and haggle. On a good day, there will be great piles of yellowtail, red roman, and Cape salmon, but these prize fish mostly vanish into the hands of the restaurant trade, leaving the rest of us to bargain for snoek, a barracudalike predator that comes in huge runs, sometimes driving the price down to a dollar for a yard-long fish, and another fifty cents to the garrulous old fishwife who guts it and tosses the innards into the harbor, to be snatched up by boiling seals. By now we're hot, so it's time for another swim, then the climb back to our mountainside aerie, where we smear the fish with the juice of figs and lemons from our garden, set it to grill on an open fire, uncork a bottle of wine, and watch the moon rise over the bay.

The next day is much the same, and the day after, the heat-stricken rhythm of it broken only by furious southeast gales and the coming and going of visitors who want to see things and go places. We take them to Boulders Beach, to swim with African penguins, or to Pcrima's, a funky little restaurant where Gayla Naicker serves the best curries in Africa, but after a few days they too subside into bewilderment. Why travel to tourist attractions when you're in one already? In season, tour buses park on the road above our house, disgorging foreigners who gape at the view and then turn their binoculars on us, clearly wondering what entitles us to live in such a place.

As our first summer wore on, I began asking myself the same question. The contessa saw it as a Calvinist problem and suggested I seek therapy, but for me it was like withdrawing from an addiction. I'd spent much of my life thinking and writing about the terrors and ecstasy of life in Africa, always half-convinced that we were heading for some sort of catastrophe: race war, revolution, economic collapse, famine, extinction by AIDS. I just didn't know how to live in a place where no one seemed particularly worried about anything, even when there was a real crisis to agonize over. "Our currency is plummeting, sir!" a wino called out as I passed the other day. "Could it be that some of it will fall my way?"

He was white, the grizzled bum beside him was not, but they seemed to get along fine. The school over yonder was integrated, as were the beaches and bars along the seafront. Sure, almost everyone is poorer than he'd like to be, and the eyes of Kalk Bay coloreds still grow hooded when they talk about the insults of apartheid, but memories are fading, and nobody's going to war about it. The only truly unhappy man in my little world is Bishop Kitenge, the glamorous *personne d'élégance* who runs the Congolese barbershop in Muizenberg, and his pain is rooted in frustrated ambition: he wants to go to America but can't get a visa. "I must be star," he says, struggling a bit with his English. "I must go to Miami, and open beautiful salon. I love America!"

And that's about it for the bad news from St. James, other than an isolated incident in which some kids broke into my pickup, and the night the contessa woke up screaming that a leopard was in the garden. I fetched a flashlight and probed the darkness, and there it was, a leopard-spotted feline eating our dog food. Turned out to be a genet rather than a leopard, but still — a wild creature from the mysterious mountain that looms above and behind our home.

In winter, when the bay turns gray and cold and the fishing harbor is stormbound for weeks on end, we turn away to the mountain, bundle up in scarves, boots, and waterproof jackets, and take the dogs along a footpath that leads onto a bleak, misty plateau, part of a national park that runs fifty miles from Table Mountain to Cape Point. You can walk and climb for hours up there, with absolutely no sense of being in a city. If a storm catches you, you might even get lost and wander in circles until you die. Some days, the clouds part, sun pours down, and we find ourselves suspended in light between two oceans, the slopes around us strewn with wildflowers, and snow on the peaks of Groot Drakenstein, sixty miles away. Then the weather closes in again and we turn back for home, where we huddle around a fire sipping Cape brandy while rain taps against our windows.

The contessa believes this is how the Cape will always be. I wonder. I lift binoculars to the barrier of mountains that separates us from the African hinterland and think of all the trouble out there — the grinding convulsions of what the *Economist* calls "the hopeless continent." It seems inconceivable that the Cape should remain untouched, but here we are, sun-drugged and stupefied. Summer has returned, and the snoek are back in the bay. We grilled one on the fire last night, and fell asleep to the sighing and gurgling of whales, happy fools in an improbable African paradise.

BILL MCKIBBEN

Small World

FROM *Harper's Magazine*

WHEN YOU THINK about Vermont, Barre is not the town you're imagining. Main Street has seen better days. There are few covered bridges and fewer rusticators in J. Crew sweaters. There is a heroin problem. The town's peculiar local geology — it is the self-proclaimed "granite capital of the world" — has given rise to a peculiar local economy. For nearly a century, Rock of Ages Corporation has been one of the town's biggest employers, providing tombstones for a nation. Barre is — literally and figuratively — a gritty town.

Thunder Road, "the nation's site of excitement," sits just down the hill from the quarry, and on summer Thursday nights (because quarrymen used to get paid on Thursday afternoons) it vibrates with noise — cars dopplering around the half-mile track, the whine rising and falling as they flash by the grandstand straight. It's glorious fun — the booth selling homemade videos of last year's best crashes, the "battle flags" of last year's champion cars flapping over the infield. Those grandstands hold ten thousand people on a big night, and most nights are big. Ten thousand — one Vermonter in sixty — is more people than gather anyplace else in the state.

"After the war, that's when all this started," said Ken Squier, who built Thunder Road. Car racing may be bigtime now, but it began as a local sport, and not just down south. "The soldiers came back from Okinawa, from Iwo Jima, from the Bulge. They were not going to play a children's game like baseball. This was their thing. It was always the people's sport. Always the sport for the unshined shoes."

I could listen to Ken Squier most of the night. He's a talker, and he comes by it honestly, having spent the better part of six decades in front of the microphone at the radio station his father helped build — "WDEV, Radio Vermont . . . the *friendly* pioneer . . . Ninety-six-point-one on your FM dial." Naturally he broadcasts races from his Thunder Road, at least on those Thursdays when the Red Sox aren't playing at the same time. And of course he discusses the races in loving detail on his morning sports wrap. He even has a weekly auto-racing hour, hosted by one of his sidekicks, Dave Moody. Any businessman would do the same — when Disney and ABC or AOL and Time Warner do it, they call it "synergy."

But here's the odd part. When Dave wraps up the auto-racing show on Monday evening, the next thing you hear is *Dinner Jazz* — two hours of Cannonball Adderley and Miles and Coltrane and Dave Brubeck, brought to you by the same advertisers (Lenny's Shoes and Apparel, Shore Acres restaurant) that bring you, at various times during the week, the bird-watching hour, *Music to Go to the Dump By,* and the station's own bluegrass band ("We don't want to be strangers . . . We're the Radio Rangers . . . from WDEV"). Some nights in the winter they'll carry two different girls' high school basketball games back-to-back or hockey from Norwich College. There's some gospel preaching on Sunday morning, and Dairyline with the latest hundredweight prices in the five o'clock hour so you can hear it during morning milking. There's a conservative talk show for an hour in the morning, of course — but oddly, in the afternoon, there's an hour of left-wing talk, hosted by socialist congressman Bernie Sanders and by Anthony Pollina, of the state's Progressive Party.

In other words, this is a very strange radio station. Forget the red states and the blue states. WDEV exists in a kind of purple state. Many parts of its schedule sound like things you can hear elsewhere. If you've got the new satellite radios, you can get bluegrass twenty-four hours a day and nineteen flavors of jazz. Modern radio stations aim for a particular niche — say, thirty-five-year-old males who want sports around the clock. But it's a rare place in our society where Thelonious Monk and stock-car racing coexist. It's radio that actually reflects the reality of local life, and it seems very strange because it's all but disappeared everywhere else.

*

A couple of miles downhill from Thunder Road, on the slightly tired main street of Barre, Tod Murphy opened up a diner about a year ago, right next to the hardware store. Ham and eggs, breakfast all day, bottomless cup of coffee. A local joint. But the Farmer's Diner is maybe the most local joint in the whole United States — something like 80 percent of the food it serves was raised within sixty miles of the kitchen. In a country where the average forkful of dinner travels 1,500 miles to reach your lips, this makes Murphy's diner perhaps the most interesting restaurant in America. Sure, other chefs work with local food — Alice Waters has been doing it for years, to great and deserved acclaim. But not at $5.50 for the hamburger platter. Diner food comes frozen in great plastic sacks on the backs of trucks.

Great local food in a diner is as odd as jazz and stock-car racing sharing a radio frequency. America has been Clear Channeled and Olive Gardened with enormous success, but it's possible that success has begun to breed a reaction. Politicians were bowled over last summer when hundreds of thousands of Americans from across the political spectrum wrote in to decry new FCC deregulation that would have let media giants own even more stations than they do now. And people are flocking in the hundreds, anyhow, to line the counter at Murphy's new eatery. Some are old hippies, and some are on their way to Thunder Road. But there are enough of them that Murphy has begun to think big — begun to imagine Farmer's Diners all across America, serving food grown from whatever region they happen to be in. "'Local' is the new 'organic,'" he said. "Everywhere that there's an Applebee's, there could be a Farmer's Diner."

In fact, the longer I spent around Squier and Murphy, the more I began to wonder if maybe "local" really is what comes next — whether as the globalized world begins to fray, socially and environmentally and even economically, people might start wanting to shorten their supply lines. Energy that comes from a windmill on the ridge instead of an oil tanker from the Gulf, say. We're not going to build computer chips in local workshops, but does every chicken need to come from some enormous Tyson shed in the Southeast? A resurgence of the local would be counterintuitive. The momentum in the direction of globalization seems too powerful to buck, the economic logic unmatchable. But in a region where jobs are draining away, and where an ethic of self-reliance remains a dim, vestigial, but honored memory, it seems at least an outside possibility. And inside the Farmer's Diner, with cops and housewives and truck drivers hunched over chili from local steers and local beans, it seems awfully appealing.

The train of thought that led to this Barre lunch counter began, oddly enough, in the 1990s, when Tod Murphy was working in a cool new coffee place in Seattle called Starbucks, soon to be the poster child for the destruction of local commercial culture. "I was a damned good Starbucks counter guy," Murphy said. "That's where I got my chops. I found out that I really liked customers. It fits in with my Aquarian personality — you don't have to make a long-term commitment to them, but you get to converse." He learned plenty of other things, too, watching Starbucks owner Howard Schultz. "He was always able to see the possibilities. He knew about the 'half-hour vacation,' and how people wanted a new public space, and all of that. He understood what was happening in the culture."

In the mid-nineties, Murphy and his girlfriend, a Starbucks manager, moved east to Atlanta to launch their own start-up — Coffee Station, they called it. The plan was to make as much money as quickly as possible. "The whole idea was to flip it, to turn it — all those late nineties words." Murphy ended up in New York as operations director. "In three years in Manhattan, I saw Patrick Stewart in a Shakespeare play and that was pretty much my tourist life. We were full-out." Coffee Station didn't turn into Starbucks — in fact it went out of business — but Murphy and his partners had sold out near the top of the boom, clearing a small bundle. "It made having a farm possible."

Ah, a farm. Murphy grew up suburban, but his grandparents were still farming in rural Connecticut (just down the road from what's since turned into Mohegan Sun, the gaudiest of the Indian casinos). He knew what he wanted to do: "I would get the Sears and Roebuck farm catalogue and price out what a laying flock would cost me," he said. So when he sold off his stake in overpriced Manhattan latte, he drove north to Vermont and started looking.

He found a place — a beautiful, scraggly hill farm ten miles south of Barre, where he started raising veal calves. "Great organic veal calves, nursing off old dairy cows. They were out on pasture, too, so they actually had some flavor from grass. I went to start selling them because shortly they were not going to be veal anymore; they were going to be young beef. The first chef I talked to said, 'Great, I'll take three cases of top round.' Well, Christ, the entire herd didn't have three cases of top round. And no one wanted the front legs."

Murphy had discovered the essential fact of modern agriculture: veal calf, ear of corn, gallon of milk, what you've grown is a commodity. Either you sell it into the huge industrial food stream, at a price set by the lowest-cost, highest-volume grower in some distant market, or you can begin the laborious task of figuring out how to market your product for a higher price: at a farmers' market, or through an organic co-op, or maybe marinated in some special sauce and FedExed from your Web site. (You could also do what most small farmers in Vermont or elsewhere in America have in fact done: sell your farm to someone else, who will either try one of the above strategies or turn it into ski condos.) In this case, Murphy sold his veal calves to the New England Culinary Institute for use in their meat-cutting class. But that was clearly a limited market. And anyway, he was cursed with the brain of an entrepreneur.

"I started to ask myself, how do you create a company that will take food off the farmer's hands in the easiest way for a farmer, and set it in front of the customers in the easiest way for them, and do it at a price point everyone could live with? And a diner was the answer I came up with. People know what to expect from it. It's a ground-beef business. Nothing fancy."

In fact, though, a diner was not so intuitively obvious. Virtually all the other restaurateurs who want to use high-quality local produce have gone high-end, for the obvious reason that a $50 check covers a multitude of sins. You can afford to pay the higher price of hand-raised organic veal, and the high price of having a chef take the time to hack it apart, and the higher price of going down to the farmers' market to shop for it, and the high price of the fresh flowers on the table to make your customer feel as if $50 was money well spent. If you're going to try to use the same ingredients to compete with, say, Denny's, you're going to have to think a lot harder. And if you're going to try it in Vermont, where winter lasts awhile, you're going to have to think harder still.

*

Local sounds good, but most of American history has been spent transforming local into national and now global. The result is the society we inhabit. Considering only just these two categories, food and communications, it's easy enough to see what's happened. Whereas once most people grew their own food, and perhaps a small surplus to sell, farmers now make up 1 or 2 percent of the population. The rest of us have moved on, making the economy vastly larger by doing other things. We now can get fresh food from around the planet, flown or shipped in at every season, and it's all incredibly cheap — once upon a time an orange was a rare treat in the bottom of a Christmas stocking for most Americans, and now orange juice is a staple of our lives, available in low-acid and high-calcium and everything in between. It's kind of a miracle that consumer capitalism can deliver you an apple from South Africa for forty cents. Similarly, communication was once largely confined to the people in your immediate vicinity, unless you were willing to write a letter. Now we are entertained virtually nonstop by hundreds of channels of television and radio and Internet radio and legally and illegally downloaded tunes and you name it. There is no vaguely musical sound emitted by anyone on the planet that is not available, again for a vanishingly low price, to any of the rest of us at any time. Vermont alone has seventy-eight radio transmitters — the dial is pretty crowded even in this small state.

Or, of course, you could say it another way. We now grow our food with so few farmers that lots of rural communities have simply shriveled up and disappeared, and many of the rest are impoverished and hopeless. Farmers working thousands of acres apiece can't take good care of the land — soil erodes, pesticides and herbicides go on by the ton. Animals grown in vast factory farms are, by definition, animals abused. Flying and trucking food from one end of the world to the other spews carbon into the atmosphere. By the time the apple from New Zealand reaches your supermarket it tastes like nothing special. Vast quantities of cheap food have, in the last couple of decades, helped to make us, well, vast.

When a train car overturned in Minot, North Dakota, last year, a large quantity of ammonia spilled out, sending up a cloud of poison gas. Local officials quickly tried to contact the town's seven radio stations to send out the alarm — only to find that there was no one actually working in six of them. They were simply relaying a satellite feed from Clear Channel headquarters in Texas — there was plenty of country music and golden oldies and Top 40 and right-wing chat, but no one to warn about the toxic cloud drifting overhead. It's true that you can hear anything from anywhere at any time, but, oddly, it's gotten a lot harder to hear much about your immediate vicinity. All fall, talk radio covered the fine points of the California recall in obsessive detail — did Arnold grope all those women? But try spinning the dial to find out about, say, the extent of domestic abuse in your own county. That's one reason people rose up last summer to fight the FCC when it moved to make the world even safer for the Clear Channels. It was supposed to be a quiet backroom deal, but pretty soon activists of every stripe were fighting the regulation: when Bernie Sanders held a hearing in Vermont, for instance, there weren't enough seats for all the people who wanted to testify; Congress got so many e-mails that the Senate actually tried to reject the new regulations. Michael Powell, the shocked and peeved chairman of the FCC, whined to the *New York Times* in September that "there was a concerted grassroots effort to attack" the new regulation. "I've never seen that," he added.

Here's another way of saying it. A couple of clicks up the dial from WDEV, you come to a Clear Channel Vermont station, one of a half-dozen area signals controlled by the $8 billion corporation. It styles itself The Zone, and it carries Rush. After Rush, it carries the Don and Mike show. A few days ago, I listened to Don and Mike for an hour. They tried to fry an egg on the sidewalk because it was so incredibly hot (in Washington, D.C., where they're located; in Vermont it was raining). They also had a big discussion about a porno film they'd recently watched on a cable channel and whether or not it was gross that the male actor had an uncircumcised penis. This turned disputatious, and either Don or Mike told either Mike or Don to kiss his ass. "Kiss the inside of my ass. Kiss the eye. Kiss the eye!" Then a woman came into the studio who had tanned the words "Don" and "Mike" onto her breasts in order to win a hundred dollars. There was more dispute, this time about whether or not she'd tanned them low enough, "across the round part, the aureole."

An economist would argue that we've chosen this world — that if we didn't want the Sysco truck unloading frozen dinners into the back door of the family-casual chain dining house, we wouldn't go there. That if we wanted to listen to local radio, local radio would ipso facto exist. And there's plenty of truth in all that — by and large we have picked (with the assistance of immense quantities of advertising) the cheapest, the easiest, the saltiest, the greasiest. Something in dirty talk appeals to many of us, and community has often seemed like more work than it's worth. Our choices *have* in some ways built our world. On the other hand, it's hard to test whether these are the choices we really, or *still*, want to make. If most every radio station in your town is owned by some big broadcaster, you need many millions of dollars to buy a frequency, if indeed one is even open. If your choice of restaurants is confined to twenty places with a loading ramp at the back for the tractor-trailer, then it's harder to make a statement of your desires.

In other words, if you wanted to find out whether, in the early twenty-first century, local "works," or whether it's simply a romantic fantasy, you'd need to have some test cases, some examples to look at. A few places that exist slightly outside the conventional economy. Like the Farmer's Diner, or like WDEV.

One way to have such a place is to inherit it from your father, which is how Ken Squier came by his radio station. "This was a print shop in 1930," he said, waving his arm around the small suite of offices in downtown Waterbury where WDEV still operates. "They published the Waterbury *Record*. My father was working here for Harry Whitehill, who was also the customs collector for northern Vermont. In those days that meant chasing liquor, and Mr. Whitehill spent quite a bit of time up at St. Albans near the Canadian border, where they happened to have the first commercial station in the state. And one day he came home and said to my dad, 'Lloyd, more people can hear than can read. I think we ought to have a radio station too.'"

The Pony Boys, and Beedie's Troubadours, and Doc Kenyon of the Moonlight Ramblers — they stayed up night after night, playing away as Squier Sr. tested the signal. By July 6, 1931, all was ready. Miss Kate Lyons, the daughter of Mr. and Mrs. Arthur Lyons of Waterbury Center, sang "The Rose in the Garden," followed by Stanley Nevin singing "The Hoot Owl." Mrs. Beryl Thibuilt played the first instrumental solo — a violin rendition of Fritz Kreisler's "Liebesfreud." The president of the local bank spoke, as did the general manager of the Eastern Magnesium Talc plant and a number of preachers. The state's poet laureate, Dan Cady, offered a poem:

> Vermont now goes upon that screen
> That wondrous screen, the air:
> We'll show that things can happen here
> As well as anywhere:
> We'll give the world the news it needs
> And still have news to spare

Soon the station was on the air three hours a day; soon it was carrying live chats from the governor's office and broadcasting the state basketball championship. But the bread and butter was country music. "Dance pavilions were the social activity in those days. There were six or seven really fine local bands, and all through the 1930s each band would come in and play for half an hour, talk about where they were performing that night. They'd take requests and sell their pictures over the air. Texas Slim and the Northern Ridge Runners. Bud Bailey and the Down Easters." And the local towns got an hour a week — the Morrisville hour, the Montpelier hour. "My father met my mother because she came for the Hardwick hour," Squier said. "All the towns took it very seriously."

WDEV offered full-service radio in part because it paid off nicely, and in part because Whitehill and Squier Sr. saw it as their responsibility. In fact, the idea of businessmen owning radio stations was controversial. In the 1920s, as the medium got off the ground, licenses went mostly to colleges, to labor unions, and to groups like them — they seemed the obvious rightful custodians of the public airwaves. But in the 1930s, as it became clear what a commercial gold mine broadcasting could be, business managed to convince Congress that their "well-rounded" programming should get the edge over "narrow special interest." Washington did demand, however, a certain modicum of accountability. "Right from the very beginning, from like 1934, you were supposed to assess your community," Squier said. "The government told you to assess the needs, and say how you were going to fulfill them, and if you didn't they would take your license away from you."

So at the time, there was nothing in the least unusual about WDEV — every radio station on the dial was busy trying to entertain and inform local audiences. But by simply doing pretty much the same thing for seventy years, the station has turned into a kind of relic; there are others like it, mostly scattered around rural parts of the country, but the landscape of the medium has changed dramatically. With the advent of television, radio turned more and more into a mere music box; then, in the eighties and nineties, big companies discovered they could knit together huge networks and feed them the same formatted top hits, the same nationwide talk shows. The cost of a frequency skyrocketed — any signal in a major metro area now brings in tens of millions of dollars — but the opportunities to save money were also enormous. Instead of a staff of forty, like the one Squier maintains, you could run a radio station for next to nothing, enabling you to pay off the cost of acquiring the license and still make lots of money. The same ad salesmen can pitch all of Clear Channel's local stations, and it's simpler for advertisers to buy their package.

"Literally now, if you can prove you haven't been busted for drugs and you've got the money, you get a place on the dial," Squier said. "They pay lip service to need and necessity, but that's horse pucky." Indeed, Clear Channel brags a good deal about its "public service," which mostly involves running those free ads from the Ad Council. That's different from the idea that the radio station is there to actually *serve* a community. "A few years ago a big flood hit Montpelier," Squier said, "and after a couple of days they asked Governor Dean how he was keeping track of what was happening. And he said, 'Well, I'm listening to WDEV.' We took all our sales staff and turned them into reporters for that period. We dropped all our commercials for three days. We had someone on the scene when the railroad bridge down here moved on its moorings. That's what we're supposed to do."

As radio and TV grew less and less interested in education and service, Congress responded not by reining them in but by setting aside a little cash to create public broadcasting. Vermont has a considerably better than average public-radio service. Along with all the NPR shows, it offers a twice-a-week hour-long call-in on local topics, three five-minute commentaries every day by local residents, and an unparalleled weather forecast. But there's a sense in which it manages to appeal to a certain market segment, just like the Clear Channel stations. The only time that sports come up is on Saturday mornings between seven and eight, in a national broadcast originating in Boston; rock-and-roll gets a (remarkably lucid) hour on Saturday evening. You aren't going to hear stock-car racing, and you're not going to get a twenty-minute interview with the editor of the Addison County *Independent* about what's going on in his paper that week.

Squier insists that if Congress had maintained a vigil on commercial broadcasting, "there never would have been the need to set up what some see as an elitist network." But he understands just how far out of the barn and out to pasture that particular horse is. So he's left listening to public radio with a kind of rueful vengefulness, because so much of it sounds like what he wants WDEV to sound like. He loves jazz, for instance. He spent his college years in Boston, working at clubs run by the great promoter George Wein. "The best education I ever had. Miles, Coltrane, Ella, Sarah Vaughan, I saw them all, five or six nights a week. Brubeck, Errol Garner." And hence he runs *Dinner Jazz*, right before the Red Sox. He also loves classical music — in fact, he runs his own small classical station. "I tried to give Vermont Public Radio money," he said. "I sent them a check for $1,700 and asked that they say, 'Support for this programming is coming from WCVT, Classic Vermont, 101.7.' But they sent it back and said they wouldn't accept it because I'm a competitor. Competitor! They pay no taxes, they get $300,000 a year from the government. So on the one hand I'm up against Clear Channel. And on the other hand I'm up against this group that claims they're public." He would settle, he said with a laugh, for the chance to run *Prairie Home Companion* on his air. "I begged for that show," he said. "But they just laughed at me."

Some years WDEV makes money, though Squier is not about to say how much, and some years it doesn't. If Squier had to buy it now, though, he couldn't. "No Vermonter will ever hold a radio station license again," he said. "They'll go to the big companies with the liquidity." Which will pay the capital costs by not using the sales staff to cover the three-day Montpelier flood, and not broadcasting back-to-back high school girls' basketball games, and not mounting a microphone on a bicycle to cover the local marathon, and not going live to the woods on the opening day of deer-hunting season.

Lots of conversations in Vermont get around to milk, which has been the state's agricultural staple since the decline of the wool trade in the nineteenth century. But Vermont has lost 80 percent of its dairy farms in the past forty years — they're competing with the megafarms of the Midwest and California, which have driven prices through the floor. A few dairymen have emulated the competition and gotten very big, but many more have gotten Florida license plates. So it was a relief when one day Tod Murphy drove me out to visit the Strafford Organic Creamery, a small dairy that actually seems to be almost making it. Earl Ransom was born on the farm in 1972, and he's been running it since he was twenty-three; his milk comes in big glass bottles, from apparently happy cows who spend their time out on pasture, at least until it gets cold. (Or until something else happens. "That's Stu with the horns over there," explained Earl as he flipped burgers on his grill. "Stu's going in the freezer on Tuesday.") Anyway, Earl lives the life of a dairy farmer — which means that his property taxes have gone up 38 percent since 2001 as the land gets more and more desirable, and which means that he spends $2,000 a month on electricity to run his small farm. "It's highly unlikely we could survive at our scale without being organic," Earl said. The premium price underwrites an ecologically sensible farm.

But the milk mostly goes to natural-food stores — that is, to people who can afford, and are willing, to pay $3.50 a half gallon instead of $2. It's a niche market, the public radio of dairying. The exception is the Farmer's Diner, which buys most of its dairy products from Ransom. "I've had to educate folks that whipping cream is not supposed to be white," Murphy said. "When the cows went out of the barn and into the pasture in the spring, the half-and-half changed color noticeably. The waitresses were afraid people would freak."

It's operations like Ransom's that Murphy wants badly to support. But he didn't inherit his business. If he's going to spread it around the country, it will be on other people's money, money that's looking for a good return. A good way to lose that money would be to go entirely warm and fuzzy. So while Murphy decorates the diner with slogans from Wendell Berry ("Eating Is an Agricultural Act"), he resists the urge to hire on the basis of ideology. "My first manager, he wanted the kitchen to be a Darwinian, organic, evolving system. No. You have to be God in the kitchen, lay down how it will be, impose some divine intelligence on the primordial soup. Chaos theory is great, but you need some pretty powerful computers to see the patterns, the pretty fractals. Customers are the observers in this system, and to them it just looks like chaos."

By contrast, Murphy has evolved a careful plan for the diner, a plan that at the moment is making the rounds of investors. His Barre operation has indisputably proved people will line up to eat local food — but it's also indisputably proved, Murphy said, that you need a certain degree of economy of scale to make the idea really work. He's making two or three cents on the dollar now. Not many investors are going to sign on for a 2 or 3 percent return. So, *to a degree*, Murphy has no choice but to expand — once started, the competitive logic of globalism is hard to derail. His scheme goes like this: Murphy will build clusters of diners — maybe five or six in Vermont, perhaps fifteen in a metro area like Boston — and service each cluster from a central kitchen. "If we have a central commissary supplying four or five other places, we go from making three cents on the dollar to nine cents on the dollar. We can go from one guy with a knife cutting home fries to a machine that cuts home fries and coleslaw and everything else. In the same time it now takes him to prep one hundred pounds of home fries, he can do all the vegetables for three diners."

That's the way that Denny's thinks too, of course — and once you've started down that path it would be easy to just keep going. Doubtless there's a bigger machine that cuts French fries for three thousand restaurants at once. "That's why we have to have a stake in the ground. The food has to come from within sixty miles — that's where philosophy overrides the business model," Murphy said. "Because there's some point at which you're not local anymore, and then you're Applebee's. I contend it's the sixty-mile radius — that allows people to recognize the names of the towns the food comes from. Wendell Berry wrote me and said sixty miles is too far away. Well, he's right. I'd like it all within a buggy ride, too. But since we're playing in a 1,500-mile game, sixty miles is pretty good."

The aim, eventually, is for locals across the nation to invest in their own clusters of diners — the parent company will provide the business model and technological expertise, collecting a percentage from the franchises. "We want to be a vertically integrated company, which is evil and awful," Murphy said. "But a *decentralized* vertically integrated company. I don't think there's a model of that anywhere."

The biggest problem with this vision is that globalism has long since eviscerated the infrastructure needed for it to happen. As the food system nationalized, all the slaughterhouses concentrated around the big Midwest feedlots. A few potato-producing regions — Maine, Idaho — have enormous French fry factories, but if you want to produce a French fry anywhere else, you need a guy with a knife. Vermont literally doesn't produce pork anymore — to get a supply of bacon, Murphy has a fifteen-year-old named Andrew raising pigs on his parents' small dairy farm.

And so, in order to open even the Barre diner, Murphy had to buy or build his own miniature supply chain. His smokehouse, Vermont Smoke and Cure, is located in the back of a Texaco station a couple of miles from the restaurant. "This is the raw room. This is a pickler — we can inject brine into hams and bacons. This is the vacuum stuffer, for sausage making. It's a great machine, but the drawback is all the directions are in German. I have to get my uncle down from the Canadian border to read them for me."

In essence, by setting his sixty-mile limit, Murphy has thrown a handful of grit into his business plan. He's agreed to cook with one hand tied behind his back. In return, he gets a story to tell, one he hopes will draw customers. "I keep comparing it with Starbucks. Latte is in the culture now, but it wasn't ten years ago. Right now people are starting to care about local food. We're in the right place at the right time."

The nation's liberals are forever talking about launching some kind of left-of-center radio network — Al Franken going head-on against Rush Limbaugh. But Anthony Pollina, former gubernatorial candidate on the Progressive Party ticket, has already been doing the job, week in and week out, for half a year on WDEV. The guests are mill workers laid off as Vermont's manufacturing base contracts, and other mill workers who have restarted their old factory to do locally marketed production. They're dairy farmers fighting for higher milk prices from the big marketers. Pollina's show is wildly different from almost anything else you hear anywhere — working-class Americans voicing their resentment not of feminazis and gay people and welfare queens and so on but of their actual adversaries in corporate America.

WDEV charges both Pollina and local conservative talkmeister Lauric Morrow for their hour a day of airtime — it's a mercenary proposition for the station. But the shows fit pretty neatly with Squier's own politics, a kind of populism that has very little to do with party. His listeners often seem cut from the same mold. In fact, it makes you wonder if a gradual return to more local economies might bring with it a gradual change in the lines that divide our political life. We're used to imagining local communities as hopelessly parochial and conservative, but in fact it's the national culture that has grown right wing and intolerant — all those ranters thrive because in the nation as a whole there are enough bigots to make up an audience. But local communities are maybe more interested in finding out what works than they are in venting. Less interested in left versus right than in big versus small.

Tod Murphy, for instance, wears his hair in a ponytail and is driven by an intense concern for the environment. He also averages twenty-five hours a month filling out federal and state paperwork for the restaurant and the smokehouse — the USDA inspector, by law, gets his own room and his own bathroom in the back of the Texaco station. Is he for big government? Not exactly.

Or consider this. Last summer a Vermont state trooper named Michael Johnson was trying to stop a car driven by a suspected drug dealer. He was putting a spike strip down on the interstate to puncture the car's tires when the dealer drove into the median and ran him over. A few nights later Squier ran the main feature at Thunder Road in his honor — state troopers driving the pace car, jugs going through the grandstand to collect money for Johnson's three kids. And the next morning Squier was on the radio fulminating about the need to start executing heroin dealers. Red meat stuff — understandable in the circumstances, but red meat. What you expect from radio.

Ten minutes later, though, he was interviewing a local author, Thom Hartmann, who had written a book called *Unequal Protection,* an account of "the rise of corporate dominance and the theft of human rights." All summer, in fact, Squier kept returning to the book, urging that his listeners go out and buy a copy so they could understand how corporate campaign contributions came to have such power. The day after the great eastern blackout, he was fulminating again — this time about the way that utility lobbyists had left the nation vulnerable. It's as if Rush Limbaugh and Al Franken shared a brain.

With one big difference. When you're local, it's harder to be a

complete jerk. The day after he raged on about lining heroin dealers up against the wall and shooting them, Squier invited a local
lawyer onto his program to argue against the death penalty. "If you
ever saw someone get executed, you wouldn't be so glib about it,"
he told Squier.

"I don't think you're right about that," Squier said. "But maybe
you are." There's a phrase you'll wait a long time to hear on the national shows.

If you look hard enough, you can see a strain of this populism in
Vermont's contribution to national politics, the Howard Dean campaign. Against gun control, for the death penalty, against tax cuts
for the rich, for restrictions on global trade. And funded by $50 do-
nations from around the country. Small, not big. The Bush campaign is reportedly counting on "NASCAR dads" to carry the day,
but the view from Thunder Road is a little different.

If you took a poll and asked people if they wanted more "community" in their lives, a huge majority would say yes. Left, right, and
center, it's a lack we profess to feel. But it's not at all clear that we
mean it in anything other than a wistful, sentimental way — that,
given the choice, we have any real interest in community, or in
the institutions (like WDEV or the Farmer's Diner) that might
build it.

That's because a local community is in some ways an exercise in
inefficiency. Take the modern radio industry as an example. It's
the furthest thing from local, but it's incredibly focused on *you*. It's
entirely set up around the idea that you are a part of a predictable
demographic whose tastes can be reliably commodified. If you walk
into the headquarters of, say, Kansas City's Entercom Broadcasting,
a Clear Channel wannabe, it looks like you're in a food court. In
the center, ad salesmen work from a line of cubicles. Around them,
a ring of small sound booths house each of the company's stations
— there's a country, a classical, a smooth jazz, a news, a rock, a classic rock, an alternative rock, and a continuous soft rock (KUDL)
geared toward women. If that kind of segmentation isn't enough
for you, you can sign up for satellite radio — on XM's 101 channels, rock-and-roll comes in an endless variety of flavors, including
"stadium rock" and "hair bands." And of course the whole premise
of talk radio is that you can go all day long without hearing an opin-

ion you disagree with — Limbaugh's fans, after all, call themselves "dittoheads."

Whereas on WDEV, if you listen regularly, you hear Ann Coulter decrying the treason of the American left, but you also hear the American left, or at least the Vermont version of it, decrying plant closings and failing dairy farms, demanding national health insurance and dissing the president. You hear jazz in the evening, and you hear stock-car racing. You hear, in other words, things that *other people* are interested in. Which is pretty much the definition of community. If you're a senior citizen you find out what's going on in the schools, and if you're a jazz fan you hear some bluegrass, and everyone gets the Norwich ice-hockey scores. Television, of course, is so expensive it has to chase the largest possible audience, and the Internet, by virtue of its design, splits people off into narrow avenues of interest. Radio is the ideal community vehicle, its signal confined by the hills and mountains to a narrow area — or was, until big money figured out how to buy up those local stations and turn them into ghost repeaters.

Now there are just survivor stations like WDEV hanging on, for who knows how long. I was in the studio one morning when Squier was interviewing his grandchildren about the new Harry Potter book. Their mother, Squier's daughter Ashley Jane, squeezed into the booth too, and when she started talking it was with the practiced air of a radio pro. She'd grown up in the studio, hosting the Green Mountain Ballroom, a dance program for kids. But she took up religion instead — she's an Episcopal priest in Chicago, and her brother's the soundman for the California band the Smokin' Armadillos. Monthly, Squier said, one or another of the big outfits makes an offer for the station. "The value probably went up another forty percent when the FCC passed the last deregulation." It's a little hard to see how the station will outlast him.

The barriers to entry in the restaurant business are a lot lower than they are in broadcasting — the most important license comes from the local health department. Still, the Farmer's Diner is another difficult example of embracing a certain kind of inefficiency. Since it's always summer somewhere and we know how to fly tomatoes around the planet for next to nothing, why bother seeking out blemished local hydroponic tomatoes to top your burgers in midwinter? Lettuce is a commodity item, and it comes at $18 a box; why bother paying $21 a box simply because the local farmers say that's what they need to make a profit? Murphy took me to Thistle Hill Farm in Pomfret, where they make a stunning Tarentaise cheese; it costs $10 a pound wholesale, however, and it would be a lot easier not to use it in your version of a Ploughman's Lunch. Why bother with ice cream from the small organic herd in nearby Strafford when you know, based on experience, that they're going to run out a few times in the course of the summer and your whole menu is going to be screwed up? It's so much easier just to take it all out of the back of the tractor-trailer and serve it up.

All you get in return for the effort is a story, the story that the food comes from your neighbors, that by eating it you're helping local agriculture. It's possible that the story is worth a buck — people might pay Murphy $6 for a hamburger lunch even though Denny's would serve them the same number of calories for $5 (especially since Murphy's hamburger, from beef raised on the western side of the Green Mountains in Starksboro, is really, really good). It's possible that by cutting out the middleman and using prefab diner buildings and finding investors who think it's a good idea as well as a good scheme, Murphy can make it work.

Look — we live in a world where Wal-Mart and McDonald's, with their unbelievable efficiency, have managed to erode away most of what were once local economies — "Low Prices Always" might as well replace "In God We Trust." So it's a stretch to imagine that a really good hot turkey sandwich might matter — that the pendulum might be poised to swing back the other way. But it's sweet to imagine it too.

JOHN MCPHEE

A Fleet of One

FROM *The New Yorker*

THE LITTLE FOUR WHEELERS live on risk. They endanger themselves. They endangered us. If you're in a big truck, they're around you like gnats. They're at their worst in the on-ramps of limited-access highways, not to mention what they do on horse-and-buggy highways. They do the kissing tailgate. They do passing moves over double yellow lines. They make last-second break-ins from stop signs on feeder roads. The way they are operated suggests insufficiency in, among other things, coordination, depth perception, and rhythm. When I went to bad-driver school, the opening lecturer did not imply any such flaws in his students. He was a real bear. He wore blue-and-yellow trousers and a badge. In a voice he fired like a .45, he began by asking us, "How many of you people think you're good drivers?"

We had all been singled out in four-wheelers. My own car had a tendency to ignore stop signs without previously sensing the presence of bears. It lapsed in other ways as well. After I reached twelve points, I was offered admission to the New Jersey Driver Improvement Program, on the following voluntary basis: enroll or lose your license. Among the twenty-five people in the class, two smart-asses stuck up their hands in positive response to the instructor's question. He looked them over, then swept the room. "Well, you must all be good drivers," he said. "If you weren't, you'd be dead."

Then he darkened the room and rolled a film showing cars hitting cars in on-ramps. A, looking left, accelerates. B, looking left, accelerates. B rear-ends A, because A hesitated, and B was still looking to the left. This primal accident, the figure eight of bad driving, was the base of a graphic montage that ended in high-speed collision and hideous death on the road.

These memories of bad-driver school ran through me in eastern Oregon after Don Ainsworth, at the wheel of his sixty-five-foot chemical tanker, gave some air horn to a step van that was coming fast up an on-ramp on a vector primed for a crash. A step van is a walk-in vehicle of the UPS variety, and, like all other four-wheelers, from Jettas to Jaguars, in Ainsworth's perspective is not a truck. FedEx, Wonder Bread, Soprano Sand and Gravel — they're not trucks, they're four-wheelers, even if they have six wheels. A true truck has eighteen wheels, or more. From Atlanta and Charlotte to North Powder, Oregon, this was the first time that Ainsworth had so much as tapped his air horn. In 3,190 miles I rode with him, he used it four times. He gave it a light, muted blast to thank a woman in a four-wheeler who helped us make a turn in urban traffic close to our destination, and he used it twice in the Yakima Valley, flirting with a woman who was wearing a bikini. She passed us on I-82, and must have pulled over somewhere, because she passed us again on I-90. She waved both times the horn erupted. She was riding in a convertible and her top was down.

If the step van had hit us it would only have been inconvenient, the fact notwithstanding that we were hauling hazmats. The step van weighed about ten thousand pounds and we weighed eighty thousand pounds, minus a few ounces. Ainsworth said he could teach a course called On-Ramp 101. "We get many near-misses from folks who can't time their entry. They give you the finger. Women even give you the finger. Can you believe it?"

I could believe it.

"Four-wheelers will pass us and then pull in real fast and put on their brakes for no apparent reason," he said. "Four-wheelers are not aware of the danger of big trucks. They're not aware of the weight, of how long it takes to bring one to a halt, how quickly their life can be snuffed. If you pull any stunts around the big trucks, you're likely to die. I'm not going to die. You are."

We happened to be approaching Deadman Pass. We were crossing the Blue Mountains — on I-84, the Oregon Trail. He said, "Before you know it, we'll be sitting on top of Cabbage. Then we're going to fall down." He had mentioned Cabbage Hill when we were still in the Great Divide Basin. He mentioned it again in Pocatello.

After crossing into Oregon and drawing closer, he brought it up twice an hour. "It's the terrific hill we fall down before we come to Pendleton. Pretty treacherous. Switchbacks. Speed restricted by weight. You'll see guys all the time with smoke flying out the brakes or even a flameout at the bottom."

From the Carolina piedmont to Hot Lake, Oregon — across the Appalachians, across the Rockies — he had not put his foot on the brake pedal on any descending grade. In harmony with shrewd gear selection, this feat was made possible by Jake Brakes — a product of Jacobs Vehicle Systems, of Bloomfield, Connecticut. Ainsworth called the device "a retarder, generically — you're turning a diesel engine into an air compressor." On a grade we descended in Tennessee, he said, "If you choose your gear right, and your jake's on maxi, you can go down a hill with no brakes. It saves money. It also lengthens my life." Crossing the summit of the Laramie Range and addressing the western side, he geared down from twelfth to eighth and said, "I won't use one ounce of brake pressure. The jake is on maxi." As big trucks flew past us — dry boxes, reefers — he said, "These guys using brakes with improper gear selection don't own the tractor or the trailer. Using brakes costs money, but why would they care?" Ainsworth owns the tractor and the trailer. As he glided onto the Laramie Plains, he went back up to eighteenth gear: "the going-home gear, the smoke hole; when you got into this gear in the old days, your stacks would blow smoke." On a grade at Hot Lake, however, he tried fifteenth gear, and his foot had to graze the pedal. He seemed annoyed with himself, like a professional golfer who had chosen the wrong club.

And now we were about to "fall down Cabbage." In ten miles, we would drop two thousand feet, six of those miles on a 6 percent grade. Through basaltic throughcuts we approached the brink. A sign listed speed limits by weight. If you weighed sixty thousand to sixty-five thousand pounds, your limit was 37 miles an hour. In five-thousand-pound increments, speed limits went down to 26 and 22. Any vehicle weighing seventy-five thousand pounds or more — e.g., this chemical tanker — was to go 18 or under. A huge high view with Pendleton in it suddenly opened up. I had asked Ainsworth what makes a tractor-trailer jackknife. He had said, "You're going downhill. The trailer is going faster than the tractor. The trailer takes over. It's almost impossible to bring yourself out of it.

Brakes won't do anything for you. It's a product of going too fast for the situation. It can happen on a flat highway, but nine times out of ten it's downhill." The escarpment was so steep that the median widened from a few feet to one and a half miles as the northbound and southbound lanes negotiated independent passage. Ainsworth had chosen eighth gear. He said, "Most truckers would consider this way too conservative. That doesn't mean they're bright." Oregon is the only American state in which trucks are speed-restricted by weight. Feet off both pedals, he started the fall down Cabbage praising the truck for "good jake" and himself for "nice gear selection." My ears thickened and popped.

"Six percent is serious," he said. "I've seen some sevens or eights. British Columbia drivers talk about tens and twelves."

In two strategic places among the broad looping switchbacks were escape ramps, also known as arrester beds, where a brakeless runaway truck — its driver "mashing the brake pedal and it feels like a marshmallow" — could leave the road and plow up a very steep incline on soft sandy gravel. In winter, the gravel may not be soft. Ainsworth recalled a trucker in Idaho who hit a frozen ramp. His load, bursting through from behind, removed his head. On Cabbage Hill, deep fresh tracks went up an arrester bed several hundred feet. After trucks use a bed, it has to be regroomed. The state charges grooming fees. Some drivers, brakeless and out of control, stay on the highway and keep on plunging because they don't want to pay the grooming fees. Ainsworth said, "Would you worry about your life or the goddamned grooming fee?"

He was asking the wrong person.

A little later, he said, "Bears will roost at the bottom here."

Fulfilling the prediction, two cars were in ambush in the median where the grade met the plain. Wheat fields filled the plain — endless leagues of wheat, big combines moving through the wheat, houses far out in the wheat concealed within capsules of trees. We passed a couple of dry boxes, both of them Freightliners. Among truckers, they are universally known as Freightshakers. "What's the difference between a Jehovah's Witness and the door on a Freightliner?" Ainsworth said.

I said I didn't happen to know.

He said, "You can close a door on a Jehovah's Witness."

We crossed the Columbia River and went over the Horse Heaven Hills into the Yakima Valley, apples and grapes in the Horse

Heaven Hills, gators in the valley. To avoid a gator he swung far right, over rumble bars along the shoulder. A gator is a strip of tire, dead on the road, nearly always a piece of a recap. "A gator can rip off your fuel-crossover line, punch in your bumper, bomb out a fender."

The Yakima River was deeply incised and ran in white water past vineyards and fruit trees, among windbreaks of Lombardy poplars. Hops were growing on tall poles and dangling like leis. There was so much beauty in the wide valley it could have been in Italy. Now, through high haze, we first saw the Cascades. On our route so far, no mountain range had been nearly as impressive. We had slithered over the Rockies for the most part through broad spaces. Now we were looking at a big distant barrier, white over charcoal green, its highest visible point the stratovolcano Mount Adams. We met three new Kenworths coming east — three connected tractors without trailers. One was hauling the other two, both of which had their front wheels up on the back of the tractor ahead of them. They looked like three dogs humping. It was here that we were first passed by the scant bikini in an open Porsche, here that Ainsworth touched his horn for the second time on the journey. I was marginally jealous that he could look down into that bikini while I, on the passenger side, was served rumble bars in the pavement. I had long since asked him what sorts of things he sees in his aerial view of four-wheelers. "People reading books," he answered. "Women putting on makeup. People committing illicit acts. Exhibitionist women like to show you their treasures. A boyfriend is driving. She drops her top."

We skirted Yakima city. "'Yakima, the Palm Springs of Washington,'" Ainsworth said. "That was written by a guy on laughing gas." He reached for his CB microphone. "Eastbounders, there's a pair of bears waiting for you. They're down there right before the flats." Now ahead of us was a long pull up North Umptanum Ridge. "We're going to give 'em hell," he said. In the left lane, he took the big tanker up to 83, pressing for advantage on the climb. He was in the fast lane to overtake a flatbed hauling fifty thousand pounds of logs. The distance had almost closed; we were practically counting tree rings when the logging truck began to sway. It weaved right and then left and two feet into our lane. Ainsworth said, "Oh, my goodness!"

Ordinarily, I tend to be nervous if I am riding in a car driven by someone else. Like as not, the someone else is Yolanda Whitman, to whom I am married. On trips, we divide the driving time. I make her nervous and she makes me nervous. She was a student in bad-driver school in the same year that I was. While she is at the wheel, I sometimes write letters. I ask the recipients to "excuse my shaky penmanship," and explain that I am "riding in a badly driven car." Coast to coast with Don Ainsworth was as calm an experience as sitting in an armchair watching satellite pictures of Earth. In only three moments did anxiety in any form make a bid for the surface. None had to do with his driving. The first was over the Mississippi River on the bridge to St. Louis — the big arch in the foreground, the water far below — where we seemed to be driving on a high wire with no protection visible beside us, just a void of air and a deep fall to the river. The second was in St. Joseph, where we swung through town on I-229 for a look at the Missouri River, and the narrow roadway, on high stilts, was giddy, a flying causeway convex to the waterfront. Falling down Cabbage Hill, concern for safety hadn't crossed my mind. And now this big logger was bringing up a third and final shot of adrenaline. We got by tightly. The driver was smoking something.

The ridges were dry in that part of Washington — rainfall less than eight inches a year. At elevations under three thousand feet, the ridges were not notably high — certainly not with the Pacific Crest becoming ever more imminent at twelve, thirteen, fourteen thousand feet. We made another long pull, over Manastash Ridge, and drifted down from the brown country into another paradise of irrigation — instant Umbria, just add water. It was a dazzling scene, the green valley of hay, wheat, and poplars; and here the string bikini passed us again, goosed by the air horn and waving. By Cle Elum, we were pulling at the mountains themselves — less than a hundred miles from Seattle and approaching Snoqualmie Pass. Listening to his engine climb, Ainsworth called it "operatic."

Ainsworth thinks his chemical tanker is at least as attractive as anything that could pass it in a car. He is flattered by the admiring glances it draws. He is vain about his truck. That day in particular had started in a preening mode — at a nylon-covered building called Bay Wash of Idaho, next to a beet field west of Boise, where we drew up soon after six and went off to have breakfast before the big doors opened at eight. Ainsworth will not go just anywhere to have his truck's exterior washed. All over the United States and Canada, for example, are washes called Blue Beacon, and they are known among truck drivers as Streakin' Beacon. Ainsworth passes them by. He insists on places that have either reverse-osmosis or deionized rinse water. He knows of three — one in Salt Lake City, one in the Los Angeles Basin, and Bay Wash of Caldwell, Idaho. To the two guys who washed the truck he promised "a significant tip" for a picture-perfect outcome, and he crawled in granny gear through the presoak acids, the presoak alkalis, the high-concentration soap, and warm water under such high pressure that it came through the seams of the windows. "They're hand-brushing the whole critter," he said admiringly a little later. And soon he was getting "the r.o. rinse" he had come for. Ordinary water dries quickly and spottily. This water had been heated and softened, sent through a carbon bed and a sand filter, and then introduced to a membranous machine whose function was distantly analogous to the gaseous diffusion process by which isotopes of uranium are separated. In this case, dissolved minerals and heavy metals failed to get through the semipermeable membranes of the reverse-osmosis generator. Water molecules made it through the membranes and on to rinse the truck, drying spotless. The Army and the Marine Corps use reverse-osmosis generators to go into swamps and make drinkable water. (Deionization is a different process but does the same thing.) Ainsworth paid sixty dollars and tipped fifteen. We were there two hours. "If you go into a Streakin' Beacon, you're going to be out in twenty minutes," he said. "You see the amount of time we fuck around just manicuring the ship? If I were in a big hurry, I wouldn't be doing it. Lord help us." We were scarcely on the interstate rolling when he said, "This is as close as a man will ever know what it feels like to be a really gorgeous woman. People giving us looks, going thumbs-up, et cetera."

This is what raised the thumbs et cetera: a tractor of such dark sapphire that only bright sunlight could bring forth its color, a stainless-steel double-conical trailer perfectly mirroring the world around it. You could part your hair in the side of this truck. The trailer seemed to be an uncomplicated tube until you noticed the fused horizontal cones, each inserted in the other to the hilt in subtle and bilateral symmetry. Ainsworth liked to call it "truly the

Rolls-Royce of tanks," and then he would deliver "Ainsworth's Third Axiom: if your stainless-steel thermos seems expensive, wait till you break three glass ones." The tank looked new. He had hauled it 387,000 miles. It was so cosmetically groomed that its dolly-crank handle was stainless steel, its fire extinguisher chrome-plated — costly touches of an optional nature, not in the Third Axiom. Ainsworth uses tire blackener in the way that some people use lipstick. The dark tractor, still in its first ten thousand miles, had several horizontal bands, red and powder blue. On its roof, its two principal antennas were segmented red, white, and blue. Its bug screen — forward, protecting the nose — was a magnified detail of a flying American flag. His earlier tractors all had similar bug-screen bunting, long before 9/11.

When Ainsworth slides into a truck stop, if there are, say, 210 trucks on the premises he is wary of 209, not to mention others that follow him in. At a Flying J in Oak Grove, Kentucky, he went completely around the big parking lot looking for the space where he was least likely to get clipped. "You're inside the truck stop and you hear your name on the PA," he said. "'Meet So-and-So at the fuel desk.' At the fuel desk is a guy with a sheepish look. Nowadays, they usually don't show up." In Little America, Wyoming, he cir-cled a couple of hundred trucks before parking beside a light pole so only one truck could get near him. He said, "We're fifty percent protected and that's better than one hundred percent vulnerable." He has never been dinged and nothing has ever been stolen from his truck. "'Constant vigilance is the price of freedom,'" he re-marked. "Patrick Henry."

Ainsworth wore T-shirts with the truck's picture on them. Tall and slim — wearing tinted glasses, whitish hair coming out from under the band at the back of his cap — he had pushed sixty about as far as it would go. Only in one respect was he as well dressed as the truck. His boots, fourteen inches high, had been custom-made from the tanned hide of a water buffalo by the bootmaker J. B. Hill of El Paso. Hanging in the sleeper behind him as he drove were boot-shaped leather bags containing other boots, like fly rods in burnished tubes. His caiman boots, he wished to point out, were made from the skins of farm-raised caimans. "Most people think they're either gator or croc. They're not custom-made. They're off the shelf."

"Whose shelf?"

"Cavender's, in Amarillo."

In his boot library, as he calls it, are mule boots, eel boots, ant-eater boots, gator boots, crocodile boots. All these boots are in the Third Axiom, he says. Why? "Because they last forever." His elk and bison low walkers are made by H. S. Trask of Bozeman. Most truck drivers are content with running shoes. Ainsworth is content never to wear them.

I rode with him as "part owner" of the truck. I didn't own even one hub nut, but was primed to tell officials in weigh stations that that's what I was. I never had to. My identity in truck stops was at first another matter. Hatless, in short-sleeved shirts, black pants, and plain leather shoes, I had imagined I would be as nondescript as I always am. But I was met everywhere with puzzled glances. Who is that guy? What's he selling? What's he doing here? It was bad enough out by the fuel pumps, but indoors, in the cafés and restaurants, I felt particularly self-conscious sitting under block-lettered signs that said "Truck Drivers Only."

So, a little desperate and surprisingly inspired, I bought a cap. Not just any cap. I picked one with a bright gold visor, a gold button at the top, a crown of navy blue, an American flag on the left temple, and — on the forehead emblem — a spread-winged eagle over a rising sun and a red and green tractor-trailer and the white letters "America — Spirit of Freedom." On the back, over my cerebellum, was a starred banner in blue, white, red, green, and gold that said "Carnesville, GA Petro." I put on that hat and disappeared. The glances died like flies. I could sit anywhere, from Carnesville to Tacoma. In Candler, North Carolina, while Ainsworth was outside fueling the truck, I sat inside in my freedom hat saying "Biscuits and gravy" to a waitress. She went "Oooooo wheeeee" and I thought my cover wasn't working, but a trucker passing her had slipped his hand between the cheeks of her buttocks, and she did not stop writing.

I would pay for my freedom at the Seattle-Tacoma airport, when — with a one-way ticket bought the previous day — I would arrive to check in for home. Sir, your baggage has been randomly selected for radiation therapy. Please carry it to that far corner of the terminal. My boarding pass was covered with large black letters: "S S S S S." At the gate, I was once again "randomly selected" for a shoes-off, belt-rolled, head-to-toe frisk. I had become a Class 1 hazmat. At home was a letter from Visa dated two days before my return. "Please call 1-800-SUSPECT immediately." Yes? "Please explain the unusual activity: Georgia? Oregon? Petro? Flying J? Kirk's Nebraskaland? Little America? What is your mother's maiden name?"

"Was."

Self-employed, Ainsworth has an agent in North Salt Lake. Ainsworth rarely knows where he will be going, or with what, until a day or two in advance. "I am in a very specialized portion of trucking," he had once told me. "I have chemicals in a tanker. The whole game hinges on tank washings. Without tank washings, tankers would roll loaded one-way, then go back to origin to load again. In the old days, it was all dedicated runs. Now, due to the widespread existence of interior tank washes, we can move around, taking different things."

For example, when I joined the truck, in Bankhead, Georgia, he was hauling a load of concentrated WD-40 east from San Diego. He had called the day before, from Birmingham, to say that he had just learned that after delivering the WD-40 in Gainesville, Georgia, he would be going to the Spartanburg Tank Wash, in South Carolina, then deadheading to Harrisburg, North Carolina, where he would pick up the hazmats for the haul west. We had been corresponding for four years but had never met. I was at Newark Airport two hours after his call.

Before San Diego, he had hauled a surfactant from Salt Lake to New Mexico. He had washed in Phoenix and deadheaded west. To Hill Air Force Base, in Ogden, Utah, he once hauled parts degreaser for F-16s. From Philadelphia to Superior, Wisconsin, he hauled "a secret ingredient" to the company that manufactures Spy Grease. After bouncing to Neenah to wash, he loaded at Appleton a soap used in the making and curing of bricks. It was bound for Dixon, California. He has hauled weed killers, paint thinners, defoaming agents that form a broth in the making of explosives, latex for sandwiching plywood, and dust suppressants that are "kind to horses' hooves." To Fresno he took latex for a dye that turns brown cardboard white. Wood squeezings, or lignin liquor, is used in curing cement. He has carried it from Bellingham to Rancho Cucamonga — northern Washington to southern California. He turns down a job maybe once a year. "I don't want to haul any more cashew-nutshell oil — I believe it harms my barrel," he said. Cashew-nutshell oil arrives in ships from Brazil. "You can't make any friction device — clutches, brake shoes, brake pads — without it. It looks like creosote or asphalt. It's a hard wash. It calls for a stripper."

South of Pocatello, in a brightly greened irrigation valley, we met a Ranger reefer coming the other way. "They're out of Buhl, Idaho," he said. "They raise trout. I took some liquid fish guts up there last year — out of a tuna place in L.A. Harbor." Before the liquid fish guts, his load had been soap. Generally, the separation is distinct between food-grade and chemical tankers. You haul chemicals or you haul food. The vessels are different, the specs are different — mainly in protective devices against the aftermath of rollovers. Ainsworth used to haul wine, orange juice, and chocolate. He mentioned a load of concentrated cranberry juice worth $500,000, a load of chocolate worth $700,000. He said orange juice haulers sometimes carry sizing agents on the return trip (sizing agents control shrinkage in textiles). Very few companies carry both foods and chemicals even in completely separate tankers. Ainsworth remembers a California carrier with a fleet of about twenty trucks who carried paint thinner, washed, and then picked up wine. He said, "Your brother better be F. Lee Bailey if you're going to engage in practices like that."

In Gainesville, north Georgia, less than fifty miles from Atlanta, we arrived at Piedmont Laboratories, Inc., on Old Candler Road, at 7:59 A.M. Piedmont is an independent packer of everything from hair spray and shaving cream to WD-40. "If it's rainy and your car won't start, rip off the distributor cap and spray it in there," Ainsworth said. "The WD means water displacement." A man named Bomba Satterfield came out — brown shirt, brown trousers — and took a sample of our brown liquid. Ainsworth hooked up a Piedmont hose to force out the cargo with compressed air. By nine we were discharging. Ainsworth said, "We're flowin' and a-goin' right now, Bomba. It'll be about an hour." Satterfield disappeared. Ainsworth said, "Got to take a whiz." As he started off in search of a men's room, he said to me, "If the cargo starts to spill or all hell breaks loose, turn that stopcock and pull down the lever of the internal valve." All hell stayed put, to the relief of the part owner.

When the load was gone, air was hissing from a valve at the top of the tanker. "If we let air go into the company's tank it would roil the waters," Ainsworth said, adding helpfully, "That's r-o-i-l." He climbed up the steel ladder on the side of the vessel and began, gingerly, to undog the dome. The dome cover was nearly two feet in diameter and was secured by six dogs. "Bleed before you break," he said. "Air is bleeding. Pressure can kill you if you break early." He said he had "heard of guys being blown off the tops of their trucks and into walls and killed." He had "heard of guys having their heads blown off." Other discharging methods could result in negative pressures no less serious. You could implode the tank. If you worked on railroad tank cars, which are made of carbon steel, you could crush them with implosion and twist them like beer cans. Your head would not come off but you would surely be fired. From the dome, we looked down inside the vessel. It looked almost clean. The heel, or residue, was — as we would learn at the interior wash — scarcely more than one ten-thousandth of the six thousand gallons that had been there.

The Spartanburg Tank Wash charged him less than two hundred dollars. It consisted of four parallel bays in what had recently been country. After three pints of heel went into a bucket, a Texas spinner was lowered through the dome. "They're using ultrahot water — just below steam — and detergent," Ainsworth said. "It's an easy wash." A Texas spinner is a Gamma Jet, directing blasts of water at a hundred pounds of pressure per square inch. The procedure took two hours. "They use steam for caustic, and strippers for supercorrosive solutions," Ainsworth remarked while we waited. "You clean out cement mixers with sugar and water." He had a chemical dictionary in his truck to help tank washers break down any unusual product he might be carrying. "But wash guys usually know. Are you aware that a lot of wash guys get killed every year by nitrogen blankets? Customers sometimes use nitrogen to force a load out of a truck. Then the driver goes to a wash. A wash man goes into the tank. He dies. The driver should have alerted him." Some tank washes that service food vessels are kosher. A rabbi is there, supervising.

Directions supplied by Chemical Specialties, Inc., to 5910 Pharr Mill Road, Harrisburg, North Carolina, were written for vehicles approaching the region from the direction opposite ours. When

Ainsworth is given imperfect directions, he sometimes asks, on arrival at the company office, "How did you get to work?" Often the answer is "I take the bus." Ainsworth: "That's apparent." At Chemical Specialties, he nosed onto a scale that was under a loading rack lined with bulbous vats. Releasing air, locking the brakes, he said, "Okay, we're in the tall cotton." Variously, the tall cotton was zinc nitrate, manganese nitrate, D-Blaze fire-retardant solution, monoethanolamine. Before filling our vessel, a company handler of hazmats rattled off questions while Ainsworth nodded affirmatively: "You got a wash-out slip? Is your outlet closed? Can you take forty-five thousand pounds?" Ainsworth, for his part, had a question he was required to ask the shipper: "Do we have to display placards?" But he knew the answer and he had the four placards — diamond-shaped, bearing the number 8 and the number 1760 and an inky sketch of test tubes spilling. If you dipped your fish in this hazmat, you would lift out its skeleton, but the hazmat at least was not combustible, not flammable, not explosive. The "8" meant "Corrosive." The "1760" stood for monoethanolamine.

We took it in by hose through the dome. As we filled, Ainsworth sat in the cab plotting his way west. Hazmats had to stay off restricted routes and avoid all tunnels except exempted tunnels. With your tire thumper, you did a tire check once every two hours or hundred miles, whichever came sooner. "Any fines that have to do with hazmats you take a large number and multiply it by a grandiose number," he said. "There's a $27,500 maximum fine." A Class 6 hazmat is poison. A Class 9 hazmat with zebra stripes is "as close to harmless as you're going to get." Explosives are Class 1. Even Ainsworth develops wariness in the presence of a Class 1 placard. Seeing one at a truck stop in Cheyenne, he said, "You might not want to park next to him at night." If a placard with a 3 on it is white at the bottom, the load in the truck is combustible. If a placard with a 3 on it is red at the bottom, the load in the truck is flammable. Odd as it may seem, Gilbert and Sullivan did not write the hazmat codes. A flammable substance has a lower flash point than a combustible substance, according to the codes. "Hazmats" may soon be a word of the past. In Canada they are called "Dangerous Goods" and the term may become international. Hard liquor is a Class 3 hazmat. Depending on its proof, it is either combustible or flammable. The Glenlivet is combustible. Beefeater is flammable.

I got out of the truck to look at the hose in the dome. Ainsworth said, "Get back in. We're almost loaded and your weight has to be part of the total." He should not exceed eighty thousand pounds, and the part owner's hundred and fifty would matter. We were, after all, parked on a scale. Drawing on his knowledge of nineteenth-century rifle-sighting, he said, "Kentucky windage and Tennessee elevation is what you are doing if you're not right on a scale."

And moments later Ainsworth said, "He's hammering on my dogs. We're getting ready to get out of here." He backed away from the loading rack, stopped the truck, and went off to sign papers and receive from a laboratory his Certificate of Analysis. As if in a minor earthquake, the truck trembled for minutes after he was gone, its corrosive fluid seiching back and forth. As we began to roll for the Pacific Northwest, he said, "We're weighing 79,720, so we'll have to plug our brains in to see where we're going to fuel."

In this trade, if you were "grossed out" you were flirting with the weight limit. In weigh stations, they could "make you get legal" — keep you right there until you discharged enough cargo not to be overweight. "Grain haulers, they may know a farmer who will take it, but this corrosive stuff is something else," Ainsworth said. His twin saddle tanks, one on either side of the tractor, could hold three hundred gallons, and "a full belly of fuel," at 7 pounds a gallon, would weigh 2,100 pounds. We never had anything like a full belly. Constantly he had to calculate, and cut it fine. With no disrespect for the Chemical Specialties scale, he sought a second opinion, pulling into a Wilco Travel Plaza forty miles up the road, where he came to a stop on a commercial CAT Scale (Certified Automated Truck Scale). While Ainsworth waited, while a truck behind us waited, and while the cashier in the CAT booth waited, the load in the big steel vessel took five minutes to calm down. Ainsworth paid $7.50, got a reading of 79,660, and renewed his fuel calculations. In Candler, North Carolina, at TravelCenters of America, he took on fifty-five gallons of fuel — "just a dab" — and, to pay $75.85, lined up at the truck stop's fuel desk behind a couple of dry-box drivers with lighter loads, who paid $325.63 and $432.22 for their fuel. Always near the intersections of interstates, truck stops have also tended to sprout on the leeward side of weigh stations. Approaching a Flying J just west of Knoxville, he said, "We're going to take on some Mormon motion lotion." He paid Flying J, a company based in Utah, $65.96 for another fifty-five gallons.

Waiting behind trucks at fuel bays, Ainsworth sought to avoid being trapped, because some drivers park at the pumps, go inside, eat, and shower. Farther west, where space expanded, he could show more generosity to the saddle tanks. At the Nebraskaland Truck Stop, in Lexington, he bought a hundred gallons for $135.90. In the bays, there was always a pump on either side of the truck, one for each fuel tank. Truckers call the two pumps the master and the slave. One pump has the rolling numbers, the other is blank. As a general rule, if you take on fifty gallons or more at a truck stop, you get to shower and overnight free.

Many weigh stations have sensors that provide, as you enter, a ballpark assessment of your respect for the law. If a green arrow lights up after you go over the sensor, you bypass all other apparatus and move on. The stations have dynamic scales that you slowly roll across and static scales, on which you stop. The weight on each axle is critical as well as the gross. You obey brightly lettered, progressively stern, electrically lighted signs: "Ahead," "Stop," "Park Bring Papers." Sometimes in weigh stations the IRS is present — there to check the color of fuel. Clear fuel is the only fuel you can legally burn on the highway. Red-dye fuel is maritime fuel, farm fuel, or for use in stationary engines. If you are caught with dyed fuel, the fine starts at a thousand dollars. Ainsworth recalled disdainfully a trucker-negative television piece in which "they only interviewed people in the failure line at scales — outlawish people, running around with no sleep, pinching asses, and going a hundred miles an hour." Park bring papers. In a weigh station east of Boise, we passed a painted wooden sign that said "Leaking Hazardous Materials Next Right." We weren't leaking. We proceeded on.

While the common weight limit for five-axle eighteen-wheelers is eighty thousand pounds, in some states you can carry a greater load if, on more axles, you spread the load out. Near Lincoln, for example, when we met a seven-axled ag hopper, Ainsworth said, "He can gross maybe a hundred thousand pounds. He takes grain from Nebraska to Salt Lake and brings salt back." The more axles you add, the more you can legally carry. In 1979, westbound at Rawlins, Wyoming, Ainsworth, in a reefer hauling pork, came up behind a "Long Load Oversize Load" surrounded by pilot cars, a press car, a spare tractor, a tire truck, mechanics, and bears. A lowboy, it had eighteen axles and 128 tires. From Argonne National Laboratory, southwest of Chicago, to the Stanford Linear Accelerator Center, in Palo Alto, California, it was carrying a super-conducting magnet that weighed 107 tons. At close to half a million pounds gross, this itinerant enterprise was the largest legal load ever to move in the United States, a record that has since been eclipsed. To Don Ainsworth, the magnet was just a magnet. But the truck — the tractor! "It was a Kenworth — olive and glossy — with an olive trailer, a sharp-looking rig."

The most beautiful truck on earth — Don Ainsworth's present sapphire-drawn convexing elongate stainless mirror — gets a smidgen over six miles to the gallon. As its sole owner, he not only counts its calories with respect to its gross weight but with regard to the differing fuel structures of the states it traverses. In western Idaho, we took on fuel at $1.299 a gallon. An hour later, in Oregon, we passed pumps that were selling diesel for $1.199. He said, "It's much better for us to take Idaho fuel than that phony-assed Oregon fuel. It's expensive fuel that looks cheap." The Idaho fuel included all Idaho taxes. The Oregon fuel did not include Oregon's ton-mileage tax, which Oregon collects through driver logs reported to each truck's base-plate state (in Ainsworth's case, Utah). Oregon feints with an attractive price at the pump, but then shoots an uppercut into the ton-mileage. Passing a sign in Oregon that flogged the number 1.199, he said, "You got to add 24.9 to that to get a true price."

In general, he remarked, fuel is cheap on or below I-40, and north of I-40 it's costly. He particularly likes the "fuel structures" of Georgia, South Carolina, Tennessee, Missouri, and Oklahoma. To save a couple of thousand pounds and commensurate money, some hazmat-carrying chemical tankers are made of a fiberglass-re-inforced quarter-inch plywood with balsa core. Ainsworth's aesthetics do not include balsa cores. He would rather be caught dead in running shoes. In Idaho, in a heavy quartering wind on the huge plateau beyond Mountain Home, he could barely get into eighteenth gear and could feel the wind getting into his wallet, running up the cost of fuel. In the Laramie Basin, where we passed a collection of wrecked trucks, he said, "This place is Hatteras for box trailers. Those six wrecks, probably, were blown over in the wind. In terms of hurting your fuel economy, a side wind is every bit as bad as a headwind. The smaller the gap between the back of the cab and the nose of the trailer, the better off you are in terms of fuel economy." In his mind as on his calculator, he paid constant attention to cost efficiencies. The Wyoming speed limit was 75. Driving into a setting sun near Rock Springs, he said, "All day long I've been going seventy in an effort to save fuel." He asked if I knew what heaven is. Heaven is "this month's Playmate in the passenger seat, last month's in the sleeper, and diesel fuel at ten cents a gallon tax paid." Time and again, as we crossed the continent, he said, "I am a businessman whose office is on eighteen wheels. I have a fleet of one."

Most owner-operators own just their tractors. They haul company trailers. In the hazmat-tanker business, Ainsworth knows of only one other driver who owns his whole truck. Insurance is near prohibitive. Per vehicle per accident, the limit of liability for a dry box or a flatbed is $750,000. For a chemical tanker, the limit of liability is $5 million. So why did Ainsworth want to own the whole truck? "First," he answered, "my piece of the pie increases. Second, I maintain her. I know what kind of shape she is in." The "wages" he pays himself are $1.08 times the odometer. But that pie he referred to was filled with more than hours driven. What did he and the truck earn in a typical year? A good year? His responses were strictly elliptical. He would sooner tell you what he paid for his water-buffalo boots, and he was not about to reveal that, either. Instead, he said, "Would we be waltzing around in a brand-new Pete and a virtually new tanker if there was no money in this business? And would my banker back me up? It's good money. It really is."

He said truck drivers make about seventy thousand a year if they are Teamsters, but few are. "Teamsters don't even organize trucking companies anymore. There's no point. Trucking is overpowered by non-union drivers." And companies pay them thirty-five thousand a year. Specialists like auto haulers can make a hundred thousand a year. An owner-operator may gross a hundred thousand, but roughly half is overhead: payments on the tractor, road taxes, insurance, maintenance, and about seventeen thousand dollars' worth of fuel. There are some 350,000 independents on the road, hauling "mostly reefers and flats." And what about the people in local six-wheelers — dump trucks, delivery trucks? "Those guys who drive these little shitboxes around make thirty to forty grand a year. But, as I've said, they're not truck drivers. A truck driver drives an eighteen-wheeler. The skill level to drive those little step vans is like a kid riding a trike."

Don's father, Arthur Ainsworth, was born in Lancashire, and came to Canada, and then to western New York, after the Second World War. He became the editor in chief of *Screw Machine Engineering*, a magazine whose name a hyphen would have improved. In 1952, he gave up journalism and began rebuilding machine tools, specifically the Davenport Automatic Screw Machine. He also bought fifteen acres south of Rochester — a truck farm. "I'm a farm boy," Don says often, and that is where he grew up, one of seven kids, in the "muck empire" around Honeoye Falls, growing celery, sweet corn, onions, and cucumbers, and hauling them to the farmers' market in the city.

He went to Honeoye Falls High School, class of 1960. After four years as a billing clerk for the Mushroom Express trucking company, he joined the Army, and served in the Azores and at the Defense Language Institute in Monterey ("a lot of those people were spooks"). He was a reporter on the base newspaper. Out of the Army, he found a billing-clerk job in California, and in 1971 was married. He has two children. Jeff, who lives in Sioux City, hauls livestock in his own truck. Alisa lives in Newport Beach, California, and is a programmer/analyst.

Divorced in 1975, he has not remarried, but he calls a woman named Jill Jarvis three or four times a week and sees her half a dozen times a year. She lives in Dayton, Ohio. They met in 1989 in the lot at a Union 76 truck stop near Los Banos, California, in the Great Central Valley. She owned her own tractor in the reefer trade, and it had a crumpled fender. He asked what had happened. She said, "Man driver!" She traveled with a very large German shepherd that had flunked out of training for the LAPD. If anything made her uncomfortable in the society of her peers, she would call out, "Here, Fluffy! Come here, Fluffy," and the big shepherd would leap out of her truck.

In 1976, when he was freshly single, Don began to hang around truck stops in the Los Angeles Basin. Thirty-four years old, he was seeking informal training on the road. At a Union 76 in Ontario, near Riverside, he saw a guy changing a headlamp, chatted him up, and learned that he was independent. His name was Tim, and sure, he said, why not? Don could come along. They took a load of lettuce to Iowa, and returned with pork, team driving. Four months later, Don bought Tim's truck — "a 1973 Peterbilt cab-over with a skillet face." With it, he did "endless pork-and-produce loops," and in 1977 bought his own refrigerated trailer. When "the produce market went to hell," he sold his reefer and found a tanker outfit — Silver Springs Transport, Howey-in-the-Hills, Florida — that would teach him the ways of tankers and take him on as an independent contractor. In addition to the orange juice and the chocolate, he hauled liquid chicken feed, lard, and tallow. It was a living, but after a while he was running empty too much of the time, getting too much deadhead. So he switched to chemical transport.

He watches his diet. Ordering dinner from a Waffle House menu in Smyrna, Georgia, he asked for a salad with his T-bone instead of the eggs. In the Kingdom City Petro, Kingdom City, Missouri, he had a big sirloin for breakfast with eggs over easy and toast. We went past Kansas City, up through western Iowa, and had lunch in Nebraska that day. Typically, we had lunch eight hours after breakfast. He described himself as a teetotaler and a nonsmoker all his life. He said "nor'west" for "northwest" and "mile" for "miles" ("It's twenty or thirty mile down the road"). He spoke trucker. A dump truck was a bucket. A moving van was a bedbugger. A motorcycle was a murdercycle, or crotch rocket, driven by a person wearing a skid lid. A speedo was a speeding violation. A civilian was someone not a truck driver. A lollipop was a mile marker. A "surface street" was anything off the interstate. On a horse-and-buggy highway, look for William Least Heat-Moon. He also used words like "paucity" and spoke of his "circadian rhythms." He frequently exclaimed, "Lord help us!" He said "shit" and "fuck" probably no more than you do. He seemed to have been to every jazz festival from Mount Hood to Monterey. He had an innate pedagogical spirit, not always flattering but always warm. Twenty-two miles into Oregon, he explained the time zones of the United States. "There's four time zones with an hour's difference between them," he said. "Spread your four fingers. There's three zones between them." Or, as a Montrealer is said to have said to a Newfoundlander laying sod, "Green side up!"

Each morning, everywhere, he hunted for "the Walleye," often in frustration, because the Walleye tended not to be where his truck could go: "You just don't roll around with hazmat placards looking for the *Wall Street Journal.*" He referred to the *Journal* conservatively as "the best-written paper in the world." In the course of a day that began in central Tennessee and went on through Kentucky and southern Illinois, he found no Walleye until we pulled into a QT in St. Peters, Missouri — "a convenience store on steroids that has grown into an El Cheapo truck stop" — where we parked between the pumps in a fueling bay, left the truck, went inside, bought the *Wall Street Journal,* Xeroxed fifteen pages from *Hazardous Materials Transportation: The Tank Truck Driver's Guide,* bought sandwiches to go, took a whiz, went back to the truck, pumped no fuel, and departed.

"Do you know of a writer named Joan Didion?" he had asked me in North Carolina.

I was too shy to say, "Take the 'of' out."

"She is a powerful writer," he went on. "She was raised in the San Joaquin Valley and now lives in New York City. Do you remember an author — he's dead now, twenty or thirty years; they celebrate him up there in the valley . . . ?" Silent for a mile or two, working on it, he eventually said, "Saroyan. William Saroyan." He had Cormac McCarthy's Border Trilogy in the truck. "It's the third time I've read it," he said, "but it's like *Moby-Dick,* you learn something new every time." Out of the blue, in widely scattered moments, he mentioned other writers, editors. They seemed to come up out of the landscape like cell phone towers. On I-85, George Plimpton: "Is he head of the *Paris Review* today?" On I-40, William Styron: "He really knows his cured ham." *Esquire* materialized on I-640 in Knoxville: "I don't know how you can run a man's magazine if you're a lady." As we crossed the Missouri River for the first time, Heat-Moon rose for the first time, too. Seeing two combines and a related house trailer in Little America, Wyoming, Ainsworth said he had read "a great book, a terrific book" called *Dream Reaper* that described a new machine for harvesting wheat, but he couldn't remember the name of the author.

"Craig Canine."

The ten-acre parking lot behind the Kingdom City Petro, in Missouri, was covered with steel biscuits, by now familiar to me — yellow humps, about a foot in diameter, protruding from the asphalt. "When the Martians land and try to figure things out, the toughest thing is going to be the yellow hump at the truck stop,"

Ainsworth said, but actually any self-respecting extraterrestrial would go straight to a yellow hump and start plugging in jacks to cable TV, the Internet, and the land-line telephone system. After dark, the big parking lots appear to be full of blue fireflies, as drivers lying in their sleepers watch TV. For team drivers, many trucks have in-motion satellite TV. Tractors come with built-in television trays. They're not an option. A truck with no television is about as common as a house without TV in Van Nuys. Ainsworth's TV shelf had boots on it.

Explosives are carried in liquid form in tankers. The more prudent truck stops have designated "safe havens" — Class 1 parking spaces situated, if not in the next county, at least, as Ainsworth put it, "a little away from the rest of the folks who may not want to be there when the thing lights off." Meanwhile, the main parking areas are always decibeled with the idling sounds of diesel engines and refrigeration units. At night in Bankhead, under the full moon, six hundred trucks were idling. It was hot in Georgia but the drivers were cool. Iowa, Oregon, everywhere, the trucks in the truck stops are idling, summer and winter, adjusting personal levels of coolness and warmth. When you are walking in a lot through the throaty sound of hundreds of idling trucks, it is as if you were on the roof of a co-op beside the air conditioner. From the sidewalks at impressive distances, some drivers can hear their own trucks within the chorus, their own cicada reefers.

The concatenation of so many trucks can be intimidating to new, young drivers. Parking spaces are usually designed so that trucks can enter them and exit them moving in the same direction. But not always. Sooner or later, you have to back up, or make some other maneuver that raises the requirements of skill. "In truck stops, you see guys with stage fright," Ainsworth said as we entered the Flying J in Oak Grove, Kentucky. They take their stagefright with them when they leave. Some years ago, a young tractor-trailer driver, new in his job, picked up a load in Minnesota bound for New York City. He got as far as the apron of the George Washington Bridge, where he became so nervous and scared that he stopped the truck, left it there, and headed for a bus station.

Ainsworth's favorite line in truck-stop restaurants is "I see a lot of civilians in here, a very good sign. You see a civilian and the food is good." My own first choice comes off the public-address system like this: "Shower number 275 is now ready." While guys in truck stops are waiting for showers — or just killing time — they sit in the TV rooms and stare. One hour a week they are asked to clear the TV rooms for Sunday religious services. They gripe and yell obscenities. Ministers are provided by Truckstop Ministries, Inc., of Atlanta; Transport for Christ International, of Ephrata, Pennsylvania; Truckers' Christian Chapel Ministries, of Enon, Ohio. Some truck stops have mobile-unit chapels permanently parked in midlot. "Sometimes they take you to a real church, and return you," Ainsworth said. He seldom misses a Sunday service.

He locked the cab wherever he parked. "Dopers are everywhere," he explained. "And they know the value of everything. In truck stops it's not truckers who bother me, it's pimps and whores, people who want to steal, and people who want to sell you Rolex watches with Timex guts." He said of a truck stop in the backcountry of eastern Oregon, "At one time it was a whorehouse with fuel pumps." Generally speaking, though, the seaminess of truck stops is in inverse proportion to their distance from major cities. In fact, you could generally call them wholesome if they're out in the tall corn. He described certain truck stops in the eastern Los Angeles Basin as "dangerous" and said they were full of burglars who would "hit you over the head," pushers, fencers of stolen goods, and hookers known as "sleeper leapers," who go from truck to truck. "The stops have security, but once the sleeper leapers get in there's no getting rid of them. You don't say 'Get lost.' They might hurt your truck. You say, 'I just left Mama. I'm okay.'"

In a bitter ice-cold winter wind at a truck stop on I-80 in South Holland, Illinois, he had seen a hooker going around the lot dressed in only a blouse and a miniskirt. Outside New York City, in his experience, no regional truck stop is less safe than the service area on the New Jersey Turnpike named for Vince Lombardi. His description of it was all but identical to his description of the truck stops of Los Angeles: "The Vince Lombardi plaza is a real dangerous place. Whores. Dope. Guys who'll hit you over the head and rob you. A lot of unsavory people wandering around, and not your brethren in transport." About his brethren in transport, the most unsavory item that Ainsworth pointed out to me was lying beside a curb at the edge of a truck-stop parking lot in Kentucky. It was a plastic quart-size fruit-juice bottle with — apparently — apple juice in it. He said, "That isn't apple juice. It's urine. They generally leave the bottles by the trucks. Other trucks run over them. When you see wet pavement, that isn't rainwater."

You see children playing in the truck-stop parking lots, especially in summer — eight-year-olds in baggy short pants like their parents'. A woman in Little America was walking her dog beside a closed auto hauler with a custom sleeper. A closed auto hauler hauls concealed expensive cars. A custom sleeper is a family home, stretched onto a bobtail. Indiana Custom Trucks, of Lagrange, Indiana, makes kitchen-bedroom-parlors that cost more than the tractors themselves and, of course, have in-motion satellite TV. "People think truck drivers are all evil and mean," Ainsworth said when we were still in North Carolina, and even earlier in our acquaintance he said, "Please do not entertain any stereotypical notions about truck drivers — i.e., that they are tobacco-chewing, ill-educated, waitress-pinching folk raised on red beans and rice and addicted to country music." He is dour about the brethren's obscenities and profanities while talking with one another on CB radio. "A lot of four-wheelers have CBs," he said. "The truckers' language reinforces the stereotype that truck drivers are fourth-grade-educated grease-under-the-fingernails skirt-chasing butt-pinching dumdums. Dodos." Sometimes you look into trucks and see big stuffed animals on the passenger seat. "Lots of real dogs, too. The dog of choice is poodle."

I think it can be said, generally, that truckers are big, amiable, soft-spoken, obese guys. The bellies they carry are in the conversation with hot-air balloons. There are drivers who keep bicycles on their trucks, but they are about as common as owner-operators of stainless-steel chemical tankers. At the Peterbilt shop in O'Fallon, Missouri, we saw a trucker whose neck was completely blue with tattoos. Like many other drivers in the summer heat, he was wearing shorts, running shoes, and white socks. Some still wear bib overalls — the Idaho tuxedo, according to Ainsworth. Sometimes it's the Louisiana tuxedo. Bull racks are trucks that carry cattle. If a bull rack has a possum belly, slung down inches from the pavement, it can variously carry "hogs, sheep, goats, cattle, vicuñas — whatever." Bull-rack drivers, according to Ainsworth, are "all macho guys." In Wyoming, we passed a Freightliner driven by a slight Asian woman in a baseball cap. She wore glasses and her hair was gray. In Oregon, an England company dry box out of Salt Lake overtook and passed us. Ainsworth described the driver as "a lady who looks like a grandmother." Women are now about 5 percent of all truck drivers. "You have to have half-ass mechanical skills," he said modestly. "Women don't have such skills." Quite rare are "single lady drivers" and two-female teams. Man plus woman, however, seems to work out as a team. "For a husband and wife it can be a very simple chore. They have drop trailers at both ends. Dropping and hooking, they can easily do a thousand miles a day." The sun never sets on the languages spoken by American truck drivers.

Drug use is "not rampant" among truckers, he said. "Random drug screening is fairly effective. Preemployment screening, too. If they see you staggering around and your eyes are red, you're going for a for-cause screening — urine test, blood test, et cetera. They test for five things: cocaine, marijuana, angel dust, amphetamines, and heroin. Many times, they'll give you a saliva test, just like a horse, right on the spot." Alcohol? "I don't smell it on guys." As a teetotaler, he is a particularly qualified smeller. Truck stops sell beer, and Ainsworth approves. "Better to have it right there than to be rolling around in your bobtail looking for a liquor store."

Just as the body of a fish tells you how that fish makes a living, the body of a tanker can tell you what it contains. In Ainsworth's words, "The architecture of the tank says what is in it." If a tank has gasoline inside, it has a full-length permanent manway on top, and, seen from the rear, is a recumbent oval. If a truck is a water wagon, the tank — rear view — is rectangular. A perfect circle ambiguously suggests asphalt, milk, or other food. If the vessel is all aluminum and shaped in tiers like nesting cups, it is a food-grade pneumatic hopper full of flour, granulated sugar, and things like that. If stiffeners are exposed — a series of structural rings circling and reinforcing the tank — the vessel is uninsulated, generally operates in a warm climate, and often hauls flammables and combustibles. Ainsworth said, "That is what mine looks like without the designer dress" (the stainless mirror sheath). The double conical side view speaks of chemical hazmats. Since September 11, 2001, all these shapes have scattered more than fish.

"Since 9/11, people see a tanker and they think you've got nitroglycerin in it," Ainsworth said.

Responding to a suggestion that we use a Wal-Mart parking lot while making a visit in Laramie, he said, "There's no way I'm putting these hazmats in a Wal-Mart. People in places like that think the truck is going to explode." In the fall of 2001, near St. Louis, a cop in a weigh station asked what he was carrying. "Latex," said Ainsworth. "Latex is a hazardous commodity," said the cop, but let him go. In a weigh station near Boise with a tankful of phosphoric acid he got the "Park Bring Papers" sign, as did all trucks with hazmat placards after 9/11. Everywhere, though, drivers were being scrutinized even more closely than the contents of their tanks. Drivers quit "because they looked Middle Eastern and were stopped left and right." If not native born, drivers with hazmat endorsements on their licenses became subject to police checks. "At truck stops, you used to be able to drop your trailer and bobtail into town. Now they don't want that. Something may be ticking." Signs have appeared: "No Dropping Trailers." The asphalt pavement at many truck stops used to be laced with dolly slabs. If you wanted to drop your trailer and go off bobtailing, you used a dolly slab or you might regret it. The retractable landing gear that supports the front end of a detached trailer could sink deep into asphalt and screw you into the truck stop for an extended stay. Rectangles just large enough for the landing gear, dolly slabs were made of reinforced concrete.

September 11 did not create in Ainsworth a sensitivity to law enforcement officers that was not already in place. He describes the introduction of photo radar as "another encroachment of our rights." On I-10 once in Florida, a cop pulled him over and tried to put a drug-sniffing dog in his cab. He said, "I'm allergic to dogs." The officer said, "It's okay. We can spray the cab." Slowly, Ainsworth said, "I'm constitutionally allergic to dogs." The bear got the message. The bear, of course, had "run a make" on him — "a cop phrase for plugging me into the NCIC." The National Crime Information Center is a system within the FBI. "A cop stops you, runs an NCIC on your license, your whole history — your hit-and-runs, your DUIs, your drug arrests. He's ready to give you a field sobriety test — walk a straight line, et cetera. Around San Francisco, that's called the Bay Shore Ballet."

"What did the cop find in your record?"

"Zero. There's nothing that exists on me. We don't really believe in interviews with police. It just gums us up. I run a legal ship, and the equipment is well maintained." Ainsworth added that he can afford water-buffalo boots because he obeys the law, keeping the buzzards out of his wallet. Buzzards, a word of broad application, extends from police to the Department of Transportation and the Internal Revenue Service and beyond. In the argot of the road, DOT stands for Death on Truckers.

A female police officer is a sugar bear. A honey bear. A diesel bear is a cop who deals with truckers only. On a surface street in Puyallup, Washington, we happened by a municipal cop parked in his police car. Ainsworth said, "That's a local. That's not a real bear. Truck drivers would say, 'That's not a full-grown bear.'"

It had been well over a decade since he had acquired his last speedo. At one time, he thought "speedos were merely a form of doing business," but he had completely changed his mind. Individual bears have idiosyncratic speed thresholds that range from zero to ten miles above the limit. So Ainsworth sets his cruise control exactly on the speed limit. "Cops are suspicious of everybody," he said as we were starting to roll from Charlotte. "You have to think like a cop." His thinking is assisted by his radio scanner, which homes on the highway bands for state police. In Malheur County, Oregon, he heard a bear on the scanner say that he had a dump truck in Vale and was going to weigh it on a portable scale. "Vital information," Ainsworth said. "It's vital for you to know where the predators are." He bought the scanner mainly to detect "bears in the air." How does he know they're in the air? "You learn cop talk: 'That blue truck in lane number three — we've got him at 82.5.'" On the Pennsylvania Turnpike he once heard an air bear say to five chase cars on the ground: "We're going home early. We've got our work done for today." In other words, a quota had been met. The quota mattered more than a full shift of the cops' contribution to safety. Speedos, evidently, were for them a form of strip-mining more profitable than bituminous coal. On I-15 in Idaho, after we met a four-wheeler getting a speedo on the shoulder from a bear with flashing lights, Ainsworth turned on the scanner. "We want to know everything about cops," he said. "We want to know if that cop is going to turn and come along behind us after signing the ticket." He did.

"On I-90 in Montana it was legal to go any speed until about two

years ago," Ainsworth said. "Guys went a hundred miles an hour.
There were too many wrecks. You'd need a big parachute to stop
this thing at a hundred miles an hour. I wouldn't think of doing a
hundred miles an hour. You're going to Beulah Land."

Backing blindsided at the Peterbilt dealer's in Missouri, he said,
"Sometimes you do this by Zen." He had never been to driver
school. "I'm a farm boy," he explained. "I know how to shift. There
are two things you need to know: how to shift, and how to align
yourself and maintain lane control — exactly how much space is
on each side. In city traffic it's critical." In the open country of western Kentucky, he said, "Out here, you look way ahead. It's the same
as steering a ship. There's a silver car about a mile ahead that I'm
looking at now. When you steer a ship, you don't look at the bow,
you look at the horizon. When I'm in a four-wheeler, I stay away
from trucks, because if a tire blows or an entire wheel set comes off
I'm going to Beulah Land."

Gratuitously, he added, "Atlanta has a lot of wrecks due to aggressive drivers who lack skill. In Los Angeles, there's a comparable
percentage of aggressive drivers, but they have skill. The worst drivers anywhere are in New Jersey. Their life cannot mean a great deal
to them. They take a lot of chances I wouldn't take — just to get to
work on time."

From Harrisburg, North Carolina, to Sumner, Washington, the
load in the tank behind us kicked us like a mule whenever it had a
chance. The jolt — which he called slosh, or slop — came mainly
on surface streets and on-ramps when gears were shifting at low
speeds. On the open road, it happened occasionally when we were
gearing down, mashing on the accelerator, stepping on the brakes,
going downhill, or going uphill. Ainsworth minimized the slosh
with skills analogous to fly casting. "You coordinate shifting with
the shifting of the load," he said. "You wait for the slop or you can
pretzel your drive line." The more ullage, the more slop. The den-
sity of the monoethanolamine had allowed us to take only six thousand gallons in the seven-thousand-gallon tank. The ullage was the
difference was the mule.

We would deliver it to Sumner after a day's layover in the Cascades. We were running twenty-four hours early. For the spectacular plunge in christiania turns down through the mountains from

Snoqualmie Pass, Ainsworth's gear selection was number 14 and his foot never touched the brake. The speed limit for trucks was, of course, restricted, but not by weight, causing Ainsworth to say, "They're not as bright as Oregon." The state of Washington was bright enough, however, to require that a truck stop in that beautiful forest of Engelmann spruce and Douglas fir be invisible from the interstate, right down to the last billboard. About thirty miles uphill from Puget Sound, we turned off I-90 at a nondescript exit, went through a corridor of screening trees, and into the Seattle East Auto Truck Plaza, where a freestanding coffee hut aptly named Cloud Espresso dispensed americano one-shots and mondo latte — truck-driver drinks, strong enough to float a horseshoe. In the lot, at least a hundred trucks were parked and humming. On one flatbed, a guy had a yacht he had hauled from Fort Lauderdale for a Seattle couple who had sailed around the Horn. He was getting ten thousand dollars to take the boat home.

As we began to roll on the second morning, I asked Ainsworth what time it was. He said, "0600 local." Sumner is down near Enumclaw and Spanaway, southeast of Tacoma. On Eighth Street East at 6:50 A.M., we turned into a large, elongate, and already busy lumber mill, where lanes were narrow among high piles of raw logs and stacks of lumber in numerous dimensions, from rough-cut ten-by-tens down. We saw a machine called a C-claw, or grappler (basically a crab's claw with a six-foot spread), go up to an eighteen-wheeler that had just arrived with fifty thousand pounds of fresh wood — forty-foot logs of Emperor fir. As if the huge logs were bundled asparagus, the big claw reached in, grabbed them all, and in one gesture picked up the entire fifty thousand pounds, swung it away from the truck, and set it on the ground.

A man appeared from behind some stacked lumber and shouted, "You guys got chemical?"

"We're not here with his morning orange juice," Ainsworth muttered.

"Did you know you've got a hole in your tank?"

A living riot, this guy. He directed us to "the second dry shed" in the vast labyrinthine yard. It was a cloudless day. From the roof of that dry shed, you could have seen the white imminence of Mount Rainier, twenty-five miles southeast. But we were soon parked under the roof and looking instead at a bomb-shaped horizontal cylinder rouged with rust. This was the destination to which he had hauled the monoethanolamine 2,884 miles. "What is the capacity of the tank?" Ainsworth asked. Answer: "It's big." Eventually, he determined that the receiving tank's capacity was nine thousand gallons. He got out his tire thumper and thumped the tank. "Sounds pretty empty to me," he concluded, and from tubes on his tanker he removed two twenty-foot hoses two inches thick and a ten-foot jumper with double female ends. He hooked them together and forced out the hazmat with compressed air. As the fixing preservative in pressure-treated wood, chromated copper arsenate and ammoniacal copper arsenate were being phased out by the pressure-treated-wood industry. Some people had built their houses entirely of pressure-treated wood, and from the arsenic in the preserving compounds the people were going the way of old lace. Adults had been hospitalized. Children were at particular risk. So arsenic compounds were out now, and we had brought the base of the broth meant to replace them. In an hour, the six thousand gallons were discharged. We climbed to the dome, Ainsworth eased it open, and we looked down into the vessel. There remained what turned out to be a pint and a half of heel. It was a very dark and glistening, evil-looking blue. If blood were blue, it would look like monoethanolamine.

At 0900 local we were back on the road. Ainsworth was headed for a wash in Portland, and then would bounce to Kalama, near Kelso, and take a load of K-Flex 500 to Kansas City, and then bounce to Gastonia, North Carolina, for latex bound for White City, Oregon. From the lumber mill, he took me fourteen miles to the Flying J Travel Plaza, Port of Tacoma Truck Stop, Interstate 5. As he departed, the long steel vessel caroming sunlight was almost too brilliant to look at. I stood on the pavement and watched while the truck swung through the lot and turned, and turned again, and went out of sight. As it did, the Flying J's outdoor public-address system said, "Shower number 636 is now ready."

GEORGE PACKER

Gangsta War

from *The New Yorker*

FROM MY BALCONY on the eighth floor of the Hôtel Ivoire, I could see downtown Abidjan across the lagoon in the mist. Sky-scrapers rose along the waterfront, a blue neon sign blinked "NISSAN," and the plate glass of the commercial banks reflected the silver afternoon light. At this distance, it was easy to pretend that these skyscrapers weren't emptying out; that the African Development Bank hadn't abandoned the city; that the shipping traffic at the port, on which all West Africa depended for an economic pulse, hadn't dropped by 50 percent. From the balcony, it still looked like the glamorous capital of twenty years ago, before de-cline and civil war, when young men and women from all over French-speaking Africa came to Abidjan to seek their future in the city of success.

I was living in a small village in Togo then, two countries east of Ivory Coast; in the evenings, I would listen to the mother of the family in my compound describe the time she had spent in Abidjan as a kind of dream. There was abundant work in Ivory Coast, and foreigners like her were thrilled to find themselves in a truly cos-mopolitan city, one where everyone spoke the same Abidjanaise French. The ambitious students in the village school where I taught knew that, short of Paris, Abidjan was the best place to be. An Afri-can privileged class of bureaucrats and professionals ate in fine res-taurants downtown and kept the nightclubs open till all hours. A robust economy based on coffee and cocoa exports employed sev-eral million African immigrants to do the manual labor and forty thousand French expatriates to run businesses and advise the government. The French, some of them third- or fourth-generation, enjoyed a slightly updated version of the colonial life. In the eighties, a French teenager in Abidjan could celebrate his birthday by racing his moped around town and then jumping off a bridge into the lagoon, to the cheers of an Ivorian crowd. The French who have remained in Abidjan now call that time *la belle époque.*

In Togo, I was a Peace Corps volunteer, living in a village without electricity, and one detail I learned about Abidjan struck me as miraculous. The Hôtel Ivoire, I was told, had a large skating rink with ice that kept a perfectly glazed surface even when the temperature outside topped a hundred degrees. The capital also had world-class golf courses, because President Félix Houphouët-Boigny, the relatively benign dictator who had led Ivory Coast since its nominal independence from France, in 1960, considered the sport to be a mark of civilization. He had turned his home village of Yamoussoukro, 125 miles north of Abidjan, into a grand political capital of wide boulevards lined with street lamps. He built a Catholic basilica there that rises out of the palm forests like a hallucination of St. Peter's, of which it is an actual-size replica. He also erected a vast presidential palace and surrounded it with man-made lakes that were filled with crocodiles. (Houphouët-Boigny, who died in 1993, is buried in a mausoleum near the cathedral.) While the rest of the region was becoming mired in coups and wars and deepening poverty, social scientists talked about the "Ivorian miracle." The country was one of the most prosperous in Africa, and Ivorians weren't killing one another. The residents of Abidjan said that their country was "blessed by the gods."

As soon as I went down to the hotel's lobby, my vision of old Abidjan began to fade. The skating rink, on the grounds behind the hotel, was closed. An artificial lake that once was dotted with paddleboats had been drained because of chronic scum, and blue paint was peeling off its concrete walls. In the restaurant, a Liberian lounge singer was belting out "Yesterday" and the theme from *Fame* for a handful of lonely white mercenaries and West African peacekeepers and their prostitutes; she had the desperate brio of a resort performer in the off-season. I hailed a taxi, and as I sat in back, listening to my driver — who was garrulous with rage, like most men in Abidjan — complain about the traffic, the heat, the economy, the government death squads, and the ongoing civil war, it was hard to believe that the ovens of the Pâtisserie Abidjanaise, across the Charles de Gaulle Bridge, were still disgorging sheets of warm, perfect baguettes. But so they were.

Abidjan valiantly clings to the idea that it remains the refined city it was twenty years ago. The University of Abidjan, once an impressive institution, now decrepit, continues to turn out thousands of graduates every term for government jobs or foreign scholarships that no longer exist. In the nineties, the French began to restrict immigration and opportunities to study abroad, just after a catastrophic drop in commodity prices plunged Ivory Coast, the world's largest cocoa producer, into deep debt. Today Abidjan is populated with educated young men and women who have no outlet for their ambitions. "All the generations until 1985 found work — state work, private work," Ousmane Dembelé, a social geographer at the university, told me. "All goals were satisfied. But after '85, '90, '95, all these generations of youth in Abidjan could find nothing. Nothing."

These days, Abidjan looks less like Paris and more like a decaying Third World city. Residents encounter symptoms of decline on every street, from collapsing infrastructure to violent crime. "It's not Lagos yet," the financial manager of an architecture firm told me. "But we're headed straight there."

The northern part of Ivory Coast is largely Muslim, and poorer than the mostly Christian south, with its cocoa plantations and Abidjan. On September 19, 2002, rebel soldiers from the north mutinied against the government. The civil war has regional, religious, and economic dimensions, but its basic cause is political. The mutiny was a violent reaction to several years of anti-northern and anti-immigrant policies pursued by the series of southern presidents who succeeded Houphouët-Boigny. During the 2000 election, the presidential candidate from the north, a former International Monetary Fund official named Alassane Ouattara, was disqualified on the dubious ground that he was not of Ivorian parentage. The winner, a history professor named Laurent Gbagbo, from the cocoa region, took office amid riots, during which his supporters killed hundreds of Ouattara's primarily Muslim followers. Since the civil war broke out, at least three thousand people have been killed and more than a million have been displaced from their homes. Throughout the conflict, one of the government's favored weapons has been the rhetoric of xenophobia.

The taxi was taking me to a rally of Ivory Coast's Young Patriots, a coterie of young men paid by the government to stir up nationalistic feelings against the rebels, who, soon after starting the civil war, occupied the north of the country. The Young Patriots railed with equal intensity against immigrants, blaming them for the country's soaring unemployment rate.

At the Young Patriots' rally, I wanted to get a glimpse of their leader, Charles Blé Goudé. The drive to the rally took me near the Place de la République, a public square of cracked concrete, where, in late January, Blé Goudé had spoken to tens of thousands, denouncing the French government for failing to rescue Ivory Coast from the rebels. (France, refusing to take sides, had pushed Gbagbo's government to reconcile with the insurgent forces.) The iconography of those demonstrations was remarkable. It was virulently anti-French and desperately pro-American. "U.S.A. WE NEED YOU AGAINST THE 'OLD EUROPE,'" one sign pleaded, just a few days after Donald Rumsfeld coined the term. Blé Goudé waved an American flag and delighted the crowd by refusing to speak French. "Are you ready for English?" he yelled, and the crowd roared as he spoke a few clumsy sentences in the tongue of the superpower, which, in Ivory Coast, is the language of youthful resistance. The January demonstrations had led to anti-French riots, and thousands of French expatriates fled the country while young Ivorians spat on them, attacked their businesses and schools, and tried to block the departure of Air France jets from the airport.

The rally this afternoon was in a slum called Port-Bouët, on a waterfront strip near the airport. My driver got lost in Port-Bouët's labyrinthine streets, which were choked with the blue taxis known as *woro-woro*. About fifteen years ago, the city government of Paris sent Abidjan a fleet of used green-and-white municipal buses, which grew filthy, broke down, and were never replaced or repaired, even as the city's population exploded. The *woro-woro* run local routes to fill in the gaps, but their drivers are notoriously reckless. We passed clogged roads, shantytowns, and entire neighborhoods without decent water, power, or sewage systems.

The taxi turned a corner, and suddenly there were hundreds of people crowding around the perimeter of a dirt rectangle the size of a football field. This was Place Laurent Gbagbo.

Port-Bouët is a government stronghold. High-rise housing projects in advanced states of decay ringed the field, and residents hung out from the windows, their arms dangling beside their laundry. A young MC was warming up the crowd with a call-and-response that always ended in the word *bête,* or "stupid." The rebels who held the northern half of the country were *bête.* The neighboring countries suspected of arming them, Burkina Faso and Liberia, were *bête.* The immigrants in Abidjan with Muslim names, who supposedly sympathized and even conspired with the rebels, were *bête.* And the French, who had failed to defend their Ivorian brothers and sisters in the hour of crisis — the French were more *bête* than anyone.

For all the hostility in the slogans, the crowd was cheerful, like spectators awaiting the main act of a show they'd seen before. Almost everyone in the crowd was young; most of them clearly had nothing better to do. Boy vendors were selling hats in the national colors, orange and green, with the warning "Don't Touch Our Country" and T-shirts declaring "Xenophobe — So What?"

In the front row of a tented seating area were the Young Patriot leaders, local stars in their twenties who were dressed like American hip-hop singers: gold chains, tracksuits, floppy hats. Their scowling bodyguards sat behind them, wearing muscle shirts and mirror glasses; a few were armed with Kalashnikov rifles. Sitting quietly and pathetically in the back rows were the neighborhood elders. In the traditional hierarchy of African villages, the old are elaborately deferred to by the young. Here the elders had no role other than to applaud while the Young Patriots took turns swaggering and jigging out on the speaker's platform and the loudspeakers blasted reggae or *zouglou,* the homegrown pop music of the movement. A favorite anthem, by a *zouglou* group called the Bastards, was "Sacrificed Generation":

> They say students make too much trouble
> They say students go on strike too much
> At the start they took away our scholarships
> They made us pay for rooms and meal tickets
> Students are poor . . .

> When we present our demands
> They answer us with tear gas . . .
> The big brothers are angry
> The old fathers don't want to get out of the way!

Each speaker tried to outdo the last in scabrous wit and extremist views, before boogying back to the tent to touch fists with the others, like an NBA star returning to the bench. At another Young Patriot event, I had heard a heavyset demagogue pronounce the true "axis of evil" to be Liberia, Burkina Faso, and France, and then declare, with malicious irony, "Yeah, I'm Jean-Marie Le Pen!" Meanwhile, at night, immigrants were being hounded from their homes under the pretext that they were supporting the rebels, entire shantytowns had been bulldozed, and the corpses of opposition politicians were turning up at dawn in remote corners of the city. Everyone knew that paramilitary death squads were at work, though no one could prove the rumor that they were directed by the president's wife, Simone, an evangelical Christian with a taste for inflammatory rhetoric against Muslims, immigrants, and whites.

This spring, President Gbagbo, under pressure from France, agreed to include rebel ministers in a new cabinet. In July, the civil war was declared to be over. But late last month rebels started boycotting meetings of the unity government, and threatened to resume the war. This was fine with the leaders of the Young Patriots, who had thrived during the civil war, making regular appearances on television; many had become national celebrities. These young men have no desire to return to the ranks of the eternal students and the jobless street-corner orators.

Blé Goudé arrived very late, in a convoy. "They're coming! They're coming! I see Charles!" the MC informed the crowd. By the time Blé Goudé, his figure lean and tense, made his way with an armed bodyguard to the tent, and then out across the open dirt to the speaker's stand, the moon was rising over Port-Bouët.

Blé Goudé, the son of a peasant from President Gbagbo's region, rose to prominence in the nineties when he became a leader of the national student movement. The group clashed frequently with police during the chaotic years following Houphouët-Boigny's death, and Blé Goudé was sent to prison many times. At the end of that decade, when the student movement split into two factions, the university campus became the scene of a small war. Blé Goudé, whose side won, earned the nickname Machete. (He never received a degree, however, though for years he pretended that he had.) The leader of the losing side was Guillaume Soro, an overweight, soft-spoken student from the north. Soro is now the political leader of a major rebel group, the Patriotic Movement of Ivory Coast. The country's destiny is being shaped by former students who have never held a job.

Blé Goudé took the speaker's platform. He was wearing baggy green army pants, a tank top, an Adidas pullover tied around his waist, and a black baseball cap with the bill turned up — the imitation-gangsta style of the Young Patriots. But he didn't strut; his hungry, liquid eyes and knowing smile projected the self-containment of a leader. As he spoke, darkness fell, and gradually he became a disembodied voice. He didn't shout, unlike the others; his was a deep, calm voice.

Blé Goudé denied press reports that he was getting rich off his leadership of the Young Patriot movement. "They don't understand that some people fight for their beliefs," he said. "They think everyone can be bought. They say my belly is getting bigger." Shrieks of laughter rose from the crowd as he patted his flat stomach. "All this stuff about xenophobia and exclusion is just a cover," he said. "The Ivorian youth is showing the whole world its attachment to democratic principles. I'm not just talking about the Ivory Coast of today. I'm talking about the generation that will rule Ivory Coast. Because the little kids of ten or eight all say France is no good."

Other Young Patriots had been funnier and nastier. But when Blé Goudé finished speaking and the music started up, the crowd swarmed around him. For a moment, he had actually made them feel that the future was theirs.

The Young Patriots represent a new kind of African success story. They're celebrated by many young people in Abidjan for beating and cheating a system gone rancid. With the corrupt "old fathers" refusing to get out of the way, and with all the old channels to success — emigration, foreign study, state employment, family connections — blocked, the new hero is a young trickster with a talent for self-promotion. The model is no longer the formal bureaucratic style of the French colonizer; it's the loud, unrestrained style that everyone in Ivory Coast calls American.

When Blé Goudé drives around Abidjan in his armed two-car convoy — Renault in front, four-by-four behind — he's saluted as "the General of the Youth." According to one well-connected Frenchman I spoke with, the government, at the height of the demonstrations in January, was giving Blé Goudé eighty thousand dollars a week to distribute to his fellow Young Patriots and their crowds of followers. I was told by a Western diplomat that he runs a Mob-style racket in the campus dorms, taking a cut off the illegal lodging of students, who sleep two to a cot or on the floor. Blé Goudé has become a sort of urban warlord.

He hasn't completely grown into his success, however. When I sat down to talk with him over lunch, it was in his mother's under furnished cinder-block house, across a rutted dirt road from a small shantytown. Blé Goudé was wearing gray socks monogrammed with his initials, CBG (a friend had made him ten pairs), and, along with half a dozen hangers-on, he was eating the peasant dish of rice and sauce.

"Our elders deceived us," he told me. "Our predecessors, the political leaders and others, have shown us clearly that our future doesn't matter. That's why I've organized the Ivorian youth. To give it a political arm."

Blé Goudé says he is thirty-one; others claim he is older. In his mother's living room, without the charmer's smile I had seen in Port-Bouët, he looked hard-featured and edgy. He said that he was tired from his work, but he mustered the energy to urge an American intervention in his country along the lines of the Iraq invasion — a request that his followers had presented to an American official outside the United States embassy. Blé Goudé hoped to exploit the Franco-American rift over Iraq, and he explained that Ivory Coast's struggle was the same as America's: for democracy and against terrorism. The rebellion of September 19, 2002, splintered Ivory Coast, and to him the connection with 9/11 was obvious. "There's only eight days' difference," he pointed out.

"And a year."

"And a year. That's all. It's the same thing. Only it wasn't helicopters here, that's all. It wasn't the World Trade Center, that's all. So, *voilà* — the connection."

I asked whether he thought Americans even knew what was going on in Ivory Coast. He didn't respond, but it was clear that the youth of Ivory Coast thought they knew what was going on in America.

"Even if the United States didn't colonize our country, they should come to our assistance," he said. "Ivory Coast is a land to be taken. Above all, the generation today has been educated in the American spirit. The American spirit is freedom. The American spirit is integrity in action." Blé Goudé extended his arm in front of him. "When the U.S. says what they'll do, they do it. They don't say one thing at night and the opposite the next day, like the French." It was just as true, he said, of the American celebrities worshiped in Ivory Coast, like Mike Tyson and Jay-Z. "Boxing has no tricks in it. When someone hits you, he hits you. Basketball — it's all straight up and down. Rap comes out of the ghetto, to convey the suffering of the young people there. When they sing, you listen, and the message comes straight at you."

In the eyes of Blé Goudé and the Young Patriots, Amadou Guindo is the enemy. Guindo, an immigrant's son, lives in Koumassi, another Abidjan slum, separated from Port-Bouët by a land bridge across the lagoon. It smells of oranges and sewage. Because there is a high concentration of northerners and foreigners in Koumassi, the government regards it as a hotbed of rebel sympathy. One morning, a month after the war began, several gendarmes stormed down an alleyway, entered a cinder-block compound where the landlady was washing clothes, and broke down Guindo's door. (He happened to be out.) The landlady convinced the gendarmes that it was a case of mistaken identity, but not before they had rifled through all his belongings.

Guindo, thirty-three years old and unemployed, is known as Cool B, for Cool Boy. On the wall above his bed hung a large American flag; overhead, taped to the low ceiling panels, were posters for B movies like *War Dog* and *The Arrival*. A Richard Wright novel was on his bedside table, next to CDs by Stevie Wonder and R. Kelly. Outdoors, when he cruised the crowded dirt roads of the neighborhood he calls *mon ghetto,* where someone yelled out his name every few yards and the teenage prostitutes approached to flirt and the guys sitting in doorways exchanged fist-to-chest salutations with him, Cool B, his head shaved and his eyes concealed behind a pair of Ray-Bans, carried himself in a manner that he called "the American style." It bore a close resemblance to the style of the young men on the other side of the conflict. Cool B told me that 90 percent of the young people in Abidjan imitate the American style, which he defined as "total independence. Liberty to express yourself. Economic independence, too. A way of talking and walking." And he demonstrated by sauntering up the road with a novel combination of the pimp roll and the keep-on-truckin' stride.

Though he has spent his entire life in Ivory Coast, Cool B is technically a citizen of Mali, to the north, where his father comes from. This is how he acquired Malian citizenship: One night in 1996, Cool B was walking through his ghetto in the company of his German girlfriend, Petra, when a group of policemen approached and demanded his papers. He produced his Ivorian identity card (his father had had him naturalized when he was sixteen), but this only enraged the police. "Amadou Guindo," one of them said, seeing that the name was foreign. "What name is that?"

"It's *my* name."

The police pocketed Cool B's card and told him to come with them to the station. When he asked why, they fell on him and handcuffed him. His white girlfriend's presence seemed to provoke them to ridicule, Cool B recalled. "I said, 'It's because of my name you arrest me, you humiliate me. Okay, you don't have to be Ivorian to be happy in life. Go shit with my card, I don't give a fuck. From now on, I'll keep the nationality of my parents.'" Instead of going to the police station to ask for his card back and suffer more abuse, he took citizenship from the Malian embassy. "I'm proud of it," he said. "I know nothing of Mali. But if I try to get Ivorian nationality they'll humiliate me every time."

Cool B speaks with a slight stutter, and as he told me this story, in the privacy of his sweltering ten-foot-square room, the stutter grew more pronounced, his crossed leg jiggled, and the lines deepened in his face, which, with the Ray-Bans off, looked older than his years. Stripped of the American style, he seemed vulnerable, as if he were trying to ward off disappointment.

In 1996, the same year Cool B became a "foreigner," a new word emerged on the political scene in Abidjan: *ivoirité*. The English equivalent that best captures the word's absurdity might be "Ivoryness." In practice, *ivoirité* meant that immigrants were subjected to harassment and shakedowns and restrictive new laws. Ivorians from the north, who tend to share family names and the Muslim faith with immigrants from Mali, Guinea, and Burkina Faso, came in for similar treatment. If a single word can be said to have started a war, *ivoirité* started Ivory Coast's.

Cool B's father worked as a nurse in Abidjan for thirty years before retiring and returning to Mali in 1991. Cool B didn't go beyond high school — instead, he pursued an early career in what he calls *voyousie,* or the hoodlum life. The scale of his activities was small, but he made it a habit to insult pretty much everyone who crossed his path. "The troublemaker doesn't know why he makes trouble," he said. "He's just proud of himself. He has a certain pride." One day in 1990, when Cool B was in high school, a Frenchman came to his drawing class and asked the students to do illustrations showing the proper use of condoms. Cool B found the assignment foolish, and at the end of the class he stood in the doorway to block the Frenchman's exit.

"You're going around the world showing people pictures of how to use condoms?" Cool B asked mockingly. "I'll show you what to do." He snatched away the man's prospectus and, reading from the text, improvised an anti-AIDS rap on the spot in the manner of LL Cool J.

The Frenchman was impressed. Within a couple of days, he had arranged for Cool B to record the rap at a downtown nightclub, and the song made him a momentary celebrity among Abidjan youth. It also began his long association with white people — among them Petra, his girlfriend, who eventually went back to Germany, and Eliane de Latour, a French filmmaker who employed him for a while as a researcher on a feature about Abidjan youth. Cool B keeps pictures of them on his wall, and he tries to figure out why, in spite of these connections, he remains stuck in Koumassi. He spends his ample free time and his limited funds at a local Internet café, surfing international dating sites and chat rooms where people he knows have found marriage opportunities that got them out of Africa. Or he visits a green-card lottery Web site. His ambition, short of leaving Africa, is to open his own Internet café.

"I don't understand my situation," he said. "I'm still blocked. I want to get out of my problems one day. I don't have the totality of independence." Cool B's residence permit expired last year, making him an illegal alien in the only country in which he has ever lived.

When the room grew too hot for us to stay inside, even with a fan blowing, we went around the corner to pay a visit to Cool B's gang. A dozen young men were seated on facing benches under a ramshackle tin roof; they spent twelve hours a day there, like a conclave of village elders, except that Cool B was the oldest person in the group. The others regarded him with respect and sought his advice. They were all immigrants or northerners, keeping an eye out for the police. They wore gold chains, tank tops, and Nike caps. When I asked what kind of work they did, most of them replied, "Tent rental," which began to seem like a euphemism for unemployment, though some of them had part-time work fencing stolen goods.

At noon, a communal basin of rice and sauce appeared, and the young men plunged their right hands into it. The gang argot of Abidjan, which combines French, profane English, and the language of Ivory Coast's north, is called Nushi, or "mustache," a reference to the way bad guys look in Hollywood movies. The inferior type of rice that Cool B and his friends had to eat is derisively referred to in Nushi as *deni kasha,* or "lots of children." The young men all came from poor and enormous polygamous families in which there were as many as thirty-five siblings. "That's what spoiled our future," a surly fellow with a shaved head told me. "When our parents worked, they didn't think of us first. In Europe, they set up an account to help the kids when they grow up, right?"

This was the story they all told: fathers who did nothing for their sons, extended families that might have made sense in a rural village but crushed the life out of them here in the city. Cool B's closest friend in the group was a rangy twenty-five-year-old, wearing wire-rim glasses, who introduced himself as McKenzie. He'd taken the name from a character in an action movie. Growing up in a northern town called Odienné, McKenzie (whose real name is Morifère Bamba) used to watch American westerns on a communal TV. John Wayne made a particularly strong impression. These movies lit a desire to live in his "dream country," which remains McKenzie's sole ambition.

At twelve, he quit school — his mother was dead, his father too poor to support him — and the next year, 1990, he came alone to

Abidjan. I asked how he had imagined the city then. "It was the city of success," McKenzie said. "The city that would give me the ability to realize my dream." Abidjan was a way station on his escape route to America. This, I thought, was the difference between Cool B's gang and the Young Patriots: they all copied the American style, but the Young Patriots had found a way to make it work for them in Abidjan.

After a few years in the city of success, McKenzie realized that he was entirely alone. "Succeed how?" he said. "You have to have lots of connections and acquaintances. Guys go into banditry to realize their success." McKenzie joined a gang, began smoking cocaine, fought, stole, and saw a friend die at the hands of the police. Movies like *Menace II Society*, which seemed to glamorize the gangster life, finally convinced him that it was a dead end. McKenzie left the gang and learned the electrician's trade, at which he worked irregularly, trying to save money for the trip to America, until the war started and jobs disappeared altogether.

The war was out there somewhere. In Abidjan, a ten o'clock curfew enforced by gendarmes at roadblocks had shut down night life, but the city was no longer a conflict zone. It was hard to believe that a couple of hundred miles away, in the interior, teenage militias were machine-gunning children and cutting old men's throats. Like so many African wars, Ivory Coast's had degenerated into looting and massacres by bands of loosely controlled, generally underage fighters; it became part of a larger conflict that had been spreading through the region for years — ever since the outbreak of Liberia's civil war in 1989 — producing hundreds of thousands of corpses and millions of refugees.

Seen from a distance, Africa's man-made disasters look senseless. But to the participants, who tend to be young and poor, these wars have meaning. The war in Ivory Coast began as a struggle over identity — over the question that haunted Cool B, the question of who gets to be considered Ivorian. The country's decline made identity a political issue, but it also extends to the larger, almost existential question of what it means to be a young African living in the modern world.

After a week in Abidjan, I drove north to Bouaké, Ivory Coast's second-largest city and the main rebel command center. Behind the ceasefire line patrolled by French and West African peacekeeping troops, the town hadn't seen fighting in months. At rebel headquarters, in a former nursing school, a polite, bored young official was doing a Yahoo search for Uzis and grenades. Out on the half-empty streets, every civilian vehicle had been commandeered, license plates had been removed, doors had been ripped off, and young rebels had painted the sides of the vehicles with Spider-Man logos and self-styled unit names: Delta Force, Highway of Death. Without a war to fight, they were turning into gangsters.

At the hospital, the staff of Doctors Without Borders reported that the most serious injuries were sustained by the young rebels who routinely smashed up cars or accidentally shot themselves in the foot. One night while I was in Bouaké, a notoriously violent young commander named Wattao threw himself a lavish birthday party, with a fawning MC, cameramen, hundreds of guests who watched themselves live on video screens, and gatecrashers who ended up exchanging gunfire.

The rebel military leadership, which had maintained fairly good discipline since the outbreak of hostilities, was turning to a local priest called Abbé Moïse to rehabilitate the restless underage recruits. "They haven't killed a lot," the Abbé told me. "They're recoverable here. The children of Bouaké aren't as traumatized as those in the west."

That was where the real war was taking place. In November 2002, two new rebel groups had suddenly appeared near the Liberian border. The western groups claimed an alliance with the northern rebels, but they had no clear political motivation, and their rebellion quickly took on the violent, anarchic quality of Liberia's and Sierra Leone's civil wars. In fact, some experts have concluded that the western rebellion was the inspiration of Liberia's president, Charles Taylor, who has had a hand in all the region's murderous and intertwined wars, organizing and arming rebels in Sierra Leone and Guinea as well as terrorizing his own country for a decade and a half, until his forced departure this past August. Although Taylor is out of power, the widespread instability he fomented won't dissipate in West Africa anytime soon. The region is now populated with young fighters who float from country to country, looking for war.

The conflict in the west was a catastrophe. Both the rebels

and the government were recruiting Liberian mercenaries to do their fighting. The Ivory Coast government also used MI-24 helicopter gunships with Eastern European or South African mercenary crews; the rebels used the feared Sierra Leonean warlord Sam (Mosquito) Bockarie and his battle-hardened teenage fighters. (Bockarie was killed in Liberia in early May, most likely on the orders of Taylor, against whom he might have testified at the war crimes court in Sierra Leone, which had indicted him in March.) Hundreds of civilians were being slaughtered in western Ivory Coast, and entire villages had been looted and left empty. It was in the west that the "Ivorian miracle" met its final demise and Ivory Coast became just another West African nightmare.

Before the civil war broke out, the journey from Bouaké to Man, the biggest town in the west, took eight or nine hours. It took me two days, because I had to pass through at least fifty roadblocks. In some places, there was a roadblock every quarter mile. They were makeshift affairs: a tree limb, pieces of junked machinery, concrete blocks. The boys on guard roused themselves from the shade of a tree. When they noticed a white face in the car, they put on angry expressions and went back to grab their AK-47s. Glowering behind sunglasses, they stalked over to the car, fingers on triggers. Around their necks hung leather thongs with polished wooden or stone amulets, which they believed made them bulletproof. Carved fetish figurines stood guard alongside the roadblock. The boys ordered me to open the trunk, they pretended to search inside, they demanded to see my travel permit. A standoff: everything was in order, but they hadn't given the signal to go, and they had the guns. This last detail made all the difference, yet I found it hard to accept the obvious power relation. Most of them looked the age of the middle school village boys I had taught twenty years ago in Togo. Those boys had called me Monsieur and left presents of papaya at my door. It was as if I had come back to the region to find all my students armed and snarling, ordering me to get out of the car.

I tried to talk my way through the roadblocks in the old jokey Peace Corps way. And it usually worked: the boys' faces softened, the barked orders turned into requests for cigarettes or money or aspirin, which were only half serious and then even a bit sheepish, and, as the car started rolling forward, we exchanged a thumbs-up, and a boy began giving me breezy compliments — "If you Americans were here, we'd already be in Abidjan!" — as if the guns had just been props and everything were friendly between us.

The farther west I drove — past the ripe anacard-fruit trees that no one was tending and the storehouses of cotton that couldn't be sold and the carcasses of vehicles that the rebels had wrecked and abandoned — the less useful my Peace Corps skills became. In Man itself, picturesquely nestled in a ring of steep green mountains with waterfalls, the boys at the roadblocks, drunk or high, muttered about stealing the car. Pickup trucks bristling with Liberians carrying rocket-propelled grenade launchers slalomed wildly through the rebel army's obstacle courses. The walls of government buildings were bullet-riddled, and the freshly turned mass graves gave off a sharp smell. It was hard to tell who was in charge of Man — the rebel commanders or their underage Ivorian and Liberian recruits, who, according to townspeople, were becoming indistinguishable.

In the middle of town, the young rebels hung out at a *maquis,* or open-air eatery, called the Tirbo, which smelled of porcupine stew. The youngest I saw, toting his AK-47, was no more than nine. I ordered a plate of rice and looked around. A boy with a red checked kaffiyeh on his head was staring straight ahead, filled with some private rage. Draped around the necks of other boys were leather clubs or sheathed knives or bandoliers. There was no one over thirty in sight.

At midday, a group of four Liberians arrived and sat down at a table. The young men, who propped their weapons between their legs, began making their way through a bottle of Mangoustan's rum. Their names were Sha, Shala, Johnson, and Romeo. Shala wore an American-flag bandanna, Rambo style. Sha, the most intoxicated of the group, lifted his shirt to show me his wounds.

I asked how much he was paid for his services to the rebels.

"The cause is much more important than pay," Sha said. "I don't appreciate pay."

What was the cause?

"Peace and unity in Africa," he said.

After the war, Sha said, he wanted to go to New York and become an American marine and learn to fly helicopters and use heavy weapons. "I love America," he slurred, making an effort to lean for-

ward. "America is my culture." He waved his glass at the others. "All
of them love America."

Romeo's glass fell to the floor and shattered. He stared at the
fragments without moving. Johnson told the waitress that they would
pay for it. Romeo slouched, sunk in a dark mood.

A few months earlier, a recruiter had come to a refugee camp
along the Liberian border and persuaded Romeo to join the rebels. There was no better offer on the horizon. "I want something
because I don't want to be suffering, I don't have nowhere to go,"
he said. "Someone say, 'Take money, go to war. You will not go
there? You will go.'" He turned his dead-eyed stare on me. "If you
can't pay the young stuff, the war will go all over the world. The war
will enter America — let me tell you today. Because you don't give
them money. The man we want to see is bin Laden. We want to see
him, to join him. Because he can pay revolutionaries. You think you
can get pay for this?" Romeo held up his left calf to show me a bullet wound. "You can't. Bin Laden can pay it."

I had seen bin Laden's face painted on the side of a rebel vehicle. Some fighters wore T-shirts with bin Laden's face and Bush's
face side by side. In this part of the world, there was no ideological
contradiction. Both men stood for power.

At a hospital in a town not far from Man, an Italian doctor
named Albert Brizio described the imagery of this war as "a per-
verse effect of globalization," adding, "It's what I call the Liber-
ianization of war." Brizio had seen the effect in other African countries: young fighters styling themselves after performances, often
brutal ones, that they'd seen on TV or in movies. "It allows people
to see events or situations they would never have thought of, and
they imitate them. These situations have always been contagious,
but then you had contagion by contact. Now you have contagion by
media."

But contagion by media can go in both directions, as I discovered when I met a young woman in Man named Jeanette Badouel.
She was moving around town in the company of rebels, but, unlike
the handful of girl recruits in their ranks, she carried herself with
an air of blithe authority and pop stylishness. Jeanette was impossible to miss, decked out in sparkly gold jeans labeled "Pussy" and
rolled to the calf, six-inch platform shoes, and a pink frilly blouse;
her hair was dyed blond and done in short braids. She shopped for

her Liberian-made American-style T-shirts and shoes at Saturday markets along the border, which was one of the most dangerous places on earth. She was born in a village twenty miles south of Man but had been living with her French husband and their children in Rennes, where she directed a nonprofit group called Association Métissage, whose Web site says that it "realizes projects favoring cultural diversity and solidarity among peoples." When the western rebellion broke out, just as Jeanette was visiting her parents in Man, she refused the French government's offer of evacuation and decided to set up a rebel television station, using the digital equipment she happened to have brought. Though she claimed to operate free of political interference, it was clear that TV Grand Ouest served up pro-rebel propaganda to the region, if anyone was watching.

I sat in the station's bug-filled studio with Jeanette and watched programming. There was a traditional dance, performed to express villagers' happiness with rebel rule, the voice-over explained. There were Eddie Murphy movies. And there was footage of the aftermath of a recent massacre by government and Liberian forces — the hacked and bullet-ridden bodies of peasants lying in houses and on roads just south of Man — with Jeanette conducting breathless interviews.

I had trouble figuring Jeanette out. She loved fashion and reading *Paris Match,* yet rebel-held Man seemed to suit her fine. The rebellion looked to her like a wonderful example of cultural diversity and solidarity among peoples. It was almost like America. "For me, it's democracy," she gushed. "Everyone is here — the Liberians are everywhere. You'll see a lot on the way to the border. Guineans, Malians. For me, it's the people."

Twenty years ago, V. S. Naipaul published an essay in this magazine called "The Crocodiles of Yamoussoukro," an account of life in Ivory Coast at the height of the "miracle" under Houphouët-Boigny. Toward the end of the piece, Naipaul has a dream: the bridge on which he is standing starts to melt away. The concrete and steel of Abidjan turn out to be perishable. "The new world existed in the minds of other men," he writes. "Remove those men, and their ideas — which, after all, had no finality — would disappear."

Naipaul's prophecy that Ivory Coast would slip back into a primordial past seemed comforting compared with the new reality that was taking hold. Cool B and his gang, and the Young Patriots, and the rebels in the north and the west are severed irrevocably from the traditional sources of meaning — the village, the elders, the extended family — that I found in West Africa two decades ago. Their heroes are American celebrities, local warlords, gangsters, and demagogues. In the cities and the ragtag armies, they live in a society consisting of only the young. Tempted and tormented by images and words from elsewhere, trapped in a money economy with nothing to sell, they have no ready way of realizing their desires. But they can't go back. To some hardheaded observers in the West, they are "loose molecules," mindless forces of anarchy or a new primitivism. In fact, the opposite is true: the struggle in Ivory Coast, and perhaps in other parts of Africa, is recognizable as the unlovely effort of individuals to find an identity and a place in a world that has no use for them.

In Abidjan, I spoke with Ruth Marshall-Fratani, a researcher with the French journal *Politique Africaine.* "The gap between aspirations and possibilities — I think that gap has widened incredibly in the last fifteen years," she said. "Access to global images has increased it amazingly." The phrase she borrowed to describe the situation of the young Africans I had met was *lèche-vitrines* — window-licking. "It isn't window-shopping," she explained. "That means you can go in and buy. This is just licking the window. And, basically, that's this generation's experience." She went on, "Everybody wants to get a part of the action. They have these aspirations and they're not prepared to give them up. Politics is one way. Religion is another. And war is another."

On one of my last days in Ivory Coast, I went back to Koumassi to see Cool B. He wanted to introduce me to two young men he knew. Madness and Yul, twenty-six and twenty-three, had both done time in prison and had the razor scars to prove it. Madness, whose real name is Mohamed Bamba, had been on the street since the age of twelve, working as a petty thief and drug dealer. His eyelids were heavy and his voice slow from years of smoking heroin. Yul, born Issouf Traore, hustled stolen pharmaceuticals. Both of them were trying to go straight as barkers at a *woro-woro* station, snagging passengers for local runs. Cool B, Madness, Yul, and I sat in a *maquis* and drank Guinness. Madness was stoic; Yul, whose nickname came from his shaved head, grew frantic as he talked. It was the same story I'd heard from the others — a father who hadn't taken care of him. "He told me, 'If you come back here I'll put you in prison again.' I said, 'You're my father, you put me in the world.'" What agitated Yul to distraction was the fact that his father had gone back to Mali and died and been buried before they could reconcile. "He died when it still wasn't okay with us. He spoke to me, but I don't know what was at the bottom of his heart."

From his trouser pocket Yul withdrew a piece of folded officialdom. It wasn't proof of citizenship — his father had failed to naturalize him. Nor did Yul have Malian papers. But when his girlfriend gave birth, Yul, who never attended school, needed to establish himself as the legal father. He bribed the police to give him a document stating, falsely, that he had lost his identity card. The document was called a "Certificate of Declaration of Loss." It wasn't sufficient to confer his last name on his son, but it was the sum of Yul's identity in Ivory Coast.

"A man has to have a father at his side to help him. If he doesn't —" Yul stared at me a bit wildly, his toothy mouth open. "Who's going to help me? Who? I don't see."

Madness said calmly, "If you talk to a thousand youths, there isn't one who will tell you it's going okay for him."

I asked Madness and Yul what they imagined Americans thought of them.

"They've forgotten us," Yul said.

"They don't know what we're living here in Africa," Madness said. "Africa is misery. Africa — really — it's hard, hard, hard. People of goodwill are interested in us. But there are others, with means, who aren't interested at all. Because Africa — it's a continent of hell."

ELIZABETH RUBIN

The Road to Herat

FROM *The Atlantic Monthly*

SAMI HAD DISAPPEARED. We were planning to head out of Kabul that morning on a road journey to Herat, in western Afghanistan. Sami was to be my guide, and I couldn't find him anywhere. I'd traveled with him in late autumn of 2001, when Kandahar fell, and though he was an unpredictable character — a thirty-four-year-old manic-depressive Pashtun poet and former Taliban intelligence man — his predictions on Afghan affairs had always been flawless.

It was the summer of 2002. Kabul was often swathed in dust storms and rains in the same afternoon. The long-awaited *loya jirga*, which elected Hamid Karzai as Afghanistan's leader, had ended in dissatisfaction for many, but relief for most that under the great white tent, more than 1,500 Afghans from around the country, including the warlords, had assembled and talked and shouted for ten days, and no one had been killed.

Sami, however, had come a few days earlier from his home in Kandahar and said that things were not all right. The Pashtun tribes were angry. Discontent and plots of sabotage were brewing down south. As he put it, "They're saying Karzai is a motherfucker and a U.S. spy."

On our trip we planned to find out about these plots and about how volatile the Pashtun discontent really was. Herat lies due west of Kabul, near the border with Iran, and the only passable road there from Kabul dips south in a 650-mile arc through the southern Pashtun belt. I was bringing along Habib, a thirty-one-year-old human rights researcher, who I hoped would defuse the unexploded ordnance that was Sami. Habib was half Baluch, half

Hazara, and a secular humanist — ethnically, politically, temperamentally, and philosophically the polar opposite of Sami. If Sami was the Confederate, Habib was the Yank.

Habib would be translating for me and collecting data on the civilian casualties of U.S. bombing and on political repression in Herat, where Ismael Khan, a powerful warlord, had appointed himself the city's emir. For Sami, however, our most important goal was to meet his latest national hero, Amanullah Khan, an old rival of Ismael Khan's, whose turf lay south of Herat. Sami painted an image of him out of *Arabian Nights* — the isolated warrior in his mountain redoubt, leading his horse-mounted brigade into battle against enemy Iranian invaders. And there may have been a morsel of truth in it: Ismael Khan, who had been allied with the Northern Alliance, was now not only rebuffing the central government but under the influence of the Iranian Revolutionary Guards; Amanullah Khan, a Pashtun, was under the wing of Gul Agha Sherzai, America's favored warlord down south.

Habib entered my hotel room with bad news: "The security agents took Sami." Before I could set off after Sami and the agents, Habib politely suggested that I stay put and not make matters worse. We looked over the balcony helplessly, imagining Sami's terror — because he had a lot to hide. As he often said wistfully about his Taliban past, "I was very dangerous."

Sami had joined the Taliban in their early days, in 1994, when they were Islamic guardian angels spreading peace and the end of warlord rule. As a lifelong devotee of the former king, Zahir Shah, Sami, like many other Pashtuns, had believed that the Taliban would finally end Zahir Shah's exile in Rome. The Taliban extinguished that hope as soon as they seized Kabul, but Sami stuck with them. He was educated, and thus rose fast in the ranks of the semiliterate Talibs, soon becoming a director of investigations in Kabul, where he had responsibility for six thousand prisoners, many of them from the Northern Alliance — the same sort of men who had ambushed him at my hotel. His power lasted only eight months before the Taliban higher-ups turned their fickle favor away from him, accused him of plotting a coup and supporting the "infidel" Zahir Shah, and threw him into solitary confinement, in the same chambers where he himself had interrogated many a prisoner. He escaped execution when a Taliban friend intervened, and then fled to Pakistan, where for a time he survived by selling his thirty Kalashnikovs for $200 apiece and by selling carpets.

Since then he's assumed a variety of aliases, but to me he always said, "Just call me Sami." He had just enough education to turn Western culture into scrambled oddities. "Do you all have credit cards that say whether you have HIV?" he once asked me. He was an ethnographer's dream, and his brain was a databank on nearly every Afghan who'd ever touched politics or guns. He knew where many of the old Taliban gang were and what they were doing. He knew, he said, that sixty members of Al Qaeda — from Uzbekistan, Chechnya, and other places they couldn't return to — were hiding in a gorge in the north. He knew about plots to rally the Taliban around Gulbuddin Hekmatyar, a Pashtun career warlord. And he knew how to play dumb, as I learned when he finally showed up at my hotel room, shaking. "I will slaughter a sheep," he said, whipping his shawl around the room, "as soon as we're out of this fucking Kabul." It turned out that the intelligence mafia who controlled my hotel were in a fury that I'd rejected their car and driver. So when they saw Sami, who they knew was with me, they rerouted him into a back room to investigate why. Putting on his naïve and humble act, he told them, "Because she's crazy."

Late that afternoon Sami rounded up a driver and a Toyota Corolla with jammed rear windows and no air conditioning (it was above 100° most days), and we set off as the waning sun brushed Kabul's parched hills with amber and gold. Soon we were moving through the fertile green pastures of Maidanshar, a valley known as the gateway to Kabul — partly because it's only fifteen miles south of the capital, and thus within artillery range.

The valley was home turf for Sami, where he'd found his wife, and he was back in his element. He pointed to a mountain peak that he'd occupied with Taliban forces just before they swept into Kabul in 1996. He cursed the little mosques that spring up like Mc-Donald's arches on the interstate, erected by the Al-Rashid Trust, a charity of "the motherfucker Pakistanis who occupied our Afghanistan." He told us about an old blue-domed shrine we saw in the distance, where infertile or unhappy women go to expel the devil spirits. "She goes mad, shouts, screams, lather comes from her mouth, and with hypnosis the mullah can cure the madwoman," he said. "Or just get her pregnant."

Some sixty miles from Kabul, Sami directed us off the main road and through the desert hills. Our feeble headlights were the only signs of life in the darkness. After two hours of bumping and twisting, we saw a faint light appear and then resolve into an oil lamp, a checkpoint, a squat mud-walled shop, and a boy with a Kalashnikov. Life. We had entered Governor Ruhani Nangialai Wardak's territory. A guide squished into our car and led us to the governor's isolated compound.

In Afghanistan a stranger rolling up unannounced in the night is almost always guaranteed the hospitality of the desert. Dinner, cushions, and blankets were all delivered by one of Ruhani's men. That night we all slept together in Ruhani's communal room, which had bookcases stuffed with books of Islamic law, Persian poetry, and a surprising collection (for a Pashtun commander) of French and English paperbacks — Françoise Sagan's *Un Certain Sourire*, Antonin Artaud's *Voyage to America*, and even *Lolita*.

The next morning Ruhani arrived for breakfast to greet us. He was a tall, thin man with a regal yet modest bearing. A supporter of Zahir Shah, Ruhani spoke English and had traveled to the United States three times during Taliban days to encourage U.S.-Afghan relations. He must have been thrilled to have company. He drove us up through a gorge, past emerald waters, to a high mountain range, where in Russian times he'd hidden an explosives laboratory, and where Bernard Kouchner, a founder of Doctors Without Borders, had hidden a field hospital for the mujahideen. But all day, no matter what the story, Ruhani kept returning to one theme — America. He couldn't understand us.

These loathed old warlords and fundamentalists making trouble everywhere, for example. Why were we supporting them — again? In the eyes of many Afghans, America had created the mujahideen to keep the Communists from the warm sea, had bankrolled their return to fight Osama, and had then allowed them to be sanctified under the great white tent of democracy.

And why did we pull this trick — pushing for the return of Zahir Shah, only to render him powerless? Here was the heart of the matter for many Pashtuns, whose royal dynasty, the Durrani, founded the Afghan kingdom in 1747 and reigned until 1978. The Pashtuns, who make up about 40 percent of the population, still regard themselves as the rightful rulers of Afghanistan, but they fear that for the first time in the country's history power has shifted from Pashto speakers (southerners and easterners) to Dari speakers (northerners and westerners). (Dari is the name of the Farsi spoken by Afghans.) Zahir Shah, a Durrani, was meant to ease their way back into the palace. Hamid Karzai is a Pashtun, but he's seen as a caged bird of the former Northern Alliance minorities — particularly the Tajiks — who fill the ranks of the power ministries, people like General Mohammed Fahim, the Tajik defense minister. Before the *loya jirga* Fahim had warned diplomats and journalists that he would start a civil war if the old king ran for power. So when the U.S. envoy got wind of a petition, signed by a majority of *loya jirga* delegates, to nominate Zahir Shah as leader of the country, he panicked and convened an emergency press conference at the American embassy to announce that Zahir Shah would not run. It was a public relations gaffe, a trifle in recent Afghan history, but it sent an alarm to the suspicious Pashtun tribesmen: This was a coup against the people! Americans are not only occupiers, they're anti-Pashtun!

Then, when the eighty-seven-year-old king stood up to open the *loya jirga,* his microphone died. TV screens snapped and frizzled. A minute or so after his speech ended, the technical glitch was miraculously fixed. That was the final mockery. "Everyone knows it was a plot," Sami said, delighted that Ruhani had brought up the matter.

Ruhani kept saying, "I'm confused," and I could see why. America has shaped not only the political history of Afghanistan but also the personal narrative of nearly every Afghan, and yet America is a fickle benefactor, bestowing graces and acknowledging the attachment only when it suits her.

As we traced our way back down a ravine, a shepherd dog nearly attacked us to protect his masters — a Kuchi nomad family, tucked under a rocky outcropping. A white-bearded man with scrawny legs waved down Ruhani: Come for tea, yogurt. We'll kill a sheep. You'll spend the night. We shared some tea with rancid milk, and the old man told us his family had just been kicked off the Hazara lands that lay behind the high peaks. His wife stared at me: What was this girl doing in the mountains with men? "Don't worry, Auntie," Ruhani said. "Western girls are just like men." She nodded, thinking about that. She was a beautiful but worn woman with thirteen children. She wore paint on her forehead, silver bangles in her ears and up her arms, and a dusty embroidered dress. She was prattling away, her dazzling green eyes still staring at me, and I asked Habib what she was saying. "Alas," he translated, "I don't have any heavy artillery or I could have killed all those motherfucker Hazara and grazed my sheep back there."

The next morning we sat with Ruhani amid his apricot orchards and poplar trees. Sami was puffed up now by the fresh, safe Pashtun air, and he began briefing Ruhani on the mischief down south. The Taliban forces were regrouping, he said. The man primed to replace the fugitive one-eyed Taliban leader, Mullah Omar (largely disgraced for losing the war to the Americans), was Hekmatyar. Though he was probably the most anti-Western and most brutal of the seven Soviet era mujahideen leaders, Hekmatyar was plied with the most money and guns by the Americans and the Pakistanis. Most Afghans despised him and had been comforted to know of his exile in Iran. But after Bush's "axis of evil" speech, Tehran booted him out, and he sneaked back into eastern Afghanistan, near the border of Pakistan.

Sami said Hekmatyar was promising Mullah Omar's followers that he would organize them and fund a jihad against the new government and the American invaders. Sami sounded worried. But then he slapped his hands together and said, "Even I will give my money and ammunition to anyone who rises up and lays mines to destroy the U.S. Army, because I am so dissatisfied with this northern government, and motherfucker America is supporting it." He laughed and laughed. And Ruhani laughed. And Habib laughed. And we all laughed. But Ruhani was also shaking his head. His four wives and sixteen children were refugees in Pakistan. Though war had been his craft for twenty-two years, since he was eighteen, he'd now lost his appetite for fighting. When we got in our car to leave, Sami said, "He's not so important. He's from a weak tribe."

We traveled south, past nomad camps and camel caravans, toward the Dasht-i-Margo, or Desert of Death. Eerie rock formations and ancient fortresses melded with sand dunes. Variety outside the car dried up altogether, and my thoughts drifted to Sami and Habib. On the road Sami would often tell stories about the arbitrary and dangerous nature of Taliban rule. In Ghazni, between Kabul and

Kandahar, he recalled a friend whom the mullahs had caught sleeping with a woman not his wife. The mullahs sent him to Sami. They wanted a military tribunal and death. Sami overruled them and saved the friend's life. "Every year," Sami said, "he sends me a — how do you call that one? Gift. Yes. A two-hundred-kilogram sack of almonds." Once he had to prepare two seats in an aircraft flying from Kabul to Kandahar for some friends who were transporting four containers of uranium. The uranium belonged, Sami said, to a businessman who had bought it in Russia, and the Taliban planned to sell it to Pakistan. Whenever we met recalcitrant Talibs who were thwarting Karzai's attempts to extend his weak rule to the provinces, Sami embraced them. Yet he also regularly railed against Islamic fundamentalists for sinking his people into the Dark Ages — just as he railed against deceitful America for fertilizing Afghanistan with weapons, not education.

Habib — who liked to call himself our "cold-blooded, laconic translator in the back," and who always carried with him a collection of Tolstoy, Chekhov, and Hemingway short stories, in English — watched Sami with bemusement and even respect, for who knew when this human information bank might come in handy?

When we heard that the Americans had bombed a Pashtun wedding party, killing dozens, it was Habib — Sami's Farsiphone nemesis — and not Sami who rushed us to the hospital in Kandahar to interview the survivors. In one room a wounded seventeen-year-old girl wrestling with her bedsheet surveyed me and Habib with loathing and in a delirium spat out, "Yes, motherfucker, I was there, at the wedding. Why not? I fucked the wedding." Her mother and father and brother, she said, had been killed. "Why do you Americans bomb us first and then come and ask us stupid questions?" she asked. Then she rolled toward the wall. Habib suggested it was time to leave.

Unlike Sami, who entertained us for hours with his war stories, Habib was reserved about his past. Only later did I discover the Dickensian saga that lay behind his self-possession. He had been born into a family with prospects. His father was a successful doctor with a beautiful wife and a car. "Life was sweet," Habib said — until the Communists staged their coup, in 1978, and arrested his father. He was never seen again. The family moved in with his father's brother, Anwar, who wanted revenge and helped the mujahideen with nighttime ambushes. His house became a bomb-making factory. One night Habib was jolted awake by a shattering explosion. One of the bomb makers was killed, others emerged blackened. One, Habib said, had "the meat falling out of his shoulders." His injured uncle Anwar told Habib and his family to flee for their lives. They ran into the night so fast that his grandmother and mother forgot their chadors.

The police swept the neighborhood, and Habib's mother, rather than see her children tortured, surrendered herself along with her infant. She was given electric shocks but still refused to betray the other resisters. Though she developed rheumatism and lost her breast milk, she kept her baby alive. Habib, his grandmother, and his siblings, now a marked family, hid with a relative down south. Nearly a year later, when the Russians invaded and installed a softer Communist leader, Habib's mother was released, along with thousands of other political prisoners. At one point on our trip Habib began to describe the reunion with his mother but then melted under the memory. "It was such a — okay," he said. "Leave it."

It was then, he said with a nervous laugh, that "the difficult times in our life began." It was wartime. His family had no food, no decent shoes, and lived on a cold Kabul mountain. Habib was nine. He went to work in a candy factory, squatting for nine hours a day to guide sweet steaming paste as it oozed out of a machine. He was paid enough for ten pieces of bread a month.

Twice he was chosen for a scholarship to study in the Eastern bloc, and twice it was rescinded at the last minute. Then, in the 1990s, after the Russians had withdrawn, a local commander in their district was nearly assassinated and accused his uncle, who quickly escaped. Habib and his brother were imprisoned instead, until the townspeople protested and the two of them were released. His face still bears scars from the branches with which his jailer whipped him.

A soft time in Habib's life soon followed. A friend offered his sister as a bride to Habib, and he accepted. Was he happy with her? "Why not?" he asked. "It's not good to be unhappy." An uncle working with the United Nations gave him money for law school in Mazar-i-Sharif. Just as he was finishing his last exams, the front lines fell to the Taliban. Habib fled on what became a twelve-day odyssey through the mountains, where Taliban forces twice nearly executed him. As soon as he made it to his hometown, he and his friends began plotting sabotage. They practiced making and laying bombs. They met with exiled intellectuals in Pakistan, who promised them money, and drew up a charter for a secularist rebellion — just to make a constant hell, he said, "for those Taliban invaders." But the money never materialized; the group dispersed, and Habib went miserably defeated into exile in Pakistan, where a friend set him up as director of a new computer-and-English school. He remained there until after September 11, when he heard President George Bush's voice accusing the Taliban on the radio. "Oh, God, happy thanks," he said to himself. "This is the end. We are going back."

Our rendezvous with Amanullah Khan, not far south of Herat, was arranged by satellite phone. Because Amanullah was an outlaw in the eyes of Herat's self-appointed emir, Ismael Khan, he couldn't venture near the main road. Sami led us down several side roads in search of Amanullah's men, but night was falling, and it was impossible to distinguish one stretch of desert from another. Ismael Khan's soldiers stopped us at the edge of a small canyon and said we couldn't go on. "We can't guarantee your safety," one of them said. "Amanullah Khan's bandits work these roads, and we don't work at night."

A rational man. But Sami was not. We had a date to keep. Besides, a fox had just streaked across our path — "a sign in our culture," he said, "that your travels will be a success."

Habib believed the soldiers and didn't want to move. Besides, an hour before, Habib had seen a hare flit across our path — "a sign in our culture," he said, "that your travels will fail."

We settled the matter by hiring two of Ismael's soldiers to ride with us. We dropped them at a small bazaar, switched off our lights, and then drifted off the road. We flashed our high beams a few times. Nothing happened. Finally we saw faint beams signaling back in the distance, and soon we were surrounded by Amanullah's soldiers — a band of men crammed into three pickup trucks, their white sneakers dangling over the edges. As the western vanguard of the Pashtuns, they were well stocked with uniforms, weapons, and food by the governor of Kandahar, Gul Agha, who was in a cold war with Ismael Khan.

After another hour of desert travel we pulled into Amanullah

Khan's isolated compound. We found Amanullah folded up on a red cushion, leaning against a hanging prayer rug, surrounded by guests. Unlike the other warlords I'd met, who were burly and well fed, Amanullah was reptilian, small, and sickly — an old host to malaria and tuberculosis. He picked at dinner and then swallowed a dose of tablets from several packets. Sami, meanwhile, was on a roll. The uprising against Karzai and the northerners, he said, was about to begin in the east; soon it would spread to the south. He leaned closer to Amanullah, as if offering inside information. "Even Kandahar won't tolerate it any longer," he said, lying.

That night I realized the extent to which Sami had been traveling on a frolic of his own, hoping to stir his listeners to action with exaggerated stories of rebellion elsewhere. When I suggested that he lay off the rabble rousing while we were together, he hissed, "At least I'm not an Iranian spy," and then glowered at Habib as he entered the room.

Iran, Karzai, America, Tajiks — they all swirled in his confused mind like satellites of the same enemy who'd conspired to destroy the purpose of his entire adult life, which was to bring back Zahir Shah. It was irrelevant that the old king suffered from shingles and was too feeble to rule. For millions of Afghans like Sami, the king had become a mythic figure. He represented a long-lost Afghan Eden of peace and fertility. And then along came America and Karzai, who snuffed him out.

Sami's futile quest had been fueled, in part, by the abrupt loss of his idyllic childhood and of his father, who'd been a judge in the kingdom for thirty years. When Sami was nine, his father disappeared, and was assumed to have been executed during the Communist purges, along with more than twelve thousand people, mostly from the educated elite, like Habib's father.

Sami's family fled to Pakistan, where he was forced to stay with his sister and her radical husband, who belonged to Gulbuddin Hekmatyar's executive committee. Sami ran away, studied politics and religion, fired rockets at the Russians during holidays, joined a Pashtun royalist party, and had a rude awakening to Cold War politics when he discovered that the Americans were backing extremists like Hekmatyar, over the moderates and the royalists, to fight the Russians. As a friend in the U.S. military explained to him, "They're better killers." This time around Sami had imagined that America might get it right, clean up its Cold War mess. Instead

Hekmatyar was back in action. The Americans were funding warlords. Sami was bewildered, and someone had to be blamed.

The next day Amanullah took us for a ride through a valley of wheat fields, orchards, and villages of beehive-shaped houses. He stopped by the river and fished lazily, with grenades. He had been fighting Ismael Khan for several years, and thousands were dead — many here on this land. Though Amanullah believed he was protecting persecuted Pashtuns from Ismael, now, with all the ideology stripped away, the two men looked just like old rivals battling it out for control of the lucrative drug-smuggling and trade routes that run through the region and into Iran.

Amanullah told us that after the most recent clash between the two men, which had come on the heels of the Taliban's retreat, the Iranian Revolutionary Guards had stepped in and taken both of them out to the desert. "The Iranians told us, like a father advising his sons, 'It's not the time to fight among yourselves,'" Amanullah said. "'Analyze what's around you. Infidel American troops have invaded and captured your country. They'll give you no power. Forget your hostility, and face the Americans together.' They told us to hug, and we hugged, and the Iranians shouted, '*Allahu Akbar!*'" The Iranians said they would go home and get approval to bring supplies from Iran for the fight against the United States. "I refused," Amanullah said. "I knew they'd deceive us. We're with Gul Agha and Karzai" — America's men. But Ismael is with the Iranians, who have helped to fund and train his standing army of fifteen thousand soldiers, the largest private army of all the warlords.

We left Amanullah Khan behind and drove toward the ancient walls of an extinct castle on a rocky peak, where Ismael Khan's men were perched with binoculars and artillery. Sami, who views Iran as an evil encroacher, said of Amanullah, "This great man would be so useful for Americans against the Iranians. But they'll never use him properly."

We arrived in Herat, the former capital of the Timurid Empire. Red rock and forests of jack pines had replaced the desert. A fourteenth-century citadel still towers over the city, and five of ten minarets designed by Queen Gawhar Shad, the daughter-in-law of Tamerlane and the patroness of the Timurid Renaissance, still stand, tilting in the distance like giant dead palm trees.

We were back in the Dari-speaking world. Sami's Pashtun jingo-ism grew into a flaming rash, but Habib relaxed visibly. He noticed, however, that his old friends here, along with everyone else, were more afraid to speak about politics than people elsewhere had been. Everyone we talked to implied that Ismael Khan was indeed dictatorial, but that Herat, unlike most of Afghanistan, was flour-ishing and relatively safe — as long as you didn't challenge the emir. Business was booming. Construction was everywhere. Ismael Khan was building an ambitious new library. Still, Taliban-style so-cial laws had darkened his image — despite his visits to the hospi-tals where two or three women a week were being brought after dousing themselves with petrol and setting themselves on fire, be-cause they saw no other means of escaping their domestic misery.

Inside the vast courtyard of the Masjid-I-Jami, or Friday Mosque, which had been restored over the past fifty years to reveal exuber-ant lapis, green, yellow, and red mosaics and Koranic script, a woman in a burka ignored a soldier who was trying to push her away from the central altar, where she was praying. There, a few days earlier, Ismael Khan had led a mourning ceremony for Haji Qadir, a vice president of Afghanistan and an old mujahid, who had just been assassinated in Kabul. Ismael railed against the "coali-tion forces" (that is, the United States), who, he suggested, were be-hind the killing, and excited the crowd so much that some chanted back, Iranian-style, "Death to America!" and "Long live Ismael Khan!"

We visited Queen Gawhar Shad's mausoleum, where a crew of American military men in civilian dress were also sightseeing. An Italian aid worker later remarked, "Their visibility is a message to Iran: 'Take your nose out of Afghan affairs.'"

At the shrine of a famous Sufi poet Sami prayed, kissed the tomb, and then lay on the ground, his head on a small stone and his arms crossed over his face. He rolled over and over to the edge of the garden. The aim was to roll straight. He tried the roll twice, each time arcing too far south. "It means you're still disturbed inside," a young man who was watching told us. "You haven't attained spiri-tual health."

Sami knew this. He was a frustrated man. It partly explained his poor Tom act. He had things to tell. Information. He was on to all the troublemakers, and he was used to a double life. When he fled the Taliban, the man who harbored him, at a refugee camp in Paki-stan, was the Wahhabist Abdul Rasul Sayyaf, an avowed enemy of the king and of the United States. Sami played the mole, nodding his head to Sayyaf's plans for sabotage, even writing subversive letters for Sayyaf. But all the time he was collecting facts. Now he wanted to tell America of the dangers. "America is only controlling the public highways," he said, "but the village roads and mosques are still under control of her enemies." And he wanted to be important. Everyone touched by America bloomed in his fellows' eyes. The United States may have been the great infidel, but it was also the bestower of power.

Earlier in the year Sami had called me from the desert, in the middle of an anxiety attack. "I'm so unhappy," he said. He'd made a deal with the Americans to coax the former Taliban commander of Jalalabad, Abdul Salam "Rocketi," out of hiding, to negotiate an amnesty. Or so the Americans had told him. At the last moment Rocketi had received a message that he was on the Americans' blacklist. He was sure they would arrest him, so he reneged on the deal. "I am so ashamed," Sami said. "What will I tell them?" He wondered if he should return the expense money that the Americans had given him. "Finally, God gave us this opportunity for peace and development, and we will lose it," he said miserably. He'd seen plots to sabotage the new administration being hatched everywhere by Hekmatyar and former members of the Taliban. But after Rocketi the Americans had little use for him.

There are thousands of Samis today, wandering Afghanistan's deserts and mountains like zombies created by the twentieth century's big ideas — communism, Islamism, Americanism. If they get their own people back in power, with guns if need be, at least then, they think, the future will be secure. In the meantime, they are governed by the irrational, by unknowable foreigners, by conspiracies, and by God's plans.

Sami's predictions have since all come to pass. Hekmatyar has met with powerful troublemakers, including, allegedly, Ismael Khan, and was most likely behind an attempt to assassinate Karzai in Kandahar. So I had an ominous feeling when Sami called me again the other day, on a friend's satellite phone. He wanted to tell me about a commander he had met, not far from his wife's village, who was plotting to burn schools and to attack Kabul. There was a delay on the line, and then he asked, "Who should I tell?"

Places of Darkness

FROM *National Geographic Adventure*

1. Rutshuru, North Kivu Province, Democratic Republic of the Congo

"HOW ARE YOUR GORILLAS?" Colonel Bonane asks. The brigade commandant of the RCD (Congolese Rally for Democracy) rebel forces terrorizing eastern Congo, he steps out of a night so complete and starless that it is as if the darkness itself has produced him. Well over six feet tall, wearing camouflage fatigues with a green beret folded neatly under an epaulet, he has the powerful, arresting physique of a warrior. All of us — including the park warden, a Congolese mountain-gorilla conservationist named Vital who is acting as my interpreter, and an RCD official assigned to monitor me — stumble out of our plastic chairs, give deferential bows, smile lavishly and painstakingly. We need the colonel to like us. This man can, with a word, save or destroy us.

Bonane is pleased by our display, entreats us to sit down, make ourselves comfortable. "And you," he demands in French of me. "Why are you here?" There is instant silence around the table; his officers level sharp, steady stares at me.

Vital jumps in, explaining that I'm a journalist come to Congo, to their war, in order to see the mountain gorillas. Or, at least, what's left of them. I don't reveal my own, deeper interest: that I'd like to know what motivates people, such as the late Dian Fossey, to save these animals in an area of the world that seems hell-bent on its own destruction.

"Ah, the gorillas!" Bonane laughs. His laugh is deep, resolute, like the crack of a whip. We all come to attention at its sound, wait for whatever is expected of us. "The gorillas!" Bonane exclaims. "I love the gorillas!" He grins and sits back in his chair. His men squeal in laughter: it is a joke. All of the men with me, many of whom have devoted their lives to saving the rare gorillas and who work for the Dian Fossey Gorilla Fund Europe (DFGFE), laugh along with him. You do not want to piss off the colonel.

Overhead, a single fluorescent bulb hums and spits out light; large moths dive into it like kamikazes. The RCD soldiers eye me, their AK-47s leaning daintily against their chairs like parasols. I glare back at them, match their filmy gazes with my own. I don't know what's a more incongruous sight in this seedy outdoor restaurant in this war-exhausted town: a white journalist interested in the gorillas, or a woman. The women in these parts are noticeably absent after dark; they hide themselves to avoid being gang-raped by drunken RCD soldiers. The RCD has almost total control of this area, and I know that only the official presence of the town mayor (a high-ranking RCD crony) and the RCD government monitor keeps me in a safe, hands-off status. My two protectors are starting into yet another large bottle of Primus beer, slurring their words, sharing *mzungu* (white person) jokes with some of the soldiers nearby. I look into the darkness to the south, where the gorillas are. I wonder if they are hiding, cringing in the shadows of their jungle home. I know I would be.

It is hard to talk about the mountain gorillas and not talk about the chaos surrounding them. Perhaps more than that of any other animal on earth, these creatures' fate is inexorably tied to war. There are only about 650 of them left. Fewer than half are in Uganda's Bwindi Impenetrable National Park bordering Congo; the others reside farther south in the Virunga Mountains, on a mere 166 square miles of protected land where Rwanda, Uganda, and the Democratic Republic of the Congo (the DRC, formerly Zaire) meet. Both populations live in the heart of one of the world's most violent and unstable regions, a place rife with corruption and greed, with unchecked exploitation of natural resources and an unfathomable disregard for human life. It was in 1994 that the world got its first enduring taste of this region with the Rwandan genocide. The conflict spilled into neighboring countries as the Hutu militias, known collectively as the Interahamwe —

whose war with the minority Tutsi tribe left about 800,000 dead in a hundred days — fled into the jungles of eastern Congo to regroup and launch further cross-border assaults. Rwanda and Uganda sent their armies in after them in 1996, ushering in the Congolese civil war. It is a conflict that drew in the armies of Zimbabwe, Angola, Namibia, and other countries, and has created an unending nightmare for the UN. Only educated guesses about the number of dead can be made in a region that hasn't had an official census since 1984, but it is estimated that the war has claimed as many as 4.7 million people — the worst reported loss of life in an armed conflict since World War II.

And the war shows no sign of stopping. Local tribes, assorted militia groups, and clandestine army factions from neighboring countries have found the fighting lucrative beyond all expectation. In a country like Congo, where the average person can expect to earn no more than $120 a year, fortunes are made hourly by whoever controls mineral-rich areas. More profitable than gold or diamonds is the rare substance columbite-tantalite, known as coltan, an essential ingredient in microchips and cell phones. Found almost exclusively in eastern Congo, it can bring in $400 per kilo on the international market, giving rebel factions and neighboring governments a financial reason to keep the war going indefinitely. Only when the Congolese conflict caused a temporary suspension of coltan mining did the Western world feel the reverberations of a war it had all but forgotten: Sony was forced to delay the launch of its PlayStation 2.

As for the mountain gorillas, the animals have so far been blessed: the mineral hasn't yet been found in their habitat. Where it has been found — most notably in the eastern Congolese park Kahuzi-Biega — the population of eastern lowland gorillas has been decimated by as much as 90 percent and the park's jungle elephants, once numbered at 350, are down to *two*. With so much wealth being pulled out of the ground, no one, neither human nor animal, is safe. "Once the gorillas cross into unprotected [Congolese] areas, we don't know what will happen to them," says Fortunate Muyambi, field staff coordinator for the Mountain Gorilla Conservation Fund (MGCF) in Uganda. If the war goes on, he says, "there will be extinction in a very short time."

The main reason for the animals' continued survival is the tourist dollars they bring into the area. Quite simply, they have been worth more alive than dead. In Rwanda and Uganda, prewar gorilla tourism was a significant source of revenue. Back when it was still Zaire, Congo had a thriving, lucrative tourist industry that included upscale lodges, gorilla safaris, and jungle treks. Now, with the lodges destroyed, the hiking trails frequented by the genocidal Interahamwe, and tourists banned altogether, Congo has lost all of its revenue from the gorillas — and thus the incentive to safeguard them. Though there is a national park authority, in eastern Congo it is run by RCD-appointed bureaucrats. Vital, a straight-talking ecologist who recently won a conservation award from the BBC, explained it to me bluntly: "It's a crony government. These people don't have any interest in conservation. The first purpose of RCD officials is achieving economic gain." The RCD does not want its exploitation of the parks publicized or interrupted — hence the man sent to monitor my every interview, to keep me always within his sight. I am not supposed to let my focus waver from the gorillas.

Before I came to Africa, I spoke with a representative of Doctors Without Borders who criticized the way people give more attention to the plight of the mountain gorilla than they do to the tragedy of the human beings. It seemed a valid and important concern. Can the gorillas' story of survival be seen as a classic parable of hope? Of grace rising like the spring of new leaves from a landscape devastated by war? The thought is grossly romantic, makes me shake my head before Bonane and his men. Grace? *Here?* *I* know this: a staggering eighty-two Congolese park rangers have been killed since the war started, making mountain-gorilla conservation one of the most dangerous professions on earth. Yet the people who have devoted everything to work with these animals tell me that there is something ineffable about them. One Rwandan park ranger, named Jean-Bosco Bizumuremyi, who endured an Interahamwe attack to return to his gorillas — he showed me a machete scar across the top of his head — said, "Unlike us, the gorillas do not try to kill each other."

Colonel Bonane sees me writing in my notebook, and he waves angrily at me, issues an immediate decree. An apologetic Vital whispers in fervent English: "Stop! Don't write anymore! Close that book."

I close it.

Bonane sighs and waxes nostalgic: "Ah, the gorillas . . ."

Later in the evening, in the dank cement cell of a room where I'm spending the night in Rutshuru, chair propped against the door, my knife out on the table beside me and opened to the largest blade, I reread Dian Fossey's *Gorillas in the Mist.* Fossey was the first person to launch a crusade to save the gorillas, under the tutelage of the famous paleontologist Louis Leakey, back in 1966. With very limited funds, she went alone into the Congolese Virungas to set up a base camp to study what was then a dwindling population of only 240 animals. Even then, she observed that "one of the greatest drawbacks of the Virungas is that it is shared by three countries, each of which has problems far more urgent than the protection of wild animals." After barely a year in her new home, she was forced to flee when war broke out. She soon returned to the Rwandan Virungas, to set up the now world-famous Karisoke Research Center. To pay for increased patrols in the Virungas, she established the Digit Fund, named after her favorite silverback, who had been killed by poachers.

I met Fossey's successor, Ruth Keesling, in the lobby of the posh Hotel des Milles Collines in Rwanda's capital, Kigali. Shortly after Fossey's death in 1985 — two assailants, believed to be local poachers, killed Fossey with a machete blow to the head — Keesling took over the Digit Fund, changing the name to the Dian Fossey Gorilla Fund Europe. These days, she runs the Mountain Gorilla Conservation Fund. Flashing bright brown eyes and an impish grin, the seventy-three-year-old Keesling greeted me with the unwavering energy you'd expect to find in a woman half her age. For the past nineteen years, the American has made frequent pilgrimages to Rwanda and Uganda in order to meet with the leaders of both countries and negotiate on the gorillas' behalf. If in-your-face coercion was Dian Fossey's specialty, Keesling's secret weapon is congeniality. Having experienced firsthand the rare influence she had over people, I could think only this: here is someone who can get anything she wants. Which has been good news for the gorillas. Though few outside of animal conservation know her by name, her campaign has been one of the main reasons why the gorillas have survived into the twenty-first century.

Most notably, she hasn't let central Africa's unrest stop her. "I don't worry about things like that," she told me over her customary predinner double Chivas, waving the instability aside. She recalled arriving in Kigali the day the genocide ended and the Tutsi liberated the city from the Hutu Interahamwe — there were bodies rotting on the streets, buildings pocked with bullet holes, corpses filling the basement of her beloved Hotel des Milles Collines.

"I just didn't think a thing about it," she said of her decision to fly in under such circumstances. "We came here all the time."

Keesling explains her commitment to the gorillas by saying that she likes "solving problems," but her love for the animals is undeniably profound. She knows many of those in the Virungas by name, refers to one adored silverback, Shinda, as her "boyfriend." Her tale of how she met Fossey in 1984 is a favorite of hers, told so many times that it now has the rote ring of legend: "I met Dian at a dumpy hotel in Rwanda. She was dynamic, in control. I was so impressed by her mission. And Dian said to me, 'Ruth, there are only 248 mountain gorillas left in the world. They're all going to die, and I'm going to die with them.'" Keesling brought Karisoke its first veterinarian in 1986, and in later years raised enough funding to see poaching almost completely eradicated from much of the gorillas' habitat.

After our introduction in Kigali, Keesling and I went to visit Fossey's grave and the remnants of the original Karisoke Research Center, all located above ten thousand feet in Volcanoes National Park in the Rwandan Virungas. On the way up, we passed large tracts of farmland — all well within the official park boundaries — that had been cut from virgin rain forest. In the years after the Rwandan genocide of 1994, international pressure called for the repatriation of thousands of refugees who had fled to camps in Congo. Only when civil war erupted in Congo did many of the refugees return, some resettling on the only uninhabited land they could find: around the fringes of Volcanoes National Park. The result is the severe deforestation of the lower portions of the park's mountains.

We trudged up the muddy path, reaching moist montane forest filled with giant hagenia trees draped in a kind of Spanish moss. The fourteen-thousand-foot peaks of the volcanoes lorded over the countryside, revealing themselves through breaks in the clouds. I half expected some gorillas to come loping toward me from out of the brush. Instead, from some faraway point in the jungle, a male gorilla thumped his chest and let out a deep bass tremolo that echoed across the mountains.

The animals' extreme habitat has been their only real defense against humans. They weren't known to European explorers until 1902, when Oscar von Beringe, a German, shot two members of the first group he discovered. In the 1920s, whites decided that the rare gorillas ought to be kept alive rather than killed, and so the Belgian government, then Rwanda's colonial ruler, formed Africa's first national park, Albert National Park, in the Virungas. By not overlapping with the habitat of other large primates, the mountain gorillas have naturally quarantined themselves from such diseases as Ebola, which is currently decimating the chimpanzees of Uganda, and they have so far avoided being caught in the bushmeat trade that has ravaged the populations of the less glamorous lowland gorilla all across central Africa.

Still, their status as a highly endangered species hurts them in unexpected ways: wealthy outsiders with their own private menageries have offered poachers upward of twenty-five thousand dollars for the capture of a single baby, which can entail killing several of the adults protecting it. There were two attempts in 2002 to steal babies — one in Uganda's Bwindi Impenetrable National Park, the other in Rwanda's Volcanoes National Park — which resulted in the capture of two babies and the murder of six adults; luckily, one of the babies was recovered and successfully assimilated into another gorilla group. Yet there are concerns that the lawlessness and instability on the Congolese side of the Virungas will make it easier to steal babies from this vulnerable population. "In the spring of this year, we saw a general increase in the wildlife trade in this area from Congo," says Gil Grosvenor, a DFGF International board member and chairman of the board of the National Geographic Society, "and the [seizing of gorilla babies] suggests that there is now a focused attack on the mountain gorillas." To counter poaching, Karisoke staff and Rwandan and Congolese wildlife authorities now engage in trans-boundary patrols.

We finally reached the meadow of Karisimbi, which Fossey describes in her diary as "the most fantastically gorgeous country I never dreamed existed." It was, indeed, an enchanting place, ancient hagenia trees rising like wizened sentinels to stand vigil over the site of Fossey's life work and grave. Appropriately, she was buried alongside her gorilla cemetery, a martyr for the very animals that had consumed her life. I read the bronze plaque on the headstone — a gift that Keesling had made in Fossey's memory. Around us, workers for the Rwandan government were busy replacing Fossey's gorilla grave markers, adding fences and footpaths, and covering Fossey's grave with a neat patio of lava rock — upgrades for the tourists. Fossey and her mountain gorillas were about to go commercial; the Rwandan government had plans to charge fifty dollars per person for permission to visit the grave.

Of Karisoke itself, little remained — just some cement foundations and rotting wooden frames. The jungle had already started to reclaim the site, beautifying its recent unsavory history with a cover of new greenery. After the Rwandan conflict erupted nearly a decade ago, the Interahamwe repeatedly pillaged Karisoke, finally using the area as a base camp for launching raids from 1997 to 1999. Miraculously, Karisoke's rangers continued to monitor the gorillas on the Rwandan side during most of the hostilities, and only three animals were killed. In Congo, however, as many as seventeen were lost.

Given the continued threat of poachers and Hutu rebel encroachment, Rwanda appointed an entire army battalion to protect the animals and the tourists who visit them. I met the leader of Battalion 69, Major Kirenga, who said that the Interahamwe has not been in the park since 2001. "I don't think they will come back to this area," he said, "because when they were here in 2001, they suffered." François Bigirimana, warden of Volcanoes National Park, was less sanguine: "Now the situation is okay, but for only a short time. The Interahamwe keeps coming back."

Few in gorilla conservation can forget the widely publicized 1999 incident in Uganda's Bwindi Impenetrable National Park, home to more than three hundred mountain gorillas, a spectacular area of jungle-covered peaks that the locals have long called the Place of Darkness. The name took on a more sinister meaning as the Interahamwe crossed into the region from Congo and attacked a tourist camp, murdered a warden, and led sixteen foreigners on a march into the jungle. Eight were hacked to death. To the locals, numb to such atrocities, it was business as usual — but it was the first time in years that Western civilians had been direct victims of the region's horrors. The massacre took a devastating toll on Uganda's tourism industry. Today, tourism has rebounded to be the country's second-largest revenue source. Bwindi now boasts a seventy-six-person-strong ranger force with paramilitary training. Still, just a couple of miles from Bwindi's park headquarters, over some nearby hills, sits Congo.

2. *Jomba, North Kivu Province, Eastern DRC*

I see about renting a few RCD soldiers to "protect" me on my journey to visit the mountain gorillas. Assorted militia groups, bandits, and warlords have been staging frequent ambushes on passing cars. The latest attack on this road, I am told, was just last evening — we had been fortunate to miss our turn.

The last time Ruth Keesling visited this place, in 1998, she, her adult son, a woman from Ohio's Columbus Zoo, and a couple of local veterinary students were captured by Interahamwe child soldiers. Keesling recalled it in her typically deadpan way: "I thought, okay, we're going to get it — I might as well die with the gorillas." The soldiers held AK-47s to everyone's heads and accused Keesling's group of spying for Rwanda's Tutsi government. Everything looked hopeless, but luck intervened: they had been giving a ride to a former official of the Zairean government, who used his influence to persuade the soldiers to set the captives free. Keesling has not tried to see the Congolese mountain gorillas since.

I have no difficulty finding RCD soldiers willing to be "volunteer" protectors — all you have to do is offer them enough U.S. dollars and promises of free beer. Vital chooses three individuals who don't appear to be drunk or stoned, and our large group, including three armed Virunga National Park rangers and the three hired soldiers, presses into the ancient Toyota minibus I've rented. We head into the countryside, past overgrown fields and mud-and-wattle huts. "There are two types of ambushes here in Kivu Province," Vital tells me. "The first is the 'political ambush,' the second the 'soft hit.'" He explains that in the former, everyone in the vehicle is shot dead in order to make a statement of protest; in the latter, people are robbed or maimed but otherwise left alive. "Soft hits," Vital assures me, "are the better ones."

We pass through frequent RCD roadblocks; at each one, the park warden or government monitor leaps out of the van to shake hands and cajole the officer on duty. The notion of our going to see the gorillas always creates a profusion of laughter. I stay in the back of the van, by the window, returning the stares of children who have the stoic, circumspect countenances of adults. Only the very youngest give emphatic waves or smiles, and the soldiers mock their earnestness.

Our minivan groans and perseveres down the boulder-strewn track past villages of round thatched huts and banana trees. Women walk along the road wearing wraps of printed cloth and carrying washtubs or bundles of firewood on their heads. Their eyes settle nervously on the RCD soldiers inside, a wave of fear passing over their faces. All you can taste in this country is fear. An inescapable vortex of it. I hope these gorillas will be spectacular, more fantastic than anything I could have imagined.

We near the Virungas. I can see mountains of jungle rising from a series of deforested foothills. The land resembles a crude checkerboard: square, empty fields baking in the sun. With no buffer zone between pastureland and jungle, there is nothing to prevent further encroachment into the park from the Congolese side. Farmers and refugees have cleared the jungle toward the cloud line; the gorillas now very much inhabit the mists.

We reach the end of the road and park the van at an outpost called Jomba. Only two weeks ago, the Interahamwe came through this area, which perhaps explains why nobody is out tending the fields. To reach the Jomba park headquarters, we begin a long hike uphill through grassy, deserted fields. "In 1994," Vital says to me, "these fields were covered with jungle and giant trees." Ten years ago, Vital worked here for a large, five-star tourist lodge; it is now a pile of burned-out rubble that we pass on our way up. It is hard for me to picture this place as a stable environment, with foreign tourists resting on lawn chairs and sipping cocktails before a majestic view of the Congolese Virungas.

Jomba headquarters — a collection of a few small huts — sits on top of a lonely, tree-stripped hill at about 7,500 feet. The jungle-covered peaks of the volcanoes act as a backdrop. It is a vulnerable spot in which to live, with no immediate cover and an imposing spread of jungle nearby that might hide militiamen, snipers, ambushers.

When I reach the round cement building that acts as the base, a group of men in olive-colored uniforms comes out to greet me: the park rangers. They smile shyly; it is not often that they receive visitors, particularly foreigners. These men confirm what I already know: no one is paying them. Not the government in Kinshasa, capital of the Democratic Republic of the Congo, and certainly not the RCD. During better periods, they receive funding from UNESCO, which allows them to feed themselves and provide for their families, but it barely suffices. It is these men who have lost eighty-two of their own in the past few years. I'm shown the photo of one of their most recent casualties, a man named Jean de Dieu — John of God.

While gorilla populations in Rwanda and Uganda have slowly climbed in recent years as a result of conservation efforts, most experts agree that the number of mountain gorillas in Congo has dropped significantly. They have been caught in snares, hunted with impunity by poachers, or killed in crossfire. An estimated fifteen to seventeen have been lost since the war started. For such a fragile population, totaling only about 355 in all the Virungas, a loss of fifteen to seventeen members is dramatic. "If you kill only ten percent of them," says Tony Mudakikwa, senior veterinary officer for the park authority of Rwanda, "and that's only thirty-five individuals, I can't imagine they'd have the genetic viability to survive extinction." It is already a concern, as gorillas are starting to be born with webbed fingers — a possible sign of inbreeding.

Dominique Bavukai, chief of patrols for Jomba since 2000, says that just a few months ago one of his men was kidnapped by the Interahamwe and never heard from again. A week later, the same Hutu militiamen attacked the station again. A lengthy firefight ensued, but the rangers were able to hold them off. Still, they lost another man during the battle.

"No one knows where the enemy is," Bavukai says to me, and he glances out of the hut at the surrounding countryside. His eyes look weary, resigned. "But our mission is to protect the gorillas as long as they are at risk of extinction."

"Some people in my country might wonder why you don't get a safer job," I say to the men. "Is there a reason why you've stayed?"

I am hoping for a certain kind of answer, I realize. A lofty reply about wanting to preserve the heritage of the mountain gorillas for future generations, about the inherent grace and beauty of a creature that must be saved at all costs. But Bavukai's reply is practical rather than poetic: "There are no other job opportunities out here in this war zone. It would be hard to just quit this job and find another."

Our long column snakes its way toward the jungle and the gorillas, through barren farmland overtaken by weeds. Each soldier rests his AK-47 on a shoulder, fist around the muzzle. The higher we climb, the closer the clouds come to touching me, coating my face with mist. We finally approach a thick jungle that stretches to the very tops of the volcanoes, an unbroken spread of primeval green. Some trackers who monitor the mountain gorillas walk over to greet us. They are stationed far from the Jomba site, on the edge of the jungle. We all head into a mass of trees and vines that requires more pushing and shoving than actual walking, the men hollowing out a path with machetes. The head tracker waves to me, and I follow him into a grassy clearing. I'm so busy looking around that I nearly walk into a giant silverback named Rugendo. He is lying on the ground, his chin resting on his hands, staring at me with liquid brown eyes. He is gigantic — his shoulder span is wider than that of two grown men — and his enormous face studies my own with eye-blinking fascination. Two of his females, smaller and furrier, seem paralyzed with wonder as they gaze at me through the bamboo.

I kneel down and stare at them all. "Hello," I whisper, our eyes meeting.

The mountain gorillas were the first gorilla species to be habituated to a human presence. Inexplicably. It is this innate trust that fascinates me. With what other jungle animal can a person readily gain such close, intimate access? Surely this helps explain why so many tourists will fly halfway around the world for a mere hour's visit with these creatures, and why, through war and famine and unrest, so many individuals and organizations are determined to save them. But there is something beyond this: these animals, with their trusting and peaceful natures, caring family units, and unconditional acceptance of others, reveal to us humans just how far we've strayed.

The females come toward me, slowly at first and then faster as the tracker attempts to wave them off with a stick. They are determined to touch me. The tracker tries to explain their strange behavior — "They haven't seen a white person before" — but I'm not sure I believe him. Rather, they seem to want to greet me, welcome me. The females regroup for another approach, but the tracker is too fast for them. He explains that the gorillas are at risk of catching human diseases, and so only researchers, who are quarantined for two weeks upon arriving here, should interact with them.

Rugendo rolls onto his back — his enormous potbelly facing up, his legs splayed and toes wiggling — and yawns. Casually, he grabs some young bamboo and gnaws on it, glancing peacefully at me and the trackers as he chews. Humans could do anything to him right now, but he simply scratches his great belly, farts, and sighs, closing his eyes to us.

I can only wonder what will happen to him. Two weeks ago the Interahamwe crossed through this park, and they will cross through it again.

My hour is up, and the females take one more daring advance toward me before the tracker intervenes and shoos them away. Reluctantly, I follow the men out of the jungle, back into the desolate fields.

Dr. Théogène Rudasingwa, the Rwandan president's chief of staff, sits calmly in the heavily guarded presidential compound in Kigali, fingertips touching lightly. When I ask him about his country's commitment to protecting the gorillas, he says, "Our agenda, first and foremost, is to protect the people. The protection of the mountain gorillas has been at the back of our minds. But it's in our interest — and the gorillas' — to establish more security in Congo and Uganda, as well as Rwanda."

In the name of "security," Rwandan and Ugandan troops first entered Congo (then Zaire) in 1996, igniting its bloody civil war. Rwanda pulled out its troops in 2002, but not before establishing local armies and governments — such as the RCD — to do its bidding. Uganda soon followed suit. The two countries now battle each other through proxy armies for control of Congo's lucrative natural resources.

The worst of their playing fields is in eastern Congo's Ituri Province, where Uganda and Rwanda frequently flip-flop in supporting the militias of the Lendu and Hema tribes, who busily engage in tit-for-tat massacres with each other. At least fifty thousand people have died in Ituri since hostilities began there in 1999, most of them civilians; half a million others have been displaced. Various relief organizations characterize this conflict as an all-out genocide, in which rebel groups take the machete to anyone — man, woman, or child — with the wrong ethnic identification. Little wonder that the mountain gorillas are on the Rwandan government's back burner.

I decide to go to Ituri Province, the epicenter of the violence, to see how bad it is. Whatever happens there can have a domino effect on this whole region, destabilizing entire countries, killing untold numbers of people, and bringing species caught in the middle — like the mountain gorillas — to extinction.

3. Bunia, Ituri Province, Eastern DRC

"Hey, journalist! I will kill you, journalist!" The boy looks at me with blood-colored eyes — he could not be older than nine or ten — and waves the muzzle of his AK-47 in my face. He is drugged up, gone. He wears a red T-shirt and a sardonic grin, his camouflage pants new and stiff-looking, hanging from his body like oversize pajamas. The back of the truck is full of others like him, child soldiers: a thirteen-year-old with a rocket launcher, a couple more teenagers with assault rifles. The driver, another kid, grinds the gears of a Toyota, trying to learn hands-on how a manual transmission works. I pause on the side of the street, intent on not showing fear. Fear is what they want, these children in control of Bunia. Show a trembling hand, throw a sidelong glance for assistance, and this weakness instantly registers in their brains. You can see the grins widen, the hands tighten around the weapons. They know they have you.

But these boys are busy with other matters. They have a truckload of looted furniture to take somewhere, and so the truck jumps into gear and roars off down the pitted street. I watch them go, still not moving. Only when they are safely out of sight do I let out my breath.

"Jesus," I whisper.

Farther up the street, a United Nations peacekeeper in a light blue helmet and a flak jacket — a Uruguayan soldier — sits on top of an armored personnel carrier, elbow resting over the stock of his machine gun. Watching. These seven hundred peacekeepers, primarily Uruguayans and none battle-tested, aren't mandated to interfere militarily unless UN personnel or property is directly threatened. (Technically, they are authorized to defend civilians as well, though to do so could invite overwhelming retaliation.) They remind me of actors going through the motions of soldiery. But they are not unaware of their impotence: a number of them, obligated to simply watch the unraveling slaughter, have had nervous breakdowns and been evacuated.

Since the peacekeepers' arrival in April 2003, civilians have continued to be killed within sight of the UN's main compound; rebel soldiers have been seen adorning their weapons with the organs of their victims. Cannibalism is rife; militias go into the jungles to hunt the local Pygmy population for "bush meat." A week ago, the Rwanda-backed UPC (Union of Congolese Patriots) guerrillas, who are allied with the Hema — those who had just wrested the town of Bunia from the Uganda-backed Lendu — tossed a mutilated corpse into the UN compound to remind the peacekeepers of their uselessness. Each day, more stories of mass killings and atrocities reach the UN ears in Bunia, while hundreds of refugees pack into its makeshift camps and hospitals with their limbs cut off or their bodies shot up, telling the same gruesome stories: how family members were killed in front of them, how they were forced to eat human flesh. The UN does nothing. It will tell you that its hands are tied by its Chapter 6 mandate.

I enter one of the crude hospitals run by Doctors Without Borders. It sits on the outskirts of Bunia near the airport, adjacent to a large refugee camp full of people — mostly Hema civilians — who are lucky to have escaped their Lendu attackers alive. In two rooms, the walls are lined with foam mattresses, most of which are occupied by children and adults in bloody wrappings and casts: the victims of machete or gunshot wounds, land mines, mortar fire. The head of the DWB mission here, who for political reasons asks that his name not be used, tells me that a handful of doctors are doing 120 to 150 new consultations a day — a staggering 3,000 a month. The Doctors Without Borders physicians and staff look haggard, yet the sheer numbers of new patients keep them almost constantly on the move and force them to send even the worst casualties on their way after a few days.

I leave the hospital and start walking past Bunia's decaying buildings, riddled with bullet holes, and the emptiness of side streets that speak of something hushed and awful. It is as if death leers from every direction. It stares out at you from the faces of the refugees in the tent camps. You hear it in the voices of the child soldiers roaring by in their stolen trucks. You smell it in the cholera-infested latrines and on the disinfectant-coated floors of the makeshift hospitals. In Ituri, to the rampaging rebel soldiers, life isn't cheap; it's irrelevant. They claim a monopoly on it, decide who lives and who dies based on the lottery of their mood.

I think back to the people trying to save the mountain gorillas. How seldom I heard them mention the region's human casualties. There seemed to be a rejection of an all too common premise: that a human being's life is more valuable than any animal's. People here have explained the carnage to me as a "loss of humanity," of humans becoming "animals." I remember Rugendo, the silverback I met in the Virungas. No: we do not become animals. We become the worst that is in ourselves, what is purely, unequivocally human.

The question of who's to blame for this mess leads one down a lengthy path of culpability. The Hema and Lendu peoples lived relatively peacefully together for centuries in Ituri until the Belgians colonized Congo in 1908 and declared the Hema to be racially superior, thus relegating the Lendu to a permanent lower-class status. When the country gained its independence in 1960, the favored Hema ended up in charge of Ituri's land, businesses, and government offices. Enmity grew between the Hema and the Lendu, but tensions escalated to wholesale violence after Western powers discovered that Ituri is home to some of the largest gold reserves in the world.

I meet with Colonel Daniel Vollot, commander of UN forces in Ituri. He is a tall, middle-aged Frenchman with a crew cut and a wiry frame, looking in every way like the career soldier. I repeat to him one of the most blaring allegations made by Rudasingwa, the Rwandan president's chief of staff: that Interahamwe responsible for the Rwandan genocide are now "linked to Uganda" and are finding "safe haven" in Ituri. This is news to Vollot; he says he's seen no evidence of it. But when it comes to finger-pointing in this part of the world, the veracity of claims is immaterial as long as they effectively get the blood boiling. Vollot is not an optimist; he has an unmistakable look of defeat in his eyes. After he describes a UN plan to send a thousand French troops here with a beefed-up mandate that authorizes the use of force, he quickly shoots it down. "We can't solve the problem of pacifying Ituri with a thousand troops."

As we speak, I think of all the civilians being maimed and massacred across the countryside. "Doesn't it bother you," I ask Vollot, "that all of these atrocities are going on right now and you can do nothing about it?"

"Yes, it's frustrating!" he declares. "But I can't change the world. I do my best here. The press's negative comments about our mission in Congo — it's scandalous. Every day we do our best."

The UN information officer who has been monitoring our interview stands up now, trying to end it. Vollot ignores her and leans close to me: "There was an old woman, eighty-five years old, who was brought in with both her arms cut off. Eighty-five years old. Sometimes I want to kill. Really. Now, I'm like a beast. It's not a problem for me. I see it, I get used to it. But that's not normal behavior. Whenever I leave this country — if I leave this country — when I have a normal life, all of these things will begin again in my brain. This will be very difficult for me, I'm sure."

I arrange to go on the UN's Alpha Route patrol to the north of Bunia, in the company of three military observers: an Indonesian, an Indian, and an enormous Zambian, nearly seven feet tall, who has surely missed his true calling as a linebacker. My request was reluctantly granted: UN officials told me that it would be bad press if a journalist was killed by rebels, especially after two of their own monitors had just been slaughtered in the Ituri countryside.

The observers give me a light blue flak jacket and helmet to wear, and I get into the back seat of their Toyota 4Runner. With the Indonesian driving, we pass through the razor-wire barriers protecting the UN headquarters, entering the long main drag of Bunia, with its omnipresent UPC child soldiers. Noticing that none of my companions has a weapon, I mention this to the observer from India.

"We can't use weapons unless we're defending ourselves," he explains. "It's against our mandate."

"Yes," I say. "So why don't you carry weapons to defend yourselves?"

"We do not want to be seen carrying weapons. It will give a bad impression. We want to remain neutral."

"We have this," the Zambian says, holding up a radio. "We can call in if we have trouble."

"You can call in so they know where to pick up your dead bodies," I say, half joking.

But the Indian nods. "That's right," he says. "So they can get our bodies."

We drive past the airport, leaving behind the UN's radius of protection. With no jungles around Bunia, we enter rolling green grassland, following a dirt road that curves to the north. A large contingent of Lendu fighters is supposed to be massed behind some approaching hills, regrouping in order to try to retake Bunia from the UPC-backed Hema. The Indian explains to me that his patrol has orders to conduct reconnaissance to find out more about this gathering from the locals.

We pass a man riding a bicycle, and the Indonesian stops our vehicle and flags him down. "Him," he tells us. "We will ask him." But the three men just look at one another. It turns out that none of the peacekeepers speaks French, the usual means of communication with the Congolese. I am assuming the UN commanders knew this when they sent these men out — yet here we are.

The Indian turns to me. "Do you speak French?" he asks.

"Somewhat," I say.

"Good. You can be our interpreter."

I find it unsettling that any potentially critical information for the UN must rely on my French language skills, but I give it my best shot. I ask the man if he's heard anything about the Lendu, inquiring about numbers of fighters, possible troop movements. He says that, for sure, a large number of them, perhaps as many as a thousand, are gathered behind the hills, but to his knowledge they haven't started moving forward yet.

The Indonesian stops me. He's angry. "What are you asking him?"

I tell him.

"Don't ask him that," he says.

"I thought that's what you wanted to know."

"We're only supposed to ask them 'What's the situation here?' Do not mention Lendu or troop movements."

"We want to stay neutral," the Indian explains.

When we stop another man on the road, I ask only what I'm supposed to ask: "What's the situation here?"

The Congolese man looks at me, puzzled, then gestures around him. "It's fine," he says.

I tell the Indonesian. "Good," he says. He turns the vehicle around and we head back to town.

Each evening I run the usual two-block gauntlet from where I'm staying — a room in the guesthouse of some Belgian priests — to the UN compound and then back again, passing down the pitch-black streets of Bunia, never knowing who or what waits in the shadows ahead. I'm reminded of childhood games of tag. My senses become sharp, fixed on sounds and sights. If I see UPC soldiers coming, I step behind a tree or the corner of a building and wait for them to pass. I have become a gambler, wagering my safety each night on the whims of the soldiers and their sporadic gunfire cracking across the otherwise silent town.

Tonight I have made it once again to the UN compound. If this is a game of tag, then the goal is the armored personnel carrier sitting on the lit-up corner before the rows of razor wire. By now, I recognize the Uruguayan soldier on top, and he invariably greets me with a smile and a wave from behind his .50-caliber machine gun.

"*Hola!*" another soldier calls out from aboard the armored personnel carrier.

"*Hola,*" I say to them, relieved to be near them and their guns. "*Qué tal?*"

Whereas during the day these men stick stoically to their job, the nights are different. The darkness, its increased danger, does something to them, turns them into consummate flirts. They will ask me quick questions, delighting in my lousy Spanish, then watch me head to the gate of the UN headquarters for my meeting with the information officer, who often doesn't receive news reports until evening. When I return afterward and pause again before their APC, they greet me as usual, only this time I have lost my enthusiasm to talk with them; before me sits the long black corridor to the safety of Father Jo's place, two blocks away. Two interminable blocks of darkness.

256 KIRA SALAK

I start walking quickly down the street. I'm hoping the Uruguayans will keep watching me, will come to my assistance if I run into trouble, but it isn't long before their white APC becomes barely discernible behind me. I hear voices. Some young UPC soldiers step out from a building, see me, rush over, and surround me. I remember the UN warnings: that the rebels want to capture or kill journalists. These men — drunk, drugged-up adolescents — ask for cigarettes or money. I glance behind me and see the Uruguayan soldier behind his machine gun, but does he see me? Do I yell out? But that would be revealing my fear to these men. I keep walking, the soldiers forming a pack around me, demanding money.

"Okay," I say to them.

I pull out a wad of dirty Congolese money and shove it into their hands. An argument erupts, and I use the opportunity to shove through them, run to the priests' compound, and bang on the metal gate. A caretaker opens it. The game is over for tonight. Safety.

If most of the people in Ituri have "lost their humanity," it is all the more remarkable that the two Belgian priests have managed to cling so strongly to theirs. Father Joseph Deneckere — known as Father Jo — is a legend here. I do not exaggerate: he has a saintly light in his eyes. Age fifty-eight, he's lived in Ituri for going on thirty-three years. He and his colleague, Father Jan Mol, are two of the small number of foreign priests who have stayed on in Bunia through all the chaos and killing. Father Jo has been threatened numerous times, but he earned a reputation as someone to be reckoned with when some soldiers burst into his compound and trained their guns on him. They decided to play with him before they killed him, so they shot bullets around his head, made him temporarily deaf. In what Father Jo describes as a moment of heavenly intervention, he gained superhuman courage and strength, grabbed the burning-hot muzzles of their AK-47s and tossed them aside, and yelled at the soldiers like a schoolmaster chastising pupils. As he puts it, "They became afraid of me because I was not afraid." Father Jo is now known throughout the countryside as the White Father who tossed death's guns aside.

He is a large, gray-haired, bespectacled man who can be found at the end of each day holding his cigarette and bottle of beer. He and Father Mol maintain a guesthouse with impeccably clean rooms, as well as a flower and vegetable garden, and a chapel in which a black Jesus on a cross gazes down with wincing eyes. Father Jo, fluent in Swahili and Kilendu, speaks to victims and perpetrators alike with a gentle hand on their wrist. He is endlessly patient, tolerating the demands of the strung-out journalists staying at his place, shrugging it off when we noisily enter the compound after curfew, reeking of whiskey and Primus beer. And he sits for long interviews, giving the same answers again and again to the usual questions from the stream of reporters who come and go: Why such chaos in Bunia? What happened?

I am curious about other things, though. For example, how Father Jo keeps that light in his eyes, given all that he's seen. Two weeks ago, two Congolese priests in Bunia, along with twenty refuge seekers, were trapped in a building surrounded by Lendu attackers preparing to kill them. One of the priests phoned Father Mol, begging him to send UN troops to his assistance. Father Mol spent hours persuading Colonel Vollot's forces — which were occupied protecting eighteen thousand refugees — to intervene, stressing that the priests were only a half mile away. In the end, twenty-two people died, most of them killed by machete. Five hours after Father Mol's frantic appeal, Father Jo accompanied Father Mol to identify the bodies. There were men, women, and children.

"I often ask, Where was God?" Father Jo tells me. "I think God was not in that killing. God gave the world to mankind, and if we follow the gospel of charity and love, it must go good once more. *God is love.*"

But Father Jo admits that his faith has been tested. He tells me Thomas Lubanga, leader of the UPC rebels, once was a seminary student, had wanted to become a priest.

"How do you explain this?" I ask him.

"People here believe they will be killed, and so they do the same thing to others that they're afraid others will do to them."

Father Mol offers his own explanation, his words coming out with deliberation. I can tell he has thought about this many times. "Do we ever convert people really? The light and darkness are always present in a person, and there are moments when the bad things are reigning more strongly than the good things. These soldiers, warlords, are all victims of the political and social situation here. What is good and what is bad? I think that humiliated people will react by doing horrible things. They're asking, 'Can we be recognized as human beings?'"

The next morning, I hear news of a Cessna that has arrived in Bunia and is bound for Entebbe, Uganda. I have no business in Uganda, and Entebbe is a long way off, but I ask a UN official to give me a lift to the airport so I can get a seat. Any place in this world seems better than Bunia. While I wait for the pilot to finish up his business, I see the head of the Doctors Without Borders mission overseeing the unloading of supplies from a cargo plane. He recognizes me and comes over to say hello. I notice how old his face looks, how grave, though he's only in his thirties.

"So you're leaving," he says.

"Yeah. I'm running out of my nine lives."

He nods. "Yesterday," he says, "we had to amputate a girl's arm. We had to wait an hour with it because we weren't able to bury it. The arm was just sitting there in the bucket — we tried not to look at it." I don't know why he decided to tell me this; it is as if he were telling me about the weather. I wonder how long it will take before he allows himself to feel again.

"Is this the worst you've ever seen, here in Bunia?" I ask him.

"No. I was in Angola. Liberia. Sri Lanka."

"So do you think there'll be peace here?"

"I don't like to lie," he says. "No." The pilot is heading toward the Cessna, so I say goodbye and get in the plane. We taxi down the runway and surge into the air, but the dangers are not over yet: the pilot must gain a high altitude and avoid flying over roads or villages, to protect us from any antiaircraft fire. Gradually, Bunia and its problems shrink below us. I see that it's better to view this land from afar, muted by clouds and distance. Then I can pretend there's beauty, at least. I can forestall heartache.

Back in Volcanoes National Park, I sit high on a slope of jungle, watching a family of mountain gorillas climb down from their trees to greet us humans. Some British tourists, perched farther below, wave their camcorders around like frenetic conductors as they try to capture their first communion with these animals. Each person has flown to Africa and spent $250 for this one-hour visit, but from the awed look on their faces they're obviously not disappointed.

I rest above them, out of the way. A gorilla baby beats his chest at us and swings from a branch. Trackers busy themselves with cutting a path higher up the slope, hoping to lead us to the silverback father. I recall a photo I saw of a gorilla touching Dian Fossey: the first known physical contact this species had ever made with a human being. Fossey's face had looked radiant, blissful. She had stepped outside herself. You could tell from looking at that picture that she would never be the same again.

I am so busy recalling that image that I don't notice a female appearing from the brush nearby and coming directly toward me. The trackers haven't noticed her either, and they yell and rush up the slope. But it's too late. She's nearly reached me, is as large as I am, with long, wild black hair, a wide, flat nose, and those liquid brown eyes. I have never been this close to a wild animal before, and I don't know what to do. Fear rushes through my body, and I freeze, holding my breath. She ambles forward on her knuckles and stops just inches away from me, her eyes running over my face. As if from some other universe, faint and distant, I can hear the trackers scream and scold me — still, I can't move. All at once, she raises her arm and rests a black, clammy hand on my cheek.

The head tracker yells — he is a few feet away now — and the gorilla (her name, I learn, is Mbere) promptly drops her hand and retreats to the forest.

I watch her go, discovering that there are tears in my eyes. As a young baby climbs up the slope ahead of her, she stops to take an enigmatic look at me over her shoulder. If I could, if it were not already too late, I would follow her back into the state of wonder.

PAUL SALOPEK

Shattered Sudan

FROM *National Geographic*

THE OLDEST CIVIL WAR in the world is being fought, on one side, by men who wander like demented hospital orderlies across the primordial wastes of Africa.

I follow them one hot morning as they flee a government ambush in the oil fields of southern Sudan. One of their comrades has just been shot dead, his body abandoned on a parched savanna that hides nearly twenty billion dollars' worth of low-sulfur crude. We retreat for hours under a scalding sun, crossing in the process a vast, cauterized plain of cracked mud. I pause a moment to watch them: an antlike column of rebels dressed in bizarre homemade uniforms of green cotton smocks and white plastic slippers, limping into the heat waves of distance. Five casualties bounce in stretchers. They suffer their bullet wounds in silence. A boy marching in front balances a car battery on his head. He is the radio operator's assistant. Every few hundred yards he puts the battery down and empties blood out of a shoe.

When we finally reach a tree line, the fighters strip off their clothes and jump into a bog. The water stinks. It is infested with larvae of guinea worms, which, once ingested, burrow painfully through the body to the legs, and are extracted by making a small incision; you reel the worm out slowly, day after day, by winding it on a small stick. All around us, half-naked people move feebly through the thorn forest: ethnic Dinka herders displaced from the contested oil fields by fighting between rebels and the central government based in the faraway capital, Khartoum. Their children, stunted and ginger-haired from malnutrition, clamber in the trees.

They are collecting leaves to eat. This awful place, I learn, is called Biem — a safe haven, such as it is, of the forty-thousand-strong Sudan People's Liberation Army.

"You cannot reclaim what is lost," the sweating rebel commander says, squatting in the shade of an acacia, "so you just keep fighting for what little you have left."

He is trying to console himself. But I see little solace for the epic tragedy of Sudan. It is April 2002, and Africa's largest country is lurching into its nineteenth uninterrupted year of warfare — the latest round of strife that has brutalized Sudan, off and on, for most of the past half century. More than two million Sudanese are dead. We just left the latest fatality sprawling back in the yellow grasses, a bullet through his brain. And thousands of scarecrow civilians stagger through the scrub, starving atop a lucrative sea of petroleum.

Numbly, I crawl inside an empty grass hut to be alone. Lying flat on my back — depressed, exhausted, stewing in my own helplessness — I try to remind myself why I have returned to Sudan: Because peace is in the air. Because oil, newly tapped by the government, is shaking up the wretched status quo in Africa's most fractured nation. Because the long nightmare of Biem — and a thousand other places like it in Sudan — may soon be over.

Bulging like a gigantic hornet's nest against the shores of the Red Sea, Sudan has rarely known stability. Civil war erupted even before the nation gained independence from Britain in 1956. (A frail peace lasted between 1972 and 1983.) The roots of the violence have never changed: British-ruled Sudan wasn't a country; it was two. The south is tropical, underdeveloped, and populated by Dinkas, Nuers, Azandes, and some hundred other ethnic groups of African descent. The north, by contrast, is drier, and wealthier — a Saharan world with strong links to the Muslim Middle East. Shackled together by lunatic colonial borders, these two groups — northern Arabs and southern blacks — have been at odds since the nineteenth century, when northern slave raiders preyed on the tribes of the south.

At present, the rebel Sudan People's Liberation Army, or SPLA, controls much of the southern third of Sudan. Its insurgents sometimes carry spears as well as Kalashnikovs and are fighting for greater autonomy. The northern government in Khartoum, now dominated by Islamic fundamentalists, drops bombs on them from old Russian-made cargo planes and employs famines and modern-day slavery as crude weapons of mass destruction. So far the death toll — mostly among southern civilians — exceeds that of many of the world's recent conflicts combined, including Rwanda, the Persian Gulf war, the Balkans, and Chechnya. Four million Sudanese have been displaced by violence and starvation. Yet the calamity of Sudan unfolds largely without witnesses — an apocalypse in a vacuum. Until now.

Two factors are bringing new hope to Sudan. Neither has anything to do with the suffering of millions of Sudanese. Both involve the self-interest of outsiders.

First, the U.S. war on terrorism appears to be pressuring reforms in the northern Islamist regime. When a military coup backed by the radical National Islamic Front toppled Sudan's last democratically elected government in 1989, the country plunged into a new dark age. Independent newspapers were banned. Labor unions were suppressed. The north's moderate Islamic parties were hounded into exile. The civil war escalated to the drumbeat of jihad — holy struggle against indigenous religions and Christianity in the south. Outlaws ranging from Osama bin Laden to Carlos the Jackal settled into mansions in Khartoum's sandy outskirts. And the fundamentalists' secret police, the feared *mukhabarat,* added a new word to the lexicon of political repression — the "ghost house," or unmarked detention center.

Recently, however, Khartoum's extremists have begun mellowing. Chafing under U.S. economic sanctions, they have begun cooperating with the global war on terror. Desperate to shed their pariah status, they have bowed to Western pressure to enter peace negotiations in the civil war. In October 2002 the government and the SPLA signed a fragile ceasefire.

The second — and perhaps more profound — force of change in Sudan is less noble. It is about something the whole world wants. It is about oil.

In May 1999 engineers in Khartoum opened the tap on a new thousand-mile-long pipeline that connects the Muglad Basin, a huge, petroleum-rich lowland in the south, to a gleaming new tanker terminal on the shores of the Red Sea. The Muglad Basin, a prehistoric lake bed, is said to hold some three billion barrels of crude — nearly half the amount of recoverable oil that lies under the Arctic National Wildlife Refuge in Alaska. This bonanza, pessimists say, is just one more prize for the warring parties to fight over. But oil also has fueled renewed international interest in Sudan. And diplomats are more optimistic.

"It's a no-brainer," says a U.S. expert familiar with Sudan's many woes. "The rebels control much of the oil country. The government has access to the sea. They need each other to get rich."

A Canadian geologist who is mapping the Muglad Basin agrees: "Every Sudanese won't be driving a Mercedes tomorrow — we're not talking about another Saudi Arabia here," he tells me, "but the reserves are big enough to transform Sudan forever."

There are good reasons for skepticism. Sudan's grievances are very old and complex. They confound even the Sudanese. For many, the north-south war is rooted in the old toxic relationship between Arab master and African servant. For the religious, it is a contest between northern Islam and southern indigenous religions and Christianity. For the impoverished herdsmen on the front lines, it is a local skirmish over a water hole or favorite pastureland: violent disputes among Sudan's hundreds of ethnic groups have been inflamed — and manipulated — by the main warring parties. Yet oil cuts, literally, across all of Sudan's overlapping wars. Better than any road, or river, or political theory, the shining new pipeline leads the way through a labyrinth of misery in the Horn of Africa that defies easy interpretation.

I have traveled before to Sudan. Like many journalists, I was sent there to chronicle a freak show of human suffering: endless civil war, recurrent droughts, mass starvation, slaving raids, and epidemics of killing diseases. Today, however, I am on a different mission. I will follow the flow of Sudan's oil wealth from the implacable war zones of the south to an ultramodern export terminal on the Red Sea; to the country's future.

This will not be an easy journey. I will be forced to complete it in disjointed segments, sidestepping battlefronts, accommodating roadless deserts, avoiding suspicious bureaucrats — an erratic process that mirrors life in Sudan.

I pressed my ear against the pipeline once: the Nile Blend crude oozing inside emitted a faint liquid sigh. I listened hard, sweating under a tropical sun, trying to discern some hidden message — a clue as to whether thirty-three million Sudanese will stop killing each other anytime soon.

We are sneaking into Unity State, the start of Sudan's pipeline, some 450 miles northwest of the Kenyan border.

Flying into rebel-held southern Sudan from Kenya, you must be prepared for certain compromises. First, the flight is illegal. The central government in Khartoum disapproves of independent visits to its unseen war. Then there is the question of facilities. They simply don't exist. For almost four hours we drone over a landscape of impressive emptiness — a sea of grass that is burned and reburned by wildfires into a mottling of purplish grays, as if the muscles of the earth itself lay exposed. Later, a huge bruise darkens the western horizon: the famous Sudd, an enormous swamp clogging the flow of the White Nile. When the chartered Cessna finally touches down at a rebel airstrip, the pilot anxiously dumps my bags in the dust and leaves immediately for Nairobi. This is natural. His shiny airplane, a target for government bombers, stands out dangerously in the bleakest liberated zone in the world.

I have come to see George Athor Deng. Deng is a Dinka fighter, an SPLA commander of note. And he has promised, via shortwave radio, to show me what oil is doing to his people. He smiles sourly when I tell him what the diplomats say, that oil can bring all the Sudanese together.

"When has the north ever shared anything with the south?" he says of the government oil fields a two-day's walk across the front lines. "In the near future we will shut them down. Shut the oil down completely."

I meet Deng where he spends most of his days, issuing orders from a folding chair under a shady acacia. His headquarters, Biem, is like an engraving from another era — from the journals of Stanley and Livingstone. Stockades of elephant grass surround his crude huts. Food is precarious. His soldiers scavenge off the land and, when possible, skim UN rations dropped from airplanes for starving civilians. (His troops' canteens are empty plastic jugs marked "Canada-Aid Soy Milk.") There are at least twenty-five thousand displaced people jammed into Deng's territory, virtually all of them Dinka herders fleeing the fighting in the nearby oil fields, and whenever groups of famished refugees trudge through Biem, begging for food, the commander dispatches a marksman to shoot a hippo.

According to Deng — and he is broadly backed up by human rights groups — oil has sparked some of the ugliest fighting Sudan has seen in years. Deng and other SPLA commanders mortar oil rigs or shoot at oil company planes. And the Khartoum regime responds by striking back ferociously against local civilians. Government helicopters bought with new oil revenues strafe Dinka and Nuer villages. Sorghum crops are torched. And the dreaded *murahilin*, Muslim raiders armed by the Sudanese army, sweep through porous rebel lines on horseback, sowing terror and taking slaves. Khartoum denies that it is targeting noncombatants, just as it has long rejected responsibility for slavery in Sudan; it calls these raids tribal abductions, and says they are beyond its control.

"It is simple," Deng declares. "The government is depopulating the area to make way for foreign oil companies."

Deng's outrage would inspire more sympathy if his own forces weren't so morally tainted. Traditionally, the SPLA has mistreated as much as defended Sudan's long marginalized southern peoples. Until the south's oil wealth helped forge a common cause, various rebel factions — especially the Dinka-dominated SPLA and a variety of ethnic Nuer militias — killed each other mercilessly, often with the encouragement of government bribes. Some commanders have kept civilians malnourished in order to "farm" UN aid. And the movement's political agenda has never really solidified. The SPLA's leader, an Iowa State University Ph.D. named John Garang, claims he is fighting for a secular, unified Sudan (as opposed to the north's theocracy), yet almost every field commander, Deng included, is gunning for full southern independence.

Knowing what I do about the SPLA, I am prepared to dislike Deng. Compact, scar-faced, blinded in one eye, he promenades around the refugee lean-tos of Biem with a lackey in tow, carrying his chair. Yet there is also an ineffable sadness about him. His entire family — a wife, child, and four brothers — has been wiped out in the current phase of the civil war, which erupted in 1983. Such stupefying losses pervade life in the south. They surface all the time in small, melancholy gestures.

Like the way Deng announces the name of his soldier who is

killed, shot down and abandoned, on the ill-fated patrol that I attempt to accompany into the oil fields. "Mayak Arop," he sighs, waving a gnarled hand over a map of the expanding government oil roads, as if wishing to wipe them away.

Or in the way a bowl-bellied Dinka girl stamps out a pretty little dance on a dusty path in Biem, oblivious to the thousands of haunted figures camped in the bush around her.

Or in the answers to a simple question.

What color is oil?

"It's like cow urine," says Chan Akuei, an old herder at Biem with a belly wrinkled like elephant skin. Government troops have shot his cows, an incomprehensible crime in the Dinka universe. The Dinka adore their cattle. They rarely kill them for meat, and compose songs about their favorite animals. Akuei cannot stop talking about his murdered livestock.

"It is as clear as water," says a boy in Koch, a nearby frontline village. He is a member of an ethnic Nuer militia. The last I see of him, he is marching off at dawn to attack an oil road along with hundreds of other rebels — many of them children.

Nyanayule Arop Deng (the name Deng is common among the Dinka) doesn't know the color of oil. She sits by her skeletal husband, who is dying of kala-azar, a wasting disease that has killed tens of thousands in the oil zone. "All I know is the lights," she says dully. "They appear at night. We don't go near them."

The tower lights of Roll'n wildcat rig number 15 click on at dusk — an unexpectedly pretty sight as the sun drops behind the iron silhouettes of the thorn trees. The quest for oil is tireless, urgent, expensive. It is like a physical thirst — an around-the-clock obsession. Before the evening shift comes on, Terry Hoffman, a sweat-soaked driller from British Columbia, runs one last stand of pipe down into the skin of Sudan.

"Killer bees, cobras, and acid-spewing bugs that give you blisters!" Hoffman hollers over the rig's noisy generator, ticking off the dangers of roughnecking in Sudan. "Boredom's the worst, though. You can't even walk around this place."

Hoffman is a prisoner of his rig. He and his crew must eat their barbecued chicken and cherry pies, read their e-mail, and lift weights inside a Sudanese version of Fort Apache: a fifteen-foot-high berm has been bulldozed around the floodlit work site. Heavily armed government troops patrol the perimeter against the likes of George Athor Deng. Deng is doubtless out there tonight, plotting under his tree.

The idea behind rig 15 — a small component in a billion-dollar complex of drilling equipment, dormitories, pumping stations, new roads, and prefabricated office buildings at Heglig, Sudan's torrid version of the North Slope — is visionary in its way.

At present, none of the Western energy majors dares to drill in Sudan. Chevron suspended its exploration in 1984 after three of its employees were shot dead by rebels, and pulled out of the country altogether in 1990. (All American companies abandoned Sudan once the United States listed it as a supporter of terrorism and imposed sanctions in the 1990s.) Yet today an improbable mix of engineers from Communist China, authoritarian Malaysia, democratic Canada, and Islamist Khartoum have cobbled together an experiment in globalization on the baleful plains of the Sahel. The Greater Nile Petroleum Operating Company, as it is called, pumps 240,000 barrels of crude a day out of a war zone. Two years from now that output is projected to nearly double. It may surge even higher should lasting peace return to Sudan, and the rebels allow French, Swedish, and Austrian companies to explore their concessions in the south.

"All these stories about us pushing out local people to pump for oil? A total lie," says Bill, a rig supervisor with Talisman Energy, the Canadian partner in the Heglig project.

Bill wears cowboy boots and doesn't share his surname. Like everyone else I meet in Heglig, he seems aggrieved. Talisman has come under fire from human rights groups for allegedly turning a blind eye to government atrocities in the oil patch. (Partly because of this bad publicity, Talisman will later sell its Sudan operation to an Indian oil company.) In response to the criticism, a wary company official in Khartoum lectures me on the value of free markets in reforming oppressive regimes. Supervisors drive me around Heglig in a pickup truck, pointing out unmolested villagers in the savanna. Few of these people are southerners. Most are Baggaras, northern Muslim pastoralists who vie with the Dinkas for grazing lands, and who have come to the oil fields to hack down trees for charcoal.

"TV at home shows these incredible stories — famines and war in Sudan," says Bill. "Well, let me tell you, I've been in a two-hundred-mile radius of this place, and I haven't seen that."

Bill may be willfully blind. But then so are his faraway customers. The only difference is, Bill must walk past a rebel bullet hole in his trailer wall every day and not see it. This is a difficult feat. But a common one in Sudan.

There is no fixed front line between SPLA territory and government-controlled Sudan. No walls. No razor-wire fences. No permanent Thorn Curtain. The war is fluid. One army cedes power invisibly to another, and what changes across the no man's land are things far subtler and more profound than claims of political control. The round grass huts of Africa give way, slowly, to the square mud houses of desert dwellers. The hot blue dome of the tropical sky recedes behind a veil of white Saharan dust. As I travel north, the twenty-first century begins to reappear — roads are graded by machines, and human beings once more begin to congregate into towns. Some of these towns have sidewalks. The sight — concrete poured on the ground merely to ease walking — is mesmerizing; a surreal extravagance after the utter desolation of the south.

The oil pipeline rockets north from Heglig and crosses the eerie rock piles of the Nuba Mountains. The Nuba people, allied with the SPLA, have been fighting their own war of autonomy against Khartoum for years. A U.S.-brokered ceasefire is in place when I drive through. I see government trucks rolling up into the hills, loaded with satellite dishes. The equipment is meant for "peace clubs" designed to lure the stubborn Nubas down from their mountain strongholds and into areas of government control. "Many of them have never seen television before," a grinning official explains in the garrison town of Kadugli. "We give them twenty-two channels, including CNN. Their leaders are very irritated by this."

The pipeline burrows onward under a mound of raw earth — a monumental tribal scar creasing the barren landscape. Construction began in 1998 and was finished in fourteen months by two thousand Chinese laborers sweating through double shifts. Workers who died in Sudan were cremated on the spot and their ashes shipped back to China.

I chase the twenty-eight-inch-wide steel tube on bad roads. Dilling.

El Obeid. Rabak. The northern towns swell, turning into ramshackle mud cities. Two days north of Heglig, the pipeline disappears into slums. A cratered highway leads me into an enormous traffic jam that backs up for miles. Buses nudge through herds of sheep. Donkey carts jockey with taxis so battered they look like the products of junkyard crushing machines. Pedestrians step unhurriedly among the stalled vehicles. Yet no one is angry or abusive. There are no honking horns, insults, threats, or curses. Silently, patiently, the drivers creep forward. They advance, inch by inch, into a city of waiting.

This is Khartoum.

"Please put your notebook away," advises Asim el Moghraby. "We don't want any problems."

El Moghraby and I are perched in a borrowed motorboat, bobbing in the middle of the Nile. I have joined el Moghraby expressly to avoid problems — to admire an overlooked natural wonder of Africa: the meeting of the Blue Nile and White Nile. The two majestic streams, tributaries of the world's longest river, swirl together in a mile-wide dance of light — one the hue of an evening sky and the other the color of a milky sunrise. Yet Sudan's troubles are insistent. El Moghraby, a retired University of Khartoum biologist and my unofficial guide in the city, is nervous. Western visitors are relatively rare in the city. And he worries that I will draw the attention of secret police. We are too close to shoreline government ministries. "The regime is loosening up," he says apologetically as we chug back to the marina, "but nobody knows how much."

Change is coming to Sudan, but few know if it is deep or real. The thinking of the small cabal of generals and fundamentalists who run the country is largely opaque. Nevertheless, the virulence of their Islamic revolution began fading even before 1998, when the Clinton administration launched cruise missiles at a pharmaceutical plant in Khartoum in retaliation for Al Qaeda's terrorist bombings of two U.S. embassies in Africa. Eager to put those years behind them, Sudan's secretive rulers claim they have expelled some three thousand foreigners linked with terror groups (bin Laden and Carlos included) and that they have released most political prisoners. Opposition parties have been invited back in from the cold, though they often remain marginalized.

Driving around Khartoum with el Moghraby — a lean, balding

scholar who reminds me of a patient turtle, with his wrinkled neck and watchful eyes that dart behind wire-rimmed glasses — I see a crumbling metropolis of seven million that seems to be fluttering its dusty eyelids after a long slumber beneath the sands. Young couples hold hands on the banks of the Nile, unmolested by the morality police. Flashes of oil money glint off fleets of new Korean-made cars. And freshly painted Coke signs and a new BMW dealership have popped up in the city's shabby downtown.

Still, it is staggering to think that this insular, puritanical city — with its turbaned Arab rulers, domed mosques, and tea shops blaring pop music — is the capital of the bleeding African south. Yet the war is here too. On a blazing afternoon I visit Wad el Bashir, one of the miserable camps where some of the nearly two million southerners are sweating away their lives in and around Khartoum. Nubas and Dinkas accost me in the maze of dirt lanes. "They are taking our children!" they whisper, describing how their young men are being yanked off sidewalks and buses to fight for the Sudanese army against their own people in the south. Behind their mud huts I spot my old companion, the pipeline. Its inert presence now seems malevolent.

Popular discontent — and profound war-weariness — is only slightly less palpable among northerners in Khartoum. University students complain about the loss of jobs and political freedoms under the Islamists. Arab businessmen bemoan Sudan's ruinous isolation. ("Please tell the world we are not all terrorists and bullyboys," pleads one wealthy trader.) And several middle-class men openly boast of evading the draft — they aren't buying jihad's promise of a direct ticket to heaven.

"What you are seeing is the northern front in Sudan's civil war," explains a human rights advocate named Osman Hummaida when I share my surprise at the cynicism I find on Khartoum's streets. "Sudan is not just divided north-south. There is a broader struggle. It is the center against the periphery — a tiny Khartoum clique against everyone else, including fellow Arabs."

My tour guide, el Moghraby, is a casualty of this subtler northern war. Bullying his Land Rover through Khartoum's downtown one day, he points to a drab building and says, "That one's mine" — meaning the old ghost house where he was detained in 1992, along with his politically active lawyer. In 1995 he was arrested with his

wife for producing a documentary film critical of Sudan's environ-
mental record. He was imprisoned yet again, in 1999, for publicly
questioning the country's oil projects.

Like many disillusioned northern intellectuals, el Moghraby has
withdrawn from public life. He has retreated into private enthusi-
asms — into the past. He takes me one day to see a weathered colonial monument honoring the charge of the 21st Lancers, a once famous skirmish in the British conquest of Sudan in 1898. Wistfully,
el Moghraby talks of an older, more cosmopolitan Khartoum of
electric trams, midnight cafés, and clean-swept streets. This nostalgia is sad, especially given Britain's divisive legacy in Sudan.

As a young soldier, Winston Churchill participated in the charge
of the 21st Lancers outside Khartoum. British horsemen slammed
into the ranks of defending Sudanese troops with such force, he
wrote, that "for perhaps ten wonderful seconds" all sides simply
staggered about in a daze. The beleaguered citizens of Sudan's capital know this feeling well. They have endured it for the better part
of fifty years. It is not wonderful.

Where is undemocratic, underdeveloped, and oil-rich Sudan
headed? For answers I must leave the periphery. I go to the center.

Sudan's president, Lieutenant General Omar al-Bashir, almost
never grants interviews. Hassan al-Turabi, the intellectual father of
Sudan's Islamist movement, is also not available, having been put
under house arrest by rivals in the government. (He has since been
locked up in Kober Prison.) So the task of explaining the policies
of the secretive National Islamic Front that rules Sudan falls to
Hasan Makki, an Islamic academic and one of the regime's leading
ideologues.

Makki greets me in a dazzling white djellaba, or Arab robe, in his
spacious home. He is a member of the elite "riverine" Arab tribes
who have monopolized power in Sudan for years. Like most of Sudan's political inner circle, he is friendly, smart, and chooses his
words carefully.

On the war: "It is effectively over, my friend. The south already
has lost. Millions of their people have moved up to join us in the
north." Ignoring the detail that the refugees have not come by
choice, he calls Khartoum "an American-style melting pot."

On Arab-black hostility: "How can there be racism? Look at my skin. No northern Sudanese is a pure Arab. For centuries our blood has mixed with Africans. We are brothers!"

On oil: "It is a blessing. It will hold Sudan together. Before oil, we northerners were tired of the south. Why lose our children there? Why fight for a wasteland? Oil has changed all that. Now our economic survival depends on it."

Regarding the unpopularity of the regime, Makki has little to say. He politely pours me another cup of tea and suggests that I go look at stones.

We have flown, walked, and driven more than six hundred miles through Sudan.

The pipeline leads on — tireless and unerring, far more sure of itself in the turmoil of Sudan than I ever will be. Its oil is kept at 95°F, the temperature required for it to be thin enough to flow freely. It tunnels through Khartoum's bleak refugee camps, then slips beneath the Nile. Emerging from the other side, it disappears north into an ocean of light: the Nubian Desert.

There, baking under the sun, are Makki's stones. They are the silent remains of ancient cities and temples.

At a city called Naga, a ruin of great beauty and stillness that juts from the eroding hills east of the Nile, I see a relief carved into an imposing temple wall. It depicts a queen grasping a handful of small, doomed captives. The queen is recognizably Nubian: chiseled in pharaonic splendor, she is a mix of Egyptian elegance and full-hipped African beauty. Her prisoners too strike me as dead ringers. They look like the far-flung citizens of Sudan's modern fringe: fierce Beja nomads from the Red Sea Hills — or even Negroid Dinkas or Nubas from the south. Blinking sweat from my eyes, I stare in amazement at this antique blueprint for governance in Sudan — a two-thousand-year-old political poster advertising the power of Nile-based elites over the weak periphery.

"Some things never change," says Dietrich Wildung, head of the Egyptian Museum and Papyrus Collection in Berlin and one of the sunburned archaeologists working at Naga. "The north always thinks itself supreme — Egypt over Sudan, Berlin over Munich, New York over Alabama."

Wildung, an almost dauntingly effusive man, pads briskly around his digs in a flimsy pair of sneakers, pointing out details on a half-excavated temple that make him exclaim with pure delight. According to archaeologists, Sudan's northern deserts hide one of the great civilizations of not only Africa but the world. These Sudanic realms — variously known as Nubia, Kush, or Meroë — were no mere appendages of neighboring Egypt, as was sometimes thought. Their intelligentsia created an Egyptian-derived writing system, Meroitic, for a still unintelligible language. And the "black pharaohs" of Sudan and their notorious archers eventually gained such power that they briefly ruled all of Egypt some 2,700 years ago.

Proudly, Wildung shows me his latest discovery: an altar excavated from beneath a fallen wall. Nile gods painted on its plaster-covered pedestal indicate Egyptian influence, and the floral designs are pure Africa — all exuberance, singing colors. Ancient Greece reveals itself too in the classical flourishes on a figurine of the Egyptian goddess Isis. Crouched over a hole in the earth, we behold the unexpected beauty of Sudan's fractured nature, the art of a continental crossroads.

Can oil dilute the age-old divisiveness of Sudan? The pipeline is my guide. But it is no oracle.

North of the city of Atbara, the steel artery is patrolled by wild-looking men in vehicles mounted with heavy machine guns: mujahideen, or holy warriors, guarding the pipeline from being blown up, as it was nearby in 1999. (That act of sabotage was carried out by northern opposition forces in alliance with the SPLA.) The oil squirts across the Red Sea Hills at the pace of a fast walk. Then it races three thousand feet down to the devastatingly hot Sudanese coast. To the Bashair Marine Terminal. To the end of the line. When I visit the high-tech export facility, a Singapore-flagged tanker is preparing to gulp a million barrels of crude.

"You are looking at our gateway to the world," a jumpsuited technician tells me grandly in the sleek control room, some 950 miles from the oil wells pocking the savannas of Africa.

I hope he is right. I hope oil helps create a new era of stability in Sudan. I hope it prods international efforts, such as those of U.S. peacemaker John Danforth, to end the terrible civil war. I hope it bribes Sudan's cruel and insulated elites into abandoning selfish power struggles that have wreaked hell on millions of ordinary people. I hope it somehow lubricates relations with Egypt, the regional superpower, which exercises powerful interests in Sudan: Egypt strongly opposes southern independence, fearing that such a development will threaten its access to the vital middle reaches of the Nile. Most of all, I hope Sudan's new oil revenues — more than two million dollars a day — do not end up stoking what one analyst calls a "perfect war," a conflict waged, at tolerable cost, indefinitely. Hope: a commodity Sudan could use more of, even, than oil.

Near the end of my journey, I camp for a few days in the parched wilderness of the Red Sea Hills. My host is Abu Fatna, an old Beja, a Muslim nomad whose ancestors have roamed the eastern wastes of Sudan for the past five thousand years. His tent is pegged only forty miles west of the pipeline, yet his life is as detached from its power and wealth as those of the southern Dinkas dying at the opposite end of the oil trail. Drought has forced Fatna to sell his camels. Saudi hunters have slaughtered all the local wild antelope. He is skinny and poor, and he has only two teeth left in his head. But he still knows which desert stars to travel by. He can still handle a tribal broadsword.

When I leave, Fatna offers me a gift: he dances goodbye in the dust. The flapping of his scrawny arms, the dry snatches of song — these are meant as an honor, though they seem more like a lament. Driving back to the pipeline, I wonder if this sadness, too, somehow gets pumped out of Sudan. Along with commander Deng's bitter hand-waving over a crude map. Or el Moghraby's demoralized retreat from the world. Or the terrible absences of so many dead.

So much heartbreak, it seems, gets burned up in Sudan's oil.

THOMAS SWICK

Faces in a Crowd

FROM *The South Florida Sun-Sentinel*

Brazil may be a little absurd. But one must admit it has perfect pitch.
— Caetano Veloso

LILIAN LIVED in the Campo Belo District, across the street from a
Shell station. There are so many Shell stations in São Paulo that the
odds of growing up next to one are not excessively low, but it depressed me that first day — before I had been made aware of the
city's pervasive Shellness — when Lilian drove me home from the
airport. To her, of course, it was a staple from childhood: some of
the older mechanics, she told me, used to help her cross the street
when she was a toddler (she was now in her late twenties). And her
parents liked the fact that it never closed, and so served as a perpetual neighborhood watch for their children who tended to come
home late.

The parents lived catty-corner, above their store (Lilian led me
across to the shingle reading Bazar Liang). It was like something
from my childhood, a little mom-and-pop operation offering everything from watches to toys. (Though, admittedly, a number of the
electronics items had come on the scene since I was a kid.) Lilian
greeted the Chinese woman behind the counter in Portuguese,
then said to me in English, "Her son studied at Berkeley too." Soon
her mother came out, stopping first to put on her sandals, a pretty
woman with wonderfully smooth skin, and welcomed me to Brazil.

This was two-dimensional travel. Americans are used to immigrants at home, but abroad we still expect the undiluted national:
the bereted Frenchman raising his wine glass, not the skullcapped
Arab toting a baguette. Yet much of the world is becoming a cross-

word of cultures, while Brazil has been in the huddled-masses business almost as long and as all-embracingly as the United States (as befits a place eternally dubbed "the country of the future").

In the late 1800s, large numbers of Germans, Poles, Ukrainians, Spaniards, Dutch, Russians, Swiss, and Italians began settling in with the Portuguese, and were joined, at the beginning of the twentieth century, by Japanese, Arabs (mostly from Lebanon and Syria), and Eastern European Jews — these last three groups, along with the Italians, getting their own neighborhoods in São Paulo, though the old Jewish quarter has gradually been turned into a Little Korea.

Lilian's father came from Taiwan, first in 1968, and then, with his wife, in 1973. To support themselves they sold the only thing they had — their clothing, which the mother-to-be in pigtails peddled door-to-door. Eventually they made enough to start a business, a shop selling *pastéis*, envelopes of fried dough lined with fillings of meat and cheese. Three children — Lilian, Eugene, Juliana — were born, raised, sent to a strict German-run high school, the University of São Paulo, and then abroad to continue their studies, the first two attending the University of California at Berkeley. After graduation, Lilian worked as an intern at the *Sun-Sentinel.* Her father now spent part of every weekend on the golf course. The Liangs' is the classic American success story, only from the southern side.

The new world reeled as Lilian drove, surprisingly fast for such a gentle soul. Highways coursed through the middle of the city, which, partly because of this, appeared to have no middle. Highrises didn't cluster, they spread out in all directions. There seemed no such thing as a vacant lot or an empty lane; the infinite crush of buildings created an eternal stream of cars. I got the impression that people pulled into Shell not just for gas but for relief.

It was extremely intimidating. Usually I feel automatically at home in cities, but that's when I'm on foot; this city, like Los Angeles, was virulently opposed to feet. And, unlike Los Angeles, it had no mountains or ocean to serve as reference points. The manmade ones — Congonhas Airport, the Bandeirantes Monument — passed in a grand, inconsequential blur.

Tourists are immigrants who audit. We feel the dislocation yet bear none of the responsibility. We pick up a few words; we don't abandon our mother tongue. We come for the enticements but we don't stay for the test.

Our fleetingness deprives us of depth but rewards us with intensity. That first day in Brazil offered:

My first taste of *pão de queijo,* small balls of dough infused with cheese that instantly joined focaccia, naan, bialys, and pretzel rolls in my personal bread pantheon.

A stroll down Avenida Paulista, the Fifth Avenue of São Paulo, except that it is paralleled not by Madison and Sixth but by two narrow streets of modest apartments and ho-hum shops. (Which makes it really more like the Las Vegas Strip, a singular showpiece, the extroverted casinos here turned into international banks.) And, halfway down the Avenida, a park rises so lushly it looks like a fenced-in pocket of the Amazon.

A search, along this financial corridor, for an ATM with a Cirrus decal, and then the rush as my first two hundred reais oozed out.

A visit to the Livraria Cultura (while Lilian went to teach her Bible class), full of serious books and passionate browsers in its three passageway stores just off Paulista.

The Pinheiros neighborhood, where Lilian joked with a scraggly young man, the self-appointed guardian of our parked car, as if he were an old school friend.

Feijoada at the Consulado Mineiro, a black bean stew with bits of sausage and numerous pig parts that is eaten only for lunch, mainly Wednesdays and Saturdays (unusually strict dietary rules for a seemingly laid-back country). It arrived in a huge pot accompanied by a small bowl of kale, a dish of pork rinds, and manioc. "This is what the slaves ate," Lilian said before dispatching a forkful of beans. "Like gumbo," I said, then crunched a rind.

A TV soap (back at home) of Italian immigrants in Brazil. (Even without understanding the dialogue, I could see it was no *Sopranos.*)

Another (relatively short) drive to the club All of Jazz: *caipirinhas* (the national sugar-and-lime cocktail deliciously capping a day of revelatory tastes) and the soothing rhythms of a modern quartet.

Sunday, I awoke to the sounds of car repair. Downstairs, Lilian was already dressed, in white sweatshirt and black spandex shorts. Eugene and Juliana were still sleeping.

We hopped in the car and drove to Ibirapuera Park, where sneakered Paulistanos crisscrossed on lanes past elephantine trees and a swan-swum lake. I was struck not just by the number of people — the place was as crowded as a state fair — but by their purposefulness. Lilian and I were about the only strollers; everybody else, it seemed, was walking briskly, or jogging, or weaving energetically along wooded paths, or putting legs under raised logs for sit-ups, or cradling loose logs for weightlifting sessions. It was as if they had decided, since there was little chance for solitude (the traditional gift of big city parks), that they might as well aim for self-improvement, and not just of the human variety. There was a training pen for German shepherds. Yet I also had an image of the ultimate urbanites (São Paulo, with a population of eighteen million, is one of the world's largest cities), finally freed from their cars, now helplessly replicating the daily Formula 1 race on foot. In Ibirapuera Park, at least, Paulistanos made New Yorkers look like slackers.

The main street of Liberdade, the Japanese neighborhood, was lined with vendors. "It's illegal," Lilian explained after parking the car, "but the people don't have jobs so they do this to make money." None of the vendors were Japanese; they were found in the restaurants and shops, a good number of which sold non-Japanese goods.

"When I came back to Brazil," Lilian said as we walked toward the cathedral, "I thought about starting a magazine about our different ethnic groups. In the States you hear all this talk about diversity. So I started asking people about their backgrounds, but nobody cared." She laughed. "People don't think of themselves as Chinese Brazilian or Italian Brazilian — they think of themselves as Brazilian. So I gave up the idea."

The beauty of the cathedral was not the interior, with its stark and newish nave, but the view from the front steps, looking down onto a textbook plaza: two rows of towering palms and, off to the left, the elegant façades of turn-of-the-century edifices. It was the first thing I had seen in São Paulo that spoke of history, graciousness, the grand South American city before overpopulation. I had found the center.

We walked past a more professional class of vendor (wheeled carts as opposed to folding tables) to the Pátio do Colégio, a reconstructed part of the Jesuit mission founded in 1554, then continued down the quiet streets of an office quarter before emerging into a large open space near a busy thoroughfare (women in provocative poses outside the Cairo Cinema) and climbing a grand staircase past classical statuary to the Teatro Municipal, which signaled to Lilian the need for a left across a sizable intersection leading, a few minutes later, to a sloping street of smart apartment houses with tasteful landscaping where, near the bottom, we joined the crowd waiting for a table at Famiglia Mancini.

Inside, painted wooden figures lined the walls, and bottles of chianti, in their raffia gondolas, hung above a sea of blue-and-white-checked tablecloths. We sat in the back with Fabrizio, who had joined us outside, and ordered a serving of wild mushroom ravioli in a cream sauce.

Fabrizio was a friend of Lilian's from Berkeley, currently unemployed and enjoying life. (He came from a wealthy industrialist family.) São Paulo, he complained, got short shrift from travel writers. "You can't have eighteen million people and nothing to do in a place," he said. "The city has great restaurants, clubs, arts, music, theater — there is a kind of Broadway here."

He admitted that it was a difficult city to navigate: hopelessly spread out and with enervating traffic. But he loved it. He had lived in Philadelphia (undergrad at Penn), partied in New York, done the Bay Area: they were not São Paulo. "I wouldn't," he said confidently, "live anywhere else."

The waiter arrived, holding the ravioli out for our approval. The single serving was enough to feed a small wind ensemble.

After lunch we walked, heavily, through Bixiga. For a Little Italy, it looked a bit dour: unmatched row houses, a couple of small-windowed bars, a few canopied restaurants. "Best steak in São Paulo," Fabrizio said, passing one. We climbed a steep staircase that put us onto the "Street of Englishmen." A few doors down sat the house Fabrizio had just bought.

The seller, a museum director, let us in. Pieces of folk art were scattered all about, going very nicely with the art deco window in the bathroom, the circular cast-iron staircase from Bahia. The view from the top floor took in a jumble of tile roofs.

"If I tell you how much I paid," Fabrizio said, "you're going to want to move to São Paulo."

"How much?"

"Eighty thousand dollars."

He was looking for roommates; Lilian seemed to be high on his list. In the last three hours I had lost track of the number of times he had put his arm around her, pulled her close, caressed her arm, kissed her cheek.

On the way out, I asked the director about one of his pieces. It was a four-foot-high wooden cross on which had alighted numerous small, hand-painted birds.

"It's from Peru," he said.

"It's lovely."

"You can have it."

"Really?!?"

We walked back down the steps, I bearing my cross. A flea market occupied the square, and Lilian and I took a seat by a food stall — I had never expected to be footsore in São Paulo — while Fabrizio browsed.

"He seems quite interested in you," I said.

"No, no." She laughed. "We're just friends. I don't even think of him in that sense."

She took a sip of her water.

"I missed that in the States — people touching, hugging, kissing."

"Well, you know, we're not allowed. By law."

Fabrizio returned, holding record albums of Nana Caymmi and João Gilberto. He liked the period flavor of the albums.

"Nana Caymmi has the most amazing voice," he said. "There's something in her — I don't know how to say it in English — *timbre*."

"Timbre," I said.

"And Gilberto is a genius. The father of bossa nova. Even now, nobody can play the songs the way he does — he puts something into them that nobody else does. And he never plays a song the same way twice. He's such a perfectionist.

"He says 'Let's have lunch' and he gets a bunch of friends and he calls them up and they all have a conference call over lunch. He's crazy, but he's a god."

In the evening, Lilian and I ventured back out into the fray, barreling down highways, pummeling through intersections. We picked up her friends Daniela and Chiaki and Chiaki's friend

Paloma — making a rich Brazilian carload: Chinese, Jewish, Japanese, Bahian — and ended up at a samba club in Vila Madalena. Waiters in straw hats brought us beers, fries made of cornmeal dusted with grated cheese, beef croquettes, fried rice balls. Up toward the front, a couple danced. I was very happy — surrounded by women (until Fabrizio appeared), tasting new foods, listening to live music — and then I realized that tomorrow was Monday, when Lilian would go to work and I would be on my own in the impossible city.

In the morning, Eugene was at his post at the computer. Thin, long-limbed, handsome, preoccupied. Lilian had told me that he had really taken to Berkeley, and was not happy about being back in São Paulo, without a job, his California girlfriend returned to Istanbul. He got up to go to the post office, and when he returned it was with two chicken croquettes for my breakfast.

Around noon he walked with me to the corner, where the taxis congregated, and gave the address in my hand to one of the drivers. A group of them studied a map, burbling in Portuguese, until Eugene's right hand, held out from his waist, formed a fist with the thumb erect in that international pop-up move which in Brazil can mean anything from approval to thanks to agreement to breakthrough. *Tudo bem* (everything's good), I thought to myself. *Tudo bem.*

And why not? I was headed to lunch at the home of a woman who had married into the family that ran Brazil's largest newspaper, *O Estado de S. Paulo.* She was a friend of a friend, though, not a media mogul with a great admiration for my work. After about fifteen minutes (I had allowed for forty-five), the cab turned down the quiet, well-manicured streets of a neighborhood called Jardins. The Garden District. We pulled into a driveway abbreviated by a high green wall. I paid the fare and started off down the sidewalk for a pleasant half-hour stroll. The cabbie leaned on his horn, motioning that he had brought me to the right address (where the hell did I think I was going?), and then a door in the wall opened to reveal a guardhouse. There was no escaping my premature arrival.

Marjorie came out and greeted me while two small dogs danced at our feet. She wore a pink sequined blouse and flower-printed slacks. Inside, we took seats on sofas in front of a fireplace. Elegant rugs patterned the hardwood floor, oil paintings decorated the walls, the songs of Louis Armstrong played from unseen speakers. A moneyed calm in the heart of the gritty maelstrom.

Her father, she said, had been American; he had come to Brazil and started a chain of five-and-dimes. She had a cattle ranch in the country and an apartment in West Palm Beach. But she could never live full time in the States. "Americans are too . . ." she said, holding her hand out straight. "Brazilians are more . . ." and the hand moved up and down in gentle waves.

"What other country," she asked, "publishes the black-market rate of exchange in the newspaper?"

Other guests arrived — the travel editor of *Estado*, a translator from an aristocratic Polish family, Marjorie's daughter — all moving easily from Portuguese to English and back again. At the buffet set up in the dining room, under a mirrored ceiling, we filled our plates with slices of beef, vegetables, gnocchi, salad, rice and beans, and the ubiquitous dried manioc. "My American friends say it tastes like sawdust," said Marjorie. "But I love it."

After lunch, the daughter drove me to the newspaper offices in a faraway pocket of the city. She wore the same clothing combination as her mother, except that her blouse was a gray T-shirt, and beneath it billowed baggy fatigues. All her sentences came out in a voice of unrelieved sadness, as if she were never free of the burden of having enormous wealth in a country where millions are desperately poor.

The tour of *O Estado de S. Paulo* took over an hour. I was shown around the modern newsroom and informed about the comprehensive on-line operation. And so, inevitably, the three things that impressed were the news editor's cubicle with a taped row of votive cards of Santo Expedito ("He's the patron saint of urgent causes," the editor told me. "I'm not religious — people give these to me as a joke"); the suspendered editorial writer leaning back from his desk and puffing on a cigar à la H. L. Mencken; and the female reporter who walked over to a colleague, rubbed his bald spot, and nuzzled his cheek.

"They gave me a driver to bring me home," I told Lilian when she returned from work.

"That's right, reporters don't have drivers in the States."

"Reporters have drivers? I thought he was *the* driver, given to out-of-town visitors."

"No. Papers here employ drivers for their staffs. It makes sense. When you go out on a story, you're busy doing other things — going through your notes, preparing questions. It helps to not have to worry about driving."

Tonight, Lilian's parents were taking me out to a *churrascaria,* an all-you-can-eat place where you are visited by skewers of meat, carried by a steady succession of waiters, until you are sated. In the morning, I'd asked Eugene if he would be coming and he had said, "Sure, free food."

Before leaving, Juliana wondered if I'd ever tasted Guaraná. I said no, and she got up and walked across the street to the gas station, returning with a large plastic bottle of soda. It had a perfumey aroma and an ambrosial taste, both of which reminded me of Vernor's ginger ale.

While I sipped, she and Eugene told me about one of their favorite restaurants — Chinese, with a delicious seafood soup but absolutely no atmosphere. "It's kinda dirty," said Eugene.

"I know the type of place," I said. "With fluorescent lights, I bet." "What are they?" he asked.

I described the long tubes that produce a harsh light. They nodded in recognition.

We set off in what looked like a new direction. Modern office buildings rose in the night sky. "They're trying to make this the new Avenida Paulista," Lilian said. And I remembered Fabrizio saying that every few years in São Paulo a new center forms, and everything shifts. At an intersection I was startled by a *favela* (slum), huddled in darkness, the silhouette of a man caught in the brazen glow of one open doorway.

In the restaurant, I took a seat across from Lilian and next to her father. I told her to tell him I'd noticed his tennis trophies in the living room. He smiled politely; he had other things on his mind.

"He wants to know why the United States talks about democracy and then turns around and sells arms to different countries." Lilian said this in a voice that was as unapologetic as it was nonaccusatory.

"It's business," I said. "An American president once said, 'The business of America is business.'" I was hoping that, as a businessman, he might appreciate the sentiment. He didn't appear to.

"And throughout history," I continued, "empires have always acted out of self-interest. The British Empire did, the Ottoman Empire did. Why should the United States be any different? I'm not condoning it, I'm simply stating a reality."

Then I admitted that my country can be hypocritical in its foreign policy. Mr. Liang lifted his *caipirinha* in my direction for a toast.

"He wants to know," said Lilian, "if you think this will be the Chinese century."

"Like the twentieth was the American century?" She translated, to utter silence. Perhaps, in the Southern Hemisphere, it hadn't been. But I was surprised by the focus on China.

"When Brazil plays Taiwan in soccer, who does your father root for?"

"*Brasil,*" he answered unequivocally.

Back in the car, Lilian said, "Brazil is my parents' home now. When they came here with nothing, Brazilians helped them get started." Eugene had told me that the Brazilians had proved more helpful than the Chinese. "So they feel very grateful to the country."

We drove to Vila Madalena again, this time for jazz. A big band, fifteen musicians in black, outnumbered the audience. At the break, I chatted with a trumpeter who grew up in Miami. I asked what had brought him to Brazil.

"The music and the women," he said. "The music brings us here, and the women keep us here."

It was after eleven when we left. Driving home, Lilian pulled up to red lights, looked both ways, and then sped through, which is exactly how the police in São Paulo tell you to do it at night to avoid getting robbed.

Tuesday morning, Eugene brought me fried chicken, bananas, and a papaya. We talked, over breakfast, about basketball, films, California, Turkey. His English was excellent, practically accentless and sleek with slang. When I was ready to go out, he walked with me to the bus stop, and then waited to make sure I got the right bus.

"That's a new store," he said, motioning to the Chinese food shop behind us. "My parents are helping them out. Because people helped them when they were starting out, they now try to help others. My parents," he said without embarrassment, "are my heroes."

A bus went past; Eugene gestured that it wasn't mine. "My father always stressed the importance of education," he said. "Not just because it can lead to a well-paying job. But because when you're educated it's harder for people to take advantage of you."

My bus took me to a subway station, where I boarded a clean and comfortable car to Estaçao da Luz. The turn-of-the-century train station was undergoing renovations, but the art museum across the way looked inviting. Its ground-floor café gave onto a park of shabby voluptuousness.

"Beautiful trees," I said to the young man standing by the tourist information booth.

"Yes," he said. "But we have some social problems in the park. For example, prostitutes."

"But at night."

"No, in the day. See that woman there?" he asked, looking in the direction of a damsel in high heels. "That is not normal. No, that is a social problem."

It took me two hours to get back. The subway was a breeze, but emerging from the station I was faced with a daunting selection of bus stops. The correct bus dropped me off on an unfamiliar street. I wandered directionless around Campo Belo until, in a vision of loveliness, the Shell station appeared at the end of a block.

Lilian's house was becoming my favorite place in São Paulo. It was a refuge from the squall with its warm and generous familial embrace. I opened the front door (she had given me my own key) and walked into the dining room to write up my notes. As I hit the switch, two fluorescent bulbs flickered to life on the ceiling.

The next day, the father of one of Lilian's friends stopped by. Jan had come from Poland as a child, and now taught economics at a private university. He said that, of his students, some were there because they didn't know what else to do, others were waiting for the family inheritance. About 30 percent were good, hardworking kids.

He believed that Brazilians had a dual personality — one persona for public life, one for private — that had its roots in the country's history: the mixing of the Portuguese with Indians, and later African slaves, had produced, in his view, one person torn between two loyalties.

He also found Brazilians insular. "They don't look outside their own country," he said. "They stand with their backs to the ocean."

Whom does this sound like? Perhaps self-absorption is the unavoidable fate of immigrant nations: forgetting the world as a way of forgetting the past. Though it could also have something to do with size — the United States and Brazil are, respectively, the fourth- and fifth-largest countries in land mass — exceptional girth making it difficult to see beyond one's own immensity.

There was, too, the frustrating constant of unfulfilled promise. "Thirty-five percent of the population makes less than four hundred dollars a year," Jan said. "Only a small percentage of land is cultivated. There is no infrastructure for tourism. They think if you just put up a hotel, tourists will come."

Yet it was a good country, he claimed, for "clever people." His daughters, widely traveled, had no desire to live anywhere else. "My one daughter says the only other places she could live are Poland and Italy."

"It's a mess in those two countries, too," I said.

"Exactly," he replied.

Thiago steered quietly through the city. Whenever a car cut in front of us, Eugene, sitting in the passenger seat, would reach over for the horn, only to have his hand pushed, gently, aside. Thiago had long, wavy hair and a splotchy brown beard and an imperturbable calm. He had come down from Fortaleza to study physics.

"People are really laid-back up north," Eugene explained.

"You can get the best hot dogs in São Paulo here," he continued, as we entered the wide, refreshing spaces of the University of São Paulo. "It's made up of two sausages, a bun, mashed potato, potato sticks, peas, corn, mayonnaise, mustard, ketchup, vinaigrette, and *catupiry* — it's a Brazilian cream cheese." It made a Big Mac seem paltry.

We looped around, occasionally passing a wrecked car on the median, a policeman standing next to it. "That's part of a campaign to get students not to drink and drive," Eugene explained. The sign by one car read, "He had only two beers."

"What's the drinking age in Brazil?"

"Anytime," Thiago said. "But legally eighteen."

We parked by the School of Architecture, which Thiago thought had been designed by Oscar Niemeyer, the man responsible for the look of Brasilia. It had seen better days; its novel blurring of the line between indoors and outdoors had opened the door to moldy deterioration.

In an upstairs room, movable partitions flowed with student *pensées:*

"There exists a woman, but I don't know her name."

"Beer, bread, and peace. Legalize the beer."

"Death to the suicidal."

At a downtown light, a soiled man with a beard approached the car with bags of candy. Thiago gave him a compassionate, unswayed smile. When he was gone, Eugene translated: "He said, 'This is me, selling you, the worst candy in the world. Now, I give you some. If it's the worst candy you ever had, you don't owe me anything. If it's not the worst candy in the world, you give me forty cents.'"

We pulled in front of the house across from the Shell station. Thiago came inside and made himself comfortable in the armchair. Eugene brought out the bread rolls that Jan hadn't touched. Shortly, Lilian walked in, expressed delight at seeing Thiago, and put on a CD. I sank into the sofa, listening to bossa nova while gazing dreamily at the panda print on the wall. Lilian asked what else I wanted to see in São Paulo. I couldn't think of a thing.

PATRICK SYMMES

Don't Fence Me In

FROM *Condé Nast Traveler*

AT DUSK, while Pancho and Claudio, my guides, were loading the boats, a single planet appeared overhead, a dim beacon in the dark blue sky. Wet and cold, I waited at the edge of Lake Rivadavia, washed by the quiet melancholy that follows a long and glorious day. Over a half hour, the sky darkened from lavender through azure to black, and a host of unfamiliar constellations emerged. When a crisp half moon rose over the dark mountains of Patagonia, I felt an icy stab of heartbreak — the pain that must have hit those three Americans almost a century ago when they looked back on Cholila like this, knowing that time was against them. Leaving this paradise was tough enough after just a couple of weeks. For three hard-living, straight-shooting adventurers named Santiago, Harry, and Ethel, who spent almost four years here, that last night in 1905 must have been painful. Cholila was the only real home they had ever had, a green valley where sweat, money, and patience had brought them peace, prosperity, and respect. But they never could escape completely.

Those weren't their real names, of course. Horse thieves, bank robbers, and train bandits are wise to reinvent themselves from time to time, and the trio in question are better known to history as the charismatic Butch Cassidy, the quick-fingered Sundance Kid, and the sharpshooting Etta Place, the most famous criminals of the Wild West. As any fan of the deservedly cherished 1969 motion picture can tell you, Butch and Sundance died in Bolivia, guns blazing. (This may even be true.) What almost no one knows — simply because it was left out of the Hollywood classic — is that from 1902 to 1905, before their fiery end, the bandits were ensconced in the Andean foothills, where they built a set of cabins, lived large, cultivated a herd of more than four hundred cattle and a thousand sheep, and, under those assumed names, tried hard to go straight.

In 1902, Patagonia offered everything an outlaw could want. In this southern part of a southern land on the southern continent, there were no big towns, no nosy detectives, no real roads, and no telegraph cables whispering descriptions of wanted men. Land for grazing and homesteading was plentiful, the local horses were excellent, and a couple of pistol-packing American cowboys blended right into the tiny community of North American ranchers, Welsh colonists, and gauchos — tough Argentine cowboys with their own outlaw traditions. In Cholila, the three were safe. They should have stayed here forever.

But only mountains last that long. When Claudio started the engine, Pancho waved me out of my starlit reveries and into the back of the truck. Perhaps only leaving a place truly preserves it. The fishing rods rattled against one another as we drove up the hill and then rumbled down deserted gravel roads toward the kind of place one can never really leave.

"My dear friend," Butch Cassidy wrote to a woman in Utah in 1902, "I am still alive. . . ." Indeed. Datelined "Cholila, Argentine Republic, S. Am.," his long letter explained how and why he had vanished into one of the most remote places on earth. He described how the outlaws had "inherited" some ten thousand dollars each — money withdrawn from a Nevada bank at gunpoint — and how, enriched by the fruits of their crime, they had headed south, taking new names, looking for a new start.

In Cholila, they finally found what they were looking for: the ultimate hideout. Four valleys meet here in the kind of verdant, high-mountain bowl common in Wyoming or Montana (*cholila* means "beautiful valley" in the local Mapuche language). On the rolling lower slopes, the Andean cordillera is forested with conifers and three-thousand-year-old alerces, a South American sequoia. Higher up, the mountains show bare shoulders of gray stone, dominated by the 8,200-foot Tres Picos, where snow is visible even in summer. Icy, deep-blue lakes — among them Lezama, Pellegrini, and Cisne — drain into a single crystalline river, the Carrileufú, which meanders down the valley for dozens of miles until it reaches Lake Rivadavia, at the northern edge of Los Alerces National Park.

Butch was punctuation-challenged and prone to misspellings, but he described Cholila and all of Patagonia with a plainspoken passion that had seduced me from thousands of miles, and a full century, away: "This part of the country looked so good that I located, and I think for good, for I like the place better every day. . . . The country is first class. . . . I have never seen a finer grass country, and lots of it hundreds and hundreds of miles." The winters were mild, the summers splendid, the grass "knee high everywhere," and there was "lots of good cold mountain water." Even more important, Patagonia offered space: space to run cattle, space to build homes, space to live unseen. There was so much empty land here that Butch predicted it would never fill up with people — not "for the next hundred years."

I returned one hundred years after Butch made his prediction, and Patagonia was still a land of hideouts, hidden valleys, and horse adventures — as vast as the American West but with few roads, fewer towns, and more scenery than one person can appreciate in a lifetime. I also found some differences — among them, Latin America's most accomplished tourism infrastructure. In northern Patagonia, towns like Bariloche, El Bolsón, and Esquel offer some glamour, bustle, and shopping. In southern Patagonia, a state-of-the-art airport has opened up a whole region of glacier country to visitors. And Argentina's rattled economy has meant deep discounts and empty hotels. But the essential qualities that drew Butch and Sundance are in oversupply.

It is still possible to mount up and disappear into the mountains. I wanted to escape that way, to ride among gauchos and live in immense spaces without regard for the law or the clock. This ambition suffered from only two flaws: I have a great deal of experience with horses — all of it bad; and gauchos are usually described with adjectives such as haughty, humorless, surly, silent, macho, and even murderous. If I was to fit into the world of these famous knife fighters the way Cassidy did, or to ride like Sundance among modern hard-luck cowboys, it was time to get in touch with my inner outlaw.

Early on a Saturday in February, under summer skies as blue as the pale Argentine flag, boys from up and down the Cholila Valley began to drift south, riding bareback. In Cholila, *caballos* still outnumber cars ten to one. They stashed their mounts — Criollo half-breeds mostly, in a kaleidoscope of brown, gray, chestnut, bay, piebald, and roan — along the river, then sat down in the dust and talked. Patagonia breeds patience.

From Tierra del Fuego to the Bolivian border, every town in Argentina has a gaucho festival — or two or three. The crucial ingredients at these national displays are a massive barbecue (the famous *asado* of beef, lamb, and sausage) accompanied by tests of horses and horsemanship. The Cholila Valley celebration, held in a meadow beside the glittering Carrileufú, was small and typical. Beef sizzled over a fire, and the appetizing smoke drew some 150 residents — much of the population — and 40 horses.

By noon, two score of wild-looking gauchos had cantered into the meadow, with more horses (and dogs) in tow. It was easy enough to pick them out from the more ordinary citizens of Patagonia. Gauchos come in all colors — their bloodlines are a mixture of Spanish and Indian, with an occasional dash of black, Italian, or even Arab — but their clothing hardly varies. They wear *bombachas* — baggy, pleated riding trousers — and flattish black hats. Their ultimate signature is the *facón*, a long knife tucked into the back of an ornamented belt or sash.

Gaucho derives from an Indian word meaning "orphan," and traditionally the gaucho is an outcast, a drifter on a horse whose great days are always said to be long in the past, before fences and cellular phones narrowed the world. Hardened by the sun, disdained by city dwellers, gauchos are still aloof, valuing independence above all. They distrust paperwork, towns, and religion. (Nick Reding, author of *Last Cowboys at the End of the World,* says a gaucho wedding is nothing more than saying *vamos,* or "let's go," to a woman.) If I turned my back on the row of pickup trucks parked along the Carrileufú, there was nothing at this fiesta that Butch and Sundance would not have recognized. Even the races would have been familiar. At one in the afternoon, an elderly gaucho lifted his hat in the air and the pounding of hooves marked the first start. The course was only a hundred yards long, and two riders sprinted down and back, the winner of each heat promoted to the next. The drumbeat of hooves continued until finally a young man with no hat outgalloped the last competitor to cheers.

One of the gauchos, already inebriated at two P.M., rolled off his horse. Egged on by dogs, his bay mare went wild — bucking through the meadow, scattering families and throwing hooves at tiny children. Instantly, horsemanship was no game: six gauchos leaped into the saddle and burst across the field. The same hatless boy was first to run down, bridle, and yank to a halt the bay. The other gauchos tried not to embarrass him with any praise.

The *juegitos,* or "little games," then resumed with a drag race; the gauchos reran the same two-way sprints, this time leaping off their mounts in the middle to don dresses or skirts and blouses. This event was organized on the theory — a correct one — that even the best horse will panic at the sight of a gaucho in a dress. One after another, the heats dissolved into chaos and laughter as the gauchos hurled their mounts down the field, struggled into flowery sundresses or flimsy black skirts, and then, tripping on their hemlines, chased their mounts around the field. The horses would have none of it. The crowd was delirious.

The *asado* sizzled, and in the heat of the late afternoon, some older gauchos sought shelter beneath the trees along the Carrileufú, sipping Mendoza wine from cardboard boxes. Cholila's other fiesta had been canceled this year as a result of Argentina's economic chaos, but in the shade of a beautiful valley, exchange rates and IMF missions meant little. "What happens in the rest of the country doesn't affect us much," an almost toothless veteran told me, handing me the wine. "We live from our own resources here."

The blast of an accordion heralded a *malambo,* the traditional gaucho dance. A dozen adolescents circled and stamped in the field, the girls in white peasant dresses, the boys wearing the finely woven belts and black *bombachas* of their elders. At sunset, the party began to break up slowly. I complimented a black-clad gaucho on his horse, and he jumped down and insisted that I ride it. I went around the field twice, shook hands, patted my steed, and missed Cholila already.

I dismounted into the hands of Jorge Graziosi, my host at the Arroyo Claro fishing lodge across the road. Graziosi collects traditional Argentine saddles and tack, and says that Butch and Sundance may have left an imprint on today's fiesta. Many of the older Cholila gauchos — grandsons of the men Butch and Sundance rode with — were wearing their neckerchiefs tied in a broad trian-

gle, the "bandit" style familiar to any American child. But in the
rest of Argentina, gauchos roll and knot their kerchiefs. The
Cholila men also buckle their spurs across the back, American
style. Gauchos elsewhere tie them with leather straps.

Graziosi bought a ranch here in 1982, fleeing the steady development of Bariloche, Patagonia's main tourist city. To the south is
the vast Los Alerces park, filled with groves of sequoias, emerald
rivers, and rippling ridges. Rolling north is the lightly settled valley
of Cholila, with gravel roads and few telephones. His main guide,
Pancho, is a wry Chilean who had dragged me from river to river all
week to catch large rainbow and brown trout, an arduous routine
interrupted only by vast meals and short naps in the gnarled forests. "I like this kind of life," Graziosi told me. "We work the ranch.
There aren't many people around. No towns with buses, no telephones. Horses everywhere. It's like living fifty, sixty, or seventy
years ago."

Or a hundred. I drove into the "town" of Cholila the next day —
a cluster of cinder-block houses down the valley, without a restaurant or a hotel but overrun with horses. Three more were tied in
front of the information booth. Patiently waiting amid maps and
handicrafts for the rare tourist, Karina Quintana confirmed what
I'd heard: the cabins that Butch and Sundance built are still standing, albeit barely. "They are in total disrepair," she said. "They are
just falling down." A plan to preserve them as a museum has been
stuck for eight years in the provincial bureaucracy. There are so few
visitors that it costs more to collect an admission fee than the fee
generates. In the meantime, the unprotected site is vulnerable.
"Don't tell people where they are," Karina insisted. Any publicity
draws souvenir hunters, who have already stripped doors, windows,
and even pieces of wallpaper from Butch's rooms. (If you want directions, just ask anyone, but first take a vow of chastity.)

Before pointing me in the right direction, Karina brushed
off her leather pants, leaped onto the counter of her booth, and
started shooting. She was imitating Etta Place, riding sidesaddle
while blasting pistols at the posse that had chased the gringos out
of town that last night in 1905.

Never mind that Etta always used a rifle, or that they slipped away
quietly. The legend — the myth — was close.

*

Even with directions, it was easy to miss the spread. I went half a mile in the wrong direction and entered the long driveway of the Casa de Piedra, a Welsh teahouse. In this stone refuge beneath tall conifers, the elderly owners fed me a stream of orange, apple, chocolate, and *dulce de leche* cakes, along with the traditional black torte of Wales. Bruce Chatwin had visited here in the 1970s while researching *In Patagonia;* he'd gotten everything wrong, they said. Stuffed with cake, I nodded and followed a pointed finger toward the cabin, which was almost in sight. "My grandmother always said that Etta was very beautiful," owner Victorina called out as I was leaving.

I parked by the road, hopped a fence, and cut through a field of daisies that smeared my trousers with yellow pollen. The fugitives had picked their site well: the cabin and two outbuildings were nestled among trees in a broad, flat valley backed by a steep Andean ridge. A small river, the Río Blanco, bursting with tiny trout, caressed a bank behind the buildings.

A century does real damage. The main cabin of four rooms had more hole than roof; the doors and windows were missing. The handiwork of two Americans was obvious in the low structure, built Wyoming style with chinked logs overlapping at the ends (Argentines build steep roofs to shed snow, don't chink, and lay even corners). I touched the adze marks and could smell the sweat and hear the cussing as Butch and Sundance lifted the timber. Etta's domestic touches are still visible: neat wainscoting and tatters of wallpaper, pink roses on burlap backing.

When it was finished, this was instantly the most famous house in the valley. Sundance and Etta had gone on an international shopping spree and filled the place with fine china, silverware, furniture, and special North American–style windows that wowed the locals. An Italian visitor in 1904 described a scene of frontier luxury, the walls lined with pictures in cane frames, magazine art, and "many beautiful weapons and lassos." Butch and Sundance hired gauchos to do the work and, under the influence of Etta, spent their spare time reading. They also did paperwork: a maze of purchases and sales, individual and joint stock companies, and a complex legal claim for homesteading the land. In short, they went straight. When the governor of the province visited, the Americans threw a fiesta for the valley. Sundance plucked out Argentine *zambas* on a guitar, and the governor danced with Etta before retiring to sleep in Butch's bed.

It has become impossible to separate Butch Cassidy and the Sundance Kid from *Butch Cassidy and the Sundance Kid*. Paul Newman's crafty, garrulous Butch and Robert Redford's silent, menacing Sundance may have reversed reality. Sundance learned Spanish and *zambas*, while Butch suffered in "Single Cussedness" and struggled to understand the local gossip. Butch made a mistake, lending a horse to an escaped prisoner: it was an impulsive gesture of solidarity with a man on the run, but there was a court hearing. The rumors reached Buenos Aires and then New York, and in 1903 one of the tireless Pinkerton detectives landed in Argentina with Wanted posters in Spanish (Pinkerton had sent them as far as Tahiti). The pressure began to mount on their idyll. When a bank seven hundred miles away in Río Gallegos was robbed by two other North Americans, suspicion fell on Butch and Sundance. After the holdup a deputy, apparently smitten with Etta, tipped them off that the territorial police were coming.

Blamed for a crime they didn't commit, hunted for those they did, Butch, Sundance, and Etta decided not to wait. They fled Cholila and rode north, outlaws again. The end of their story is still hotly debated, but Hollywood got it about right: after a botched robbery in Bolivia, the men were probably cornered by soldiers and killed.

It was easy enough to hear, above the tinkling of the Río Blanco, the ringing voices and laughter, the sound of glasses clinking out toasts, even the faint notes of Sundance's guitar. The windows must have been open, too, on that festive summer night.

"Secure," it said in my Spanish-English dictionary. Seguro isn't much of a name for a horse, and Tommy isn't much of a name for a gaucho, but Seguro and Tommy took me over the Continental Divide. By the time we turned down into the valley of Corcovado, south of Esquel, I'd learned Seguro's bad habits, like scraping me against trees, stopping for water every five minutes, and lurching automatically toward home when left undirected.

Seguro did have good qualities. An Argentine Criollo, she climbed strongly and looked where she placed each hoof, a vital habit on the almost vertical trails that led us up and over the Andes. And despite his name, Tommy was all gaucho. He dressed in black (shirt and hat) and blue (*bombachas*), spoke little, and kept a straight face even while watching me mount up. The only thing that made Tommy smile was when I asked for yerba maté. "Not many foreigners like maté," he said, grinning as he stoked a little fire to boil water.

We sipped at the bitter green tea in a small, aged shack high on a ridgeline over the Corcovado Valley. Twin threads of the Andes ran north for sixty miles. Chile was visible to the west, the great, flat Argentine Pampas to the east. Trevelin, a sweetly modest town of Welsh-descended farmers, was on the horizon.

I'd wandered down from Cholila over the course of several days, passing first through Los Alerces park and the classic Hostería Futalaufquen, a grand lodge built in the 1950s to jump-start Patagonian tourism. Thirty miles from the park's southern exit is Esquel, the Bozeman of Patagonia, bustling with rafters and backpackers. Esquel was the scene of the most famous crime the boys didn't commit. Two foreigners had killed a Welsh shopkeeper named Llwyd Ap Iwan, a murder that Bruce Chatwin blamed on Cassidy and the Kid. His *In Patagonia* convinced a generation of visitors that, contrary to the movie, a posse of outraged Welsh settlers had eventually chased down and killed the duo here in Argentina.

But Chatwin should have spent more time fishing. Heading for the notoriously trout-packed Arroyo Pescado one afternoon, I cut across the old Ap Iwan estate and promptly stumbled on a faded gravestone. "Ap Iwan," it read, "1909." Butch and Sundance couldn't have done the deed: they had fled Cholila in 1905, and by 1906 were posting letters from Bolivia, asking friends in Cholila to sell the remaining cattle. By 1907 they were probably dead. I celebrated their innocence, however transitory, by landing seven rainbow trout on the Ap Iwan stream, and then drifted off to sleep under a Lombardy poplar, muttering "They'll never take me alive" to no one in particular.

A couple of hours of gravel south was Corcovado and the Estancia El Palenque. Butch and Sundance had briefly worked for a predecessor ranch in this area, Pampa Chica, which translates roughly as "Little Pasture." Tommy (and Seguro) had led me up from Palenque to just such a little pasture. This clearing was the only flat spot in the steep terrain, and it was my theory — Chatwinesque in its inventiveness — that Butch and Sundance must have ridden these trails. Tommy used his *facón* to stir tea, cut bread, chop wood, pick his teeth, and skewer bits of steak. We made it back down to El Palenque by midafternoon, where owner Jeff Wells was gearing up for fishing. I strolled up the valley with him to a favorite hole on the Corcovado River, where Pacific salmon rested under a willow tree. At just thirteen thousand acres, El Palenque is "quite small" by Patagonian standards, Wells said in all seriousness. He'd expanded an old farmhouse into a tourist lodge five years ago, but his passion for Patagonia was more pleasure than business. Like Butch, he was a Mormon from the American West, and everywhere he looked there was a distilled essence of home, a dream of the Old West. "That letter is why I came here," he said of Butch's 1902 missive. "You can still drink from the streams. The grass is still knee high."

At the river, thousands of giant stone flies hatched out of the water, and we stayed until it was too dark to see.

I finally flew south, to the region that has changed least since Butch's day, to both the past and the future of Patagonia. Two immense lakes slid under the wingtips as we approached El Calafate: first the turquoise-tinted Lake Viedma, and then, after a bleak stretch of brown tussock, the wind-flecked Lake Argentino, also hued almost green with glacial melt. The ribbon of rugged Andean peaks was interlaced with crystalline glaciers. We set down at an inviting new glass-and-steel terminal in the middle of absolutely nothing. Less than an hour away was the grand Perito Moreno Glacier, three miles of ice sliding thunderously into a lake. The town of El Calafate has little to offer except rental cars that take visitors into a network of small towns, tourist-ready estancias, and national parks.

I headed out in a rented Fiat toward the trekking capital of Patagonia, the puny town of El Chaltén, cutting north across the mouths of lakes Argentino and then Viedma. I was on the notorious Route 40, a gravel track along the face of the Argentine Andes where flat tires and muffler-mangling mounds of gravel are routine. The four-hour trip took an extra hour because I had to stop to stare at the glaciers so often. Dating from just 1985, El Chaltén has some two hundred year-round residents and feels freshly carved from the landscape, with tin-roofed houses, wooden restaurants, and brick lodgings along a tiny valley. Directly above the town are the needle-sharp peaks of Egger, Torre, and Fitz Roy, which inspired the skyline logo of the Patagonia clothing company. The surrounding cordillera is filled with a compact assortment of glaciers, lakes, deep forest, and superb hiking trails; the scenery and trekking opportunities are the equal of the more famous Torres del Paine park in Chile, but without the crowds or the trash. The idea of this outer space ever "filling up" with people is still laughable a century after Cassidy dismissed it. Within minutes of checking into El Puma, the best lodge in the valley, I heard the refrain I would encounter again and again: "We like it so much better than Torres," an American couple told me.

In uncrowded El Chaltén, the biggest problem was finding anyone to hike with, and I had to set out alone before dawn on a trail that led me up a twisted canyon and two hours along a milky river to a cluster of expedition tents. There I joined guide Yamila Cachero and a Brit, a German, a Canadian, and two Uruguayans for a daylong assault on the Torre Glacier. We pulled ourselves over the river on a steel cable, then hiked to the face of black, gravel-strewn ice (glaciers are filthy at first glance). Once we had strapped on our crampons and climbed on top, we faced a sea of white rippling moguls, broken and craggy, riven by deep-blue cracks filled with ice water. A slip was a bad idea. Yamila shepherded us over the crevasses and then spent several hours on belay, instructing us in the basics of scaling ice walls with an ax and ropes. The white expanse was really four separate glaciers that flowed together into a single frozen river, thundering with unseen avalanches. The ice steadily cracked, rumbled, and vibrated under our crampons.

The scale of Patagonia has always impressed me — indeed, it is the central characteristic of the place — but the next day's trip to Perito Moreno National Park must have been a hallucination. Route 40 unrolled from the horizon for a full ten hours. The lack of traffic — a car an hour — was unnerving, and in the solitude, even the static on the radio had a comforting sound. On a high hill, the Fiat's AM band finally caught a whisper: "Pops, I'm out of the hospital," a voice said. And then, "Murillo, I will call Thursday at four." This was a "messages" broadcast, where families sent missives of startling intimacy over the public airwaves to gauchos in remote pastures ("Your children need you," I heard once, and "Alejandro, there isn't anyone else"). The silence that engulfed me in the next valley made Patagonia a synonym for loneliness. At sunset, a sign for the Perito Moreno park greeted me — and then nothing. Only six hundred people visited the 284,000-acre park last year. Eighty percent of it is closed to visitors, permanently, a wilderness for pumas and condors. There is no infrastructure beyond a single dirt road, some campsites, and two places to stay, both working ranches.

The first was Estancia Menelik, where I landed in the midst of preparations for an *asado*. Inside a tin wind shelter, manager Augustine Smart, round and red-bearded, was overseeing his gauchos as they banked a red-hot fire, skewered an entire lamb, and staked it over the coals. Estancia Menelik is the showcase property of Cielos Patagónicos, an investor group aiming to save failing ranches — and the gauchos on them — with green tourism and a dash of development. Smart spoke of Cielos Patagónicos as a project whose goal was "to conserve the ecology, the history, and the culture of each place." But part of the funding to save a failing ranch like Menelik might come from developing two hotels and vacation homes in El Chaltén. Cielos Patagónicos president Lionel Sagramoso conceded that the Chaltén proposal was "a total real estate investment," but the money raised would fund the group's conservation mission elsewhere.

Like some locals, Yvon Chouinard, the founder of Patagonia, Inc., is critical of this blend of development and preservation. "I've made lots of trips down there and I just love that place," he says of Patagonia. But the plan to build a lodge outside El Chaltén in order to fund preservation elsewhere is "horrible," Chouinard says. "Development like that is something we want to stop." He thinks El Chaltén is already overbuilt (something of a purist, he calls the adorable town "a horrible, junky, trashy little place"). He is a board member of the Patagonia Land Trust, which buys up large estancias in southern Argentina and dismantles rather than develops, ending ranching and removing fences in the hope of someday converting the land into national parks.

Around the fire at Menelik, as we tucked into slivers of seared and tender lamb, this duel between development and preservation seemed totally abstract. Like Butch, I could not foresee Patagonia "filling up." The park's six hundred visitors a year don't justify development of anything. Ten hours from the nearest airport, with snow closing the roads for two months every year, this region will probably still offer a terrific hideout for some twenty-second-century Sundance.

The next day, I moved to Estancia La Oriental, the other lodging in Perito Moreno National Park, where I slept in a cold but comfortable room and saw a condor while drinking coffee at eight A.M. The bird's eleven-foot wingspan was silhouetted against the sky like a splayed hand as it drifted over the house into the backcountry. Guanacos — fleet, short-haired cousins of the llama — galloped everywhere in herds of a dozen or more. Gray and red foxes slinked through the dry sage grass. Armed with binoculars, I spent a cold and fruitless morning hiking on the Belgrano Peninsula, scanning the windfalls of timber for a puma. The population has stabilized at about twenty-two cats.

The last morning at La Oriental, owner Manuel Lada just handed me a horse. Like Butch helping that fugitive, Lada didn't ask where I was going, or why, but simply caught, bridled, and saddled a chestnut for me at the first suggestion of need. He didn't even know the creature's name. There were abandoned horses all over the property, and they ran feral in the park approaches.

No Name took me over a ridgeline and then across a wet valley to the base of the thousand-foot cliff where that condor had come from. Dozens of broad white guano stains made it easy to spot, high overhead, the nests of the rookery, one of the largest gathering sites for these rare birds in all of the Andes. No Name was jaded from long exposure to condors; she merely ate her way across the meadow while I waited, binoculars in hand. After an hour, I was rewarded by the sight of a single condor stretching its neck, shaking out its massive wings, underlaid with white, and then awkwardly heaving from the cliff to soar high into the park.

It is still easy to get lost in Patagonia, deliberately or not, and on the way home I forced No Name down the wrong path, detoured somewhere, and encountered a wire fence. I dismounted and put a hand on the steel strand cutting through this immensity, convinced that if I turned back, we could head wherever we wanted. We'd live off the land for a while. No one would find us down here, in 1903 or 2003. Overfull with light and space, I burst into an off-key rendition of "Don't Fence Me In."

No Name snorted with derision, a throaty sound that flushed a pair of tall brown guanacos from the underbrush a hundred yards away. They ran and took the fence in a bound, their hooves clicking over the top wire, thump, thump. Under the tips of my fingers I felt the instant telegraph of their break for the backcountry.

A hundred years from now, you'll find them here.

PATRICK SYMMES

The Kabul Express

FROM *Outside*

WHEN THE WORLD COMMUNITY of do-gooders arrives to rescue a nation from itself, the first sign is the blinding white traffic jam. White Land Rovers stack up thick at the airport; white Nissan Pathfinders block the streets at lunch; miraculous white-on-white Toyota Land Cruisers choke the traffic circles of the lucky target country.

This caravan of chariots was triple-parked outside the Mustafa Hotel in downtown Kabul on a Saturday night. Late-model four-by-fours filled the avenue and circled the block, churning up dust as the chauffeurs maneuvered for parking. I threaded my way through a cluster of acronyms: UN, UNESCO, UNDP, UNHCR, FAO, UNICEF, UNICA, UNAMA, UNOPS, UNEP, MSF, ACF, MAP, MACA, IRC, WFP, IOM, IMC. Even the hotel was painted white. I could hear Shakira playing faintly from above.

The ground floor of the Mustafa holds a dank cybercafé that doubles as a bar, the only public place in Kabul to get draft beer. A Turkish de-mining technician sat typing homebound messages at a terminal while a Brit, a white South African, and a black Kenyan sat on stools, nursing beers and ignoring one another.

"You want the roof," the Kenyan told me.

Many NGOs — nongovernmental organizations — had banned their staff from frequenting the Mustafa after the owner's son went on a window-smashing rampage during a particularly violent business feud. Now that the hotel was off-limits, everyone was here. Spread out on the roof was the full cast from the theater of charity: UN staff, humanitarians from the 1,800 aid groups registered in

Kabul, suit-wearing security ninjas, and ubiquitous consultants. By some estimates, there are 10,000 or more foreign civilians in Kabul — about the same number as there are U.S. military personnel in all of Afghanistan, and twice the 4,800-person NATO-commanded International Security Assistance Force that keeps the peace in the city. This moths-to-the-flame aid tribe moves from global trouble spot to Third World crisis, Africa to Asia, Bogotá to Beirut. The roof looked like a cross between a kegger and a siege.

It was, in fact, a book party. *The Survival Guide to Kabul*, a kind of underground tip sheet for expats, had been circulating in a 16-page photocopy edition for a year, but tonight it was coming out as *Kabul*, a 178-page paperback crash course on first-aid kits, bad hotels, and who really makes those rugs. The two British authors, Dominic Medley and Jude Barrand, both NGO aid workers, were selling it through a network of street children, who took it on a five dollar commission and hoped to sell it for fifteen, keeping the spread.

"Who are these people?" I asked Dominic, gesturing across the roof.

He leaned up from signing books and grinned. "I have no idea!"

A few spooks, certainly. Two American men put their gray heads together and whispered about Cuban-run hotels in Prague, while a chatty Brit fumbled the introduction of an American to his friends: "Are you clandestine, or do you just tell people you're from —" he asked, before being abruptly shushed. A claque of NGO folks groused about the way house rents in Wazir Akbar Khan, the city's best neighborhood, had shot up to five thousand dollars a month. Righteously nonprofit, they held themselves aloof from their cousins, the BONGOs, or business-oriented NGOs, who mingled charity with actual profits. German soldiers knocked back three-dollar Bitburger pilsners, and militaryspeak flashed through the night: "Green on green" fighting (Muslims versus Muslims) had "gone kinetic," and the world's most wanted man was referred to only as "OBL."

There were journalists, of course — the television flesh puppets had fled for Iraq months before, but a few lean stringers complained about the Mustafa's moldy rooms. And diplomats. A cultivated European in his fifties rhapsodized about his recent first encounter with opium, sounding as tripped out as any hippie on the

Kathmandu trail, at least until he admitted he'd spent the entire drug trip — rave on! — cleaning his house.

There were Afghans on the terrace, too — they were the ones drinking the free water. A few had stayed in-country under the Taliban; others were exiles back from Virginia or Munich, full of schemes for exporting mulberries and converting monastic caves into B&Bs.

The night was soft and utterly black. The shape of TV Mountain — named for the transmitter on top — was sketched out by the tiny lights of shanties on its slopes. Shakira was replaced by a trio of traditional musicians in the courtyard, their wailing melodies drifting up to the roof. An Afghan man began to dance Sufi style, spinning with his eyes closed and arms outstretched. The foreigners tossed the musicians small bills of afghanis, a currency worth pennies fluttering down into the dark.

The party lasted until after three. The first call to prayer echoed out at 3:42 A.M., just a few winks away.

Way back in that era of naïve joy known as the 1960s, Afghanistan was a symbol of something other than war. It was the luminous mystery at the center of Asia, a kingdom of infinite skies and peerless peaks. Kabul was the antique capital of a romantic nation, and Chicken Street, the city's enclave of hotels and restaurants, was a ghetto of global hippies and seekers. By the late 1970s, Afghanistan had become perhaps the most storied name on the trekkers' road less traveled, the famous "overland route" where strangers banded together in VW vans, sharing love affairs and mimeographed tip sheets en route to the "Three K's" — Kabul, India's Kullu Valley, and finally Kathmandu. Islam was musical, mystical, and embracing, the prices cheap, the dope wicked. Afghanistan was, in the idiom of the age, mellow.

And it will be so again.

Yes, Afghanistan. After twenty-five years of war and civil war, the people and politics are beginning to come full circle. In the sixties it was the hippie trail that brought change; this time it was B-52s, dropping loads of modernization, leaving foreign troops and civil schemes in their wake. Since the American overthrow of the Taliban, in late 2001, the UN and its acronymic camp of followers have parachuted into Kabul, pursued closely by the shock troops of low-rent globalization: entrepreneurs and actual tourists. The future — however tentative and fragile — is back.

"There are a lot of cultural similarities between then and now," one of the veterans of both eras, Nancy Hatch Dupree, said. "They're trying to open it up again." In 1977, Dupree, an American expat, published the definitive — and, for the time being, last — guidebook to the country, *An Historical Guide to Afghanistan*, a 492-page odyssey down every bumpy road of delights. A friend to prime ministers, rebel commanders, and even the Taliban, Dupree now lives in Peshawar, Pakistan, but returns often, at age seventy-six, to oversee various organizations she has founded — like SPACH, the Society for the Preservation of Afghanistan's Cultural Heritage — and to advise the Ministry of Information and Culture.

"Travel today is about like it was in the 1960s," said Dupree. This was partly a promise and partly a warning — the highways are in shambles, the land is still scattered with up to ten million land mines. In many ways, I'd picked a terrible moment to venture into the provinces: the country is littered with unexploded ordnance; attacks by Taliban holdouts, mostly in southeastern Afghanistan, have been increasing; and even the pro-government warlords ruling the "safe" provinces have their own armies. In early October, the White House formed a "stabilization group" for Iraq and Afghanistan, a tacit acknowledgment of the "deteriorating security conditions" cited in a June 2003 joint report on Afghanistan by the Council on Foreign Relations (CFR) and the Asia Society. President Hamid Karzai's government has international clout but neither the money nor the troops to back it up in the provinces. At the current rate of training, there will be only 9,000 soldiers in the Afghan national army by mid-2004, compared with 100,000 militiamen for the various warlo — I mean "local leaders."

According to the World Bank, Afghanistan will need $15 billion in reconstruction money in the next five years, above and beyond relief aid. Meanwhile, opium has been reborn as a $2.5 billion shadow economy, twice the amount of foreign aid received in 2002 and more than the government's entire $2.25 billion budget. Last year, according to the report, one warlord, Ismail Khan, of the western city of Herat, reportedly levied $100 million in customs duties; the central government took in $80 million nationwide.

But as one veteran of the UN's de-mining program reminded

me, it used to be so much worse. Just over a year ago, Taliban rockets were still hitting close to Kabul. The memory of chaos is so fresh that, in one of those undiplomatically honest comments made only on background, she said, simply, "Warlord is *good.*" Afghans want order, and are slowly getting it. "It's too early to talk about success or failure," said David Haeri, special assistant to Lakhdar Brahimi, the UN envoy to Afghanistan. "Whether the glass is half full or half empty, there is water in it."

The CFR/Asia Society report concluded that "even though the international effort is not perfect, it has functioned reasonably well." Land mines are slowly being cleared; Karzai is collecting pledges of disarmament and (some) taxes from regional warlords; and European military personnel are gradually expanding their control beyond Kabul. Things that have been impossible in Afghanistan for decades are suddenly within reach.

The new age has its contradictions. A blob of opium, for eating, costs twenty-five cents in the back alleys of the Kabul bazaar, while a bottle of Absolut goes for thirteen dollars at the foreigners-only liquor store near the airport. Wine is available by the case now, but the drug of choice, as it was in the 1960s, is hashish — Afghan Prozac.

Chicken Street is being remade again. Foreigners are back. Nancy Dupree is back. Even ailing King Zahir Shah, exiled since 1973, came back from Europe long enough to accept the empty title of Father of the Nation. Everything banned by the Taliban (dancing, cameras, alcohol, opium, kites, pet birds, and Christians) is back. Everything old is new again.

The Gandamack Lodge, in Kabul, was full of excellent loot. The proprietor, a veteran British cameraman named Peter Jouvenal, had just returned from Iraq carrying a carpet from one of Saddam's palaces over his shoulder. His gun collection had also expanded, as his regular dealers delivered an armory of loosely stacked trophies to the Victorian manor's front hall. One hot noon, I found the bathroom blocked by a dozen Americans in tan vests and army boots — a grinning Special Forces A-Team — busily racking imaginary rounds on ancient Czech Mausers and vintage Lee Enfields.

House rules at the Gandamack stated that only sidearms are permitted in the dining room, so I got used to finding stacks of rifles here and there. It had always been thus: before Jouvenal marched into town for the BBC as Kabul fell in 2001, this was an al Qaeda safe house, where Yemeni men used my own cement room, number 7, to store rocket-propelled grenades. After just a few hours in my airless cell, the Gandamack began to feel more like Guantánamo.

Setting out on foot, I hoped to discover some remains of the capital described four centuries ago by the Mogul emperor Babur as a city of gardens and promenades, surrounded by orchards and fresh springs, with mountains "like rows of clover." Babur would be crying about now: Kabul 2003 is a spectacular dump. Sitting in a treeless valley at six thousand feet, the city is circled by barren, stony ridges. The Kabul River is a putrid trickle. The trees in the parks have been cut down for firewood. Half destroyed buildings sit next to half-built ones, making it unclear whether Kabul is coming or going. The airport, with its fleet of UN planes and the occasional commercial interloper, is surrounded by a graveyard of blasted, abandoned Soviet-era Tupelovs. Luggage is distributed via the time-honored method of full-scale riot.

The streets of Kabul are named, in the medieval style, by what is done there. I was staying on Passport Lane; I made a right on Interior Ministry, then turned left onto Chicken Street. Half a century after the first foreigners made this street famous, the stores cater mostly to foreign soldiers — Germans, Canadians, Norwegians, Brits. The best-selling souvenir is a small rug showing the World Trade Center in flames against a map of Afghanistan, with a pair of F-16s passing overhead, and any crudely lettered, misspelled sampler of these commemorative phrases:

WAR ON TERIRISM 9–11
AFGHANSTAN AND AMERICA!
TOGETHER VICTORY!!!

The Americans always get blamed for bidding up the price of rugs, which is totally unfair: except for a few Special Forces teams and the embassy Marines, most of the U.S. troops in Afghanistan never set foot in Kabul. Instead, blame Canada, which had two thousand soldiers in town when I arrived. Street kids tailed every giant warrior in Oakleys, offering Pakistani newspapers, thirty-year-old maps, and both the old and new *Survival Guide*.

The only thing you can't get on Chicken Street is chicken, which is available straight ahead on Flower Street. I bargained for a pirated edition of Eric Newby's *A Short Walk in the Hindu Kush,* the 1958 classic about his bumbling assault on a peak in the northeastern province of Nurestan, and paid an argumentative nine dollars for an original edition of Nancy Dupree's book. Twenty-six years out of date, this was still the best guide to the countryside.

In 1969, sixty-three thousand tourists visited Afghanistan. As the Cold War rolled on, the Soviets and Americans competed for influence in the latest iteration of the Great Game, and Kabul was awash with Afghan royals back from ski vacations in the Hindu Kush. "The social scene was the best," recalled Greek diplomat Michaelis Maniatis, who came to Kabul in 1975, fleeing a coup back home, and returned last year as Greece's chief of mission. Reclining on a sofa in the garden of his official residence, dressed in a traditional black shalwar kameez, he remembered Kabul as "a green city, full of peonies," where "people were casual, very Westernized, but close to traditions."

But in 1978, tensions among Afghan Communists and Islamic traditionalists broke into civil war. The disastrous 1979 Soviet invasion turned into a bloody guerrilla war, and the humiliated Red Army withdrew ten years and tens of thousands of casualties later. In victory, the mujahideen warriors simply turned their guns on each other for most of the 1990s. An obscure group of religious students (*taliban*) parted this sea of chaos, rising first in Kandahar and then blitzing the capital in 1996. With the help of Al Qaeda's money and men, the Taliban controlled 90 percent of Afghanistan by September 11, 2001. America's foremost Afghan ally, Ahmed Shah Massoud, the charismatic Lion of Panjshir, was assassinated just days before the 9/11 attacks, but by October his U.S.-trained Northern Alliance army was rolling toward Kabul behind a barrage from B-52s.

The visitors didn't even wait for the dust to settle. The first tour group arrived in August 2002, nine months after the Taliban was routed, and left unscathed. In April 2003, Orfeo Bartolini, an Italian motorcyclist, lost the adventurer's gamble. Bartolini was en route to India when his bike broke down east of Kandahar, the former Taliban stronghold. Two men described as Taliban shot him dead, sparing the Afghan driver who'd picked Bartolini up.

During the first seven months of 2003, fourteen American soldiers died in Afghanistan, five of them from enemy fire. But by summer, hundreds of regrouped Taliban fighters were on the offensive, and Osama bin Laden was reported to be in either Konar or the Pakistani border region of Waziristan, inspiring the jihad. Four GIs were killed in August alone; another soldier died in Paktika in late September. A series of allied offensives — joint operations of the new Afghan army, U.S. troops, and even the Royal Norwegian Air Force — cornered large groups of Taliban, killing more than two hundred in skirmishes near the Pakistan border. Meanwhile, assassinations of foreigners and Afghans who helped them were increasing: a Salvadoran from the Red Cross was killed in March, an Afghan driver for an American aid agency in August, and four more Afghans working for a Danish relief group in September.

Then again, exaggerating the horrors of this country has been good business since Marco Polo. In a 1928 book called *Adventures in Afghanistan for Boys,* blowhard American radio correspondent Lowell Thomas described a harrowing journey to Kabul in which he escaped "bullets and bandits" and "wily Pathans," mostly thanks to the fact that he never encountered any of the above. This February, *Smithsonian* magazine had a correspondent "dodge terrorists and tribal skirmishes," while failing to spot either. Most areas outside Kabul were "considered no-go areas by the UN and aid agencies," I read in London's *Sunday Times Magazine* — on the same day the UN published a map showing most of the country open for travel.

Afghan tourism has already reached its third wave. The first was, of course, the Afghans themselves. Next came the hundreds of mostly independent travelers who have already visited the country since the war ended. Now come the people Dupree calls "moneybags." During my stay, fourteen Europeans from an Italian-led expedition team were climbing 24,580-foot Noshaq, the highest peak in Afghanistan; four Americans were in the Wakhan corridor looking for rare Marco Polo sheep; and a group of Japanese travel agents was casing the countryside. In addition to the Brits, the Japanese dominate travel so far, captivated by this far edge of Asia. One tour company, Nippa Travel, already offers weeklong tours on the "If this is Wednesday it must be Jalalabad" model.

Half a dozen more tour groups were expected by the end of 2003, most bound for Bamiyan, the site of the Buddhist statues so famously destroyed by the Taliban, or for the Panjshir Valley. Asked whether this kind of travel was safe, Dupree said bluntly, "It's fine." That's true only if you know as much as she does about where not to go, but the areas north and west of Kabul are generally considered safe, at least by Afghan standards. However, she added, "I wouldn't go to Konar at this moment, for example."

I wished she'd mentioned Konar earlier. My traveling companion, Irish photographer Seamus Murphy, and I had just spent four days planning an excursion to Nurestan to retrace Newby's steps. Nurestan is best accessed through Konar Province. Our truck, translator, and supplies were all arranged, and our worries had been dismissed by both the 101st Airborne and a UN security briefer. But last-minute research warned of fresh fighting and a possible kidnapping in Nurestan. Even worse, the country's most infamous warlord, Gulbuddin Hekmatyar, a pro-Taliban fanatic known for throwing acid in the faces of unveiled women, had been spotted in the area.

We canceled the car, unpacked the groceries.

There had to be a safer place. Just off Chicken Street, I met Gul Agha Karime, the proprietor of the Karime Super Market, a dry-goods shop, as well as the leader of an Afghan initiative to rescue the mysterious Minaret of Jam, an ancient tower on the Harirud River, 340 miles west of Kabul. Leaning badly and vulnerable to looting, the tower is listed by UNESCO as one of Afghanistan's most endangered treasures. Karime gave me tea, a candid assessment of travel in Afghanistan ("Is no problem"), and two things to deliver to Jam: a letter of introduction and a heavy piece of brass. This last item was an official seal for the headman of the local village, a three-pound relic that I would now carry across the country — westward, along the old Central Route to Bamiyan, and beyond that to Jam, and Herat, the storied Persian capital of old Afghanistan.

It doesn't take long to fall off the map here. Just sixty minutes outside the capital, I was teetering on the edge of a half-blown bridge with a wildly grinning Pashtun man. "This is most far from Kabul I have been," he shouted, "in twenty-three years!"

We were waiting out a massive traffic snarl — three lines of cars, trucks, donkeys, pedestrians, fruit vendors, and vans from two directions trying to fit over a single surviving lane of bridge. (In perfect symmetry, the U.S. Air Force had blown up both lanes, and the U.S. Army had rebuilt one of them.) There was wreck and destruction to the far horizon. Scores of burned-out Soviet tanks and ruins of mud villages were everywhere. The green flags of martyrdom snapped over graves. The air was unfiltered tailpipe.

But it was mango season. The mangoes were cheap. They were cool, and sloppy with a sweet, spicy juice. To a throat rubbed raw by dust, by heat, by the choking soot of traffic, they were perfect. I was slowly beginning to realize that Afghanistan is a 1 percent country. The ninety-nine bad things are what make the one remaining thing so indescribably good.

The Afghans know how to find that 1 percent. Just outside Kabul, in the ancient hilltop retreat of Istalif, a place burned by the Taliban in 1999 and bombed by the Americans in 2001, I'd found scores of families spread out beneath the mulberry trees, training for the day when picnicking becomes an Olympic sport. Boys were throwing water balloons, men were playing volleyball, women in burkas were eating pilaf, and everyone was complaining about the lack of parking.

I was invited to join the largest picnic, a group of thirty-six men and boys arrayed along a tablecloth spread beneath the broad canopy of a plane tree. The turbaned man on my right, Sher Ahmed Barak, had run a fried-chicken restaurant in the Bronx for ten years. "The Bronx is very dangerous," he said, shaking his head. "People are getting murdered all the time." Now he lives in Kandahar.

We were served skateboard-size pieces of flatbread; salted yogurt with herbs; salads of peppers, tomatoes, and radishes; a pilaf with carrots and raisins; bowls of cherries; and huge joints of mutton in onion gravy. Everyone got a can of Pepsi.

The man at the head of the tablecloth was a security official who claimed to be a secret agent for the FBI and therefore wouldn't tell me his name. Despite the unsettled conditions in Afghanistan, he said, tribal and ethnic divisions no longer matter. He addressed the thirty-five men and boys in Dari, and they called out their tribal affiliations: "Tajik!" "Pashtun!" "Hazara!" "Uzbek!" As the day wore on, little boys climbed into the trees and shook windfalls of mulberries loose. They couldn't do enough to welcome a foreigner.

Right across the Shomali Plain, past a few hundred thousand land mines, we could make out the vast Bagram air base, where GIs waiting for anti-Taliban missions are confined in tent camps, fed imported food, and entertained by flown-in Washington Redskins cheerleaders.

It was the summer solstice, the longest day of the year. After sixteen hours of daylight, the Afghans quit the groves, rolled up their small carpets, loaded nine people into each TownAce van, and with the indifference of survivors, piloted their runty, overloaded vehicles back toward Kabul. They crossed the wide plain three abreast, surging forward in both lanes like a cavalry charge before being stopped dead in gridlock at each checkpoint, turnoff, or, in our case, blown bridge. Then, unleashed after a minute or an hour, the Afghans raced forward again, optimists in spite of it all, until they abruptly ground to a halt before the next obstacle of misery.

That's Afghanistan. You eat a mango in a mine field. Things that are easy have no flavor.

The dirt road west to the Buddhist caves of Bamiyan led into the stark and grand mountains at the heart of the Hindu Kush. Wide, parched valleys gradually withered into narrow gorges.

Bamiyan itself was a shock. After seven hours of brown on brown, we twisted up a narrow defile and spilled over into an immense valley, serene beyond description, with miles of pastel grass, all of it dwarfed by the sixteen-thousand-foot Koh-i-Baba range. The rarest thing in Afghanistan — water — flowed in careless abundance.

On the west side of the valley was a huge wall of eroded red rock, pockmarked with caves and two colossal, empty niches. In March 2001, the Taliban had used artillery shells and dynamite to destroy two giant statues of Buddha here, an event of atavistic intolerance that shocked the world. Carved between the third and fifth centuries, the statues — 125 and 180 feet tall, respectively — were among the first representations of Buddha in human form, blending Eastern and Western artistic traditions; the Enlightened One was wearing Greek robes. For centuries, pilgrims and traders thronged Bamiyan, a centerpiece in the chain of oases along the Silk Road.

Despite once again becoming the top tourist site in Afghanistan, Bamiyan boasts no real infrastructure for visitors, but they keep showing up anyway. "There are backpackers, up from India and Pakistan, who try to come here," Guillaume Limal, the lone local staffer of Solidarité, a French NGO, told me late that night in his bare room. Lean and sunburned, Limal had been running irrigation projects here for eight months. "Sometimes there are three or four [tourists] at a time," he said. "Last week a couple came — Koreans. The woman without a veil."

According to Hessamuddin Hamrah, head of tourism at the Ministry of Civil Aviation and Tourism, the government plans to erect a fake nomad encampment at Bamiyan, like it had in the seventies, with cement yurts and plumbing. Then there will be a one-hundred-room hotel at the foot of the niches. Under pressure from UNESCO, the Ministry of Information and Culture has agreed not to reconstruct the actual statues. But Hamrah brushed this aside, insisting the Buddhas will be rebuilt, quickly. "We will give them the same image as before," he told me when I interviewed him in his office back in Kabul. "I think we will start reconstruction in this year."

For now, Bamiyan remains bereft and timeless. There are almost no motors, pollution, or trash, no electronic hum. At dusk, the cry of the muezzin was the thin wail of an actual human throat, stretching to touch us from over the fields.

Afghanistan had a national park once, briefly. It lay a few hours west of Bamiyan, over flinty roads that now meander, split, rejoin, and sometimes vanish completely. As we drove, red-painted rocks marked mine fields, but it was becoming apparent that the most dangerous thing in this dangerous place was the road itself: at one point the track crested a ridge and simply ended, without warning, at the edge of a precipice. Fatema, our driver, was a former army commando, and his combat instincts saved us now as he flung the car sideways, scraping pebbles into the void. When the route disappeared, we consulted with nomads, who pointed vaguely onward.

The park, Band-i-Amir, was created in 1973 to protect and showcase five large, mineral-rich lakes, the largest of which, we now saw, is a vivid four-mile-long sheet of sapphire-and-turquoise water lined with yellow-and-pink cliffs. Dupree had avoided describing the lakes in detail, she wrote, lest she "rob the uninitiated of the wonder and amazement" that the sight of cold blue amid such hot brown inspires.

The national park was never more than a short-lived notion, its single small hotel now in ruins. The only sign of new life was a nameless tea shop made of plastic sheeting and decorated with tiny Afghan and American flags. I ordered the special: grilled fish from the lake. It tasted like copper and was full of tiny bones. A red plastic rowboat with an outboard came puttering over the water carrying four Afghan tourists in turbans, sitting stiffly upright and quietly thrilled.

Back in Bamiyan we'd stumbled into a couple of American soldiers down in the small bazaar — Special Forces guys in T-shirts, their M-4 carbines propped against a wall. In June, there were a hundred GIs living in a fort at the far end of the valley, dispensing school supplies between security patrols.

The soldiers — a friendly older guy and an unfriendly younger one who was movie-star handsome, movie-star short, and equipped like a movie-star soldier, with fingerless gloves — were skeptical when I predicted a flood of tourists someday.

"Why would they come here?" the old guy said, shaking his head.

"That's for sure," Movie Star added. "Why would you ever come here?"

There were two guns under my pillow at Jam. To reach this spot in central Afghanistan's Ghor Province, we'd doubled back to Kabul and flown west to Herat on Ariana Airlines, a.k.a. Air Inshallah — "God Willing." (The ticket's fine print noted that my family was entitled to 32,200 grams of pure silver if I died.) In the disappointingly dusty old city, we'd commandeered a Toyota HiLux four-by-four and a new driver — shopkeeper Gul Agha Karime's car and his nineteen-year-old nephew — plus a twenty-one-year-old translator. Both young men were named Wahid. We headed back east on the Central Route, through a wide valley dotted with camels, following the Harirud upstream. Here Afghanistan seemed to be made of kitty litter, piled into mountains.

The two Wahids promptly blew their young minds. During a short break along the Harirud, we caught them smoking hashish — the famous Afghan Black, dark and oily. Driver Wahid was already a virtuoso nitwit, but as we climbed into the tortuous Qasa

Murg range, his judgment collapsed. When we slid toward a thousand-foot precipice, he simply giggled, looking in the mirror to see if we were mad at him.

We were. We confiscated the hashish and ground onward, through the sad village of Chest-i-Sharif, where the teahouse television offered a documentary about Sebastian Junger in Afghanistan that left the crowd stone-faced. The next day, after six more hours, we finally reached the valley of Jam. In a narrow gorge we picked up Bahabadin, the headman of the tiny Persian-speaking Jam community, dressed in a plaid vest with a plaid turban tailing down his back. I made a show of handing over the brass seal, and he made a show of being pleased. He piled in, and after Wahid rammed us into a sharp rock, causing our third flat, we came to the confluence of two streams, and stopped, and got out, and stared, speechless.

At 215 feet, the Minaret of Jam is the second-tallest minaret in the world, after the mosque of Qutab Minar in New Delhi. Covered in terra-cotta lacework with geometric and floral patterns, it was built in the twelfth century and retains a richness of detailing lost in every other ancient site in Afghanistan, preserved here only by the utter isolation of this tiny canyon.

The tower is tilting, its base partly eroded, and in 2002 a UNESCO team led by Gul Agha Karime and a French archaeologist threw up a stabilizing wall and erected a primitive guesthouse, a cement hut with eight small cells and no furniture. The two complimentary AK-47s under my pillow were loaded; the metal was rusty and battered. Even the guns here were exhausted with war.

Some barefoot shepherds appeared and removed the rifles, under Bahabadin's orders. I had settled in with Dupree's guidebook when a red SUV skidded in, parked ten feet from the base of the leaning minaret, and discharged two foreigners.

Finally, Western tourists — women in their thirties, a Swiss-German redhead and a Hong Kong Chinese. They were in western Afghanistan on NGO business. They took some pictures and then sipped tea with us inside the cool guesthouse.

You can still travel from one end of this country to the other without ever meeting or speaking to a female Afghan. The foreign women deal with it differently: some go about as honorary men, unveiled, while others adopt a respectful cover of Afghan ways. These two wore traditional burkas and veils, and traveled everywhere with two Afghan men, their driver and translator. They had

had no problems, they said, but they wouldn't say much else: they wouldn't give their names and were eerily shy. It was only when they signed the guest book — the twenty-fourth party in three years — that I realized why. Their employer was International Assistance Mission, a Christian humanitarian agency. The IAM was thrown out of the country by the Taliban two weeks before September 11 for proselytizing, but now it's back and keeping a low profile. Christians — whether wearing humanitarian veils or U.S. Army helmets — have been deeply controversial here, but that is nothing new: the tower at Jam bears a Koranic inscription warning against Christian doctrines. It is a message to the heathen, and still valid.

After the women left, I clambered through a hole in the base of the tower and scrambled up the crumbling spiral stairs inside. Archaeologists have argued for decades over why the tower is here. It can't have been a watchtower — thanks to the enveloping mountains, I couldn't see a mile in any direction. But as a pilgrimage site, Jam still offers the necessary ratio of extended suffering to sudden enlightenment. Coming out of the burning desert into this oasis lent the trip an almost spiritual dimension, as is true in all of Afghanistan, really, where 80 percent of the land is arid mountains and only 12 percent is arable. Centuries ago, Babur wrote of the "pleasant shocks" of traveling in his country, passing "from distress to ease; from suffering to enjoyment." It was at once exhausting and exhilarating, the natural state for revelation.

Alas, the real purpose of Jam may have been more political than divine. The next day, we crossed the Harirud on a frayed wire cable, and Bahabadin led us up a canyon. Local people have always claimed that Jam was the great capital of Firuzkoh, the fabled "Turquoise City" of ancient narrative. Archaeologists dismissed this idea in the 1970s, but they didn't dig deeply enough: scattered up the canyon, less than a mile from the minaret, were hundreds of new holes, dug by looters who'd uncovered ancient homes beneath the soft loess. Every scrape of my boot uncovered green, blue, and turquoise potsherds.

Many of Jam's secrets have been lost to looting. In recent years, Bahabadin's own people have rushed in to dig up artifacts, until Bahabadin himself was hired to stop the looting — the poacher turned gamekeeper. "This is illegal now," he explained. "Last year, yes."

UNESCO is supposedly protecting sites around Afghanistan too, but some are skeptical. "I don't think anybody thinks [looting] has really stopped," said Rory Stewart, a thirty-year-old Scot on the staff of the British Foreign Office. In early 2002, Stewart walked from Herat to Jam and on to Kabul, researching his forthcoming book on central Afghanistan, *The Places In Between*. "The number of sites is so many, it is impossible to monitor, and the demand for objects is growing all the time." The best pieces migrate upward, Stewart said. He described stolen artifacts passing to Peshawar and on to New York, London, Tokyo, and Paris.

The only real hope was that the many sites like Jam could eventually divulge fresh artifacts to replace the ones stolen or, like those in the National Museum, bombed. It's not impossible. Charred wood lies about Jam in profusion, perfectly preserved for eight hundred years by the dry climate. Bahabadin held up a blackened timber: "Genghis," he said.

After dark, Seamus and I sat by the minaret and watched a perfectly Muslim crescent moon set on the peaks. We were leaving the next day, and to prevent the Wahids from getting dangerously stoned, we decided to get rid of the confiscated hashish — by burning it. The Afghan Black was harsh, and I coughed badly.

Ten minutes later I was laughing so hard I was crying. For the next hour we lay on the rough ground, giggling, watching the planets give way to magnitudes of stars. The earth shook with the tromp of a khan's 200,000-horsepower army. We ate candy bars. I resolved to throw out my furniture and live entirely on rugs. A meteor flashed across the sky, exploding in silence.

So there you have it. Thirty years later the drugs still work.

Thank God there are some adults in charge. Back in Kabul, I started tracking down the people who can improve things. Soldiers can only draw a line in the sand; it is the humanitarians who must create development and hope. And these people are found in one place at one time: the UNICA guesthouse on Thursday night.

Because the Islamic weekend consists only of Friday, Thursday night is Kabul's big party scene. And the bar at the UNICA guesthouse, really a block-long residential compound for UN staff, is where the bright caravan gathers.

Peter Jouvenal had warned us that UNICA parties were closed to journalists. Security looked high and tight when we arrived — steel walls, sandbags, razor wire, rock walls to keep suicidal cars out — but we blew through with shameful ease, signing false names and mystifying the guards with Seamus's suddenly exaggerated Irish accent. ("We're from UNFIT. That's correct — excellent, you're a darling little man.") We trailed a gaggle of Euroblonds past dozens of parked white SUVs and then down a pitch-black path toward a lot of noise.

I fumbled my way through a bamboo curtain and — who let the dogs out! Beneath a row of palm trees, a hundred people were spilling over a lawn around two swimming pools, wiping out a free bar of Johnnie Walker Black, Australian shiraz, and Chilean merlot. Thirty people were on the dance floor between the pools. The sound system was run by a slim Afghan who said his "DJ name" was "DJ Music."

He boosted some Gloria Gaynor, but as more people crowded in, he was replaced by a new mix master, a UN staffer who identified herself as Juliana from Guyana. She plugged in a laptop and ran a remix of "Like the Deserts Miss the Rain" off her hard drive, packing the lawn with a whirling crowd of grooving Afro-elites and Italians spinning with Colombian hotties.

Juliana segued into ABBA, and then "Rivers of Babylon," with its desperately inappropriate lyrics: "How can we sing the Lord's song in a strange land?"

Was it really a good idea to get drunk on whiskey and send biblical reggae booming into Kabul's wary nocturnal psychosphere? To treat Afghanistan like it was any other place? Was that the price of our help — a blank check to do as we liked, to stay unchanged by the place we were assisting? Kabul had a rockin' party scene back in the seventies, too, but when the world came to Afghanistan last time, Afghanistan eventually bit back, hard.

Most UN folks hardly seemed aware of life outside the safety of Wazir Akbar Khan. The bombing of the UN headquarters in Baghdad made it plain that security concerns are real, although, of course, common sense argued that the UNICA guesthouse itself, a liquor-swilling target writ large, was probably one of the most dangerous places in the country. Though some UN and NGO workers push out to provincial capitals like Herat or Mazar-i-Sharif, where there are far fewer aid workers, too many seem content to stay in Kabul and pass paper around in a circle.

An Afghan with ten years' experience in aid work told me that USAID, a State Department agency, is the most efficient foreign program; next best was the European Union; the worst was the UN, where urgent requests for development assistance were met with the meticulous scheduling of meetings, usually in Paris. One high-ranking diplomat insisted that more than seventy-five cents of every UN dollar targeted for Afghanistan was being spent outside the country.

Of the $5.2 billion in promised aid — including a pledged U.S. increase from $928 million in 2002 to $1.2 billion in 2004 — as little as 20 to 30 percent of it reaches villages, observers say. The rest is absorbed by administration and personnel. Rory Stewart — now serving for the Coalition Provisional Authority in Iraq as deputy governor of Maysan Province — returned to Kabul this year and was shocked to find that friends of his were earning $800 a day working for the UN. "The cost of keeping a single expat on the ground is between 300,000 and half a million U.S. dollars a year," he says of the UN staff, "if you take into account the cost of salary, all the allowances, the per diems, the white Land Cruisers they ride around in, the equipment in their offices."

"The idea that we only know Wazir Akbar Khan is just not true," the UN's David Haeri told me. He agreed that international staffs are expensive but said the UN's goal is to "work ourselves out of a job." He cited the organization's Mine Action Program, a mine-clearing operation that employs some seven thousand Afghans and only a few dozen foreigners.

"It is no secret that the UN has a huge overhead problem," notes David Rieff, author of the 2002 book *A Bed for the Night: Humanitarianism in Crisis*. Still, he defends the UN's work in Afghanistan, despite a few problems ("incredibly inflated staffing and overhead structure," "double bureaucracy," "incompetence," and "mismanagement"). More fault lies with the United States, he says, citing an American refusal to extend international peacekeepers beyond Kabul.

"Incorrect," counters Ambassador Bill Taylor, the U.S. special coordinator on Afghanistan, in Washington, D.C. "We are actively exploring the expansion of international peacekeepers." Taylor, who spent nine months as U.S. reconstruction coordinator in Afghanistan, lists some successes: improved roads, a stable currency, and an infant army "loyal to Hamid Karzai, not the warlords." Nonetheless, he agrees that the security situation is getting worse.

The real risk for America, preoccupied as it is with Iraq, will be failing to sustain our efforts in the long run — a decade or more. So far, on balance, achievements do outweigh failures, most notably from NGOs in the field: Doctors Without Borders, Solidarité, ACTED, Action Against Hunger, and the Agha Khan Foundation, among others. A Kabul staffer for the Catholic charity Caritas told me that aid projects seem slow but are making real-world progress, fixing irrigation works, clearing roads, and building schools. "A year ago, yes, there really was a shortage of money and people," she said, with the innate caution of a bureaucratic infighter. But now the aid taps are open, the staffs up and running. "It's amazing how the NGOs have been able to reach every corner of the country, rebuilding houses and so on, in the last year," the Caritas staffer added. "People are a bit impatient."

I'm one of them. I left the UNICA party for a while, wandering the compound, pushing open doors. There were bungalows, dormitories, and a lodge with dark beams, where suspiciously earnest people were poring over paperwork as the party raged. Down past the gym were a few pool tables, where Photo sent Edit down to a narrow defeat. And outside again, the Afro-Swedo-Deutsche-funk vibe was in full swing. It looked like an episode of *The Real World: Kabul* shot in a British officer's mess during the Great Game.

Juliana from Guyana finally got me. Unwilling to miss the last-night, last-chance-forever, goodbye-farewell party to this brief Kabul between unknowns, I hit the dance floor, the only place in Afghanistan with a huge crowd of unveiled women, and set about embarrassing myself.

We dance. We wave our hands in the air like we just don't care.

Contributors' Notes
Notable Travel Writing of 2003

Contributors' Notes

Roger Angell is a 1942 graduate of Harvard. He worked for several magazines in the 1940s and 1950s before joining *The New Yorker,* where he has been ever since. Now a senior fiction editor, Angell has written about baseball for *The New Yorker* since 1962, and for many years his holiday poem was a year-end tradition at the magazine. Angell's many books include *Game Time, A Pitcher's Story, Five Seasons,* and *The Stone Arbor and Other Stories.* He recently edited *Nothing but You: Love Stories from The New Yorker* and also wrote an introduction to the fourth edition of *The Elements of Style,* the classic book on writing by his stepfather, E. B. White, and William Strunk.

Frank Bures has attended high school in Italy, picked apples in New Zealand, taught English in Tanzania, and, most recently, lived in Thailand. His work has appeared in *Salon, Tin House, Mother Jones, Audubon,* and other magazines. He is a frequent contributor to the *Christian Science Monitor* and currently lives in Madison, Wisconsin.

Michael Byers is the author of *The Coast of Good Intentions,* a book of stories, and *Long for This World,* a novel. His first book received the Sue Kaufman Award from the American Academy of Arts and Letters. He is the recipient of a Whiting Writers' Award, and his work has appeared in *The Best American Short Stories* and *Prize Stories: The O. Henry Awards.* A native of Seattle, he teaches at the University of Pittsburgh.

Tim Cahill is the author of nine books, including *Hold the Enlightenment* and *Lost in My Own Backyard.* He writes for *National Geographic Adventure* and numerous other magazines. Cahill cowrote the Academy Award–nominated IMAX documentary *The Living Sea,* as well as the IMAX film *Everest.* He lives in Montana with his wife, Linnea.

Richie Chevat is a screenwriter, playwright, and now, apparently, a travel writer. He's also written numerous children's books. He lives with his wife and two children in New Jersey, where there are always plenty of inciting incidents and second-act reversals.

Douglas Anthony Cooper is a novelist (*Amnesia, Delirium*) who divides his time between Montreal and Manhattan. He also writes and photographs articles for various publications, including *Travel + Leisure, Food & Wine, Rolling Stone*, and the *New York Times*. His first piece of travel journalism won a National Magazine Award in Canada; the piece included in this collection received a gold medal in the Lowell Thomas Travel Journalism Competition. For years he has collaborated with artists and architects: a mock documentary on the human foot, written and narrated for the architecture firm of Diller+Scofidio, was recently shown at the Whitney Museum in New York. His work in various media is documented at www.dysmedia.com.

Joan Didion is the author of five novels, including *Run River*, and seven books of nonfiction, including *Miami, Salvador, The White Album, Slouching Towards Bethlehem*, and, most recently, *Where I Was From*.

Bill Donahue is a contributing editor for *Outside* magazine. His writing has also appeared in *The New Yorker*, the *New York Times Magazine*, the *Atlantic Monthly, Mother Jones*, and *The Best American Sports Writing 2003*. He lives in Portland, Oregon.

Heather Eliot is a writer and educator in Santa Cruz, California.

Kevin Fedarko is a freelance writer living in northern New Mexico. He has worked as a correspondent for *Time* and now contributes regularly to *Outside* and *Men's Journal*, reporting primarily on mountaineering, back-country skiing, and other aspects of outdoor adventure.

Tad Friend has been a staff writer at *The New Yorker* since 1998, where he writes the magazine's "Letter from California." He is the author of *Lost in Mongolia: Travels in Hollywood and Other Foreign Lands*, a collection of articles published in 2001. He is married to the *New York Times* food writer Amanda Hesser and lives in Brooklyn.

Adam Gopnik has been writing for *The New Yorker* since 1986. He is the author of *Paris to the Moon*, about the five years he spent in Paris as the magazine's correspondent there, and is now organizing a new book about life in

New York, rooted in his work writing the magazine's "New York Journal," from which his essay here is drawn.

Michael Gorra was born in New London, Connecticut, and received an A.B. from Amherst College and a Ph.D. from Stanford University. Since 1985 he has taught the history of the novel at Smith College, where he now chairs the Department of English. His books include *The Bells in Their Silence: Travels Through Germany* and *After Empire: Scott, Naipaul, Rushdie*. He is a regular contributor to the *New York Times Book Review* and other journals, and his reviews of new fiction received the 2002 Nona Balakian Citation from the National Book Critics Circle. Gorra lives with his wife and daughter in Northampton, Massachusetts.

Tom Haines is the staff travel writer of the *Boston Globe*. He spent much of the past decade as a news reporter, traveling to such places as Microsoft's manicured campus, the depths of a Ukrainian coal mine, and a sunlit Lapland film festival. His reporting about economic change in South Wales won the top prize of the Journalists in Europe Foundation, in Paris, where he was a fellow in 2000. As the *Globe*'s travel writer, he has covered plummeting pesos in Argentina, guns and cricket in Guyana, and trumpets and nationalism in rural Serbia. In 2003 he was named Travel Journalist of the Year by the Society of American Travel Writers. Haines, who is thirty-six, lives near Boston with his wife and son.

Peter Hessler is a freelance writer who lives in Beijing. He writes primarily for *The New Yorker* and *National Geographic*. His first book, *River Town: Two Years on the Yangtze*, was published in 2001. He has lived in China for eight years, since arriving as a Peace Corps volunteer in 1996.

Mark Jenkins writes the monthly adventure column "The Hard Way" for *Outside*. He is the author of three books: *Off the Map*, detailing a coast-to-coast, 7,500-mile crossing of Siberia by bicycle; *To Timbuktu;* and a volume of collected works from *Outside*, titled *The Hard Way*. Jenkins has been an editor at *Men's Health, Backpacker, Adventure Travel,* and *Cross Country Skier,* and his work has appeared in *Bicycling, Condé Nast Traveler, Playboy, GQ,* and many other publications. He lives in Laramie, Wyoming, with his wife and two children, and is currently at work on his second volume of collected essays.

Rian Malan is a South African journalist and an author best known in the West for his award-winning memoir, *My Traitor's Heart*, published in the United States in 1990. He is forty-nine and lives in Cape Town with an

American wife and two dogs, and writes screenplays in addition to journalism for a variety of American and European publications. His next book, soon to be published, is *Bridges of Our Own Dead.*

Bill McKibben is the author of eight books, including *The End of Nature,* that have been translated into twenty-one languages. He is a former staff writer for *The New Yorker,* and his work appears regularly in *Harper's Magazine,* the *Atlantic Monthly,* the *New York Review of Books, Outside,* and many other national publications. Currently a scholar-in-residence at Middlebury College, he lives in the mountains above Lake Champlain.

John McPhee was born in Princeton, New Jersey, and was educated at Princeton University and Cambridge University. His writing career began at *Time* and led to his long association with *The New Yorker,* where he has been a staff writer since 1965. He is the author of twenty-six books, including *A Sense of Where You Are* (1965), *Oranges* (1967), *The Pine Barrens* (1968), *The Survival of the Bark Canoe* (1975), *Coming into the Country* (1977), *La Place de la Concorde Suisse* (1984), *The Control of Nature* (1989), and, most recently, *Founding Fish* (2002). Both *Encounters with the Archdruid* (1972) and *The Curve of Binding Energy* (1974) were nominated for National Book Awards in the category of science. *Annals of the Former World* was awarded the Pulitzer Prize in 1999.

George Packer is the author of two novels, *The Half Man* and *Central Square,* and two books of nonfiction, *The Village of Waiting* and *Blood of the Liberals,* which won the 2001 Robert F. Kennedy Book Award. He is also the editor of *The Fight for Democracy: Winning the War of Ideas in America and the World.* He is a staff writer at *The New Yorker.* Two of his recent pieces for the magazine won Overseas Press Club awards.

Elizabeth Rubin is a contributing writer for the *New York Times Magazine.* She has traveled through and written about Afghanistan, Russia, the Caucasus, the Middle East, Africa, and the Balkans. Her stories have appeared in the *Atlantic Monthly,* the *New York Times Magazine,* the *New Republic, Harper's Magazine,* and *The New Yorker.* She lives in New York City.

Kira Salak is a contributing editor at *National Geographic Adventure* and the author of two books: *Four Corners: One Woman's Solo Journey into the Heart of New Guinea* and *The Cruelest Journey.* Her work has appeared in various publications, including *The Best American Travel Writing 2002* and *2003, Best New American Voices 2001, National Geographic,* and *Nixon Under the Bodhi Tree and Other Works of Buddhist Fiction.* She lives outside Bozeman, Montana.

Paul Salopek is a roving correspondent for the *Chicago Tribune* who won the Pulitzer Prize for international reporting in 2001. He was formerly a general assignment reporter on the *Tribune*'s metropolitan staff. In 1998 Salopek won the Pulitzer Prize in explanatory journalism for a series on the controversial Human Genome Diversity Project. Prior to joining the *Tribune*, he worked as a writer for *National Geographic* for three years. Before that, he reported on U.S.-Mexico border issues for the *El Paso Times*, and in 1990 he was the Gannett News Service bureau chief in Mexico City. Salopek began his journalism career in 1985 when his motorcycle broke down in Roswell, New Mexico, and he took a police-reporting job at the local newspaper to earn repair money. Since then he has covered conflicts in Central America, New Guinea, and the Balkans. Besides journalism, he has worked off and on as a commercial fisherman, most recently with the scallop fleet out of New Bedford, Massachusetts.

Thomas Swick is the travel editor of the *South Florida Sun-Sentinel* and the author of two books: a travel memoir, *Unquiet Days: At Home in Poland*, and a collection of travel stories, *A Way to See the World: From Texas to Transylvania with a Maverick Traveler*. His work has appeared in the *American Scholar*, the *Oxford American*, the *North American Review*, *Ploughshares*, *Commonweal*, and *The Best American Travel Writing 2001* and *2002*.

As a contributing editor at *Harper's* and *Outside* magazines, **Patrick Symmes** has traveled with Maoist guerrillas in Nepal, parleyed with the two main guerrilla groups in Colombia, profiled drug gangs in Brazil, dirt-biked across Cambodia to visit the Khmer Rouge, and worked his way through the Panama Canal as a deck hand. He is the author of *Chasing Che: A Motorcycle Journey Through the Guevara Legend*, which describes a twelve-thousand-mile ride across South America, retracing the journeys and guerrilla campaigns of the revolutionary icon Che Guevara.

Notable Travel Writing of 2003

SELECTED BY JASON WILSON

JONATHAN AMES
Club Existential Dread. *McSweeneys.net*, November 17–21.
BARBARA LAZEAR ASCHER
When Travel Serves to Comfort. *New York Times*, February 23.
STEPHEN BENZ
A Communion of Souls. *South Florida Sun-Sentinel*, April 27.
JON BILLMAN
Bumming on the Powder Hound. *Outside*, February.
ALEXANDER BLAKELY
The Place Without Roads. *Harper's Magazine*, December.
WILLIAM BOOTH
The Keys to Happiness. *Washington Post Magazine*, January 26.
CHARLES BOWDEN
An Insistent Silence, Stillness, and Space. *Arizona Highways*, January.
CHRISTOPHER BUCKLEY
Mr. Lincoln's Washington. *Smithsonian*, April.
TIM CAHILL
The Lure of Impossible Places. *National Geographic Adventure*, October.
The CO_2 Chronicles. *National Geographic Adventure*, November.
JUDY COPELAND
The Art of Bushwhacking. *Florida Review*, Fall.
LYNNE COX
Swimming to Antarctica. *The New Yorker*, February 3.
WILLIAM CRONON
Wild Again. *Orion*, May/June.
WAYNE CURTIS
In Seach of Tiki on Built-Up Waikiki. *Preservation*, September/October.
KEVIN FEDARKO
The Coldest War. *Outside*, February.
BRUCE FEILER
Prayers and Lamentations. *Gourmet*, March.

LUCY FERRISS
When the Heart Sets the Itinerary. *New York Times,* February 9.
BORIS FISHMAN
Morocco, May, 2002. *American Scholar,* Winter.
RICHARD FORD
I'm New Here. *Preservation,* November/December.
IAN FRAZIER
Invented City. *The New Yorker,* July 28.
BILL GIFFORD
Siberia: The Exile Trail. *Slate.com,* July 31.
CHARLES GRAEBER
Our Man (and His Song) in Brazil. *National Geographic Adventure,* December/
January.
ILAN GREENBERG
When a Kleptocratic, Megalomaniacal Dictator Goes Bad. *New York Times
Magazine,* January 5.
ELIZA GRISWOLD
Where the Taliban Roam. *Harper's Magazine,* September.
TOM HAINES
Balkans in the Balance. *Boston Globe,* October 5.
Far More Than a Place to Sleep. *Boston Globe,* September 7.
PETER HESSLER
Underwater. *The New Yorker,* July 7.
CHRISTOPHER HITCHENS
Saddam's Long Good-Bye. *Vanity Fair,* June.
PICO IYER
The Magic of Flight. *Via,* November.
The Thrill of Arrival. *Condé Nast Traveler,* January.
ROBERT D. KAPLAN
The Holy Mountain. *Atlantic Monthly,* December.
SUKI KIM
Night Ride Home. *Gourmet,* December.
MICHAEL KINSLEY
Hurry Up and Relax. *Condé Nast Traveler,* November.
PETER LASALLE
Metaphysical Messages: With J.L.B. in Buenos Aires. *Agni,* Number 58.
DAVID LEAVITT
Out from Under the Tuscan Sun. *Food & Wine,* April.
KATHERINE LEROY
Morning, Not Smart. *WorldHum.com,* April 16.
MICHAEL LOWENTHAL
A Loss of Orientation. *The Advocate,* March 4.
ARTHUR LUBOW
A Laboratory of Taste. *New York Times Magazine,* August 10.
PETER MAASS
The Rough Guide to Iraq. *Outside,* July.
PETER MATTHIESSEN
Emperors at the End of the Earth. *National Geographic Adventure,* November.

FRANK MCCOURT
  The Pope and I. *Gourmet,* March.
DAISANN MCLANE
  Coming Home. *National Geographic Traveler,* January/February.
  The Return Policy. *National Geographic Traveler,* September.
TOM MUELLER
  Inside Job. *Atlantic Monthly,* October.
ROB NIXON
  Traveling with an Accent. *New York Times,* June 8.
JENNY OFFILL
  American Pie. *Travel + Leisure,* April.
AMY O'LEARY
  An Open Letter to Spanish Host Family. *McSweeneys.net,* August 8.
TOM O'NEILL
  Korea's Dangerous Divide. *National Geographic,* July.
THE ONION
  Disney Family Vacation Ruined by Walt Disney Company. June 18.
GEORGE PACKER
  The Children of Freetown. *The New Yorker,* January 13.
ALLISON PEARSON AND ANTHONY LANE
  Two Sides of Paradise. *Town & Country Travel,* Fall.
ROBERT YOUNG PELTON
  Kidnapped in the Gap. *National Geographic Adventure,* June/July.
TONY PERROTTET
  Romantic Interlude. *Archeology Odyssey,* May/June.
ROLF POTTS
  The Hidden Valley. *Condé Nast Traveler,* January.
RACHEL HILLIER PRATT
  Negotiating Bride Price. *Missouri Review,* Volume 26, Number 1.
RICK REILLY
  The Importance of Being Ernest. *Sports Illustrated,* July 14.
MARK RICHARD
  Rolltop Mantra of the Outer Banks. *Harper's Magazine,* May.
DAVID SEDARIS
  Our Perfect Summer. *The New Yorker,* June 16 and 23.
LOIS R. SHEA
  Come Away! O Human Child! *Boston Globe,* August 31.
MINDY SINK
  Rocky Peaks, Bared Souls. *New York Times,* June 29.
LIZ SPIKOL
  Long Day's Journey. *Philadelphia City Paper,* August 27–September 2.
SETH STEVENSON
  Tokyo on One Cliché a Day. *Slate.com,* October 17.
THOMAS SWICK
  The Party Beneath My Window. *South Florida Sun-Sentinel,* March 2 and 9.
ERIK TORKELLS
  In Search of the Perfect Swimming Hole. *National Geographic Adventure,*
  June/July.

THE BEST AMERICAN SHORT STORIES® 2004

Lorrie Moore, guest editor, Katrina Kenison, series editor. "Story for story, readers can't beat *The Best American Short Stories* series" (*Chicago Tribune*). This year's most beloved short fiction anthology is edited by the critically acclaimed author Lorrie Moore and includes stories by Annie Proulx, Sherman Alexie, Paula Fox, Thomas McGuane, and Alice Munro, among others.

0-618-19735-4 PA $14.00 / 0-618-19734-6 CL $27.50
0-618-30046-5 CASS $26.00 / 0-618-29965-3 CD $30.00

THE BEST AMERICAN ESSAYS® 2004

Louis Menand, guest editor, Robert Atwan, series editor. Since 1986, *The Best American Essays* series has gathered the best nonfiction writing of the year and established itself as the best anthology of its kind. Edited by Louis Menand, author of *The Metaphysical Club* and staff writer for *The New Yorker*, this year's volume features writing by Kathryn Chetkovich, Jonathan Franzen, Kyoko Mori, Cynthia Zarin, and others.

0-618-35709-2 PA $14.00 / 0-618-35706-8 CL $27.50

THE BEST AMERICAN MYSTERY STORIES™ 2004

Nelson DeMille, guest editor, Otto Penzler, series editor. This perennially popular anthology is a favorite of mystery buffs and general readers alike. This year's volume is edited by the best-selling suspense author Nelson DeMille and offers pieces by Stephen King, Joyce Carol Oates, Jonathon King, Jeff Abbott, Scott Wolven, and others.

0-618-32967-6 PA $14.00 / 0-618-32968-4 CL $27.50 / 0-618-49742-0 CD $30.00

THE BEST AMERICAN SPORTS WRITING™ 2004

Richard Ben Cramer, guest editor, Glenn Stout, series editor. This series has garnered wide acclaim for its stellar sports writing and topnotch editors. Now Richard Ben Cramer, the Pulitzer Prize–winning journalist and author of the best-selling *Joe DiMaggio*, continues that tradition with pieces by Ira Berkow, Susan Orlean, William Nack, Charles P. Pierce, Rick Telander, and others.

0-618-25139-1 PA $14.00 / 0-618-25134-0 CL $27.50

THE BEST AMERICAN TRAVEL WRITING 2004

Pico Iyer, guest editor, Jason Wilson, series editor. *The Best American Travel Writing 2004* is edited by Pico Iyer, the author of *Video Night in Kathmandu* and *Sun After*

Dark. Giving new life to armchair travel this year are Roger Angell, Joan Didion, John McPhee, Adam Gopnik, and many others.

0-618-34126-9 PA $14.00 / 0-618-34125-0 CL $27.50

THE BEST AMERICAN SCIENCE AND NATURE WRITING 2004

Steven Pinker, guest editor, Tim Folger, series editor. This year's edition promises to be another "eclectic, provocative collection" (*Entertainment Weekly*). Edited by Steven Pinker, author of *The Blank Slate* and *The Language Instinct*, it features work by Gregg Easterbrook, Atul Gawande, Peggy Orenstein, Jonathan Rauch, Chet Raymo, Nicholas Wade, and others.

0-618-24698-3 PA $14.00 / 0-618-24697-5 CL $27.50

THE BEST AMERICAN RECIPES 2004–2005

Edited by Fran McCullough and Molly Stevens. "Give this book to any cook who is looking for the newest, latest recipes and the stories behind them" (*Chicago Tribune*). Offering the very best of what America is cooking, as well as the latest trends, timesaving tips, and techniques, this year's edition includes a foreword by the renowned chef Bobby Flay.

0-618-45506-x CL $26.00

THE BEST AMERICAN NONREQUIRED READING 2004

Edited by Dave Eggers, Introduction by Viggo Mortensen. Edited by the best-selling author Dave Eggers, this genre-busting volume draws the finest, most interesting, and least expected fiction, nonfiction, humor, alternative comics, and more from publications large, small, and on-line. This year's collection features writing by David Sedaris, Daniel Alarcón, David Mamet, Thom Jones, and others.

0-618-34123-4 PA $14.00 / 0-618-34122-6 CL $27.50 / 0-618-49743-9 CD $26.00

THE BEST AMERICAN SPIRITUAL WRITING 2004

Edited by Philip Zaleski, Introduction by Jack Miles. The latest addition to the acclaimed Best American series, *The Best American Spiritual Writing 2004* brings the year's finest writing about faith and spirituality to all readers. With an introduction by the best-selling author Jack Miles, this year's volume represents a wide range of perspectives and features pieces by Robert Coles, Bill McKibben, Oliver Sacks, Pico Iyer, and many others.

0-618-44303-7 PA $14.00 / 0-618-44302-9 CL $27.50

HOUGHTON MIFFLIN COMPANY   www.houghtonmifflinbooks.com